MY TIMES

IN BLACK AND WHITE

MY TIMES
IN BLACK AND WHITE

Race and Power at the *New York Times*

GERALD M. BOYD

Afterword by Robin D. Stone

Lawrence Hill Books

Library of Congress Cataloging-in-Publication Data

Boyd, Gerald M.

    My Times in black and white : race and power at the New York times / Gerald M. Boyd.

        p. cm.

    Includes index.

    ISBN 978-1-55652-952-8 (hardcover)

    1. Boyd, Gerald M. 2. New York times. 3. Journalists—United States—Biography. 4. African American journalists—Biography. 5. United States—Race relations. I. Title.

    PN4874.B638A3 2010

    070'.92—dc22

    [B]

                                                 2009035506

INTERIOR DESIGN: Monica Baziuk

PHOTO CREDITS: Page 1 – courtesy of Robin D. Stone / Page 2 – top: courtesy of Robin D. Stone; middle: by Bruce W. Talamon © 1984; bottom: official White House photograph / Page 3 – top and middle: official White House photographs; bottom: James Estrin/*The New York Times* / Page 4 – courtesy of Robin D. Stone / Page 5 – top and middle: courtesy of Robin D. Stone; bottom: Gerald Peart / Page 6 – top: Gerald Peart; middle: courtesy of Robin D. Stone; bottom: David Frank/*The New York Times* / Pages 7 and 8 – courtesy of Robin D. Stone

Published by Lawrence Hill Books

An imprint of Chicago Review Press, Incorporated

814 North Franklin Street

Chicago, Illinois 60610

ISBN 978-1-55652-952-8

Printed in the United States of America

5 4 3 2 1

CONTENTS

TO THE MEMORY OF EVIE,
AND TO ZACHARY,
WITH LOVE.

INTRODUCTION

E VEN NOW, the dreams still come. Vivid images intrude on my nights, snapshots of a life in journalism all too real and yet unimaginable for a little black boy up from the streets of poor St. Louis. The dreams play again and again, as if on some video loop. In them, the sounds of a newsroom come alive, faces come and go, and as they do, I make my way through familiar surroundings, ghostlike and from another world. Everything seems real and tangible, yet it is all just beyond my reach.

In some dreams, I am at the *New York Times* staring into the faces of men and women with whom I spent twenty years working, worrying, celebrating, even crying. There is the thrill of putting the *Times* to bed—another exclusive, another smart analysis, another page one story interpreting an event or an issue just right. Then we say our good nights and part ways, heading toward all the compass points of Manhattan and its 'burbs, looking forward to company, dinner, a drink, a good night's sleep, and whatever the next day's news will bring.

Often, I emerge from this fantasy of my old life in a sweat. In the darkness, I struggle to cling to that high, the deep satisfaction that came from being a top editor at the *Times,* the memories of the *Times* when it was really good, and good to me. As my mind clears, I snap awake—angry, spent, heart racing, my breathing loud and labored. I search for my wife, Robin, who is sleeping soundly in spite of my latest fit. At one time she would ride out these nightmares with me. But she has moved on. The world has moved on. *And you must, too,* I tell myself as I stare at the ceiling. *That life is finished. It will never come again.*

But it had been real. It had been mine.

————

I AM fortunate to have had the opportunities to do my very best work in the profession that I love and at the place where I had longed to work since I wrote my first newspaper story as a high school student. The *Times* is not just any institution; it is a public trust. There are larger media empires and more profitable ones, but none wields the power and influence, none has the reach and the scope, of the broadsheet produced in Times Square and delivered each day to homes throughout the New York region and across the nation.

With its distinctive Gothic logo, more Pulitzer Prizes than any other newspaper, and some of the most preeminent journalists in the world, the *Times* is exhilarating for nearly everyone fortunate enough to work there. To join its ranks is to join a succession of greats. Abe Rosenthal, Max Frankel, Scotty Reston, Flora Lewis, Tom Wicker, Anthony Lewis, Russell Baker—powerful men and women, courted and cursed. They broke the big stories. They connected the dots. They told a nation what to think and why it mattered.

I never expected to join this illustrious band of journalists. But as a young man, I came to regard journalism as a one-way ticket out of poverty as well as a tool to make the world better. Both were lofty goals, part of the unchecked, unbounded fantasy of youth. The young have no clue of the commitment, sacrifice, and struggle required to become successful in a profession. Many of us tell ourselves when embarking on a career, If A doesn't work out, I can always try B. For me, there was no plan B. The *Times* is where passion, fate, luck, and skill took me.

My rise at the paper was smooth and steady, and the view from the top was spectacular: as the *Times'* managing editor, second in command, I witnessed and shaped history. I reveled in the paper's legend, guarded its secrets, learned to analyze and strategize in the tradition of its best editors. Second only to my family, the *Times* defined me; I was addicted to the paper and all it represented, cloaking myself in its power and prestige. Beyond the status and security, I simply enjoyed working there. Most of my friendships were formed there—people I cared about and who I thought cared about me.

Throughout my career, I had shattered one racial barrier after another. I had paid my dues, and when I attained the position as the first African American managing editor in the *New York Times*' 150 years, I knew I was on track for the top job of executive editor—if I played my cards right. But I made a critical mistake: for a moment, I saw myself as invincible.

Then along came serial plagiarist Jayson Blair. And suddenly, in the credibility crisis that forever will be known as the Blair Affair, the prospect of my running the *Times* newsroom was gone. I realized: I am not invincible. I could be replaced. And from my lofty perch, I had to watch, day by torturous day, as calamity unfolded with a surprising fury. Blair's exposure led to one of the most tumultuous periods in the paper's history and further eroded an already shaky relationship between newspapers and skeptical readers. It also exposed fissures in the management structure on which I was standing and in many professional relationships that I had assumed were solid. And because the plagiarist was black, across the country the goal of newsroom diversity—hiring multicultural, multiperspective staff to serve an increasingly multicultural, multiperspective society—began losing ground.

Of course, it was not the first time that a plagiarist had damaged the trust between a newspaper and its readers. But this debacle occurred against a different backdrop: the *Times* staff was exhausted from living through and covering 9/11 and its aftermath, followed by the nonstop crises of wars in Afghanistan and Iraq. Staff dissension over decisions made by a new management team was simmering, and the traditional decorum among *Times* colleagues faltered, leading to a rare breach. Information—and misinformation—spewed from within the newsroom to eager outside media, exposing the inner conflicts of the paper for all the world to see. I found myself in the painful position of watching the decency that defined the *New York Times* devolve into a street-fighting mentality. Reporters and editors faced off, impugning one another's integrity and violating their own professional codes of fairness and adherence to facts.

Anyone who followed the news industry in the summer of 2003 knows how the story ended. The events that rocked the institution shook the world of journalism at large, supposedly ushering in a new era of transparency and introspection. Indeed, because of what happened at the *Times*, mainstream media stepped up efforts to become more accountable, less defensive, and more transparent in their decision-making. The *Times* itself, where for years senior editors had dismissed the need for an ombudsman, reversed course and appointed a reader advocate.

Summer 2003 also showed the dark side of today's journalism. Some journalists accept what other journalists present as truth without question or challenge, and with lightning speed the Internet spreads not just well-researched news but also reporters' errors presented as news—and once erroneous stories are out there, they can be extremely difficult to make right. The scandal also exposed the proliferation of journalists-as-celebrities and the institutional arrogance that continues to define mainstream media.

In the industry, the *Times* is still regarded as a mighty entity. But its might has been publicly questioned. The specter of such a highly regarded newspaper itself becoming the fodder for news, the butt of late-night TV jokes, is one of the saddest chapters in American journalism.

———

THE *NEW York Times* is not and probably never will be a media conglomerate—a company with significant resources also invested in television, film, radio, magazines, and the Internet. Its chief currency is quality, trustworthy journalism. With its fundamental principles in jeopardy in the wake of the Blair Affair, the *Times* did what its leaders thought was best for the franchise. Their message to me, however, was that I had intentionally jeopardized the franchise, something I would have found akin to drowning my own child.

While the credibility crisis and the *Times*' response to it are worthy of a business school case study, the entire affair cast me into my own personal hell. Initially, I felt alone, abandoned, and afraid as I searched for new bearings and a way to continue to support my family financially. I faulted myself, replaying my last two years at the paper; second-guessing every conversation, every memo, and every meeting;

asking myself what I could have, should have, done differently. The answers came, amplified by hindsight.

In time, I recognized a Shakespearean tragedy as much as I did a powerful company forced to do the hard work of reexamining itself. To look deeply into what happened is to see ugly twists and surprising turns, stories of loyalty, ignorance, arrogance, and betrayal. Add to that toxic mix a potent dose of racial animosity, which was there all along, of course, but far more sinister than I allowed myself to believe.

Eventually, though, I recognized that continually retracing my steps and assessing what went wrong was futile and damaging both to me and the *Times*. It is all too easy to hurl insults and cast blame and whine that things just are not fair. I needed to look beyond the events that severely wounded the world's greatest newspaper and ultimately ended my newspaper career. I needed to let go of the anger that gnawed at me in the still silence of those interrupted nights.

———

AT A Nieman Foundation seminar at Harvard in October 2004, a combative questioner asked me why she should read *my* book. It was a fair query, since others had already used this particular scandal to turn out articles and books filled with half-truths, whole lies, personal attacks, and oft-repeated rants about the *Times* and its staff and the tenuous state of American journalism.

Those are not my goals, I assured her. I wrote this book for those who want to understand how I rose to the top of the *New York Times* and how I experienced the *Times* as an editor and a black man who came of age in urban St. Louis in the 1960s and 1970s.

I wrote this as something of a primer on the culture of corporate America and the corporate game of trying to get a leg up on one's peers. I mastered this routine on my rise to the top; I became proficient at getting more from others than I gave to them. I kept the Real Gerald M. Boyd tucked safely out of sight while the newspaperman navigated the corridors of power. Right or wrong, this was the only way I thought I could function, survive, and succeed. This approach served me well throughout my life and through most of my career. But if you are hiding a part of yourself, you are not truly living life at its fullest.

I wrote this to show how race played a larger role in my working relationships than I ever imagined—far more than any person of color would want to believe. I never ran away from being black; in fact, I understood precisely how my differences made the paper better. I realized far too late that my belief left me vulnerable to those who did not tolerate differences. Naive, I know. Throughout my journey, I was often one of the few leaders of color, if not the only one, at the table. White colleagues give little thought to this fact, but being the first, or the only, challenges professionals of color every time they pull up a seat. It should not be surprising that being present, being yourself (or as much of yourself as you can be), being vocal, come with a price. But few of us take the time to explore the toll. My story explores those consequences in great depth.

And I wrote this for the next generation of journalists, those who are going where I have gone. I hope, but don't expect, that my story will spare them some of the mistakes I have made.

Finally, and quite fundamentally, I wrote this for my son. I want him to understand the people and forces that shaped his father, and by extension, that shape him. The *Times* used to be my life, but my life was more than the *Times*. Fortunately, I came to appreciate this before it was too late.

As I answered the question from the woman at Harvard, I recalled my childhood, my beginnings. No one back in St. Louis could have predicted my career. I covered some of the biggest stories of a generation, met with presidents, and traveled the globe. And I did so often as the odd man out, the lone black face, strikingly dissimilar from anyone else in the room.

Now away from the *Times* for three years, with a deeper understanding of who I am as a father, a husband, a son, a brother, and a friend, I can look back on the peaks and valleys in my life and newsman's career with a clarity that comes from time and distance. I tell of the highs and lows of this life at the *Times* with an honesty that comes when there is nothing to hide or lose.

July 28, 2006

MY TIMES

IN BLACK AND WHITE

"THIS IS REALLY HARD"

It's October 2006, and after an exhaustive day of testing, Gerald and I are leaving Memorial Sloan-Kettering. We climb in a cab, and the driver starts uptown. Gerald says, "You're going the wrong way." The driver says, "But I'm going uptown." Gerald says, "I know, but you need to go downtown to get on the FDR, then go uptown." The driver says, "Well, you should have told me that when we first started." Of course, it's on now.

Gerald says, "You're a licensed cab driver—I shouldn't have to tell you the best way to go!" The driver complains. He won't give up. They go back and forth, back and forth.

We're about three quarters of the way to the house. Gerald looks hard at the license posted on the back of the driver's seat. He says, "Young man, your license has expired." The driver says, "No, no. I just got that renewed." Gerald says, "Yeah, but it starts tomorrow." All of a sudden, no more arguing, no more debate.

At the house, we get out of the cab, and Gerald looks at me with that grin of his. "I got him," he says. "I won." I always knew he was determined to succeed, but it wasn't until that moment that I realized just how competitive he was.

—GARY B. BOYD

"**T**HE PUBLISHER wants to see you at six."

My assistant, Christine Moore, reminded me of an appointment with Arthur Sulzberger Jr. as I passed her in the newsroom. I was on my way to the desks of section editors to mention stories I thought should get more attention from the *New York Times*. Some had already appeared in rival papers like the *Washington Post* and *USA Today*, putting the *Times* in the unenviable position of playing catch-up. Other stories were follow-ups or new ideas to pursue.

Meddling. This was one of my primary responsibilities as managing editor. While the publisher buys the car, and the executive editor sets the course, the managing editor does the driving. Twenty years after joining the paper, I was second-in-command in the newsroom, relishing my turn at the wheel. This ride was a classic—thoughtfully crafted, meticulously preserved, updated only on occasion and only after careful consideration of timing, economics, and what the market would bear. I took my job seriously. I paced the newsroom, determined to inspire, encourage, and debate, and to focus on anything other than the saga unfolding inside the newspaper.

It was June 4, 2003, one of those sluggish days in late spring when the work gets done simply because it has to. No mega event was driving the news cycle, no economic crisis, no congressional scandal, no sensational trial to captivate or titillate the public. Those are the fly times, when the work of journalists is actually far more simple and straightforward than on a slow news day. When news happens, the newsroom operates as if on automatic pilot. Everyone worth his or her salt knows the questions to ask, the angles to cover, the stories that must be told.

That was not the case on June 4. A leisurely air permeated the newsroom. Some reporters and editors were using the time to engage in other matters, like planning weekend escapes from Manhattan or researching destinations for summer vacations. That time of year, just after Memorial Day, always changed the rhythm on West Forty-third, and the change often lasted straight through Labor Day. Men left their ties hanging in closets back at home, and barring major news, everyone shifted to a lower gear.

The shift was calming, familiar. And I needed that badly.

Since Jayson Blair's serial fabrications were exposed on April 28, top executives at the *Times* had been consumed by problems that seemingly defied solution. Our newspaper, the crown jewel of journalism, was under attack both inside and out. Blair's actions not only shattered the paper's trust with its readers but also ignited a newsroom rebellion over everything from favoritism to arrogance to diversity. Like me, Blair is black. He was twenty-seven years old, a reporter whose zeal and skill at staying on the right side of some in the newsroom masked what he later described as a history of mental illness.

This was not the first time the *Times* had come under heavy criticism, but this time the criticism seemed orchestrated and personal. With an unprecedented front-page article published on May 11, the focus of analysis shifted from assessing the damage from Blair's plagiarism and inaccuracies to an indictment of the top managers of the *Times*. It did not help that Sulzberger described the situation as a "huge black eye." I was fighting two wars at once: one against outsiders who wanted to see the *Times* knocked down a few pegs and the other against insiders seeking blood and revenge.

Almost daily the paper's credibility was pummeled, from the towers of academia to news talk shows, from emboldened Web bloggers to even the likes of late-night comedians David Letterman and Jay Leno.

Inside, the staff was clearly divided. The most vociferous critics openly challenged my boss, executive editor Howell Raines, and me by complaining on the record to practically any news outlet that inquired. Internal, supposedly confidential conversations and memos ended up quoted verbatim on media Web sites and in rival newspaper columns. Morale was in free fall.

Senior executives gathered for crisis-management meetings as many as four times a day. We strategized, argued, and eventually cooked up plans that were little match for the dozens of daily battles. We were taxed. We were weak. We were outmaneuvered. I would look around the table wondering whom I could trust. Former *Times* colleagues, who still took the paper's welfare to heart, weighed in with calls and e-mails, and their messages were anything but reassuring. The *Times* seemed a mess, they told anyone who would listen.

I rode out this storm feeling more and more isolated, deeper in the muck, far from safe shores. In the office, I walked the newsroom floor struggling against emotional and physical fatigue. I had lost what had come to define me—my poker face. Instead, I was vulnerable, and I just knew that anybody who looked could see my despair. When I could not lose myself in journalism, talking up the editors, I would try to distract myself from the chaos with routine management tasks. I approved the appointment of a new deputy editor for the Arts and Leisure section and sent flowers to a talented Sports columnist who was recovering from surgery. I was briefed about the latest developments in the *Times'* purchase of the Paris-based *International Herald Tribune*. And I plotted a way to stop a recently hired writer from returning to his old job at *Newsday*, the Long Island–based newspaper.

I sorted through invitations asking me to give a speech or make an appearance. The Council for Opportunity in Education, a group of education professionals devoted to helping low-income students move from high school to college, wanted me to address its annual convention in a few weeks.

"Your accomplishments in the media are well known and could be inspirational to millions of low-income, disadvantaged students," the organization wrote. It noted that I had first become interested in journalism while attending an Upward Bound program in St. Louis. I smiled at the reference to that highlight of Lyndon Johnson's War on Poverty. It had allowed me and thousands of other high school students to spend summers on college campuses. My summer, in 1968, opened my eyes to the possibility of a career in newspapers. I would later attend the University of Missouri on a four-year journalism scholarship, work as a reporter for the *St. Louis Post-Dispatch*, cover the White House for the *New York Times,* and then rise to senior management.

Now my rags-to-riches story was being rewritten. And my paper was fighting for its reputation. I declined the invitation, knowing my attention would be better spent on the home front.

Fulfilling managerial duties gave me no relief at all. The image I had worked so hard to cultivate was being recast wholesale, viciously; I was being carved up, one piece at a time. It was no surprise when my position, which I had held since September 6, 2001, was a target of sniping, but the latest accounts lacked context and balance. Many were flat-out wrong. Reports portrayed me as weak and incompetent, not a man whose vision, passion, and talent helped produce superior journalism that earned the *Times* ten of its eighty-nine Pulitzers.

Even more striking were those reports that presented me as a henchman to Howell Raines, the executive editor. It was as if I had no identity other than that of a nondescript black man holding the coat of my larger-than-life white boss. So much had been written trying to lay blame for the scandal—and much of that had been written so hastily—that many reporters abandoned one of the basic tenets of journalism and built their stories upon hearsay and previously reported lies instead of tracking down the truth themselves. The *Times* did not help matters by asking executives not to speak to the media and instead to funnel all inquiries through an overwhelmed PR department. I had the sick feeling that, from the outside, *Times* management looked like Keystone Cops, stumbling, bumbling, colliding into one another.

I felt helpless to reverse increasingly warped impressions of who I was and what I stood for. Each new picture of me seemed to be worse than the previous one. I began to assess the gravity of each day's developments by how many hours I slept. By then, even a five-hour night was rare.

I would often awake around four and head downstairs in our brownstone on Manhattan's Upper East Side. There in the stillness of the morning, I would turn on the family computer in the kitchen and, while it booted up, brew myself a fresh pot of coffee and prepare to read the latest assaults on the integrity of the *Times* and its leadership. This routine was a form of self-torture, but I was so obsessed that I could not break it. Our six daily newspapers would not be delivered for another couple of hours. Sipping coffee with milk, I would go online and read what the *Washington Post, Daily News, New York Post,* and other newspapers were saying about the *Times*, about me. It was a moment of sharp contrasts—a quiet, peaceful predawn world outside, and the raucous, roiling crisis that kept me from a restful sleep.

———

AS I headed to the newsroom lobby to catch an elevator for my meeting with Sulzberger, I thought back to Christine's announcement earlier that day. *The publisher wants to see you at six.* Christine, a dignified and stylish black woman who had worked for me for more than a decade, knew my every mood. The look on her face told me she could tell I was stressed and stretched.

And curious: six o'clock is a strange time to pull a top editor away for a meeting. For editors and many reporters, 6:00 P.M. is the witching hour. With a first-edition deadline only three hours away, writers are wrapping up stories, editors are anxious to get a first read to raise questions and fine tune, and photo and design teams are selecting their final images, finishing layouts, refining maps and graphics. At six, the work of putting out the next day's paper is in high gear.

So while Sulzberger's request was odd, I attached no significance to it since we had been meeting regularly in this crisis mode. While riding up to Sulzberger's office on the fourteenth floor, I thought about how in some ways I had drawn closer to the publisher since the Blair scandal erupted. I had spent so much time in his office, and we had talked so much and so candidly lately, that I was feeling comfortable enough to tell him the truth even when I knew he did not want to hear it.

I knew these were difficult times for Sulzberger, who, at fifty-two, was not just the publisher of the *Times*, arguably the world's most important newspaper, but chairman of The New York Times Company, a multifaceted and highly profitable media company. For me, the publisher had always been a tough read. He was personable enough and actively worked to project an image of an everyday guy. He began most mornings in the gym, punishing his body in a successful effort to stay slim. He often ended his day by punishing his body with his favorite drink, Grey Goose vodka. Sulzberger exuded privilege, not intentionally, but by birthright. He was the fourth generation of the storied Ochs-Sulzberger newspaper dynasty that had built and nurtured the *Times* into the media brand it is today. As such, he could summon the corporate jet at will, set the course for the empire he headed, and determine my future, something always in the back of my mind.

It would be all but impossible for a man of his station and background to understand where I came from. It was a place of wanting, not having, and that want creates a nagging insecurity that remains no matter how high you rise. After my mother died and my father disappeared, I was reared in the stifling poverty—and love—of my grandmother's home. I had no family dynasty to fall back on; my survival depended on me. Whereas Sulzberger was direct, blunt, at times irreverent, I had to tread carefully; an irreverent black man is likely to find he is not taken seriously. Reality made me cautious and guarded, weighing my words and actions. Blacks in the workplace want their white colleagues to know they have passions and obsessions, just as whites do, but we don't want those interests and obsessions to be used against us. More often than not, I tried to let my performance speak louder than my words. And always, I worried that a display of too much of the real me could be dangerous.

———

I PROBABLY was not Sulzberger's first choice for managing editor. As a professional, I had attended ten years' worth of meetings and dinner parties with him. But we did not know each other personally. He had never been in my home, and outside the *Times* and journalism events, we did not socialize. Nearly all of the time we had spent together in the last decade was related mostly to business.

I would not have been named managing editor without the recommendation of Raines, a Birmingham, Alabama, native who had worked and clawed his way up the ranks and now moved about the *Times* with a swagger of extreme confidence. When Sulzberger offered Raines the executive editor's post, Raines liked to recount, Raines told Sulzberger I was his first choice to be his number two. Sulzberger, trusting Raines, agreed. So Raines and I were a package deal.

Our appointments to run the *Times* newsroom created one of the oddest teams ever assembled to run a New York City newspaper: the white Southerner, who had come up at a time when the region was embroiled in battles for civil rights, and the black Midwesterner, who was raised in an inner-city neighborhood and had grown up flexing newfound black power.

While those experiences helped to draw us closer to each other, they made us outsiders in the insular world of *Times* journalism. With

Sulzberger's invitation, though, we were not only welcomed by the media elite, we sat at the head of the table.

Of course, being a part of a package deal has its own set of perils for a number two. Unless you quickly and clearly define yourself, you're at the mercy of the whims and actions of your other half. Unfortunately, the extent to which I was at Raines's mercy was just becoming clear to me. When my appointment to the managing editor's position was announced, one former *Times*man who knew Raines well warned me that one of my most important jobs as managing editor would be to save Raines from himself. If only I understood then what I did now.

The Blair crisis had brought out sharp disagreements between Raines and me over how to run the newsroom. We disputed each other privately—I had vowed to myself never to air our disagreements in public. Our relationship was like a marriage, I believed, and parents should not fight in front of their children. But since the crisis began, we clashed almost daily, so much so that Raines asked me to promise that I would never criticize his decisions in public. I granted him that, but the pledge did not prevent me from challenging him, which I did constantly.

———

AS THE elevator doors opened to fourteen, I realized that I was looking forward to catching up with Sulzberger. He had requested this meeting only hours after returning from a brief visit with the *Times* Washington bureau, where he had lunched with many of the bureau's fifty or so members. When Sulzberger and I had chatted briefly while he was in Washington, he was uncharacteristically guarded. He described the meeting as "brutal," gave no other details, but said that he would fill me in later.

More than twenty-four hours had passed since the Washington lunch, and I still did not know a word of what had been said. Journalists gossip, especially about one another, and I have spent my career giving and receiving. But now, even friends in the Washington bureau were mum. Their silence made me eager to know what had happened.

That morning the *New York Observer* had yet another article about the *Times*. It included the answer to a pointed question that Sridhar Pappu, the media reporter, had asked Raines: "Are you going to make it through this time?" Raines had tried to deflect that question with a nonresponsive response: "We intend to do an even better job of tapping the collective industry and intellect of our 1,100 journalists who make up the most talented news staff in the world." As I read the *Observer* over coffee that morning, I could not help but wonder whether Pappu already knew the answer to his own question.

Had I been able to see beyond each day's turmoil, had I been paying the slightest bit more attention, I would have seen all these signs for what they were. A while earlier, as I sat in my office with another editor trying to finish up some work, Raines opened the door, leaned in, and said he was leaving for the day.

"Krystyna is sick," he explained without elaboration, referring to his wife. It was plausible enough, and I thought nothing further as he strode swiftly down the corridor to the elevator.

He already knew.

The fourteenth floor is reserved for the Times Company's top officers—the vice chairman, chief executive officer, president, and senior vice presidents. Together they oversee the $3.2 billion company, which includes thirty-six newspapers, twelve television stations, Web sites, and the *International Herald Tribune.*

A portrait of Sulzberger's father, Arthur "Punch" Sulzberger, the paper's previous publisher and the company's previous chairman, greets visitors as they exit the elevator. Plush carpet runs the length of corridors. Down one corridor heading north is the wood-paneled boardroom with its commanding mahogany conference table. Signed pictures of presidents, heads of state, and other prominent people line the walls, including one autographed by Sulzberger's hero, Churchill. Here is where the board of directors meets at least four times a year, where senior managers meet, and where world leaders often give off-the-record interviews to *Times* editors, reporters, and columnists.

Except for me, the hallway leading to Sulzberger's office, which is next to the boardroom, was empty. The lights were dim. It was quiet and unusually still.

As I passed the office of Martin Nisenholtz, the head of New York Times Digital, I heard classical music coming from his computer as he sat typing away. Next door was the office of Janet Robinson, the *Times'* senior vice president for newspaper operations. Her door was closed. Cindy Augustine, the senior vice president for human resources and a friend for years, was still in her office, at her desk. Instead of her usual beaming hello or a quip, she said nothing. She glanced at me. She seemed to be fighting back tears. I made a mental note to stop by or call the next day if she was gone by the time my meeting ended.

Before I could reach his office, Sulzberger stepped into the corridor. His eyes widened as if he were surprised to run into me, but he quickly recovered and motioned for me to join him as he turned around and walked back inside. Characteristically, he was coatless and without a tie. Uncharacteristically, he seemed tired and somber. We headed to his back office, where he sat across from me at a conference table. In his hand was a bottle of water. He offered one to me. I declined.

He quickly took control of the meeting.

"This is really hard," he began. "But I've decided to make a change. I had hoped we could turn this around, but..."

Sulzberger's words trailed off as his voice cracked and tears welled in his eyes. He was silent. I could not speak. I did not know what to say. I felt as if I were a voyeur, watching someone else's tragedy play out in slow motion. The silence lasted only a few seconds, but each second was an eternity.

Sulzberger continued. I heard the words; but my mind raced to a thousand other places, and unconnected thoughts crashed around in my head: *What will happen to me? How can I tell Robin? How will I help support my family? What will my friends think? How had it come to this?*

"This is how we will do it," I heard him say through the din. "Tomorrow morning, at ten-thirty, we will announce that you and Howell are resigning." It occurred to me that he had never said that I was being fired, and in some ways I found that a relief. I don't know how I would have reacted if I had heard those words.

Sulzberger said that he had already talked to Raines, and now Raines's sudden exit made sense. Raines had given me no warning as to what was about to happen, but Sulzberger said that he had expressed concern about my future.

They had agreed, Sulzberger said, not to discuss whether we had been asked to resign or were doing so on our own accord. Whether we would speak to the staff was still being decided. Raines would be leaving the building immediately after the announcement and was not planning to talk to the media. Sulzberger suggested that I avoid the press as well.

Years before, as a senior editor, I attended a seminar for *Times* managers in which we learned how to fire people. First, we were told, let them know what was happening in a way that was clear and unambiguous. Then talk about their leaving at a specific time, so there is no doubt. After that information has sunk in, relax and have a dialogue.

Whether intentionally or not, Sulzberger seemed to be following that script. He leaned back in his chair. He turned to my future, reassuring me that he thought I would have opportunities to work as an editor again. He pledged to do all he could to help, once the paper got beyond the crisis.

I felt no anger or bitterness toward Sulzberger or any of the unseen hands that had a part in my dismissal. That would come later. Right then, I was tired and welcomed the chance to get away from what I saw as madness. In a way, knowing it was all over was calming. I no longer had to worry about what people said about the *Times*, about me, or about the scandal. It was as if I were going on to a better place after a hard, painful illness.

I was too proud to plead for my job, and I knew that this decision was not about to be reversed. But for some reason, I felt it important to share how I felt.

"I have never in my life failed at anything," I said, looking into his eyes. "I'm scared."

Sulzberger again reassured me that I had a future in journalism and that I would be all right. But his words sounded empty. This indelicate task behind him, he was thinking ahead to next steps in damage control. My future, whatever it would become, was now my problem. I knew it would be extremely difficult, if not impossible, to bounce back. No other executive had been forced out under such intense media scrutiny. How the hell would I be all right?

But those were not concerns to share with the person who had just informed me that I had been dismissed. They were questions for another day, with other people who cared about whether I really would be all right. Sulzberger was trying to save his paper and perhaps his own job, and I needed time and distance to think about how to start over after twenty years at the *Times*.

We had said everything that needed to be said. It was time to go.

I rose and backtracked down the corridor. I had walked this path to the elevators hundreds of times before, but now each step was difficult and painful.

I left the building and headed into the twilight, my head foggy, my pride wounded, and every illusion about my value to the *Times* shattered. I was being cast out and pushed away from everything that defined me as a journalist and, in many ways, as a person. I had devoted nearly half my life to this job, which was really more my calling.

Anyone who is falling will frantically reach out for something to grab, to cut the speed, cushion the crash landing. A safety net. I grasped only cool air.

In the days and weeks that followed, I mourned my loss as if it were the death of a dear friend. I shifted from anger to disbelief, then moved on to sadness, and finally slid into a deep depression. I would never regain the life I left behind, and I had no idea what lay ahead.

To save myself, I needed to move forward as soon as possible. But to move forward, I needed to do something I had never seriously done while on my way to the top.

I had to look back.

1

LOSS AND LOVE

When did Gerald become cool?

When we worked together on Soldan High's newspaper and he reproached me for being "too emotional" an editor-in-chief, I didn't think he was cool. When he went to Mizzou, I thought Gerald was worthy, but I didn't think he was cool. I felt he was too serious, and wondered if college would help him lighten up and make cool friends. When he arrived very late for a party I threw for him and my then-husband (in the 80s; they shared an October birth date), Gerald was in some kind of funk, and I didn't think he was cool. It was a party, dammit. Months had passed without a word. Was it so hard for him to be . . . well, nice? To be cool?

When I saw him last in 2004 on a bright Sunday morning, it was the final hours of a weekend in St. Louis at our Soldan class's thirty-fifth reunion. He sat alone in a restaurant booth, his cherished *Times* before him, and suddenly, Gerald was cool. Today I find comfort in those reunion memories: the warm hug between Gerald and my husband, Larry, upon their first meeting on Friday; Gerald's heartfelt keynote speech infused with love for Robin, Zachary, and journalism on Saturday; our tender farewell at breakfast on Sunday. The Gerald Michael Boyd I knew, scolded, and loved for more than forty years could be frustrating, stubborn, distant, provocative, and a bad dancer even on the slow songs. But you know what? My friend was so cool.

—JACKI (GREEN) MOFFI

W E BURIED my mother on a clear, frigid January morning in 1954. She wore a white dress that matched her casket. To the left of the casket lay a flower arrangement with a clock set at four, the time she died one morning the week before. The death certificate listed her as a female Negro and a housewife. It said her stillborn baby was at eight months' gestation and that my mother was felled by cerebral thrombosis, or a blood clot in her brain. Pregnant women have a higher risk for forming blood clots, and Odessa Thomas Boyd, who had acute anemia, was carrying her fourth child.

My sister never received a name, which was, I suppose, acknowledgment of how fragile we were as a family. Another loss would be too much to bear, and naming the baby would only make that loss more real.

We sat in the front row at Ellis Funeral Home on Stoddard Street in central St. Louis, I have been told: my father, Rufus, and his three children. The choir sang sacred standards, "Amazing Grace" and "Nearer, My God, to Thee." My uncle Clarence and his band ended the service with "Until We Meet Again." I slept through most of the somber proceedings, comfortable on my aunt Laura's lap. If I had been awake, I would not have known what to make of it all. I was three years old.

None of it registered with my younger sister, Ruth, either. Only my brother, Gary, who was seven, was able to grasp the meaning of losing his mother. He knew she was never coming back.

Try as I might, my memories were not strong enough to keep her with me. No kisses good night, no tuck-ins, no hugs, no gentle wipes to clear a spot of jam from my chin. I never knew my mother, not in the way most children do. We did not spend our evenings on the living room sofa listening to stories about how she met and fell in love with my father. I do not remember her laughter around the kitchen table at dinnertime, or her voice at all for that matter, or any of the treasured moments that more fortunate adults replay from childhood.

The few fleeting glimpses I am lucky enough to have of my mother —if you can call it luck—haunt me. I see them as if I am staring hard through a waterlogged lens. At times, I can almost picture the vague form of her face, but long before the scene crystallizes, it disappears again.

Though I could not see her and could not feel her, as I grew up I would imagine that she was with me. My mother was my secret weapon, this angel who watched over me and argued with the rest of the angels on my behalf.

Odessa came to rest that cold morning in Booker T. Washington, a segregated cemetery across the Mississippi River in East St. Louis. Grave 6, Row 2, Lot 2. And when we put her in the ground, we buried much of my childhood. Losing her has been a taint on my life, a stain throughout my years, in ways that I came to grasp only late in adulthood.

She died six months shy of her twenty-seventh birthday. It was amazing that she had seen twenty-six. Throughout childhood, she suffered from what was most likely sickle cell anemia, a malformation of red blood cells that impaired her body's ability to absorb oxygen from her lungs. She learned to live with the agonizing pains in her joints, the fatigue and nausea, the headaches, the shortness of breath. She also tolerated infections and a persistent sore on one of her thin legs that, no matter how much liniment she put on it, never healed.

There were the constant trips to the hospital for transfusions to boost her healthy red blood cell count. She had been punctured and pricked and probed by so many needles that, over the years, doctors and nurses could barely find a vein that was not near collapse. With fresh blood coursing through her, Odessa would lie in a hospital bed for days or even weeks until she regained enough strength to return home.

When she was home, relatives told me, Odessa tried to be the best mother and wife she could be. She cooked and kept a tidy house when she was able. No matter how tired or weak she was, she still doted on us children, smothering us with hugs and kisses. She so wanted another daughter to make her family complete.

Becoming pregnant again was extremely dangerous for a woman with her compromised organs. How could she ever sustain a growing fetus? Odessa's weakened system could barely support her, let alone any baby she carried. Each of her pregnancies had taxed her body more than the previous one. Doctors warned her that she was flirting with death. They urged her to have her tubes tied, an option she rejected outright.

And she never complained. "I was worried and so were others," my aunt Laura recalled. "But not Odessa." Perhaps she was resigned to her fate, Aunt Laura said. "She once said to me, 'I'm not going to get well anyway.'"

———

ODESSA AND Rufus met in 1946 in St. Louis, one of the dozens of northern cities receiving an infusion of southern, rural blacks. Their experience mirrors that of hundreds of thousands who were part of the Great Migration, one of the most significant movements of the twentieth century. The migrants shaped not only the cultural, political, and social fabric of urban areas but also black culture as a whole, adapting southern traditions to a northern lifestyle to create thriving communities that influenced everything from employment to the arts. The relocated relatives clustered around one another in the city. Uncles, aunts, and cousins lived across the street or a block or two away, flowing freely from house to house.

Odessa was a tall, slender country girl with smooth cocoa skin and deeper brown eyes. She was a looker, as fine women were called then, feisty and sweet—she drew young men like flies to honey. She was soft-spoken and a great listener who loved to sing in low soprano and dance to the latest pop songs. Though she was quiet, she was not afraid to speak her mind. She had a streak of stubborn determination with which she pursued anything she wanted. And she wanted Rufus, who was solid, dependable, and worldly, having gone overseas in the navy in World War II.

At three years Odessa's senior, Rufus was quite mature and charming, especially when he put on his suits and the attitude that went with them. He also was known as a man who liked his drink. He was not a cruel or abusive drunk, and unless you studied him closely, it was difficult to determine when he had had too much. There was no doubt that he was madly in love with Odessa.

They dated by slipping off to the movies or popular St. Louis nightclubs like the Riviera, where they listened to Lionel Hampton or Duke Ellington. When the club scene became too rowdy, they hung out with friends, playing cards on weekends. Mostly they spent time just talking in the yards in front of their homes, where my father would impress my mother with his countless stories about how people lived in lands far away.

Rufus and Odessa married the same year they met, in a small ceremony at the home of a minister. They were simple people, my parents, and wanted nothing more than to make a life for themselves and the family they hoped to have. Like most of the migrants, both grew up on farms, and the paths that brought them north were quite similar. St. Louis was a world removed from the fields and farms where the Southern transplants had barely eked out an existence, where they were still beating back Jim Crow, where the change of the seasons dictated the rhythm of life. Another thing my parents had in common: they were both poor.

Rufus was not yet eighteen in 1941, when the War Department found him deep in the small Mississippi Delta town of Itta Bena in Leflore County, where he had been sweating alongside his parents, brothers and sisters, cousins, uncles, aunts, and grandparents in the fertile cotton fields that governed their lives. For his family as for so many others, life had two realities—little money and a load of kinfolk.

My parents' individual family histories are similar to those of many other black families shaped by the African diaspora and slavery. The Delta that Rufus abandoned to become a navy cook had been home to his family for more than one hundred years. Jacob and Betsy, his great-great grandparents, were enslaved on a plantation there in 1819. They took the last name of the owner, a man called Waits. The sale of Jacob and Betsy's son Jake, along with other children of enslaved parents, was recorded by a white man in a worn and dusty book in the Leflore County courthouse: "I warrant that they are sound and healthy and free from disease and slaves for life."

When emancipation came, Jacob and Betsy's children stayed around Itta Bena working the land. Jake, unlike many slaves separated from their parents, had not traveled far. He and his wife, Katie, produced thirteen children—seven boys and six girls. Their youngest, Evie (or Eva—she spelled it both ways), who was born May 9, 1897, was my grandmother.

Jake, my great-grandfather, was known as Big Jake to distinguish him from his son and because of his imposing stature. Tall and dark, proud and robust, he rode around his ten-acre farm astride a brown horse, with a thick cigar dangling from his mouth. He was self-sufficient, working the land, saving his money. Eventually, he managed to buy a patch of property that he and his family worked, then another, then another. Even through the Great Depression, his family held tight because the farm produced almost everything they needed. The rich Delta soil yielded an abundance of corn, sweet and white potatoes, sugarcane, and all kinds of greens. Cows gave them milk, butter, and meat. From hogs, the family got hams at Christmas and the pork niblets for the cracklin' bread they ate regularly. What they did not eat in season, they pickled or preserved or salted away for later.

September, the time for picking cotton, was one of the most brutal months but also the most rewarding. The whole family joined in the harvest—from children to the oldest of the elders. With burlap sacks over their shoulders, they tugged at the bulbs gingerly to keep from getting cut by long needles that could be sharper than sharp. From this and the pecans they planted and grew, Big Jake put away enough to carry his family through the winters.

Eventually, Jake Waits owned enough land for almost all of his children, including my grandmother, to build their own houses. As a lord of the manor, every few days Jake would ride from home to home, paying each of his children a brief visit and making sure they were all right.

In 1920, Jake and Katie's baby girl, Evie, a tiny woman who topped out at five feet tall, met and married a man named Charles Boyd. They built a house close to the main house, the big house where Jake lived. By all descriptions, Evie's place was not much to look at, with its simple wooden floors and small rooms. But like all of the homes, it was clean, with neatly pressed sheets on the beds and fresh linen on the kitchen table.

A year after they married, Evie and Charles had their first child, a boy named Robert, who was born on the Fourth of July. Four more babies followed: Katie Mae; Larry; my father, Rufus; and Bertha.

But Evie was walking a tightrope. Charles was "a mean man," she once said, leaving it at that. He was a wanderer, leaving the house for destinations unknown and returning whenever it suited him. One day, he came home and watched my grandmother combing one of the girls' hair, and suddenly and without explanation, he grabbed the comb from her hand, threw it into the yard, and walked off. She never saw him again. Whenever people asked about a husband, she replied simply that she was widowed. My grandmother would later have a couple of male "friends," but she never remarried.

With an extended family so nearby, Evie, a single mother of five, found ready support. Her three boys grew up in the house with her, while the two girls lived in the big house under the watchful eye of Grandmother Katie. Evie and her brood did almost everything with her sisters and brothers, especially on Sundays, when the entire family filed into the same African Methodist Episcopal church. They spent the day in worship and followed that with more fellowship and feasting. Each family brought a dish or two to share in a communal repast.

Then came the Great Depression. Jake lost Katie. He remarried and in 1935 became ill with pneumonia. When he died that same year, he left behind thirteen children and dozens of grandchildren. He also left the land to his family, but they did not hold it for long.

Several of my grandmother's brothers moved to Jackson, Mississippi's capital, where they bought a plot of land large enough to build several houses. Evie, just past thirty, remained in Itta Bena on what was left of the farm, trying to hold on to her land. With sadness, she would later describe how unscrupulous whites swindled the family out of one acre after another.

With her three sons in the military, and one daughter, Katie Mae, married and living in St. Louis, my grandmother, alone and weary from struggling over land, decided to leave Mississippi altogether. She headed north to live with her daughter and son-in-law, figuring she could make a living doing housework for white people. It was drudgery but one of the few options available for a black woman with more farm than formal education. And anyhow, the wages would be considerably higher than what she could make in Mississippi.

She headed up Highway 7 through Greenville to Interstate 55, following that through Memphis and on to St. Louis. Under the rules and rigors of Jim Crow, colored travelers knew not to stop their cars along the highways and to pack whatever food they wanted to eat, because they would not be served along the way.

For a farming woman from small-town Mississippi, St. Louis had to be overwhelming. It counted more than eight hundred thousand residents. Streets swarmed with cars and people, and blacks filed off the highways and out of the train depots into slums that were already brimming with new transplants. Jobs were plentiful in huge plants producing everything from beer to bricks, from shoes to steel. But not everybody found work, and in close quarters, crime and illness were on the rise.

Odessa's lineage had a similar profile. She too grew up on a farm, in a small Arkansas town called Camden. It was owned by her grandmother, Fronia Evans Turner, a striking woman, with long straight hair and high cheekbones, born in 1885 somewhere in Oklahoma. While in Oklahoma, she met and married a man with the last name of Thomas. They had one child, my grandfather Elige, who in 1922 married Georgia McDuffie Wilson and settled into life on the farm that Fronia owned, growing cotton and corn, and having and raising children. In 1923, a year after their wedding, Georgia bore a daughter, Laura Bell. Two years later, my mother, Odessa, was born. Georgia's third girl, Dorothy Lee, died in infancy the next year. Two boys followed: Clarence in 1928 and John Henry in 1931.

From her earliest years, Odessa was known as "sickly." She would romp around with her siblings, but every so often, she would disappear for a week or so, staying at the local hospital for transfusions and rest. She would return home and for weeks appear to be healthy, then she would wear down, and off she would go to the hospital again.

Elige always kept a car with enough gas to whisk his daughter away in a crisis. Her sickness spared her from many chores that her sister and brothers were assigned around the farm. And it made her a favorite of her parents. They pampered her, as if trying to compensate for genetics.

Elige did not care much for farming, so it stood to reason that he would convince Fronia to sell the farm. The family moved to Parson, Kansas, where they had relatives, but made that a pit stop. Then they headed to St. Louis, which boasted, among other things, Homer G. Phillips and City Hospital Number 2, medical facilities that served most of the city's blacks. Although the hospitals were largely segregated, they offered decent medical care to poor and black communities.

––––––

AT THE end of the war, Rufus came to St. Louis to live with his mother, Evie, who was working as a maid at a downtown hotel. So was Odessa's mother, Georgia. The families lived one house apart on Papin Street, in a bustling black district called Mill Creek Valley. Rufus and Odessa first spotted each other on a hot summer evening when they had both gone outside in search of a breeze. The attraction must have been instant. Odessa, who was still attending Vashon High School, had her grandmother's cheekbones and shoulder-length shiny black hair. Everyone proclaimed her a striking beauty.

Rufus was not a bad catch himself. He was a little on the thin side, not too tall, but solid with big, strong hands. Piercing brown eyes dominated his face, and unless he smiled, he appeared to be perpetually sad. He was not one who turned heads when he walked by, but was marriage material nevertheless. In addition to the worldliness he had acquired in the navy, he had a well-paying job as a linesman at Wabash Railroad. His flashy clothes, shiny car, and sharp wit added to his value. And he wanted as much as Odessa to have a family.

My father did not talk much at all, and rarely about his wartime experiences. But he once told Gary and me that he was at Pearl Harbor on December 7, 1941, the day of the Japanese attack that drew the United States into World War II. Desperately trying to escape the flames in his building, he leaped from a second-floor window. My father cried as he told us what he had witnessed: ships aflame and hundreds of sailors taking their chances in the waters below rather than suffer certain death by fire. Then he fell silent. In his body, he carried two constant reminders of that day: a metal pin that navy doctors inserted in a leg injured in the fall, and a limp. He also had a medal that he kept tucked away.

My father spared us of the harsh degradations of serving in a segregated navy, and the wonder of a young man going from Itta Bena to places on the opposite side of the world. Mostly, he shared his thoughts with the bottle in the brown bag that became his constant companion.

After Rufus and Odessa married, they moved in with Georgia, Odessa's mother, who was separated from Elige. They stayed on the first floor of her house on Papin Street. Evie had moved to the second floor. In 1947, Odessa gave birth to a boy, my brother, whom they named Gary Bennett. In 1950, in the early hours of October 3, I came along, and my parents named me Gerald Michael. I would be called by my middle name for much of my childhood.

Mill Creek Valley, my first neighborhood, was the center of life for some twenty thousand African Americans, some, but not all, in tenements. The People's Finance Building provided offices for many black doctors and professionals. The *St. Louis American* and *St. Louis Argus*, local black newspapers, were based there; along with two black hotels, the Booker T. Washington and the Calumet; black theaters like the Star, Strand, and London; and the St. Louis Stars, a team in the Negro Baseball League. At one time Mill Creek boasted more than eight hundred black businesses, churches, and other institutions.

But more than 99 percent of the structures there were in disrepair; 80 percent were without private bath and toilet; 67 percent lacked running water; the crime rate was four times the city average; and the infant mortality rate was two times the city average.

About fifteen years after my parents moved there, Mill Creek Valley would cease to exist, razed for an expressway, apartments, and an extension of St. Louis University. This ghost of a community, teeming with the vitality and the challenges of an influx of Southern migrants, is a place where I can envision my mother and father, like hundreds of other black couples, striving and staking their claim on the American Dream.

———

WITH TWO children to care for, Rufus and Odessa carried out their distinctive roles. She looked after the boys and the house while he went out to earn enough to keep everyone fed and clothed. I don't know if my father ever thought about using his GI benefits to go to college or purchase a home. I can only imagine that my mother's illness forced him to focus on what was immediately before him. With so many health crises and practical matters to attend to, there was no time for dreaming.

For a black man who did not mind hard labor, jobs were plentiful. Rufus had steady work at Wabash Railroad—a good job with good benefits. And he was skilled at fixing almost any engine around, especially after he had a drink or two in him.

For some strange reason, my father left Wabash to drive a truck for Gershon's, a neighborhood grocery store. We never knew why he left a comfortable railroad job at that time. But Gershon's was at least convenient, about two blocks from our house, close enough for Rufus to walk there.

I can only guess about my father's motives, about how the delicate seams connecting our lives started to unravel. Gershon's must have paid much less than the railroad job, and that must have put considerable strain on my father, who was trying to feed and clothe the four of us, and possibly on his marriage as well. Still, my parents endured. Odessa was almost twenty-seven when she and Rufus had their third child, a girl who they named Ruth Etta. I was two when my sister was born, another mouth to feed.

Bringing Ruthie into the world further weakened my mother's frail body. And so it was that, in 1953 when she conceived that fourth baby, Odessa tried again to beat the odds.

After a bedridden pregnancy, Odessa began 1954 with yet another trip to the hospital. Relatives and friends rushed to give blood and hovered around the waiting room, praying that she would pull through. She had always pulled through. But this time the transfusions were futile, and the doctors were unambiguous. Odessa was going to die.

Doctors suggested a cesarean, at least giving the baby a chance at life. But Odessa's father, Elige, argued that three children were enough to handle without a mother. My father complied.

Despite her weakened state, Odessa organized her affairs. She told her husband to do whatever he could to keep their children together. She wanted them raised under the same roof. Her older sister, Laura, was bringing up four children clear across the country in Oakland, California, but said she would take Odessa's children in. My father agreed to his wife's deathbed wish.

Along with the doctors, whom the family blamed, Rufus was on the firing line for my mother's going to an early grave. His drinking somehow must have worsened her condition, my mother's kin whispered. He was not worthy of her anyway, they said. Rufus was an easy target, since he was taking to the bottle even more. When Rufus did not have enough for the funeral that Odessa's family wanted, they blamed his drinking for that, too. Elige helped foot the bill to bury his baby girl. And the tension wedged itself between the Boyds and the Thomases, pushing our families apart.

With my mother, the anchor, gone, our little family was cast adrift. My mother's mother, Georgia, took in Ruthie while my father took Gary and me and moved in with his mother, Evie. When Georgia went west to be near her daughter Laura, she took Ruthie with her. Despite my mother's wishes, Odessa's three children would never again live in the same house. Sometimes the longing for my sister, for having my family whole again, would bring me to tears.

———

I CANNOT imagine why Evie Boyd would want to take in two more children—especially two boys—at the age of fifty-seven. By then, she already had the children of her youngest daughter, Katie Mae—the same daughter who had brought her to St. Louis and who had died in 1944. Grandmother was convinced that her child had been poisoned, that someone slipped something in her drink while she was at a club. Katie Mae left two boys, Ronald, thirteen months at the time, and Walter, three months. Seven years later, their father, a cab driver, was murdered in an apparent robbery. The crime was never solved.

While Evie took care of four grandsons, Rufus continued to punch the clock at Gershon's. He piled the brown boxes of groceries high in the back of the big brown truck and made one stop after another on his delivery route. Some weekends, I would get the thrill of riding with him, watching as he maneuvered the stick shift to negotiate the busy St. Louis streets. I wanted to drive a stick just like him.

Our evenings were filled with anticipation of what goodies my father would bring home from Gershon's. Day-old cakes and pies and damaged cans and other items supplemented the government cheese and powdered milk that my grandmother received each month as a part of the public assistance that, along with the domestic work, helped stretch her money. Gary and I would rush to greet my father as he walked in the door, where his mother and four boys awaited him.

However disjointed, however ragtag, we were a family. Gary and I had someone we could call Daddy. To my cousins, he was Uncle Rufus. As a young boy, I was keenly aware of that difference, that Gary and I were bound to my father with stronger ties. I felt special and wanted.

I thought my father was doing his best to take care of us boys. His gentle demeanor was no doubt mellowed by the constant flow of liquor. By now, his drink of preference was white port wine, a bottle of which he always carried in a brown paper bag. Drinking must have eased his pain, at least temporarily, because the routine of raising the bottle to his lips clearly gave him comfort.

In 1955 Evie decided to move her family "uptown" to a neighborhood on the West End of St. Louis, where my father's big brother, Larry—or L.A.—owned a house on Temple Place. The once predominantly Jewish community on the outer city limits boasted small, neat homes on expansive lawns and was changing rapidly. Blacks flowed in to be close to jobs at the Scullin Steel plant, the General Motors plant, and the post office. All six of us crowded into my uncle L.A.'s empty second-floor flat.

Uncle L.A. was a hard man, strict and firm. He understood the importance of family, but he was not sentimental about it. Everyone was expected to pull his weight, and those who could not, he discarded. L.A. worked long hours at Scullin Steel, while his wife, Rose, worked at Jewish Hospital. Together they provided their children, Kenneth and Alison, with the middle-class trappings that we, Evie's charges, could only dream of. We boys came to know Santa Claus through the gifts that L.A. put under the tree for my cousins downstairs. Santa left nothing for us children living in borrowed space upstairs.

Under Uncle L.A.'s rules, we had to tiptoe up and down the stairs; he did not want to hear the commotion of a bunch of kids above his head. The front porch was not a place to hang out, and never, ever, a place to bring and eat food. That would be too unrefined, too country, for L.A.

Of course, Uncle L.A.'s rules were too hard for four rambunctious boys to live by. Tension grew between Evie and L.A. Something had to give, and it did.

One day we were camped out upstairs in my uncle's house on Temple, and the next we were dragging our boxes, bags, and tattered suitcases out of there. There had been a falling-out, and we were asked (or ordered) to leave. We must have been some sight, and I felt embarrassed that people could see we were homeless. Fortunately, a lady who lived several houses away, whom Evie had befriended, agreed to take us all in.

We moved onto her third floor, with the woman's family scattered beneath us on the first and second floors. We boys piled into one room with my father, and my grandmother took the other. One bathroom serviced the whole house.

The woman below had several children herself, and there seemed no end to the running and ripping under her roof. Her two boys were several years older than I was. One had a job selling the *St. Louis Post-Dispatch* on Sundays. Somehow, I became his assistant, selling a luxury item. In our home, newspapers cost too much to buy.

Once a week, my "boss" and I would wake before dawn. Rubbing the sleep from our eyes, we headed to a nearby corner to wait for the boxy truck to rumble through the streets, dropping off bundles of the bulky Sunday paper. We then set up shop, hawking to drivers and pedestrians making their way to church, dog walkers, and other passersby. It was a brisk business.

My boss netted slightly more than a nickel from each copy and split that with me. After our shift, I would skip home, proud of the pennies jangling in my pockets. It was the first money I ever earned. My first job, at seven years old, taught me a powerful lesson: I did not have to ask my father or grandmother for money they did not have. I could earn it myself.

Evenings found us lined up and waiting for our turn to take a bath in that solitary bathroom. The boys took theirs in the earliest part of the evening. We would crowd in front of the mirror, primping. We would oil our hair down with Dixie Peach pomade, rubbing and brushing rigorously enough to coax our coiled strands into the waves that many a black person coveted. To hold the waves in place, we slept in stocking caps made from Grandmother's worn hosiery. Then we slapped our faces with generous portions of Old Spice. We were a greasy, reeking bunch, but we thought we were the height of cool. It was a warm memory, one of the brighter aspects of our itinerant life.

———

THE HOUSE on Temple was severely overcrowded, and that put Evie and Rufus on a nearly constant search for more room. John Jeffries provided another temporary fix. Mr. Jeff, as we called him, was a Korean War vet with a steady job at the post office. Using his GI benefits and government salary, he had bought a two-story house in the same vicinity but a very different setting. Mr. Jeff, who was black, dated Aunt Rose's sister, Margaret, so he was already familiar with my grandmother and father and their brood.

In 1957 we moved to Mr. Jeff's at 5845 Romaine Place. He lived on the first floor and rented the second floor to my grandmother. We were the first black household to move onto the street, with its two-story brick homes and well-tended yards. It would be my home for eleven years. With three bedrooms, a kitchen, bathroom, and a back porch, the flat seemed huge to my seven-year-old eyes.

We may have moved up a notch by being in Mr. Jeff's house, but we were still poor. Our new place had its own particular problems that reflected our tentative state. Everything was old and tired. The bedrooms held a hodgepodge of shabby cast-offs. Grandmother took one room, and my cousins took another. My father, Gary, and I crammed into the third. The double mattress that we shared was frayed and so full of bedbugs that no amount of pesticide could get rid of them. A banged-up dresser held our clothes. Sitting on the warped and blistered linoleum floor of the kitchen was a three-legged dining table propped up against the window ledge for balance and a battered refrigerator that seemed to lean into a rickety old stove. Mice and roaches scurried for cover as soon as the kitchen light went on. Grandmother cleaned as best as she could, and we grabbed the roach spray and mouse traps and went to war.

But this was our home, and we slept well on that bed, bugs and all, with my father in the middle, arms outstretched as pillows for Gary and me.

Our neighborhood reflected the ethnic stew that had come to define St. Louis: blacks, whites, Catholics, and Jews. The block had a synagogue on one end of the street and a Catholic church on the other. But not too long after we settled in on Romaine, moving vans lined up as real estate speculators played on whites' racial fears so they would sell their properties. The whites who remained owned most of the stores and shops, including a grocery store around the corner that we frequented, called Cooper's.

We were treated politely but kept at arm's length. Our white neighbors stayed out of our business, except for the family next door who would converse with my grandmother as they stood on the front porch. A teenage girl, Barbara, lived there, but we never exchanged more than a hello with her.

———

WE SETTLED into a comfortable routine, with Grandmother setting the pace. She rose around four or five in the morning. She would wash up and head into the kitchen, where she began boiling water for rice, the staple of our diet. Then she would go from room to room, waking us up for school. There was no debate, no ten minutes more to sleep. If we moved too slowly, she would splash cold water in our faces. She made her point.

Then the babies came. At some point Grandmother stopped doing domestic work and kept the infant son of a cousin. The father would drop him off each Monday and return Friday evening to retrieve him.

Grandmother also cared for Mr. Jeff's baby daughter. There seemed to be no end to the number of children she was willing to have in her house.

My grandmother's influence was profound. Each child received exactly the amount of attention needed, never more or less. This was perhaps the only way that a petite woman pushing sixty could manage to keep order in a house with four growing boys.

Evie ran the tightest of ships, and I suppose she had to. I took her strictness as meanness and harshness, probably because she resisted all of my efforts to wear her down with that Boyd charm that I must have inherited from my father.

My grandmother went to bed early, around seven or eight, but she rarely slept. She kept her bedroom door wide open, and whenever she caught wind of something not to her liking, she would yell, "Cut it out!" She had no qualms about using the belt for punishment, and no amount of pleading would deter her. Once, when I was talking about a girl to a friend, I shouted, "She is, she is!" Grandmother, misunderstanding what I had said, accused me of cussing, and ordered me to get the belt, which she immediately put to use.

She never missed a thing. When I was nine or ten, I tried to smoke, as I had seen my father do. I took one of Daddy's cigarettes and hid it until the coast was clear. The next day, I snuck out on the back porch and lit up. When I saw Grandmother through the kitchen window, I quickly stubbed out the cigarette and went back inside, tucking it behind my palm, out of her view. As I made my way through the kitchen to my bedroom, I was horrified to see curls of smoke coming from below. It was still lit. She did not say a word.

That evening, when my father arrived home from work, she apparently told him what I had done and ordered him to whip me with the belt. But I feigned sleep, and he let the matter slide. It would be years before I smoked again.

When friends called on the one telephone we owned, which she kept next to her bed, she would pick it up.

"May I speak to Michael?" some girl would ask.

"No, you can't," Grandmother would answer, slamming the receiver down.

Grandmother, the disciplinarian, also had a wicked sense of humor. For her health, she drank a brew of garlic that she boiled and kept refrigerated. She drank several glasses each day. Every once in a while, as a joke, she would pour a tall glass of her elixir for an unsuspecting visitor. Their startled reaction always cracked us up.

She was very superstitious. A broken mirror really did mean seven years of bad luck; eating fish and drinking milk or eating ice cream at the same time could make you ill or kill you; and, depending on which hand was itching, you were going to get some rain or some cash.

But she seemed at peace with her life and her destiny. Once, when we were crossing a busy street, she stepped out just as a speeding car turned the corner to beat a red light.

"Grandmother!" I shrieked, grabbing her arm as the car nearly brushed against her leg.

She looked me in the eye and said matter-of-factly: "It was not my time. Only God decides when you die."

———

I CANNOT think of food without thinking of my grandmother. Breakfast always featured rice. Most of the time, it was only rice—River Rice. I grew to hate rice, especially when it was the days-old rice that Grandmother never threw away. She would just mix in yesterday's and possibly the batch from the day before that. I tried to spice mine up with sugar and butter and wolf it down quickly to avoid the taste. I also grew to hate leftovers, which always reminded me of when they were not an option but a necessity.

Our small kitchen always smelled of serious cooking: long-simmered beans or greens, fried pork chops or chicken, cornbread, oxtail soup. Grandmother prepared breakfast and dinner at the same time. She could cook any dish, usually what was available and cheap. With the rice going, she would throw a huge pot on the stove and fill it to the top with pinto or navy beans or white potatoes, all seasoned with cheap pieces of pork, such as neck bones. Any time she served meat, we would devour it and suck the bones dry.

Once I watched my grandmother take a live chicken and snap its neck with one quick motion of her hand. She plucked it clean, discarding the feathers in a brown paper bag. I was amazed by the ease and the efficiency with which she performed both tasks. And I was sickened. So much so that when that chicken was served for dinner, I took only one bite. The bird just did not taste right.

Grandmother was also the family healer. Throughout childhood, I suffered from debilitating stomachaches. I don't know if they were brought on by stress and anxiety or ancient leftovers. At times, the pains would leave me crumpled, barely moving. If the stomachaches occurred while I was in school, I would be sent home. We had no money for store-bought remedies, so Grandmother would concoct a mixture of baking soda and vinegar and direct me to drink it. If I didn't throw up, I would lie in bed with her rubbing my stomach until the pain eased.

Weekdays meant we could expect meals, but on Saturdays, we were all on our own. We subsisted on leftovers from the week, and when we could scrape up some change, a sandwich or burger from a local diner.

On Sundays, we feasted. Grandmother would bake a chicken or cook a chuck roast. She would prepare mashed potatoes, greens, fried corn, or string beans. Sometimes, she would also make a dessert, like a cake with an icing of butter and sugar, a sweet potato pie, banana pudding, or coconut cake, my favorite.

Grandmother expected us to be independent. As soon as we were old enough, she taught us how to wash, iron, and sew our clothes and to fix our own meals. A few times, when she went away to a funeral or to visit siblings or her son Robert in New York, she left the oldest boy in charge while my father was off to work. It was every boy for himself. She would leave enough money for food, but the choices were up to us. I would stuff myself silly with sugar-laden cereal, three-for-a-dollar cookies, and tall glasses of milk.

Once I confused government-supplied white powdered milk with flour and used it to fry chicken. I could not figure out why the "flour" melted away, clouding the grease. When Grandmother returned and saw the heap of slimy chicken, she just smiled and then showed me where to find the flour.

Since we seemed to put down roots on Romaine, I looked forward to Christmas. Santa would finally be able to find us. I woke up looking for games, balls, and shiny new toys, but they never appeared. Grandmother did her best to pinch hit. She would go to the Salvation Army and bring back the most decent of used toys, like the Chinese checkers set that we played until we wore the colors off the marbles.

As disappointed as we might have been, she made it clear that she would not accept whining about what we lacked and what other children had. "I just don't care," she declared. But she would temper our disappointment by cooking each of us our favorite cake. She started several days before Christmas, keeping our "presents" wrapped tight under her bed so that neither we nor the mice could attack them before Christmas morning.

So while other kids were busy unwrapping toys, I was slicing into a coconut cake, which I would wash down with a tall, cold glass of milk. As a boy, I saw the gift as a consolation prize for all the gifts we couldn't afford, but once I grew older, I knew its true meaning: Grandmother's abiding love.

———

WITH SIX people to feed, stretching one meal into three, we learned to make do. The cure for a rotting tooth: a bus ride downtown to the dentist who charged ten dollars for each extraction. At least a few times, I went in and left missing a tooth.

Since money was tight, I never attended any end-of-the-year field trips for my classes. I stayed home those days, trying to imagine the fun my classmates were having at amusement parks and museums.

Like many of my classmates, I wore the same outfits day in and day out. No one made a big deal about that. I was, however, embarrassed by the holes in my shoes and socks, so I learned to darn at an early age, and whenever I had money, I would get my shoes fixed. When a sole could not stand another patch-up, I would slip cardboard into the bottom to keep the flesh of my feet off the pavement.

For school, Grandmother insisted that our clothes be clean and pressed and sharply creased until they looked "like a million bucks." Just before the school year started, she would pull out the few dollars she had squirreled away over the summer. I received two pairs of tan khakis (I was a college student before I owned my first pair of jeans), two shirts, a new pair of shoes, and a winter coat, which we always found on sale. Any other clothes I wanted, I had to buy myself.

Despite my best efforts to hide my circumstances, I always felt that I was about to be found out. In first grade, for example, students brought their lunch from home or went to the corner store. Grandmother made it clear that lunch was a luxury—we did not have enough money for three meals a day. From time to time, my father gave us a dollar or two, but we could never count on that.

In the first week of school, when a bowl of leftover spaghetti was absolutely the only food in the refrigerator, I piled some between two slices of bread, smashed it down, and put it in a brown bag. When the time came to retrieve our lunches from the cloakroom where they were stored, I realized that a classmate had taken my brown bag by mistake. I took the only bag that was left, with a ham sandwich, an apple, and a few cookies. By the time I returned to my seat, he was wailing.

"Someone took my lunch and left me this—this spaghetti sandwich!" he cried.

The children laughed in disbelief—everyone but me. I did not let on. Somehow, the mystery remained unsolved. For the rest of the year, though, I never brought lunch again. Fortunately, Warren, a white boy I had befriended in that year, often came to school with enough money to buy lunch for himself and for me. Whenever he was short or absent, I would tell my classmates that I was going home for lunch, since I lived around the corner. I would walk home, spend thirty minutes with Grandmother, and return to school. For lunch, I would drink water.

———

NO MATTER how dire our circumstances, as the youngest of four boys, I had it better than my brother and cousins. I enjoyed the benefit of their protection, experience, and encouragement. I would hang on their every word as they talked about girls, sports, music, and school, normally in that order. As I grew, I would rummage through their closets, looking for something cool to wear.

Like all the kids in the neighborhood, I got into fights, but I also knew that I had backup. One day at school, I took a pounding from a much larger boy whose siblings were well-known bullies. I quickly found Gary, and with one of his friends, we went chasing after the offender. My tormenter became docile at the sight of my bigger brother and his bigger friend. Gary ordered me to punch the kid in the mouth, which I did without a second thought. Then I did it again for good measure, and the three of us walked home triumphantly.

Gary may have been my protector, but in those days, my father was my hero. I was both embarrassed by and in awe of him. I learned to expect teasing whenever someone mentioned where my father was born. Itta Bena was considered the sticks, with its country ways, far lesser than the sophisticated city. Even my father's name bespoke of a life without indoor plumbing, store-bought clothing, televisions, or telephones. Rufus. No child I knew had that name.

His was a life that he never lamented nor fondly recalled. It was what it was. I inherited this kind of attitude, accepting whatever fate came my way. But, unlike my father, I was concerned about what I had and what people thought. As the youngest in my family, I realized early on that I needed others, and I became skilled at seeking people out, asking questions, gaining their assistance. I was ever conscious of their reactions. I wanted to win them over rather than ignore them. To me, appearances were important.

In truth, like many children of parents who knew how to provide but not how to parent, I really did not know my father. We rarely spent time with him because he worked six days a week. Once home from work, he spent much of his time in our room listening to the radio. The brown bag was always there with him, on the floor next to the banged-up dresser. Perhaps I was so enamored with him simply because he was there.

I knew this: there was not much joy in my father's life. He would search for it in the storefront Baptist churches he attended. My grandmother was a regular at St. Paul's AME Church, which she had attended since she first came to St. Louis. St. Paul's, one of the city's oldest African American churches, was in the Mill Creek Valley district. Grandmother expected us boys to attend services, and for many years, we did. Rufus never felt comfortable in that church, perhaps because most of the family attended.

If Rufus had a "lady friend," we never met her because he never brought her home. And I can't remember his going off to spend time with such a person. But maybe I was too young or naive to notice.

Every once in a while, on a Sunday after church, my father would borrow his brother L.A.'s car and take Gary and me out for a drive. We would cruise around town with no particular destination or objective other than being together. Those were some of my most pleasant moments with him. He never took us to the cemetery where our mother was, and I did not ask. I wish I had.

I never heard words between my grandmother and father. But Grandmother showed a quiet tolerance toward him—not disrespect, but not respect. I never got the sense that she was proud of him for sticking in there with her and the boys. Neither did he, I imagine. What I know is that somehow the responsibility, the disappointment, the routine, and probably the loneliness became more than he was willing to bear.

I cannot remember the first mention of his moving to New York. I can only recall snippets of hopeful talk, like he was going there to do better. He would live with his brother Robert and get work. Whether he said it or not, I convinced myself that once he had enough money, he would send for the two of us, and my sister Ruthie in California, and that we would all be together. It was 1962 when he left. I was eleven years old.

I knew his leaving was supposed to help us, and that I had no choice but to accept it, but that loss stung more than when my mother died because I was old enough to understand what it meant to say *Daddy's not coming back*. I tried to rationalize his extended absence: *he needs to make more money to send for us, he has to find another job, maybe he got sick and is resting for now*. Families were supposed to be together.

Yet I don't recall ever crying over my father's leaving. My stoicism, my fatalism, had already set in. I expected bad things to happen to us. And I was already learning to improvise. If there was no money for a basketball, we made one by balling together some old socks and shooting it through a cut-out milk carton or shoebox that we had nailed to the wall in a corner of our room. I could pretend to be Oscar Robertson,

Elgin Baylor, or Bob Pettit, dribbling down court, and then with two seconds left, *swish*, I made my shot.

In the end, I accepted the inevitable. Until it became apparent that he would never reply, I wrote him letters every couple of weeks. For years, I would tell anyone who asked that my father had moved to New York for our benefit. That hurt less than to tell the truth: that we were abandoned. That we were orphans.

2

SEEDS OF AMBITION

Michael was different from the other boys his age. He was serious about school—and about being in the band. He was also reliable and dependable—except when he chose the band over work. There weren't a lot of young people from the neighborhood who were going off to college, but you had a sense that Michael was on a mission—that he was going to do something with his life. His perspective wasn't what was on the next corner but what was around the world. Michael always put himself in a position to be exposed to bigger things. Years later, I would see him on TV, in the presidential press corps, and my brother Marvin would call and say, "Do you see Michael?" I was very proud that we had crossed paths.

—SIDNEY COOPER

THERE WERE the five of us now: Grandmother, Ronald, Walter, Gary, and me. From what we heard, Rufus was living in New York in his own apartment, down the street from his brother Robert. He rarely called.

With Rufus gone, I looked to Gary for guidance more and more. At twelve, I needed all I could get. Despite Grandmother's firm hand, I was a knucklehead, trying to prove my budding manhood by joining friends in stupid pranks.

We would approach unsuspecting women and, with big, broad smiles, suggest something crude like wanting to have sex with them. Or we would swipe a handful of candy from the open bins at the neighborhood department store. After our offense, we would take off running, laughing at the rush that came from being up to no good. Fortunately, we never got caught.

But truth is, guilt or, more specifically, Grandmother, kept me from venturing too far down the road of a delinquent. I stole that candy only once; when I got home, I could not eat one piece. In fact, I threw all my loot away. As for harassing women, it wasn't long before I started to imagine Grandmother's horror if she ever found out: "Michael, that lady's somebody's mama!"

Despite my halfhearted efforts to be cool, I am sure I was seen as a nerd among my peers. I tried not to make waves and strived for respect, an asset that toys or sharp new clothes or a two-parent family could not bring. That meant being smarter than they were or more skilled or accomplished. And it was just as important to win over the adults in my life.

To some degree, those skills would become strengths as I polished them and adapted them to different situations. I would listen more than talk and always try to show respect. In time, I learned how to win people over.

As the youngest child at home, I was encouraged to be seen and not heard. I became an astute observer. I would sit for hours, soaking in the conversations of Gary, my cousins, and my grandmother's visitors (I noticed that older people often mistook children's silence for ignorance and dropped their guard), and then struggling to make sense of them. I usually saved my questions for later, when it was just Gary and me. Gary did his best to be father, teacher, and brother, even though he was only three years older. Losing our parents pushed him into manhood whether he was ready or not.

Gary and I were alike in many ways. Physically, we had the same dark brown skin and stocky Boyd physique and, unfortunately, even as adolescents, the same receding hairline. Like me, Gary was cautious and deliberative, considering all sides of an issue before making a decision. I was smarter, so everyone said, an assessment reflected in our grades. But he was wiser; he had experienced more. Whatever wisdom he passed on, I took without question. I knew he had my interest at heart.

There was no sibling rivalry between us—we did not have time for that. Instead, we tried to support each other, especially in the face of outsiders. Around the neighborhood, children teased Gary by calling him Bus, a reference to what they said was a great big head. As his little brother, I was known as Little Bus. Whenever Gary got in a scrape with another boy, I would rush to my brother's aid, pushing, shoving, and punching away. I probably hurt more than helped, but I came out swinging anyway.

Gary tolerated my friends and me. Once, he chaperoned us when we went to the theater to see *The Great Sioux Massacre,* the 1965 western about Custer's defeat by Sitting Bull and the Sioux. For days afterward, we played a game of soldiers and Indians. None of us wanted to be General Custer. Sitting Bull was the hero, and we all wanted to be Indians.

While my brother was my role model, my cousin Ronald was my idol. Ronald was cool and smooth. In high school, he ran track and won the state championship in the hundred-yard dash. (He inspired me to run track, and I did for a while, proudly collecting a few handfuls of first- and second-place ribbons.) Ronald was a halfback in football, and everyone expected him to get an athletic scholarship, to go some place far from Romaine. As the oldest, Ronald garnered the most respect. If we were all at the table, Grandmother served Ronald first and gave him the biggest portions. I so wanted that position of honor. Plus, Ronald had a girlfriend whom I spied him kissing once or twice.

Ronald even had a television set—the first in our home—which he bought from the Jewish merchant with money earned from babysitting Alison and Kenneth, Uncle L.A.'s kids. Neither Gary nor I could turn on the set unless we got permission from Ronald or Grandmother.

Ronald always welcomed us into his and his brother Walter's room, where they kept the TV on, volume turned low, for whatever was airing. On Sunday evenings, that meant *Daniel Boone*, my favorite show, which starred Fess Parker.

Then in early 1963, Ronald was gone. After it became clear that he would not get a sports scholarship, he enlisted in the army. I remember Grandmother sitting in the living room, listening as her oldest grandson explained how the army was his best bet, even with a war raging in Vietnam. It was a good alternative to the jobs available to black high school graduates, he said. He could send money home each month, which she clearly needed, he added. For the longest time, she did not respond. I do not remember what she said when she finally spoke, but it was clear that she was not happy.

I did not know what the big deal was. I only knew that my cousin made a striking figure in his olive greens with sharp creases in his pants and muscles bulging in his sleeves. He was going on a great adventure, first to basic training in Texas and then to a place called Germany. Not too long after he left, Walter followed, joining the air force.

That November, my family of three sat glued to Ronald's black-and-white TV, watching the burial procession for President John F. Kennedy move through the streets of Washington, D.C., and out to Arlington National Cemetery. I was ignorant of Camelot and the dashing president and his striking wife, but from overhearing Grandmother's conversations with other adults, I regarded President Kennedy as a champion of black people. I did not trust Lyndon B. Johnson for reasons that, as best as I can recall, had something to do with his being a Southerner and the hushed talk that he somehow played a role in Kennedy's assassination.

While Gary would take time to help me understand confusing events like the death of a president, he showed no empathy regarding our own predicament. Like our grandmother, he never expressed fault or made excuses for why life was the way it was. He spoke directly, without sugarcoating to make the reality easier to digest. Sometimes he delivered his honesty with sharp edges.

Once, when we were on the front porch, where we often fled to escape the suffocating summer heat in the flat, I was filled with envy watching our next-door neighbors play. I longed to be like them, with their new toys, new clothes, and working parents who seemed to provide for their every need. Gary listened to me carry on, then said simply: "But we're not like other kids. They have fathers and mothers."

———

IN MANY ways, our neighbors on Romaine became our extended family. After all, 5845 Romaine was our first real home. By the early sixties, most of the whites were gone, replaced by working-class black families. I roamed the streets with friends like Vondell, Lamar, Eddie, Darrell, and Taylor. We kids banded together, though not as gangs by any stretch of the imagination. The friendships Gary and I formed lasted for years, sealed by shared adversity, secrets, dreams, and everyday experiences. We knew which kids did not get much to eat at home, which parents fought, who had their lights cut off, who had relatives in jail, and which boys had crushes on which girls.

We would spend hours on the street, playing stickball in the summer and football in the winter, under the watchful eyes of Grandmother or other neighbors. Long before Hillary Clinton popularized the African expression "It takes a village to raise a child," adults on Romaine were living this wisdom. Grandmother certainly did. She was ever vigilant and rushed out at the first sign of trouble. If somebody else's children misbehaved, she ordered them to stop. And they did—there was no arguing with Grandmother Boyd.

———

AS MUCH as we tried to keep the rougher parts of the neighborhood at bay, sometimes they intruded on our lives, and sometimes it was scary. One day on a schoolyard playground, a bully was picking on one of Gary's best friends, a boy named Robert Lee. Robert Lee normally pulled his punches, but this time, he fought back. He was actually getting the better of his attacker, when the boy's older brother ran up behind him and bashed his head with a railing.

Robert died almost instantly, his blood staining a corner of the playground. Staring at the spot, I could not help but wonder how Robert must have felt when the metal struck him, and whether he was in heaven, and did he see my mother. Robert was the first person whom I can remember dying. And whenever I thought of him, I tried mightily to forget what happened.

Ignoring death became my way of coping with it. It was the only way I could feel secure, as if nothing more could be taken away from me. It was easier to ignore than to allow myself to feel such a deep sadness. If it did not happen, it did not hurt.

———

SEPTEMBER BROUGHT not only relief from August's heat, but also an end to summer's endless days of nothing to do. Gary and I were stuck at home while everyone else seemed to be somewhere, anywhere, on some adventure. For us, there were no visits up north or trips down south. I never posed for pictures with Mickey at Disney World. In fact, the only mice I knew of were the ones that scurried across our kitchen floor.

September also meant that school soon would start again. I loved the rhythm and order of schooldays, and the recognition and validation from my teachers. Outside of my home, school was where I felt most comfortable.

At Edward Hempstead Elementary School, which was named after an early benefactor of the St. Louis public school system, I was pegged as smart and an achiever and placed on the accelerated track. Two black teachers, moved perhaps by my circumstances or by my charm, adopted me, so to speak. One was Dorothy Vaughn, a stout woman with big emotions and a big heart. Miss Vaughn would often lose her cool over some edict that the principal or the Board of Education handed down. She coped by going shopping. For some reason, she started to take me with her on her excursions.

We would head downtown to one of the big department stores, like Famous-Barr or Stix, Baer, and Fuller, and she would buy me khakis and shirts and sweaters. I knew she was kind, but I was also convinced that she was rich. How else could she afford to spend money on a child who was not her own?

While Miss Vaughn boosted my self-esteem with her dollars, another teacher, Mildred Smith, did so with her words. I felt I could tell Miss

Smith anything, and she would listen to my boyhood mutterings and help me shape them into coherent thoughts about how I felt about life and the world. In class, I shamelessly became her pet, and when she left teaching to become a counselor, I remained in touch with her through my years in high school.

Miss Smith taught me to trust in my own opinions.

"Just remember you're not wrong," she would say. "You are seeing the world through fresh eyes and calling it as you see it. That's a good thing. Don't let anyone tell you you're wrong."

Hempstead grew more crowded as the trucks and vans ferried more black families into the neighborhood, filling homes hastily vacated by whites. First, portable classrooms were added behind the building to accommodate the surge of children. When it seemed the students would overwhelm the space, the Board of Education began busing us across town to predominantly white schools that were less crowded.

For two years, I was among the black children riding buses to white schools, first Kennard and then Wheatley, in South St. Louis. None of us complained about the long, bumpy bus rides across town. They gave us a chance to play the dozens. "Your mother's so ugly..." or "Your mother's so fat..." somebody would yell out to get things started. Then another boy would jump in and trump that punch line with an even worse insult to somebody's parents or siblings or circumstances. I participated but was not very good at it. I would laugh at the cracks, but I did not enjoy the sport of attacking others.

Forced busing in the late 1950s and early 1960s was not the explosive issue it would become in the late 1960s and 1970s, because it was not weighted with the lofty ideal of integration. In fact, the educators were determined to keep blacks and whites separated. We Hempstead students had our own classrooms, a kind of school within a school. At recess, teachers kept us away from the white children. They even directed us to use separate water fountains. The significance of the segregation was lost on me. But I felt alien in those schools. Hempstead was my home, while Kennard and Wheatley were like temporary housing. By the eighth grade, the busing experiment ended—at least for me. I was back at home at Hempstead.

———

I DON'T know when a child becomes conscious of race and the differences related to skin color. I knew that white families on my block were different, but for a long while, I thought it was only because they had money. I did not realize race and money went hand in hand. Grandmother never talked negatively about whites or anyone else around us, and she never discussed racial discrimination or the need for equal rights. Sometimes, I would hear my cousins call white folks "honkies," but that word did not register with me. What mattered more, by Grandmother's example, was the kind of person I was.

Actually, I had a hard time imagining that some whites could be poor, since they owned all of the stores in the neighborhood and appeared to have the best jobs, like teachers. That thinking was reinforced later when we watched Ronald's TV, where shows depicted whites with all the trappings of success.

Then there was the Jewish department store merchant who gave credit to my grandmother that she used to buy appliances and furniture. He would stop by the house from time to time to pick up his payments. Everyone called him "Mister," Grandmother included, even though he was much younger. It was not hard to believe that he was powerful; he could provide a refrigerator or a kitchen table.

I would hear about white families living in big fancy homes in areas west of the city, communities like University City, Clayton, and Ladue. They were off limits to blacks, but exclusion was not a concept that I understood yet. Even so, we had our own house and our own neighborhood, and that was just fine.

Every October, I looked forward to attending the annual Veiled Prophet Parade, oblivious to how the tradition underscored deep race and class divisions in the city. The Veiled Prophet was founded in 1878 as a secret organization for prominent St. Louisians, including the descendents of some of city founders. It was strictly blue blood—no blacks or Jews allowed. Everyone in the city knew about the parade, and thousands lined the streets to see huge floats pulled by tractors and carrying white debutantes. The "maids" and their "queens" sat in flowing gowns high above the crowds, waving at their "subjects" below. I never wondered why there were no black maids, and I knew nothing about the debutante ball that followed, which also excluded blacks.

Each year, Gary and I would join other boys from the neighborhood and walk several miles to see the parade and its elaborate "Mother Goose" and "The Story of St. Louis" themes. The experience was the high point of the fall. Years later, as a journalist, I would try to understand how sitting on the outside looking in, watching the floats of untouchable white debutantes waving to the crowd, affected my psyche. At the time, I looked up and waved back, not realizing that my enthusiasm signaled an acceptance of a celebration of separatism.

I suppose my enlightenment began when I entered my teen years, thanks to the Coopers, the Jewish family that owned the grocery store around the corner where Gary and I were regulars, always running Grandmother's errands, and where I would work for four years. In the aisles of their tidy shop, I found not just the eggs or milk or bread that Grandmother sent us for, but a wider view of the world and a deeper understanding of myself. I did not realize how much my values and even my politics were shaped by what I saw and heard at Cooper's store until many years later.

Mrs. Cooper, whose first name was Eva, like my grandmother, owned the store. She and her oldest son, Sidney, could usually be found at the front, running the cash register, while her daughter's husband, Irv, handled the meat department. Another son, Marvin, a college student, would help out on weekends and in the summers. Mrs. Cooper's husband had died some years before.

The family drove in each morning from Creve Coeur, a suburb north of St. Louis, arriving to open at 7:00 A.M. each day except for Sunday, when they opened at 8:00. They closed each evening at 7:00.

One day, I was waiting in line when the customer in front of me asked for her order to be delivered. Carl and Charles, the two neighborhood boys who worked there, doing everything from bagging and delivering to stocking shelves to sweeping the floors, were not available. I volunteered, and Mrs. Cooper vouched that I could do the job. I was amazed when the lady reached into her purse and gave me a generous tip.

After that, every weekend I would plant myself outside the store just before 7:00 A.M., waiting for the Coopers to arrive in Sidney's convertible Bonneville and asking if they needed help. *Yes* meant a few dollars in my pocket. *No* meant a day of playing in the streets.

No doubt it was hard for the Coopers to send me home when they had no work for me. After all, they were businesspeople not philanthropists. But I would just stand there before them with big pleading eyes.

Finally, the Coopers had had enough. In the summer of 1965, just before I started high school, they told me to come in full time. I worked alongside Carl and Charles for thirty-seven dollars a week plus tips. I learned to bag groceries, stock shelves, freshen up the produce, cut meat, and clean everything from the bathroom to the stock rooms to the aisles. For thirty-seven dollars a week, I was an eager student.

Sidney, the oldest Cooper brother, took me under his wing. I had never met a man like him. He was smart and fun and kindhearted and a natural teacher. He never seemed to tire from answering my nonstop questions. Actually, work was like an afterthought. We talked constantly, about education, responsibility, making good choices, race relations, and other news of the day. Working there was like attending a seminar on life and the best way to live it.

Sidney made most of the work a contest, one I was determined to win. When we stocked the shelves, we would see who could empty the most boxes the fastest. My box cutter ripped open the tops at hyperspeed, my marker blazing as I scribbled prices on each item. Then I quickly unloaded can after can, breaking up the empty boxes and tossing them aside. There was an easy rhythm to our work, and our contests were always close, no matter who won.

I knew that the Coopers were Reform Jews, but I knew little about their religious practices or their history. I listened with sadness and anger when they explained how Jews were demeaned and murdered in the Holocaust. I saw how they beamed when they spoke of the Israeli Defense Forces' performance during the Six-Day War in June 1967, when Israel took on and defeated the military might of Egypt, Jordan, Syria, and Iraq. I could not locate Israel on a map, but I cheered for it about as much as I did for the Cardinals. One of my first real heroes was Moshe Dayan, the dashing Israeli defense minister, identified throughout the world by the black patch he wore over his left eye.

I rode in Sidney's Bonneville, sometimes with Carl as the driver. He lived up the street from me on Romaine, and our friends took to calling him Little Cooper. I fantasized about Sidney driving out of our neighborhood each night and into a glamorous life in the suburbs. There he had everything I did not: a nice house, a great car, and most of all, no worries.

I learned Yiddish, or at least a few key words like *shnorrer* and *shmuck*. Mrs. Cooper had a routine of keeping the day's receipts in a brown paper bag that she placed in the trash basket under the cash register. Perhaps she figured that would be the last place a robber would look. Once when I was emptying the trash, I found the brown bag and returned it to her. I was no *gonif.*

Half of the money I earned went to Grandmother. The rest I used to buy everything from haircuts to new clothes for school. The first summer I worked at Cooper's, I used some money for a down payment on a stereo that I bought on credit from the Jewish merchant Grandmother had credit with. He was trying to be helpful when he offered the following advice: "Most black people use stereos like this to play their music. Use yours to also play opera, classical, and other music. Don't limit yourself."

It was the first time I heard a white person underscore racial differences. I took no offense from his advice. In fact, I embraced it.

―――――

THE COOPERS entered my life at a time when I needed them the most. That fall, I started high school. Gary, who played the clarinet with considerable skill, had received a partial music scholarship to attend Lincoln University in Jefferson City, Missouri. As it turned out, his graduation from high school was the final break in our tenuous relationship with Rufus.

A letter from the school administration said that Gary could not graduate unless he paid some bill. As much as we tried, we could not raise enough. Grandmother even allowed Gary to call long distance to plead with Rufus to send money. He promised he would, but never did. At the last minute, his brother, our uncle Robert, came through. I would never forget how hurt Gary was and how disappointed I was in our father. I knew that Gary would never forgive him.

I missed Gary once he was gone, but it was strange and comfortable being alone with Grandmother in the flat. There were few pressures or worries as our relationship took on a new dynamic. Finally, I became her favorite. She was still the adult and I was still a child, of course, but she treated me as if she understood that I was becoming a man—one in whom she had growing confidence. I put an extra lock on the back door off the kitchen and tried to secure it with nails. Each night I would push the nails over the door to make it more difficult for a burglar to get in. By default, at fifteen, I went from being the baby in the family to looking out for Evie Boyd.

When I entered the "hallowed halls of Soldan High," as the school's song proudly proclaimed, I joined a long line of luminaries, none of whom I knew a thing about. For years, Soldan was where many promi-nent white and Jewish families sent their children. Among its students were Tennessee Williams and Clark Clifford, who would become a prominent Washington attorney and a close confidant of several presidents.

F. Louis Soldan High School, like Hempstead, reflected the rap-idly changing neighborhood. By 1965, the year I entered, Soldan was a refuge for blacks who had moved uptown from Mill Creek Valley and other poorer communities to the east. One white student remained.

Gary tried to prepare me for high school life: the teachers, which students to seek out and which to avoid, the separate stairwells for going up and down, the elevator passes that upperclassmen sold to freshmen, even though the school had no elevator.

I started Soldan before the school year began in order to play foot-ball, trying out for junior varsity, where all freshmen were assigned. Practice was in early August. Football was a passion at Soldan, consid-erably more popular than basketball and baseball. Part of the allure was the coach, Leon Anton. He was short and stocky, but because he was so demanding and tough, he seemed to be a giant, a high school version of the tough Green Bay Packers' coach, Vince Lombardi, white with thick black glasses and no tolerance for excuses.

Anton's teams, draped in the school colors of maroon and gold, were always competitive and, more often than not, in the running for the city's public school titles. The Saturday games were must-see events, much like Friday-night high school football in Texas.

Anton pegged me as a defensive end, even though I was considerably smaller than other linemen. Since there was no second-guessing the coach, a defensive lineman I became. Daily practices in the sweltering August heat were torture. We ran wind sprints for hours and then lined up for one-on-one drills that resembled hand-to-hand combat. Anton would draw a circle in the grass and put an offensive and defensive lineman in its center. The object was to force the other player out, however we could. My turn was a bloody affair; the other lineman and I punched each other in the face, or at least the parts we could reach through our helmets. Finally, I managed to knock my opponent out of the circle before falling to the ground in exhaustion. From the grass I looked up and saw Coach Anton towering over me.

"What's your name, son?" he asked with a broad smile.

"Boyd. Michael Boyd," I stammered, delighted that I had gotten the coach's attention.

I made the roster for junior varsity, but I never played a game. Since the team practiced after school every day and played on Saturdays, football meant not working at Cooper's. Sidney was understanding but firm—I had to choose. There really was no choice. I needed the money more than the glory.

In the eighth grade, I had taken up the clarinet, following in Gary's footsteps. Gary had been a mainstay in the high school band and a favorite of the music teacher, Ernest Nashville, who was not only a teacher but also a real musician who played trumpet in gigs around St. Louis. I practiced long hours at home with Darrell from next door, trying to replicate Gary's success. We learned Rossini's "William Tell Overture," Tchaikovsky's "1812," and Gershwin's "Rhapsody in Blue." For football games, we rocked with tunes like Hugh Masakela's "Grazing in the Grass" and Fontella Bass's "Rescue Me." I held my own, but try as I might, I could not match Darrell, who was the first seat, or even begin to approach my brother's finesse. My problem: I was uncomfortable improvising. Take the sheet music away, and I was hesitant and lost. I needed the security of those notes in front of me.

And then came marching. At the band's first parade practice, it was clear I could not walk and blow at the same time, and Nashville quickly noticed. At one point, he walked alongside me, barking "Left! Right! Left! Right!" When that did not work, he yelled, "Don't play, just march!" He seemed amazed that anyone in his band could have so little rhythm. Every evening, I would practice marching, *left, right, left, right*. Eventually I learned not only how to march and play, but also how to make turns.

Clearly a music career was out, and with no chance of a varsity letter in football, I was left with academics. Those days, students were tracked based on academic abilities. I was in the group expected to go to college. Some of my fellow students in this anointed group were already dreaming of the Ivy League, planning careers as doctors and lawyers, perhaps hoping to become the first generation to truly topple racial barriers in education and the professions. Back then, I had none of those ambitions, probably because I had no passions, other than a thing for Victoria Johnson, another freshman. She was gorgeous, with long black hair and an inviting smile. Victoria was regarded as a "nice" girl, with a sister already attending an Ivy League college and a father who was as strict as they came. I worked hard to impress her, using one of the few tools I had confidence in. I took to writing long letters oozing with devotion. I even tried my hand at poetry, struggling to find images that captured my feelings but that did not make me look silly.

At the end of the first semester, Gary returned home. Even with the partial scholarship and a part-time job, he was unable to afford college. He would spend the next year working as a janitor to save enough money to go to the University of Missouri at St. Louis. He would set aside his dream of becoming a musician and pursue the more practical career of a financial analyst. I was glad to have him home.

For once, the Boyds did not obsess about money. With what Gary and I earned, as well as the bit that Ronald sent to Grandmother, we were able to supplement Grandmother's food stamps and government-surplus cheese and powdered milk. We had something in the refrigerator and a few dollars in our pockets. We could afford luxuries, like taking our clothes to the cleaners to be pressed. That Christmas, I did something that I wanted to do all my life. I bought Grandmother a present: a box of her favorite stockings, a shade called Red Fox, with the seams up the back.

The next summer, Gary and I pooled our money and bought a cheap blue and white Pontiac from a buddy of Gary's at work. It was a steal, but it did not make a bit of sense. Neither of us knew how to drive, and I was months away from turning sixteen, the legal age for getting a license. I was confident that once Gary learned, he would teach me.

Gary took his sweet time giving me lessons. He drove that Pontiac so much that the neighbors assumed it was his. I would wash and polish the car the way that Grandmother cleaned our kitchen. And then I would spend hours sitting parked in front of our house, pretending I was going somewhere.

———

PASSION CAN erupt in the strangest of places, and my true love took hold in the summer of 1968, thanks to President Lyndon Johnson's War on Poverty. One of its programs, Upward Bound, placed impoverished high school students on college campuses for eight summer weeks in the hope of enriching their lives. I applied in my junior year when a counselor suggested the program would "expand my horizons." When Gary dropped me off at Webster College in suburban St. Louis for my Upward Bound summer, I said good-bye to much of my past.

The campus was like nothing I had ever experienced up close. Commanding Gothic-style buildings surrounded by lush green lawns. Air that smelled clean, and sky that went on forever. Nights interrupted only by the chirps of crickets and buzz of other insects going about their business. Life was unhurried and unbothered by whatever lay outside the campus. Even more amazing than my surroundings: our group of about sixty students from all over St. Louis was coed and integrated.

For the most part, the teachers were young white college students whose enthusiasm and spirit resembled those of the Freedom Riders, civil rights activists who had gone to the South some years earlier to fight segregation. They probably held similar political views, although their mission was less about changing the course of a nation than instilling confidence and self-worth in the minds of hopeful high school students.

During my first week there, I became infatuated with a white girl named Barbara. We spent hours talking about the similarities in our experiences of growing up poor. Then our relationship was over almost as soon as it began. Over the next seven weeks, I had five other girl-friends, each fling lasting about a week. I was in demand and had never felt so cool. But it was not the girls who were driving this new sense of self-assurance. It was the words.

Upward Bound had its own "newspaper," a publication of several pages typed onto a stencil and run off on a mimeograph machine. I joined the first week, eager to write. Each staff member received a title, and I was named the layout editor, my first position in journalism. Somehow I ended up writing editorials more often than assembling stories on the page. The more I opined, I realized early on, the more teachers and students noticed me.

I had always liked writing, but I had never experienced the high that came from having my words in a newspaper. I could be angry or didactic or whimsical and light-hearted. And I could hide behind my byline, engaging and enraging readers as I saw fit. It was as if I were onstage speaking to everyone but without having to endure stage fright. Here, I could improvise. I could riff. I could solo like nobody's business. By the time I left Upward Bound, I knew what I wanted to do with my life.

I returned to high school for my senior year with a calling. I joined the school newspaper and became a fanatic. I read journalism books as if they were the local sports page. At a library, I found Gay Talese's history of the *New York Times*, *The Kingdom and the Power*, and could not put it down. I set out to become a successful writer—successful enough to work at the *Times*. Somewhere I read that Ernest Hemingway drank scotch, so I tried it, out of sight of my observant grandmother, of course. Like Hemingway, I bought a pipe and tried to smoke it, even though I didn't know the first thing about stuffing the bowl with tobacco and puffing incessantly until a good fire started.

Through journalism came a quiet confidence. In my senior year, I ran for student body president, something I never would have done before. This was my first taste of politics, of selling myself to others. I came in a respectable second, which was fine, since the defeat gave me even more time to devote to working for the paper.

By then, I sported an academic letter and a band letter, although I still envied the jocks for their sports letters. They wore the jackets that girls really wanted, and I became determined to earn one. I looked around for a sport that a senior could compete in and settled on cross-country track. I was out of my mind. Throughout the fall after school, instead of going to Cooper's, I trudged for hours with teammates through the streets and nearby Forest and Penrose Parks. There were no adoring fans, even on race days. At the end of the season, the first seven with the best times lettered; I finished eighth.

The setback didn't matter, though. I had journalism. I still had Cooper's. And I was man enough to date Phyllis, a girl I had met at Upward Bound, even though she was older and far more mature. She smoked, drank, and partied hard. She taught me many lessons, few of them good. Grandmother had no use for her.

"That girl is too fast," she said.

I would feign ignorance and argue that Grandmother couldn't know Phyllis since she hadn't even met her. She went to a nice Catholic school, I stressed. Then I would leave the house and drive over to her place, where I realized all of Grandmother's worst fears.

———

WHATEVER COMFORT my sheltered existence at Soldan and Upward Bound offered from the racial strife tearing through the city and country ended in April 1968 with the assassination of the Reverend Dr. Martin Luther King Jr. I was away from school that day, representing Soldan at a Model United Nations session for high school students in St. Louis County. I heard that teachers and students walked the halls in tears, and that well-respected teachers like Coach Anton stepped forward and appealed for calm. Back at home that evening, I watched in horror the nonstop television coverage of the assassination and its aftermath. Then came the riots, as city after city erupted. Rumors flew that blacks were attacking whites and that militant hit squads roamed the streets.

Grandmother kept us close to home. For the most part, I felt as if I were a bystander watching the events but not feeling their effects. I was more confused than afraid. And I was angry.

I was angry that King was killed; I knew he was fighting for my rights. I tried to imagine the grief that his family was experiencing—especially the four children. And I blamed white racists for his death.

But Dr. King was not real to me. And the whites in my world—the Coopers and my teachers—were not racist. They were decent and fair. In fact, they helped me improve my life, and I felt extremely loyal to them. From my earliest days, it made sense to remain devoted to those who were devoted to me.

At the grocery store, the phone calls started—the threats to kill Sidney and his family. Then the cowards would hang up. Everyone was on edge. I was furious. I could not believe that blacks would do the same thing they accused whites of doing. How could anyone want to hurt this man, who never uttered a racist word? The injustice for both races kept me from sleeping some nights.

———

IN SENIOR year, it was time to get serious about my future. I harbored no illusions about becoming a Scotty Reston or Abe Rosenthal, men I had read about in Talese's book. But with the way that people responded to my writing, I knew I had a future in journalism. I applied to colleges with strong programs—University of Missouri, Northwestern, Iowa State, Drake, and Marquette. Eventually I decided on Northwestern, which offered a generous financial aid package. Then I heard about a scholarship offered by the *St. Louis Post-Dispatch* to minority students throughout the region. Editors chose based on financial need, character, interest in journalism, and literary and scholastic achievement. The scholarship paid tuition and room and board at the University of Missouri, and guaranteed a summer job at the newspaper and full-time employment upon graduation.

I sent in the application, along with a transcript, an essay, samples of my work, and letters of recommendation from Mildred Smith, my counselor, and Sidney Cooper.

To my surprise and great relief, they wanted to interview me.

As I walked into the *St. Louis Post-Dispatch* on a school day, I was both terrified and calm. I wore a suit, blue, pin-striped—the first I ever owned—that I bought from a friend. From the moment I stepped into the lobby, I understood the significance of the enterprise and wanted to be a part of it. Etched in marble on a wall was the paper's platform, written six decades earlier by the owner, Joseph Pulitzer:

> I know that my retirement will make no difference in its cardinal principles; that it will always fight for progress and reform, never tolerate injustice or corruption, always fight demagogues of all parties, never belong to any party, always oppose privileged classes and public plunderers, never lack sympathy with the poor, always remain devoted to the public welfare, never be satisfied with merely printing news, always be drastically independent, never be afraid to attack wrong, whether by predatory plutocracy or predatory poverty.

While waiting for my meeting, I tried to soak everything in. I peeked into the newsroom and saw a group of black men seated on a bench. *Who are they and what wonderful jobs do they have at the* Post-Dispatch? I wondered. I stared at the front page of the day's edition and tried to act as if I read the paper all the time. I rehearsed what I wanted to say. I wanted them to understand me, how much I needed the scholarship, and how much I wanted to become a good journalist.

I was escorted into a conference room where three of the paper's top executives—Arthur Bertelson, the executive editor; Evarts Graham Jr., the managing editor, and Robert Lasch, the editorial page editor—were waiting. I can't remember their questions, but years later, I could still recall how good I felt by the time I left. I believed I had hit all the right points. There were no awkward silences. In fact, the session seemed to end far too early. I even remembered to smile at the end and to shake the hand of each interviewer. No matter what, I had done my best, I reminded myself afterward, echoing Grandmother's encouraging words.

The editors were to make their decision in only a couple of days, but the wait was torture. I would wake each morning hoping to learn my fate only to go to bed each night disappointed. Finally, Bertelson called with the news that the paper published on page three on May 11, 1969. Under a headline and a picture, it read:

> A young man who has worked at a grocery store as much as 40 hours a week, yet has maintained an excellent record at school, is the 1969 recipient of the *Post-Dispatch* scholarship to the University of Missouri School of Journalism.
>
> He is Gerald Michael Boyd, a senior at Soldan High School. He will enroll at Columbia for the fall term.
>
> The scholarship is awarded annually to a Negro high school senior or junior college student. It carries a stipend of $1,500 a year that is renewable for four years. The scholarship is designed to encourage a career in journalism.

In three paragraphs, a whole new life.

3

FROM UGANDA X
TO CUB REPORTER

As I sat listening for Gerald's footsteps that fall afternoon in 2006, I found myself smiling unexpectedly at a memory of his willful, confident younger self.

It was the dawn of the 1970s, and Gerald was *the* black militant on the University of Missouri's Columbia campus. That brother was about change—NOW! His passion and politics bubbled over in the pages of *Blackout*, the black student newspaper he founded and nurtured.

He and those of us in his small cadre of disciples were particularly interested in changing the hearts and minds of fellow black students. With self-righteous indignation, we bemoaned their lack of consciousness, their partying over progress. Of course, we partied, too. But we told ourselves that partying always took a back seat to "the struggle."

At some point, with Gerald at the helm, we decided to meet black students where they were. So we threw a party, and people came. Then we locked the doors, turned off the music, and started a serious discussion about the struggle. People stayed and even participated, a reflection of the respect they held for Gerald. The parties continued, and our cadre of militants remained small, but Gerald always had the respect of students and even some of the virtually all-white faculty and administration. I would see him garner that kind of respect through the decades.

It was respect for Gerald—and a love for him that transformed itself from romantic to familial through the years—that brought me to his and his wife's home that fall afternoon, that had me sitting in their dining room listening for his footsteps. When I heard them—painfully slow and tentative—I turned toward the doorway. Gerald appeared, frail and fragile. As I hugged him and guided him to a chair, the smile his youthful image brought forth lingered on my lips.

—SHEILA RULE

I N THE summer of 1969, I left Cooper's to report to the *Post-Dispatch* for my job as a copyboy, which came with my scholarship. I felt so proud to go to work that first day, even though I had to struggle against a new shirt starched and pressed so hard by Grandmother that it felt like cardboard. I joined the ranks of the black men who sat on the bench, the men whom I had spied during my interview. Most of those "boys," I learned, were full-time employees, and most were full-grown men.

I also learned quickly that being a copyboy—running errands, delivering mail, carrying copies of stories from place to place—was one of the lowest jobs in the newsroom. My coworkers took the job in stride, moving at their own slow tempo. For them, the work seldom led to anything more in the newsroom. To me, it was a step to the next step. My job paid slightly more than one hundred dollars a week, compared with my thirty-seven-dollar salary at Cooper's. I was working fewer hours and doing less work for more money—in fact more than I thought anyone could make in a week. For the first time in my life, I had a bank account. I became Zealot Copyboy.

I anticipated the needs of reporters and editors so much so that if one of them as much as looked up to yell "*Copy!*" or "*Boy!*" I was already standing by his side. When I ran errands, I took steps two at a time. I never waited for the elevator. I don't know what the old-timer copyboys hated more: the fact that I seemed to relish the work they did grudgingly or that they would retire from that bench while I would be long gone.

As my confidence grew, I found ways to have fun. One reporter kept an extremely neat desk—a rarity in newsrooms. In those days reporters typed stories on "books," sheets of manila paper separated by carbon paper to produce several copies. This reporter hated to have books stacked on his desk. But each morning before he arrived, I would scatter a bunch of used books near his typewriter. Then I would join the other copyboys on the bench, and we'd howl when the reporter arrived and cursed the mess.

I was in awe of the pros and determined to join them. I watched the calm efficiency with which many reported and wrote, and the way they leaned back with a smoke once they finished an assignment. It was as if they were enjoying a victory lap. I wandered down into the building's subbasement, where ink-stained pressmen produced the paper. I marveled at the skill of the printers as they carefully set neat rows of type from hot metal into plates.

I sought advice from journalists about what I needed to succeed. Most often, I heard that I needed to write as much as I could. Letters, poems, stories—the medium did not matter as much as learning from the process. One reporter said that once I threw my first million words in the wastebasket, then I would be a real writer. Reporters counseled me to identify my strengths and weaknesses and to look for assignments that maximized the former and minimized the latter. That advice was among the most important to me.

As my internship wound down at the end of summer, I sought the executive editor's advice about how best to use my time at college.

"Learn everything you can about computers," Arthur Bertelson said. "They will change journalism and everything else."

I nodded approvingly, although I did not believe him one bit.

———

THAT FALL, Gary dropped me off at the Greyhound terminal in downtown St. Louis. I carried several suitcases, books, and a beat-up clarinet, a hand-me-down from my brother. I watched out the window as the bus barreled west on Interstate 70, and the place that had been my home for eighteen years faded into the dust. I studied the signs as unfamiliar towns like Mexico, Moberly, and Jefferson City, sandwiched between vast stretches of farmland, came and went. I worried about what to expect.

Gary tried to prepare me, but although Lincoln University, the small, predominantly black college that he had briefly attended, was about an hour away from the University of Missouri, the two were worlds apart. I knew that Missouri, the older, larger institution, enjoyed a better reputation and was more challenging academically. The journalism school, founded by Walter Williams, ranked among the best in the world. At his college, Gary had been part of the majority; I was going to Missouri as a minority. This move was more than either of us could imagine.

The University of Missouri sits in Columbia, roughly halfway between St. Louis and Kansas City. Recognized by the six pillars, the only structures standing from a fire in 1892, it was the first public university west of the Mississippi River when it opened in 1839. I could not get over the size of the campus as I made my way from the bus terminal to Stafford Hall, my dorm. It was a city within a city, and my astonishment must have been similar to Grandmother's the first time she arrived in St. Louis from Itta Bena.

I adjusted easily, finding my way to Jesse Hall, where I picked up my financial aid package, paid tuition, and registered for classes. I headed back to Stafford, one of a dozen or so dorms housing male students. It was an older unit in an undistinguished building on the southern end of campus.

My roommate the first year was white. I suppose that should not have surprised me, but for some reason, I had not thought of what it would be like to share a room with a white person. He was a student from Iowa. Polite, even friendly. He had arrived first, chosen his bed, and unpacked his belongings. He had no posters on the walls spouting antiwar slogans or featuring favorite singers or bands. We would come to spend a lot of time together in that room, studying and talking. We never argued, but I do not recall either of us ever asking the other for a favor—not even to make sure we woke up in time to take an early morning test. Mostly we respected each other's independence and privacy and space. Once we left the room, we went our separate ways. We never ate together or socialized. Few black and white students did. I do not remember his name.

I found that my four years at Soldan prepared me well for the University of Missouri. I was not overwhelmed by any of my subjects and, in fact, found some surprisingly easy. At Soldan, I had always struggled with algebra. But in my first semester, I breezed through the course, receiving an A.

I decided to major in journalism and political science. A second degree would make me more marketable as a journalist, I believed, though I later came to realize that a good journalist needs only a keen interest in a particular subject. Curiosity plus legwork becomes expertise.

I also decided to try out for the campus newspaper, the *Maneater*. To qualify, I had to write a story based on information on a handout. Many of the so-called facts were misleading or wrong. I knew from the start to check everything. I also knew not to assume the words were correct just because they appeared on paper. My story showed two qualities critical to journalism: accuracy and skepticism. I passed and joined the staff.

It was not long before I began to chafe from openly racist attitudes and slights. The university, with an enrollment of about twenty thousand, had fewer than five hundred black students. The year I arrived, the college had just appointed its first black faculty member, Arvarh Strickland, a history professor.

I knew nothing about the university's history with blacks. I soon heard stories, like the one involving Lloyd Gaines, a St. Louis scholar who in 1938 gained admission by winning an NAACP-sponsored lawsuit in the Supreme Court. The university was ordered to admit Gaines or set up a separate and equal law school for blacks. The decision was a significant legal building block for the case that led to the 1954 *Brown v. Board of Education* decision that banned segregation in public schools. Gaines, who would have been the first black to attend the university, disappeared after the court's ruling. Rumor had it the Ku Klux

Klan got him, that he escaped the public glare by fleeing Mexico, that he led a quiet life as a teacher in New York City. Whatever his fate, in the eyes of blacks, the university bore the brunt of the blame.

Everywhere I turned, I confronted racially charged displays unlike anything I had seen in St. Louis. In one part of the campus stood a pink granite boulder with a plaque of dedication to the VALOR AND PATRIOTISM OF THE CONFEDERATE SOLDIERS OF BOONE COUNTY. A local chapter of the United Daughters of the Confederacy, whose motto was "Lest We Forget," had the rock placed there. One fraternity proudly flew the Confederate flag and read the Ordinance of Secession at Old South Days every year. At football games, the band offended with a rendition of "I Wish I Was in Dixie."

The year before I arrived, a few blacks responded to the Confederate flags at a football game by hoisting a flag with the black liberation colors—red, black, and green. That prompted a small riot in which a university policeman drew a gun on one of the black flag wavers. The incident led to the creation of a black advocacy group, the Legion of Black Collegians.

It angered me that blacks were forced to operate as a student body within the student body. The troublesome incidents were a sign that the university needed to accept and adjust to the fact that its student body was changing. I saw the university as a relic out of step with the profound changes that were sweeping through the country. I became determined to do whatever I could to fix these problems, even though I had no knowledge, experience, or plan. I simply determined that the university could and should do better, and I began to say so.

I soon found myself labeled by fellow students and teachers as a campus militant. I reinforced that view with strident rhetoric and belligerence over slights I believed that the university inflicted on black students. I had not come to Columbia that way, but Columbia shaped me through what I saw and experienced.

I joined the black student rebellion, adopting as gospel the slogan of the time: "If you're not part of the solution, you're part of the problem." We segregated ourselves, ate our meals together, attended meetings of the LBC, and held weekend parties that no whites attended. We pledged "blackness"—not a fraternity but a way of life. My group included friends like Jimmy Ethern, a sophomore from Kansas City, and Gary Cook, a freshman from St. Louis. We made an odd trio—Jimmy towered over six feet, not including his huge Afro plus the black pick that jutted out the top. He appeared menacing but was one of the most gentle men I knew. Gary, the shortest of us, was the real firebrand. He was well versed in the militant rhetoric of the day, and he recited it endlessly. He idolized the Black Panthers, in particular Bobby Hutton, the diminutive Panther killed in a shootout with the police.

We formed the core, and with other students, we made our presence known on campus, sometimes to the point of the absurd. We dressed in dashikis and picked out our 'fros, the bigger the better. We reveled in the nervousness of white students and laughed when we heard that some were gullible enough to believe that we had secret ties to the Panthers or some other militant group that we could summon with a phone call. We went to sports events and cheered for the teams that had more black players. We all studied hard, not so much to master our subjects, but to make sure that we did not flunk out. We were revolutionaries, but we had to stick around to lead the charge.

On Friday nights, we gathered in one of our rooms, where we would play Isaac Hayes's "Hot Buttered Soul" and Ramsey Lewis's "Mother Nature's Son." Fortified by cheap wine like MD 20/20 or Bali Hai that Jimmy was the only one old enough to buy, we talked politics and the need for change till the sun came up. Nothing else seemed more important.

For once, I felt a part of something bigger than myself, and that sense reinforced my need to belong. Inspired by recordings of Malcolm X speeches like "The Ballot or the Bullet" we decided to lose our "slave" names—at least in the presence of one another. I became Uganda X.

I followed every Black Panther development and savored the exploits of Huey Newton, Eldridge Cleaver, and Bobby Seale as they stood up to the Man. I revered Stokely Carmichael, H. Rap Brown, and Che Guevara. I worshipped Angela Davis, the beautiful, well-educated black woman so bravely willing to die for the struggle.

While I appreciated the contributions of black leaders like Dr. King, Roy Wilkins, and Whitney Young, I saw them as passive. They did not project my passion for the need for change.

I regarded most whites as pampered, and hippies and radicals as frivolous with choices that I never would have. They could be outrageous one day and the next trim their beards, cut their hair, and rejoin the establishment. Their parents could carve a path toward success for them whenever they were ready to come back into the fold. Of course, my thinking was as simplistic and racist as a white person who believes all blacks are criminals or on welfare.

I took immense satisfaction in challenging conventional thinking. We were certainly no experts on debating, but sometimes even the most unlearned person can point out obvious wrongs and suggest obvious fixes. Almost everyone from the chancellor to the janitor knew that the University of Missouri was a hostile place for students of color, especially blacks. But we seemed to be the only ones proclaiming the emperor wore no clothes, even though everyone could see he was naked.

I had high disdain for black students who did not share my view. One of them was Tom Morgan. Morgan, a tall and handsome dude who also hailed from St. Louis, committed the sin of sins by joining the campus ROTC. Wasn't he aware that racism existed in the military? I challenged him. Didn't he care about the real struggle? How could he give his *life* to the military when it was doing such awful things in Asia? Morgan, who clearly had his own agenda, seemed to pay us no mind.

———

JIMMY, GARY, and I dated women who thought as we did. Given my commitment to the revolution, I did not have time for a serious relationship. But despite my misgivings, I started to spend time with Sheila Rule, a sophomore who was a neighbor from Romaine.

Sheila grew up in a house several doors from me, with her father, mother, and two sisters. She had attended a different high school, O'Fallon, and she was not allowed to hang on the street as many of us did, so I did not know her well. Petite, amber-hued, with a wide, stunning Afro, she had the biggest, most beautiful brown eyes I had ever seen. She was smart and warm and easy to talk to. And already she was a sophisticated writer. We began to bond over journalism, challenging affronts and correcting injustices.

Sheila was dating a former high school classmate who was serving in Vietnam. I saw her relationship as an insurance policy. We could become good friends, but no way would our connection go any deeper.

We revolutionaries took aim at the Legion of Black Collegians, which we considered far too passive. The year before, the group was embroiled in a controversy over the college's pom-pom squad. When a black woman who had tried out did not make the team, the organization complained, attributing the cut to racism. Our group thought that in order to make significant changes, the LBC needed to select more meaningful targets than the pom-pom squad. We decided to take over the leadership of LBC. Those running it were well meaning but misguided. We could do better.

I did not run for office but operated in the background, pulling enough strings to get Jimmy and others elected to key leadership positions. It was my first success as a revolutionary.

We recognized that there were too few black students to create a critical mass, and too few blacks in authority to lend any weight to our efforts. So we forged alliances with campus activists opposed to the Vietnam War and with women's groups pushing for gender equality.

We played a moral card intended to embarrass the administration. They could not defend the lack of minority professors, black students, or a place on campus where black students could gather and support one another. We spent hours debating the best way to get the Confederate Rock removed from campus and to get frat houses to stop displaying the Confederate flag.

We hinted at violence in our talks with the administration, but we certainly were not ready to take that drastic step. I could not see violence achieving any goal other than leaving us in prison or dead.

I was not just confronting authority but risking consequences that might have altered the course of my life. But my role in the movement gave me a sense of purpose that I had never had before. I drew energy from our rabble-rousing, from the possibilities and even the danger.

Our biggest problem, and one faced by all revolutionaries, was the inability to communicate our concerns to the broader campus. As we sat around reviewing our options, I threw out my idea: *Why not start a black student newspaper?* Missouri was ripe for one, I argued. The university had a healthy pool of black journalism majors, and enough freshmen and sophomores planning to pursue journalism. That would form the nucleus of a reporting and editing staff. Students from other majors could help by selling the paper or advertising.

The group loved the idea. We agreed that we could produce the paper ourselves and not have to depend on others. We had a passionate staff that was eager to work. My Upward Bound experience had taught me how to publish a newspaper. I quit the *Maneater* to devote my time to editing.

All we needed was a name. We settled on *Blackout*. I can't remember if it came as we sat in a dorm room drinking cheap wine or at a formal meeting of the newspaper staff. Whatever its source, *Blackout* reflected how we felt: black and excluded from participating fully in the university. It was not nuanced or poetic, but nothing we did those days was subtle.

We printed the first editions of *Blackout* on a mimeograph machine like the one at Upward Bound. I served as the editor, and Sheila and Jimmy were senior editors. We had a strong staff of budding journalists and bundles of energy. Staffers fanned across campus, shoving the papers in the hands of black and white students passing by and demanding ten cents. By no means a legitimate circulation strategy, but it worked; the several hundred copies we produced at a time always sold out.

Still, there was no comparing *Blackout* to other campus newspapers, especially our main competition, the *Maneater*. The *Maneater* had university recognition and funding through a student activity fee. I realized that the only way that *Blackout* could grow was to receive similar recognition and the dollars that came with it.

The debate at the newspaper mirrored the discussion then raging throughout black America: would we be selling out by accepting money from white authorities? How else to survive and maintain our own identity? Finally, we agreed: as long we did not allow the authorities to censor us or pull our punches, we could take the money. In that sense, we rationalized, we were using the system to our own advantage, just like whites. Black students paid the same student activity fees as whites. Why shouldn't we have a voice?

With our newspaper in hand, I appeared before the Missouri Students Association to argue for university recognition. *Blackout* became only the second student newspaper sanctioned by the university and the first "black student" newspaper funded by any mainstream university. The funding enabled us to produce a professional-looking tabloid newspaper, written by "revolutionaries" and paid for by the establishment. The partnership was strange at best.

As editor, I wrote editorials while Sheila's stories graced its news pages. We both edited stories, spending long nights poring over copy. When we finished, we went to the journalism school, where we set the copy into type and laid out the pages. Then we hopped into Jimmy's car and drove to the printing company in nearby Mexico, Missouri. The company sent the papers back by Greyhound. We picked them up, then raced across campus selling them.

We learned on the fly, from finding resources to everything that takes place between conceiving an edition and getting it into readers' hands. We also learned some hard lessons about the importance of inclusion and fairness.

One edition included an article that highlighted Malcolm X, my hero, while ignoring how Martin Luther King Jr. contributed to the struggle. The oversight reflected my politics as well as my ignorance. After the edition hit the streets, we celebrated that evening with a party at an apartment off campus, where we all crashed. The next morning, a loud knock on the door awakened us. The angry regional director of the Southern Christian Leadership Conference stood there, demanding to know how such smart and committed college students could sing Malcolm's praises and disregard King's accomplishments. I realized that we had done so intentionally and that I had no excuse. I regretted our decision and never forgot that lesson of putting aside personal views when editing newspapers.

———

JUST BEFORE the end of that raucous first semester, I returned to my dorm late one evening to find half of the room empty. My white roommate had left without so much as a note good-bye. I was stunned. And as I sat on my bed staring at his bed, dresser, and desk, at the empty closet where his clothes once hung, I could not help but feel abandoned. I thought of our many conversations about growing up, about pressures to succeed, about how he, too, felt like an outsider on campus, and the difficulties his paraplegic brother, who also attended the university, had fitting in. When another paraplegic student committed suicide, I wrote an editorial urging fellow students to show them more compassion.

Still, in all those talks, not once did we discuss race, civil rights, or how my group of revolutionaries stalked around campus, demanding this and that, and keeping to ourselves in the cafeteria. When we were alone in our room, our time together convinced me we were on common ground: just two freshmen with our eyes glued to our books, worried about acing some assignment or test. I just knew that he saw past my rep and regarded me as a friend.

Months later, we bumped into each other on campus, the first time we came face-to-face after he left. We were both at ease, perhaps because the time apart gave us some distance. He explained that he left at the urging of white friends who were concerned about his having a black roommate. What did they think would happen to their brother, I wondered. Would I, in a fit of rage, smother him as he slept? Or perhaps worse, convince him to join our efforts? My former roommate said his decision was a mistake. I showed no reaction. I did not want him to know how hurt I was. I would never again have a white roommate, and I kept a safe distance from the few whites I knew.

———

WHILE HOME for Christmas break, I went to visit Cooper's. Immediately, I felt a distance. I was no longer the eager, naive sponge, soaking up Sidney's perspective. I had my own opinions, especially regarding race. I cited injustices, arguing that whites had discriminated against blacks for too long, and that we all needed to commit to fixing past wrongs. The field was not level but sagging, bringing blacks down, I spouted, recalling well-rehearsed rhetoric. Sidney agreed, but he urged the need to consider the progress already made and suggested that seismic shifts in attitude and culture and law take time. He warned of the dangers of extreme action. To him, my most important goal was getting a degree, not changing the world. A degree would assure my future.

I listened, but dismissed what I did not want to hear. And I sought out those who told me what I already knew, like Mrs. Smith, my former counselor. She understood my militancy and even laughed at some of my antics. I also confided that I was worried about losing Sheila, who was technically still with Chip, her guy who was serving in Vietnam. Despite my newfound self-confidence and a feeling that Sheila and I belonged together, I could not help but worry. Chip had been a part of her life far longer than I had been. Her family adored him. Mrs. Smith did her best to steady me, to tell me there was nothing I could do to influence what would happen. I had to let Sheila decide.

On one trip home, I said my good-byes to the Coopers. By the early 1970s, the family had grown weary of the telephone threats of violence that came regularly following Dr. King's death, as well as the prevailing attitude among many neighborhood blacks that they were interlopers, just out to make a buck. Whether they were in danger or not, owning the store was no longer enjoyable, Sidney said. There were other ways to earn a living. I remember staring through the windows into the darkened and deserted store. If I stared hard enough, past the burglar bars, I could still see all of them: Eva, Sidney, Irv, and Marvin. I saw Carl and Charlie and the ghosts of all the old regulars, making their way through the narrow aisles.

———

BACK AT the university, I moved in with my buddy Gary in an apartment off campus. Between the *Post-Dispatch* scholarship and the financial aid from the university, I was able to buy a new car. Guided by my brother, I bought a white 1963 Chevy Impala with a red interior. Gary kept the Pontiac. I would make the two-hour drive from St. Louis to Columbia singing "You've Got a Friend" along with Carole King. I could not have been happier.

When the pom-pom issue again reared its fuzzy head, my friends and I decided to take it on, in a way that guaranteed that blacks would win.

Alarmed over the backlash the year before, the administration mandated that five of the ten student judges choosing the team be black. I was picked as one of the judges. I corralled the other black judges and told them how we could favor the black contestants. We each gave the highest scores to the black women and the lowest scores to the whites. Of course, this was grossly dishonest, but it produced one of the strangest sights ever witnessed on campus.

After the scorekeepers tallied the votes, they called the names of the contestants with the highest scores. Just a year after judges denied the one black contestant, the University of Missouri now had an all-black pom-pom squad. The team did not remain that way. The administration quickly doubled the squad's size to ten and added whites to fill the slots. The Man was still in control, but our momentary victory was sweet.

Because of our efforts, the university environment was becoming a less hostile place for black students. We still often found ourselves excluded from the mainstream, but the university could no longer ignore us.

My biggest benefit of attending college had nothing to do with academia. It was a deepening of my conviction that I did not have to accept racial inequality. I would never again question whether I should just get my degree, as Sidney advised, or try to change the world. It did not seem farfetched to me to do both.

———

WHATEVER ROOTS I planted were taking hold. I saw good and bad everywhere, and it was easy to choose sides. I opposed the war, supported racial and gender equality, favored women's access to abortion, resented Richard Nixon, and wanted more done for the poor. I believed in amassing and using power of any kind, economic, political, or moral, for good. To do otherwise was almost criminal.

As I began to live a life of privilege—and I felt enormously privileged to be able to attend college—my success was tinged by a sense of guilt and obligation. Many young men from my old neighborhood had made decisions that closed the door on their future. For them, life was based on limits rather than possibilities. Every day I woke up looking for the possibilities.

Still, no matter how radical my rhetoric was, I began to see the need to work within the system for change, rather than blowing it up entirely. I knew that I was part of the first generation of African Americans who had real choices regarding our relationship with whites. We could work with them, date them, eat with them, and even live next door to them. Or we could stay to ourselves, in self-imposed segregation.

I went back and forth on that dilemma. I believed that all too often, blacks who relied on whites eventually were disappointed. Yet what choice did we really have? We could not carve out a separate nation. We had to figure out how to work together, to contribute to our own good and the larger good as well.

Like many of my fellow students, I started experimenting with dating and drugs. I briefly saw a white student. Like me, she was a campus radical and involved in another relationship herself. As much as anything, our time together gave us the chance to talk across racial lines. The experience was enlightening, but it created a dual existence that I often criticized others for: I was talking black and sleeping white. Of course, I felt the hypocrite, and I lived that part of my life as a secret, keeping it from even my closest friends.

When I hit my first joint, there was no political statement behind it, just a way to get high. I believed, as just about everyone who has lit up does, that it made me wiser. Or to put it more accurately, I felt that I *sounded* more astute. Mostly, marijuana just made me hungry. I had no desire to use any other drugs.

———

AS SUMMER approached, Sheila and I acknowledged that we were deeply in love. Working on *Blackout* and spending hours together had drawn us closer, despite our efforts to avoid it. She broke it off with Chip when he returned from Vietnam and said she would be with me. Now I had a partner whom I trusted completely.

In sophomore year, our Legion of Black Collegians grew tired of waiting for the university to fund activities for black students, and we took matters into our own hands: at a meeting of the student senate we barricaded the exits and refused to leave until it appropriated money. The Finance Committee went into emergency session and allocated

$4,300. University authorities quickly rescinded the decision, arguing that the body provided the funding under duress. A second vote restored the money. We used the funds to bring black speakers and productions like Lorraine Hansberry's *A Raisin in the Sun* to campus.

The confrontation was necessary; our lobbying was going nowhere. Still, I feared that such direct actions would get me expelled. And I confided to Sheila a larger concern: that I would die young, as my mother had. That strong premonition convinced me I had no time to waste. I sensed that somehow I would succeed, although I did not know how. And somehow, I also sensed, the success would end in tragedy.

That summer, I delayed returning to St. Louis and my job at the *Post-Dispatch* to remain on campus and participate in a special program. I was one of about a dozen campus leaders of different races and genders chosen to help orient incoming freshmen to the realities of university life. The administration expected the student leaders, who had practically nothing to do with one another during the school year, to come together as if we were lifelong friends—at least for the benefit of the freshmen. I was skeptical.

They put us all together in one dorm, the university's first attempt at coed housing. We roomed together, ate meals together, and went out together. And somehow we began to connect. We spent hours talking, not just about campus life but also about families, concerns, and dreams. I had spent my first two years regarding most whites on campus as the enemy. Now I began to see things we had in common. Like me, they were under pressure too, dealing with relationships and figuring out what they wanted to do with their lives. Of course the connection did not last. Once classes resumed, we all went back to the worlds we had come from with the same friends and the same routines. But for a moment, I saw another way to relate.

Because of that vision, I decided to become a member of the dreaded administration. At the end of second year, my roommate, Gary, transferred to Cornell University in Ithaca, New York. Instead of taking on a new roommate as I began my junior year, I applied for the job of supervising a dorm floor. As a resident assistant, I had to police the floor and report safety and conduct violations. In return, I received money for room and board, a bonus on top of the scholarship.

Few blacks held that job, and I saw my selection as yet another example of progress. On weekends, I would patrol the halls searching for trouble. I was conscientious but far from rigid regarding university policy. Whenever I smelled the pungent odor of weed coming from a dorm room, or saw a woman who had been smuggled in, I would flush the dope and escort the offending female out. Eking out my own brand of justice, I saw myself as tough but compassionate.

That semester, Edwin Hutchins, the dean of student affairs, called me into his office. I had come to know him through various campaigns to change the campus environment. Although he was one of Them, the whites who were in power, I liked him a lot. He seemed decent and fair and even empathetic.

Hutchins told me of a yearlong leadership program offered by a university in Atlanta in which participants learned how to succeed in corporate America. The program would help me grow, he argued. I would have to leave Columbia for the year, but the training would be well worth it. He said that just getting me in the program would take some effort, because all the other participants were graduate students. He argued I could hold my own based on what he had seen.

The offer marked a turning point. Was I so committed to journalism that I was unwilling to explore other options? What would become of my relationship with Sheila if we put so much distance between us for a year? Sheila and I settled on a strategy that we would follow during our years together: when opportunities came up, we would not stand in each other's way. We would do our best to make the situation work.

I applied to the program and, with Hutchins's help, was accepted. In December, I went to the terminal to take a Greyhound to St. Louis, the first leg of my trip south. As I sat on a bench waiting for the bus, something gnawed at me. I could not explain to myself why I was going. I was looking for a reason *not* to go. I found a pay phone and called Sheila, who told me just what I wanted to hear: no matter what the opportunity represented, and in spite of our agreement, she really wanted me to stay.

At that moment, I said good-bye to Atlanta. I took a taxi from the bus station to Sheila's dorm, where we had a tearful reunion. I decided my future, and there would be no turning back. I would become a journalist, and I would be with Sheila.

———

BACK ON campus for good, I eyed my next challenge. A confrontation with the student government over funding for the Legion of Black Collegians opened my eyes to the cliquishness of the Missouri Students Association. Though the body was supposed to represent the interests of all students, instead it focused on the needs of a few, especially the campus fraternities and sororities.

Three Greeks were officers—the president, the legislative vice president, and the executive vice president. The legislative vice president presided over the student senate, while the executive vice president controlled the purse strings. The student body elected them, and each received a stipend for his service. In a population of nearly twenty thousand, fewer than one thousand students voted. Many did not know the organization existed.

Year in and year out, the MSA allocated money from student fees in the same way. I saw this as an old-boy network. I wanted to shake up the status quo. I decided to run for MSA president.

I figured I could create a coalition of blacks, radicals, and students who felt ignored by the MSA that was large enough to win. The organization could not become more responsive without a takeover. Someone had to lead that effort. The time had come for me to work for change beyond the black cause.

No one thought I could win, and I had doubts myself. The MSA had never had a black officer, and the fraternities and sororities had consolidated power for more than a decade. The opposition had all the perks that came with incumbency and many supporters who were determined to protect their place. As the filing deadline approached, I learned that two other "outsiders" were also considering a run: Dan Viets, a campus radical who wore long hair, a beard, and more often than not, no shoes, and Pat Farrell, a campus Greek who had spent years planning his bid for president. Pat was one of the white students with whom I had bonded during the orientation program the previous summer.

If each of us ran for president, there would be no chance of electing a new party, since we would split the vote. I sought them out and voiced that concern: "Look, each of us wants to be president," I said. "But what's more important is that we beat those guys. We have to think about what's best for the students, not what's best for us."

We negotiated for hours. They agreed, but no one wanted to give up the presidency. Finally, Pat and I left the room and took a walk. We knew we could not persuade Dan to back down. Our only option was to unite and go after one of the two vice president jobs. Pat wanted the post of legislative vice president, so I agreed to run as executive vice president.

We chose a name, the Commitment Party, and launched a furious dorm-to-dorm campaign. We posted flyers, handed out buttons, and galvanized an odd assortment of blacks, radicals, and Greeks. I threw myself into the race, learning how to connect with audiences as well as the fundamentals of campaigning. I had a blast.

Our Commitment Party won by fewer than one hundred votes, and the University of Missouri at Columbia had the first black executive vice president in the school's history.

———

SHEILA GRADUATED that spring and was hired immediately as a features writer for the *Post-Dispatch*. A reporting job at a major newspaper was a real coup.

Our relationship was strong, so much so that we talked about marriage someday. Grandmother loved Sheila, and her family welcomed me warmly. Whenever I was back home, I would spend long evenings down the street at the Rules', sitting in their living room, watching Sheila's younger sister, Diana Lynn, parrot the singing and moves of her idol, Michael Jackson, or talking late into the night with her older sister, Marsha, herself a journalist. Sheila's family became the family I always wanted.

When I returned to the *Post-Dispatch* that summer, I also started working as a reporter. After two summers as a copyboy, it was now time to show my stuff as a journalist. I was terrified when I walked into the newsroom on the morning of June 19, 1972. The city editor, a middle-aged man named Ron Wilnow, only added to my angst. I approached him timidly and asked where I should sit.

"I don't give a fuck!" he barked.

I retreated to the back of the room, not knowing what to do. I found an empty desk, only to have to move again when its owner arrived. Finally, I found the desk of a person who was off and tried to do something useful, like read the paper.

Eventually Wilnow barked at me again, this time assigning a story. Someone had phoned in a tip about small birds in suburban St. Louis attacking residents at night. I started working the phone, talking to one resident after another. My hands where shaking as I began to hunt and peck the keys to type my first story. *Don't let me screw up*, I offered a silent prayer to God. *Don't let me screw up.* I began:

A flock of small owls has been terrorizing what normally is a quiet, pleasant neighborhood in suburban St. John by making diving attacks on residents. As a result, some of the people are afraid to go out of their homes at night.

Every night for the last two weeks the owls have dived at residents and then darted away. At least nine persons in the 2900 block of Endicott Avenue have reported being attacked.

The next morning I picked up the *Post-Dispatch* and scanned the Metro section searching for my story. I was crushed when I could not find it. It was not until I lay the paper down that I saw the front-page headline: "Diving Owls Keep Residents in After Dark." The byline, in bold black letters: "GERALD BOYD."

That summer Uganda X died. I could no longer distrust or dislike whites simply because of their race. Several whites reached out to me, helping me cope with life in the newsroom. Among them were Martha Carr, the paper's Ann Landers–style advice columnist, and Dorothy Gardner, who was acutely concerned about racial inequality and gave me *Born to Rebel*, the autobiography of educator and social activist Benjamin Mays. Mary Blackburn, a secretary for the executive editor, regularly took me to lunch, which always morphed into a pep talk. She was not only kind and highly competent but she also knew many of the institution's secrets. This made her a force in the newsroom. I felt honored that she made time for me. As with Dorothy Vaughn and Mildred

Smith, my angels from my school days, it seemed that women sought to take care of me. Perhaps they sensed my longing for the mother I never knew.

———

AT THE end of the summer, I took Sheila to Lambert Field, the airport in St. Louis, where she boarded a flight to visit a relative. As I stood in the terminal watching her plane take off, I overheard airport workers discussing the hijacking of another TWA plane. I rushed to a pay phone and called the office. I could barely catch my breath.

The editors instructed me to stay on the scene and see what I could learn. Help was on the way. Within thirty minutes, about a dozen reporters and photographers arrived and fanned out to cover all the angles. I was beside myself with pride and the high of working a big story even if the more seasoned reporters were doing the heavy lifting.

As I thought about how to find out facts about the hijacking that other reporters did not have, I overheard an attractive black flight attendant talking with a colleague. She knew the number of passengers and seemed to know some crew members by name.

I flirted, using every ounce of charm I had. I ignored my fear of older women and asked her for a date, in the line of duty, of course. To my amazement, she accepted.

That evening, when I arrived at her apartment to pick her up, she greeted me very much out of uniform. She wore a low-cut, clingy black dress that revealed as much as it hid. Despite all of my adolescent bravado, I was a virgin until I went to college. I was overmatched. Then to my horror, she announced that the babysitter would be spending the night. It was more than I bargained for.

We had a lovely evening of dinner and dancing, but neither of us got what we wanted. She knew little more about the hijacking, and I dropped her home around midnight.

———

IN THE fall of 1972, I started my senior year as an editor, a student body executive vice president, and a resident assistant. I had become far more focused on my classes once I began journalism school as a junior. Most of the courses were easy, since I had already read many of the books and devoted myself to the craft.

I took an editorial writing course from Roy Fisher, the white-haired dean who was once editor of the *Chicago Daily News.* I could sit for hours listening to his war stories about running a big-city newspaper. I also took courses with professors like Ernest Morgan and Robert Taft.

Daily, I was learning the hard lesson of holding elective office: it is far easier to win than it is to govern. The coalition that had created the Commitment Party was falling apart. Pat and I constantly squabbled with Dan over goals and priorities. Dan would show up at meetings of the university's trustees shoeless and defiant. He seemed hell-bent on creating controversy rather than finding solutions. I accused him of being on an ego trip and forsaking the needs of the students who elected us. He did not seem fazed.

Finally, I staged a protest. I refused to attend student government meetings until he changed. Of course, my strategy was no better than Dan's. When that threat produced no results, I warned that I would resign. I had put myself in a box: either I made good on the threat or I faced the prospect of impeachment, since I was no longer doing the job. In a matter of months, I ended my political career by resigning my post.

In my final semester, I learned of a special program run out of the university's campus in St. Louis, designed to expose students to urban journalism. I would have the opportunity to cover stories found in larger cities and still earn my degree. I would be home and closer to Sheila. I leapt at the chance and bid farewell to Columbia.

At home over the Christmas holiday, I bought a ring and dropped to one knee, asking Sheila to marry me. She screamed with joy and said yes. We set the date for a few weeks after my graduation.

By then, I would be joining her as a full-time reporter at the *Post-Dispatch.* We would have two incomes—enough to not have to worry about money. Together we could continue the struggle, I envisioned, bringing it to journalism just as we had to our campus.

4

GROWING BUT RESTLESS

It was the summer of 1976. Inspired by the enthusiasm of a fellow *Post-Dispatch* reporter who had returned from a meeting of the newly formed National Association of Black Journalists, Gerald suggested that we establish a St. Louis chapter of NABJ. I agreed but said we also had to do something to prepare the next generation.

Over lunch at the Original Restaurant, a popular soul food place in St. Louis, Gerald and I divided the labor: he would focus on organizing the professionals, and I would concentrate on establishing a journalism workshop for high school students.

Then we sketched out the program: We would hold it on weekends over seven weeks starting at the end of February, when there were the fewest conflicts with tests, proms, and other school activities. We would hand-pick the instructors and teach as well. We would invite public officials, such as Congressman Bill Clay, to hold mock press conferences, and have students write on deadline. At the end, students would produce a newspaper or a radio or TV newscast.

The workshops were demanding. Some students quit. But many who persevered—too many to name—went on to college and success in journalism.

The St. Louis model was copied in at least fifteen cities. Although Gerald received numerous awards throughout his career, nothing was more rewarding to him than seeing our former students become our colleagues and, in several instances, start their own high school journalism workshops.

—GEORGE E. CURRY

I NERVOUSLY strolled into the newsroom of the *Post-Dispatch* in the summer of 1973 with three goals: to win a Pulitzer Prize, to make a million dollars, and to grace the cover of *Time* magazine—all in my first year.

My editors had other plans.

I was young, with a mile-high Afro, a thick beard, a wide mustache, and an overabundance of confidence and naivete. Despite my freshly minted bachelor's degree in journalism, I was hardly prepared for the realities of the grind. I had stepped out of a world of make-believe into a far harsher reality.

The *P-D* was among a shrinking group of newspapers published in the afternoon. It was increasingly out of touch with the public's evolving reading habits, but it managed to survive, although without the robust profits of morning publications like the competition, the *St. Louis Globe-Democrat*. Most of the newspaper was produced in the daytime, when anybody who mattered worked, and when I had interned in the summers. I never thought (or thought to ask) about the job of a full-time reporter with zero seniority. I pulled the graveyard shift.

Each evening, I arrived at five, just as other reporters were heading out the door. And then I sat. Night after night, in a nearly empty newsroom, I performed the always necessary, often thankless duties of the night reporter. I read the paper. I scanned the news wires. I dialed police stations, eagerly in search of death, or at least destruction: "I'm from the *Post-Dispatch*. You got anything for me?"

When some calamity struck—a crime or a fire—I got out of the office. Sometimes I went to cover public hearings. Even then, I was grateful. I would much rather be out chronicling the umpteenth turf war between activists and city officials than waiting by the phone for news to find me. Getting out and reporting was like breathing, even though I had a lot to learn about inhaling.

On one of those exceptional evenings, I was sent to a home in North St. Louis for a triple homicide. For weeks, the images haunted me— the blood, the gashes, the awkward poses in death. Another time, I covered a fire that killed a young woman. At the scene, I approached the victim's sister with a barrage of questions. I was matter-of-fact, just doing my job.

"What kind of animal are you!" she screamed, tears in her eyes, as relatives and friends glared at me. She unleashed a stream of curses and told me to get away from her and her family. Until then, I never realized that journalists need bedside manners.

Attending public hearings meant driving to small communities like East St. Louis. I would call my editor and relay the news. More often than not, the editor would declare the proceeding worthless and tell me to return to the office. Even when he requested a story, it was for only a few hundred words.

At the rate I was going, I concluded that no way would the night shift lead to groundbreaking journalism worthy of a Pulitzer Prize. Days went by, and I would have not even one byline to show for my efforts. I settled into a funk. Here I was on the staff of one of the ten best newspapers in the nation, one with a fierce reputation for tackling important issues like corruption and city blight, and I was dialing for deadheads and deadbeats. I wanted to become a star reporter like Marquis Childs or Richard Dudman or Jim Millstone, among the most prominent journalists at the paper. Eventually, I knew from my days of running *Blackout,* I would be an editor, in the mode of Oliver K. Bovard, the legendary managing editor at the *Post-Dispatch.* Under his leadership, the *P-D* soared, winning a string of Pulitzers that at one point was second only to that of the *New York Times.* Stuck on the night shift, I could not imagine how I would reach such heights.

Of course, my impatience stemmed from youth and a lack of understanding what it meant to pay my dues. The profession is especially difficult for rookies, most of whom, no matter how good they are, face the constant criticism that comes as a part of the job. Just as they need to learn to cultivate reporting and writing skills, they also need to develop a tough skin and perseverance.

My inexperience spilled out all over the place. Carl Baldwin, a seasoned reporter who was working as director of training, was one of the first journalists I got to know. Baldwin, a stout man right out of *The Front Page*, with his wide-brim hats and double-breasted suits, had a gift for assessing talent. He always played the gentleman, although you knew that behind that façade crouched a man who, if necessary, could beat the crap out of you. He was an excellent journalist, yet his *P-D* career was stalled. It was clear that he would not rise any further.

Because he was always willing to answer a question or lend a hand, I opened up to him. As we talked one day, I shared that I believed that journalism was a profession in which everyone was honorable and the people at the top fully appreciated and awarded the talents and hard work of reporters. He looked at me as if I were crazy.

Ever the teacher, Baldwin declared softly, "It is not that simple, Gerald."

Talent matters, he said, but it is never the sole factor in success. His years in the trenches had taught him that office politics and connections played a part in how a career progressed. So did a lucky break or two. If he only knew how those words stuck with me.

———

I WAS growing from my pain and disappointments, but I did not appreciate my progress. Instead, less than a year out of college, I was questioning my decision to become a reporter. I thought about pursuing other careers, like business or teaching. I spent most of my time angry. I had a recurring dream: I would walk into a packed newsroom, pull a machine gun from under my trench coat, and fire away at my bosses. Revenge on those who I thought marginalized me.

Fortunately, Sheila kept my mind off mass murder. We had married June 2, 1973, sandwiching the ceremony between my graduation and my start at the *Post-Dispatch*. The service was at St. James AME, the St. Louis church where Sheila was baptized. It was officiated by the Reverend Bennie Randle, the father of one of Sheila's childhood friends. Somehow, as these things do, the ceremony mushroomed from an intimate gathering to an elaborate affair. Sheila was striking in a simple but elegant white gown. I gamely wore the latest trend, a tux with a paisley pattern not unlike something you would find on an armchair. Sheila's big sister, Marsha, stood up for her, and Gary stood up for me. We had far too many attendants and a homegrown reception, with handmade decorations and homemade food for about 150 people. Relatives came from as far away as California. My father did not. I did not expect him to.

———

AS HUSBAND and wife, Sheila and I fell into an easy rhythm. Since we both worked, it seemed fair to me that we both take care of the house, much to my old-fashioned brother's chagrin. Our two professional incomes planted us squarely in the ranks of the upper middle class. We rented a townhouse in Bridgeton, about five minutes from Lambert Airport. We bought a new car, applied for and received credit cards, and planned vacations to places like the U.S. Virgin Islands. I was living a life that I had always coveted, with a wife, a house in the suburbs, money. No mice or roaches and, seemingly, no worries. I was content, but I was not happy.

We spent our weekends playing cards or attending parties with other couples in our apartment complex. The men, all young black professionals, formed an unofficial club. Each Sunday, we gathered to watch football and play a spirited card game called Dirty Hearts. The loser had to drink a large glass of water or his choice of liquor. We would stumble home on the verge of throwing up from too much water or alcohol and pledge to put an end to such childish behavior. Then the next Sunday, we would all torture ourselves again.

From time to time, doubts about marriage nagged me. Before the wedding, Sheila had once raised the possibility of living together, and I immediately dismissed it. If we were truly in love, I argued, we should get married and not "play" married. I saw living together as a cop-out, an easy way to avoid real commitment. But as we began to face issues like balancing two careers and the possibility of having children, I wished I had not been so cool to Sheila's proposal. I felt I was missing something. And the highlight of each week was a cutthroat card game.

Now that I was married, it seemed I had abundant opportunities to explore and experiment sexually. It did not help that I had learned some unsavory lessons about relationships while growing up on Romaine Place. Once, a neighborhood sage boasted to several in my group of friends that all married men cheated. It was normal and natural, he explained with the demeanor of a schoolteacher at the blackboard, and as long as the wife did not find out, there was nothing wrong with it. I remember thinking it odd that men would get married, then cheat on their wives. What's the point in getting married then? As an adult, watching my friends, I started to believe there was some truth in what the old man said. Among the dudes I hung out with, nobody seemed to be faithful. It had nothing to do with their love for their wives or respect for their relationships. It was in the male DNA, they reasoned, much like the old man on Romaine.

Proof: Once I was at a bar with a group of friends, and one after another, they all called their spouses at home. After assurances that everything was fine, they hung up and returned to the mission at hand: flirting with every available woman in the place. I did not flirt and did not call home. But when I got home later, an angry Sheila greeted me, demanding to know why I had not phoned her like the other husbands. If you only knew, I wanted to tell her. But I did not want to blow my buddies' cover.

I decided, at least at that time, not to become one of the gang. My decision was not based on moral or religious grounds, but wanting to be a good husband, even though I did not know what it meant to be a good husband.

———

WORKING IN the same profession, in the same office, with your wife has its advantages. Sheila and I formed our own mutual admiration society. I encouraged her, and she kept my spirits up while I was stuck on night rewrite. As we sharpened our skills, we thrived on each other's advice. I needed that support to stay anchored in the *P-D*'s choppy waters.

Newspapers, like all companies, have their own personalities, which are developed by longstanding traditions and new leadership pushing the institution in other directions. The *P-D* was a mixture of both. The paper had been slow to argue for civil rights, particularly under managing editor Bovard, the editor I wanted to emulate. At the peak of his power, in the mid-1920s, the celebrated editor refused to publish a photograph of a lynching. Bovard defended the decision, citing in part readers "who sympathize with lynching upon occasion." For years after Bovard left in 1938, the *Post-Dispatch* continued a policy of using the "Mr." honorific when naming men in its stories. There were two exceptions: criminals and blacks.

Now the paper was clearly progressive, as was the publisher, Joseph Pulitzer Jr. Pulitzer, tall and lean, was compassionate and caring, especially about the less fortunate. Urbane and sophisticated, he had a demeanor more fitting for a museum curator than a bare-knuckled newspaper executive. He was always polite, even to the lowest on the totem pole. I formed my observations of him firsthand as a copyboy who was occasionally summoned to the publisher's office to get him lunch. He would write out his order for a tuna sandwich and iced tea in neat script on a square of paper that he gave me personally with enough money to pay the bill.

The top editor was Evarts Graham Jr., a kindhearted man who usually walked the newsroom with a pipe dangling from his mouth. Graham was a graduate of Harvard and hailed from a prominent St. Louis family. His father was a noted surgeon and performed the first lung cancer operation in the early 1930s.

The junior Graham, recognizing that the culture and norms were changing, sought to wipe away some of the *P-D*'s past wrongs and insensitivities. St. Louis was shedding its segregated past, but in small steps. It was still deeply divided, with blacks concentrated in the northern part and whites in the south and in St. Louis County. There were a few all-black pockets in areas such as Wellston, Kinloch, and Meacham Park. But the outlying area mainly reflected communities of wealth, which were white.

This split explained the culture of the city, the sharp divisions of race and income and ideology. Even so, St. Louis was not exactly a hotbed of racial strife. In fact, it seemed a model of restraint, partly because of savvy political and business leaders who paid lip service to social woes like combating crime, providing adequate housing for the poor and decent jobs for minorities, and improving schools in poorer neighborhoods. *Hold on,* they kept saying. *Help is on the way.* Poor blacks accepted this approach, probably because hope was all they had to hang on to. Despite demonstrations at department stores like Famous-Barr and at the Jefferson Bank, St. Louis was one of the few major cities with large concentrations of blacks never to experience a serious riot in the 1960s and 1970s.

Unlike the other big stories of the day, the Cold War or the aftermath of Vietnam, which seemed so remote, the subject of race was thrust upon everyone at every turn. It was intimate, so intertwined in our everyday lives that it was difficult to see it in all of its complexity. Even then, I was fascinated with the idea of stepping back, trying to understand what makes it so hard to bridge our differences over race. I had some notions, but at that point I was still learning from each day's developments.

The *Post-Dispatch* was widely regarded as one of the most liberal newspapers in the county. Ideologically, it was the mirror image of its main competitor, the *St. Louis Globe-Democrat*. The *Globe-Democrat*, with prominent editorial page voices such as Pat Buchanan, seemed to oppose integration in any incarnation. Its news columns were not racist, but it was clearly unwilling to anger its conservative base with articles considered favorable to minorities.

In its editorials, the *P-D* argued that blacks should receive the same opportunities as whites. But inside the newsroom, it struggled to meet that goal. In my years there, I worked with extremely talented black journalists, including Robert Joiner; George Curry; Fred Sweets and his sister, Ellen Sweets; Linda Lockhart; and Jim Ellis. All would enjoy successful careers as journalists, rising in the ranks at the *P-D* and often leaving for better opportunities at other news organizations. Joiner and Curry, two of my closest *P-D* friends, could not have been more different. Joiner, one of the most gifted reporters I have ever known, was low-key and most comfortable letting his enormous talent do the talking. Curry, fearless and outspoken, was quick to promote himself, often in a barrage of rapid-fire words seasoned with an Alabama twang. His delivery was always crisp, clear, and on point. I learned immense and vastly different lessons from them both.

One of the nagging, and insulting, questions that black journalists often face is *Are you black first, or are you a journalist first?* No white journalist is asked to rank his race and his profession. It is as if asking *Are you a man first or a journalist first? Are you a Christian first or a journalist first?* The question may be more subtle today, but it still lingers. It has been accepted—but certainly not appreciated—as another hazard of the job. And while blacks in newsrooms had instant credibility when the subject was black people, they often were ignored when it came to other issues.

As I watched these dynamics play out in our newsroom, I became frustrated and angry. Like other newspapers, the *Post-Dispatch* had no black editors and seemed in no hurry to appoint any. The absence was noticeable and the excuses predictable. No qualified blacks could be found anywhere. Black reporters really did not aspire to the editing ranks. After a while, these excuses rang hollow.

It did not help that I felt as if my career had stalled. Young reporters really have no control of their own destinies. The higher up the food chain you climb, the more you can decide what stories you cover, how long you work, and when and what you write. That self-determination helps make the grind more tolerable. I was still a long way from such privileges.

We began to see and feel more immediate progress when James Millstone, who had covered the Supreme Court in the Washington bureau, was appointed assistant managing editor. The bearded Millstone was well schooled in the ways of Washington, liberal in his politics, and the consummate professional. The *P-D* brought him back to St. Louis to compete with other senior editors to become the paper's top editor. I don't know how much it helped or hurt his cause, but he took on the role of mentoring and lobbying for black reporters.

Millstone was my first professional role model, not just on journalism matters, but on how to lead. He had a kind heart, a gentle soul, and was a ferocious fighter for causes he believed in. He pushed to recruit more black reporters, then pushed for many to receive the same opportunities as their white colleagues. His efforts were not automatic; he fought for those who deserved it. What guided him most were merit and a commitment to excellence. I studied his approach intently. Once, as he was complimenting my work, he also praised me for being a good person. Journalism aside, he said, a display of humanity is the true measure of a man. I took that to mean that "journalist" is a noun; it's the adjectives that really matter when it comes to defining one's self.

After about a year, I successfully lobbied to be freed from Siberia. I was taken off nights and assigned to the dayside to cover consumer affairs. Newspapers everywhere were developing consumer beats, in part to attract new readers, particularly women. I had no interest in writing about comparison shopping or getting the best deal on new tires. My new assignment was a disaster. In a three-month span, I wrote one story.

They moved me to the housing beat, where I connected a little better and wrote several front-page stories, including one about the last family to leave the Pruitt-Igoe housing project, which stood for eighteen years as an example of one of the worst urban renewal projects in the nation. The assignments helped lift my spirits and taught me some things about myself as a journalist. While I was a good and serviceable writer, I lacked the flair or the polish of Sheila and others with gifts like hers. To deliver a great story I had to labor for hours, writing and rewriting.

My strength was reporting. I quickly seized on the relevant points and seemed to know the right questions to ask to get the answers I wanted. I was able to size up a subject and figure out the best way to gather information. Sometimes that meant badgering them, sometimes putting them at ease. Once I figured out the right approach, I was usually in. I came to rely on that strength more and more.

———

BORED WITH life in the suburbs, Sheila and I moved into the city. We chose LaClede Town, an integrated midtown housing complex. The high- and low-rise apartments were built under Lyndon Johnson's Model Cities Program and included an assortment of incomes and races. With large numbers of professionals, artists, writers, teachers, and activists, LaClede Town teemed with action and creativity, unlike the tame and predictable burbs. People dropped by to visit and ended up staying for long talks through dinner and wine. City living with a communal bent suited us both. In a way, we both were trying to recapture the excitement and passion of our college days, when we stood for something and tried to make a difference. Now as working journalists, we had become self-absorbed and bent on establishing our careers. We were hungering for something other than bylines and front-page stories.

In 1976 a group met in our apartment to discuss the state of blacks in journalism. One participant, Linda Lockhart, had attended a similar meeting in Kansas City where black journalists talked about forming a national organization to serve the interests of black reporters and editors everywhere. Linda reported how journalists in other cities were exploring the possibility of starting local chapters and suggested that we create one in St. Louis. We could address many of our shared concerns, from the lack of blacks in the newsroom to inadequate assignments to parity in management. We formed the Greater St. Louis Association of Black Journalists, a group of about two dozen active members. The group elected me as its first president.

I was on familiar terrain. It was as if I were back in college helping to lead a revolution. But now, away from campus, I faced larger consequences to radical action, starting with the potential loss of my job. There was also the nature of journalism itself. At its core is the need for objectivity, not advocacy. That point was not always clear to some members, especially those who worked in black-owned news organizations. But I kept us anchored, reminding everyone that journalism groups, no matter how worthy their purpose, must have excellence in journalism as first among their core values.

Our group set clear goals, like increasing the number of black journalists and ensuring they had opportunities that could lead to promotions. We also wanted to attract talented young blacks to the profession. I embraced my new mission wholeheartedly; it gave me a sense of purpose far beyond cranking out yet another housing story.

One morning I reported to work and responded to a summons from Charles Prendergast, the executive city editor. Prendergast was a veteran journalist who had been an editorial writer before joining the news department. He was always full of energy, bounding through the newsroom eagerly unloading one idea after another on the staff. He had a fresh one for me: would I like to cover city hall for the *Post-Dispatch*?

I was stunned. It was a coveted position, one that traditionally went to older, more established reporters. I had been at the *P-D* a little more than two years as a full-time reporter. Prendergast was asking me to go from zero to fifty in mere seconds. Despite all of my internal whining about not getting opportunities I thought I deserved, I doubted I was ready. But I did not let on. Ready or not, I could not pass up the chance. I certainly could not lobby for better opportunities for black reporters and then reject one when it came to me.

I knew that this would test me like nothing before. In the history of St. Louis journalism, no black reporter had worked at city hall for a mainstream publication. I would cover the mayor, the city council, and several city agencies. The beat would expose me not only to the political elite in the city but also to big, contentious issues like education, development, law enforcement, and racial disputes. It was a difficult job. I knew that I would grow tremendously or I would fall flat on my face. I accepted the offer, and for once, I dropped my usual poker face. I could not stop smiling as I said yes.

———

FEAR CAN serve as the ultimate motivator, and in all honesty, I had plenty as I took my spot in the *P-D*'s first-floor office in city hall. Fear of failure brought out the best in me. By extension, so did the competitive nature of the beat. Each day, I scanned the *Globe-Democrat* to see if I had missed a story or to compare what its reporter had written with my account. There was no hiding. Either I beat the competition or got beaten; either I wrote a better story or he did.

That the *P-D* was an afternoon newspaper made my job even more of a challenge. I had three deadlines throughout the day, and whenever news happened, I literally ran to my office and banged out a story. I was in constant motion, racing and interviewing and typing. At the end of each day, I walked back to the *P-D* and rewrote my stories for the next day's first edition.

As arduous as it was, I could not get enough of my job. The constant pressure to make repeated deadlines helped me to think and write faster. For example, in covering a big, sometimes complicated story like the mayor's proposal to cut millions of dollars in education spending, I tried to get to the heart of it by asking myself what it meant. Budget cuts equaled teacher layoffs equaled larger classrooms equaled cuts in arts and sports. I always sought to connect vast bureaucratic actions to everyday concerns. And that exercise almost always produced a lede: "Hundreds of teachers will lose their jobs this fall as a result of the mayor's new budget proposals, which he unveiled today to the City Council," I wrote. "The cutback would also mean larger class sizes and a reduction in school programs involving the arts and sports."

I also learned how the most important news sources are not always the elected officials but the people close to them, like employees, friends, or even family. It became clear that I had to work the people at the edges. That might be a secretary, for example. If her boss spent an hour in the morning meeting with Mr. Smith, and if I knew Mr. Smith was pushing an issue, that's where I would snoop.

But my most important lesson had nothing to do with writing or gathering news. I found my passion. I worked sixteen- and eighteen-hour days. No matter how tired I was each night when I fell into bed, I awoke refreshed, eager for more. I loved what I did, so much so that I would have covered city hall even if they did not pay me.

I never fully understood what drew me to politics. If I had to guess, I would say its intoxicating mix of power, ego, diplomacy, and strategy. I was fascinated by politicians' unending mission to win people over. I could certainly relate to the need to win the favor of others, whether it was my teachers or the Coopers or relatives or friends back on Romaine. I was also enamored by the game itself: the tactical maneuvering to achieve a particular aim, as well as the postmortems—analyzing why a candidate won or lost. I would sit in the back of the chamber where the board of aldermen met each Friday talking to Richard Gephardt, an alderman and future U.S. Democratic presidential hopeful, about how we wanted to do more with our lives.

I was not nearly as cynical as some of my colleagues, but I realized early on that most politicians sought to exploit me and other reporters through access, flattery, and when all else failed, threats and intimidation. It was soon obvious that the bureaucrats I covered needed me or, more precisely, the *Post-Dispatch*, to get their messages out, and that I needed them to understand what was happening. We were linked in an uneasy partnership.

Back then, for example, journalists knew much more about their subjects than they shared with readers and viewers. We did not report on the sex lives of politicians or other personal matters, like whether they drank too much or were bigots. Unless they were outright crooks or scoundrels, few of their foibles made it into the paper.

I stretched and learned and grew. I investigated abuses of St. Louis-area neo-Nazis by city police. I spent three months exploring political favoritism by local judges in appointing attorneys to court positions. My stories led to reforms mandated by the state legislature and the resignation of a judge.

One of my more difficult lessons involved investigating the mishandling of forty-five million dollars in federal community development funds and the failure of city officials to adequately monitor projects funded under the program. My page one story rattled the city's political and development communities and faulted the head of the agency in charge. On Saturday night when the early edition of Sunday's paper hit the streets, the agency head called me. He did not dispute the report, but he said his child had seen the paper and called him a crook. He would never forgive me for writing the piece, he said, prompting me to apologize for making his life miserable. I could always empathize with my subjects in a way that some colleagues did not. That became one of my stronger traits as a journalist, one that I believe made me better.

Almost two years after I started the city hall beat, Prendergast summoned me to his office again. The *Post-Dispatch* and the *Globe-Democrat* annually selected a journalist of the year. Prendergast announced I had been chosen for the award, named after Con Lee Kelliher, a reporter who had worked at both newspapers. I was the first black journalist to receive the honor.

———

MY NEWFOUND success was a mixed blessing. It made me more confident, but it also fueled my hunger to succeed. This desire became, at times, akin to an addiction. I did not want anything to knock me off course. This was not the time, for example, to start a family—even though I craved the stability and fulfillment that I thought having children would bring.

I was trading off, but not necessarily up. This would be a source of frustration over the next decades of my life. But at the time, the answer seemed simple enough. Kids, I told myself, could come later. For now, I needed to devote my energy to my job. My career took off, I was married to a lovely woman, but still I felt lonely.

I would often find myself searching for something to make my life more meaningful. Once, I was talking to Robert Knight, a journalism professor at the University of Missouri, about how much I had enjoyed teaching at a summer program at the college for minority students. One of my students, Ann Scales, won a scholarship for a story she had written, which I had edited. I took immense pride in knowing that I played a role in her success—it was an immediate and tangible result of my giving back. Ann, a talented journalist, would later work at the *Post-Dispatch* and then cover the White House for the *Boston Globe* before going into management there. She would remain a lifelong friend.

Dr. Knight and I discussed how to broaden efforts to attract more minorities into journalism. We felt that we needed to reach them as early as high school, before they were enticed into other careers. We agreed that the earlier they received training, the sooner they understood how to make it in the profession, the better their chances of success.

I shared the conversation with George Curry as we lunched at a midtown restaurant. We began to refine the idea and turn it into a plan. The workshop could be run on Saturdays by the Greater St. Louis Association of Black Journalists. Students would learn the basics, like how to write stories and master spelling and grammar. About two dozen members of the association would serve as drill sergeants, teaching, mentoring, critiquing, and cheerleading.

As far as we knew, no such program had been done anywhere. Perhaps if we had been more humble, or less idealistic, we would have passed on the notion of creating a workshop when neither of us was a teacher. We had no road map and no money. But we were full of ourselves and our grand plan, so we improvised. We "borrowed" typing paper, pencils, and notebooks from our news organizations, and someone "found" typewriters for our students. One member, Joseph Palmer, hit up area food vendors, which provided doughnuts for breakfast and hamburgers for lunch.

Once the workshop was under way at St. Louis Community College's Forest Park campus, we would wake around 6:00 A.M. so we could arrive on campus and prepare for the students. The boot camp ran from 8:00 A.M. to noon every Saturday for eight weeks. Some thirty years later, the minority journalism workshop is still going strong, having "graduated" hundreds of journalists.

That first year, I was most impressed with one high school student in particular, Marcia Davis. Marcia had the head and heart of a journalist. She was tough and cynical and asked an endless stream of questions. Marcia went on to work as a senior editor at *Emerge* magazine and as an editor at the *Washington Post*.

I threw myself into the program and our charges, allowing myself to be content with the thrills of discovering and shaping new talent. But still I longed for something more.

———

I FOUND something more in Anna Marie Jordan, a young black woman whom I met at a party that Sheila and I attended in St. Louis. Anna was not yet twenty, about four years younger than me, but she carried herself in a way that made her seem older than her years. Fairskinned and "healthy," as men describe women of a certain size and stature, she was an enticing combination of innocence and intelligence, and she had a keen sense of herself and what mattered. She did not care a bit about journalism, but from the first time I laid eyes on her, I was taken.

Anna lived with her mother and older sister in an apartment complex in midtown. The *Post-Dispatch* unknowingly aided and abetted our affair. Shortly after we met, the paper sent Sheila to the Washington bureau to fill in for reporters who were on vacation. All of a sudden, I felt free. I dated Anna as if I were single. We had lunches and dinners and drinks after work. I would hang up after talking to Sheila and rush out to meet Anna.

I knew what I was doing, I told myself, as the unfaithful do. It was just sex. It had nothing to do with my marriage or my love for Sheila. Yes, it was risky, but I could manage to do what many of my friends were doing—and what the old man from Romaine said was in a man's makeup. I had ready excuses, like working late or having last-minute dinners. I found out-of-the-way hotels where we could meet. As long as I was smart about it, I kidded myself, Sheila would never find out.

Anna knew I was married, so, I reasoned, she knew what she was getting into. In a way, I felt empowered. I was man enough to live a dual life. I did not once think of how Shelia would feel, nor did I consider what it meant to Anna to have a part-time man in her life.

But adultery is not for the faint of heart. Eventually, the lies and excuses began to wear on me. When Sheila was home, I would pine for Anna. When Anna and I were finally together, I was constantly looking over my shoulder. Perhaps it was the guilt that got me. Or, more precisely, Grandmother's voice in my head, reminding me that this was not how I was raised. I began to realize that I was living a lie.

No matter. My wife saw through the late-night meetings and sudden disappearances.

"Are you seeing someone?" she asked directly.

"Yes," I replied with relief.

"Do you love her?" she continued.

"I'm not sure" was all I could say. I don't know why I had chosen that moment to be honest.

Years later, I can still remember the pain on her face. At her insistence, I moved out. Settling into a furnished place downtown, I figured that I would find some measure of comfort since I was "free." Instead, sitting alone in my high-rise bachelor pad on the Mississippi River, I was miserable.

We told our families that we were separating. I was embarrassed that I had disappointed Sheila's parents, who saw me as the son they never had. And I was a bit hurt when Mr. Rule rallied behind his daughter, telling her to change the locks. It was advice that Sheila ignored.

Night after night, I sat in a darkened apartment staring out at the gorgeous view of the downtown St. Louis skyline and the lights of the Eads Bridge. I went to work to distract myself from the pain and shame of destroying my marriage. I stopped seeing Anna so I could sort out my life.

In the office and around most of our friends, Sheila and I kept up appearances. It was comfortable that way: Few people knew that we were no longer living together, and I believe that neither of us was ready to deal with the public specter of a failed marriage. And in spite of my confusion and her anger, I somehow hoped that Sheila and I would find a way to get back together. But before I was able to act on that hope, Sheila was gone.

Paul Delaney, a national reporter based in the *New York Times*' Chicago bureau, swung through St. Louis regularly as he traveled through the Midwest in search of stories. Delaney, who had started his career at the black-owned *Atlanta Daily World* and moved to the *Washington Star*, was the most prominent black reporter at the paper. His visits were always a big deal for local black journalists, especially when he gathered a group of us together for dinner or drinks and generously picked up the tab.

While looking for stories, Delaney also shopped for talent. He was especially interested in minority journalists, since they were in short supply at the *Times*, as everywhere else. Apparently he was impressed by Sheila's work. At the same time, Sheila was eager to move beyond what she saw as the confines of St. Louis. Paul passed Sheila's name on to New York, and about a year after we separated, she moved to New York to report for the *Times*.

I could not have been happier for her, but I was also surprised and dismayed. I was the one who focused more on career, but Sheila was the one whom the *Times* coveted. And taking a job in New York would kill any chance of repairing our marriage. When we talked, she made it clear that she did not want to pass on the opportunity, and I agreed. If it were my career, I would have felt the same way. We could still try to save our marriage, I reasoned, but later.

We split everything down the middle, including our banking accounts and most of the furniture. Once Sheila left, I returned to the apartment. Most of our friends believed we were in a commuter marriage.

It was not long before bitterness set in. New York had claimed my father and was now claiming a woman I still loved. I hated the city and despised the *New York Times*. I would remain in St. Louis and achieve greatness at the *Post-Dispatch*, I thought childishly. I did not need the city or its damned newspaper.

Shortly after Sheila left, I picked up with Anna once more. But our relationship was different. The innocent, trusting Anna was gone, replaced by a more skeptical woman who hedged her bets by dating others. She was not about to give up her freedom for a man who was still married.

———

WITHOUT A steady relationship to occupy my time and attention, I threw myself into work. I had always been an early riser, but I started arriving in the office shortly after seven. I would juggle several different stories at the same time, never sure which one would land first. I knew everyone in city government from the janitors to the secretaries to the highest elected officials. My little office on the first floor was like a command center for news and information. Nothing happened at city hall without me finding out about it.

But my job echoed the discontent I had encountered in my marriage: I loved journalism, but for reasons I did not fully understand, I was not fulfilled in my work.

Like Anna, I hedged my bets and dated others, including a woman from my old neighborhood and a reporter at the *Post-Dispatch*. I found comfort with all of them, and they saw me at my most vulnerable. Some wanted casual relationships that centered on friendship; others wanted a deeper commitment. I knew I wanted to live my life with someone, but I needed to figure out who I was and what I was about first. I was no longer the man I had been when Sheila and I were married. I had learned the hard way not to make a relationship permanent without asking all the right questions—about myself as well as the woman.

On many nights, I was alone. I would lie in bed with only the television keeping me company until I eventually fell asleep.

Sheila and I talked several times a week. Over time and distance, as we continued to share our fears, hopes, and dreams, trust returned, and our friendship grew deeper. She loved New York and was doing well at the *Times*, and she met a man who had become an important part of her life. In a way, I was happy for her. But as I watched her grow into a confident single woman navigating the challenges of New York City, I wanted her back.

I became anxious to leave the *Post-Dispatch* and move closer to the East Coast. That would improve my chances of reuniting with Sheila, I thought. I applied to the *New York Daily News* and received a prompt reply. As I no doubt knew, the New York papers were in the midst of a lengthy and nasty strike, an editor wrote. I should inquire again once the strike was settled.

I did not want to work at the same newspaper as Sheila, so I did not approach the *Times*. But I did apply to the *Washington Post* and received a polite rejection letter. I informed my editors at the *Post-Dispatch* that I was actively looking, wanting to work on the East Coast. They weighed in with their own offer: They had no reporters based in New York, but they had a seven-member bureau in D.C. They were eager for me to join it, if the assignment would keep me at the paper.

I jumped at the opportunity. Washington was a ninety-minute shuttle ride from New York. I would be the junior reporter in the bureau, covering the Missouri and Illinois congressional delegations. And I would find a way to get my wife back.

———

IN THE fall of 1978, I sold my gray Buick Riviera, watched my possessions packed and crated, and boarded a flight to Washington. I had been to the city several times before, but I had no real appreciation for its core or culture. I soon found out: the District of Columbia is indeed a self-contained entity, quite distinct from the surrounding towns in Maryland and Virginia. You can spend nearly all of your time there and never cross the borders to the south or the north. It is essentially a one-industry town: government. And within that industry, there is a clear pecking order that starts with the president and ends with the lowest GS-ranked employee.

Washington circa 1978 was also a mecca for black professionals, hence its moniker, Chocolate City. Within the District, blacks enjoyed status and operated in a unique world within the larger white world. This was so different from St. Louis, where blacks seemed to be tolerated but never accepted. In Washington, they were celebrated—at least that's how it seemed to me.

The *Post-Dispatch* put me up in a furnished apartment for a month or two while I looked for something permanent. As soon as I arrived at the temporary apartment off DuPont Circle, I dropped off my bags and headed back to the airport where I boarded the shuttle, eager to surprise Sheila.

————

IN NEW York, I took a taxi to Sheila's Upper West Side brownstone, jumped out, and leaned on the buzzer. No one answered. I went to a bar on the corner and waited, calling her every thirty minutes or so. No answer. Finally, after several hours and with time running out to catch the last shuttle back to Washington, I returned to LaGuardia. Sheila was out for the evening, and my dramatic gesture at reconciliation had no audience. I had to face reality: Although getting back together was always a notion in the air, we were never on the same page at the same time about doing so. It was clearly time to move on.

My life had been driven by a simple notion of having the family, the home in the suburbs, and the white picket fence. If that was not to be, in large part because I rejected it, then what did I want instead?

————

I DID not give myself a chance to dwell on that question. As I had done at city hall, I plunged into my new role of Washington correspondent. I trolled the halls of the Capitol and the Senate and House office buildings getting to know politicians, especially those from Missouri.

Although the *Post-Dispatch* had a strong bureau, our small band of reporters was no match for the legions of journalists up Connecticut Street, in the *Times*' bureau. We had learned to accept the fact that we would get beaten by the *Times*, the *Washington Post*, and the *Washington Star*. Even when the *Post-Dispatch* scooped the competition, our stories did not receive the same attention as an exclusive in the bigger papers.

This reality only added to my mounting frustrations. My coworkers in the bureau were quite collegial, but we all went our separate ways after work. I felt alone, and that emptiness was most pronounced on weekends, when I had too much idle time to myself. I did my best to cope. Occasionally I would go out to clubs and other establishments frequented by blacks. It was a relief to blend into the crowd for a change, after spending most of my time as the only black person in the room. I would often imagine how foreign my surroundings would be to most of the whites I covered or worked with. Usually, from Friday after work until Monday, I remained in my one-bedroom apartment near DuPont Circle, not talking to a soul.

I tried to counter the loneliness and isolation by working hard and paying my dues. But the novelty and excitement of my new beat quickly wore off, and disillusionment crept in. Covering the Missouri and Illinois congressional delegations was reserved for the bureau's newest member. Essentially, it was grunt work: each day I would make a dozen or so telephone calls to the congressmen or their aides, searching for stories of importance to St. Louis readers. In some ways, the work resembled the monotony of calls to the police that I made in my early days on the paper. Once again, I was starting over. I was approaching thirty and had been a reporter for a little more than five years, yet I felt old and tired. I started to wonder whether I had a future in journalism.

While Washington held the promise of taking my career to a higher level, it offered none of the personal comforts that I found in St. Louis. In time, I became depressed, although it would be years before I knew what it meant to be depressed. My work suffered for lack of energy, spark, or any hint of sophistication. Like riding a bicycle, my ability to perform remained, but I traveled at a much slower speed. When a supervisor who noticed my lack of passion asked what was troubling me, I avoided the real issue—that it was difficult to be the only black reporter in the bureau. I simply promised to do better. Revealing my sense of isolation, I believed, would lead him to think I was weak. But in truth, without a home life with the support and structure I craved, I was lost and vulnerable and afraid.

5

FRESH STARTS

We invited Gerald to give a lecture in March 2000 in honor of the late James Millstone. It was fitting because Millstone, a *St. Louis Post-Dispatch* assistant managing editor, had been a mentor for Gerald and a whole generation of reporters. Also, we respected the hard-hitting journalism that both Gerald and Jim stood for. Secretly, we hoped Gerald would take on Cole C. Campbell, then the *P-D*'s editor. Many of us thought Campbell was wrecking the newspaper with his notions of public journalism and his convoluted management. But in a pre-lecture phone call, Gerald politely said it would be rude to come to St. Louis and criticize Campbell.

On the first day of his visit, Gerald gave a farsighted speech about his adventures at the *Times* and the challenges facing journalism, including pressures from Wall Street and "entertainment masquerading as news." On the second day, he joined a panel discussion that included Campbell, who attacked the *New York Times* as elitist. Campbell said he didn't care much for those who "drank Bombay martinis" and "gave each other high-fives" for reading the *Times*. Gerald didn't look angry, but there was steel in his voice. Point by point, he took on Campbell, a former college debating champion. Newspapers are supposed to devote all their energies to covering news, he said calmly. Quality journalism,

not elitism, is what attracts *Times* readers. Theories like public
journalism are a distraction. Campbell grew red under the collar,
and people connected to the *Post-Dispatch* sank in their seats,
embarrassed by their leader's weak presentation.

Word of the debate filtered back to the *P-D*'s offices. Less than
a month later, Cole Campbell was out.

—WILLIAM H. FREIVOGEL
and MARGARET WOLF FREIVOGEL

I T WAS a stroke, Gary said. They did not know how severe. No need
for me to come, my practical brother counseled; there was nothing I
could do. The next morning, I was on the first flight to St. Louis.

I had never seen Grandmother seriously ill, and the thought of
what I might find frightened me. On my way there, I pictured her
petite frame as I often saw her, settled into her wooden chair in front
of the window in her bedroom. I last saw her in her favorite spot when
I was home visiting several months earlier. I remember sitting with her
for hours, watching her sleep, drawing strength from her as we talked
about everything and nothing.

That last visit, I was desperately trying to get out of my funk. I was
a Washington correspondent for a major newspaper, a measure of success by most accounts. But I was not a star. And my personal life was
a disaster. I was stuck, afraid to move forward or backward. It was an
odd place for a successful man to find himself, with a self-imposed barrier against taking risks. I felt I had no opportunity to make a mistake.
The paralysis frustrated me, to say the least. *You're better than the man
you've become,* I kept telling myself. *You have to decide what you want,
then go after it.* And looking at my grandmother, who was sleeping so
peacefully, I knew that no matter what I did in my career or my personal life, she would be there for me. I so needed that anchor.

But now she needed me. I raced from the airport to the hospital. As
soon as I entered her room, I saw her motionless body and the concern
on the faces of relatives huddled in the corner with Gary discussing her

condition, and I could tell the situation was not good. Her eyes were closed. She breathed easily. I braced myself for the news.

Evie was paralyzed on her left side and slurring her words, Gary reported. They did not know much more, including whether she would walk again. Her doctors' biggest worry was that she was not eating. She seemed disoriented and unwilling to do anything to help herself.

Sitting in the hospital waiting room, I realized for the first time that Grandmother might die. I fought back tears as I prayed for her to live.

The next morning, I found her awake, staring at the ceiling.

I tried to sound cheerful. I made some comment like "What are you doing in the hospital?"

She smiled and slurred, "I'm sick," as if to say, *Duh, what do you think I'm doing here?* At least she had her wit, I thought, somewhat reassured.

I stayed by her side for several hours, holding her small, bony hands. When lunch arrived, I gently took her face and looked deep into her eyes and made my case:

"Grandmother, all of your life, you have taken care of us, you have taken care of yourself, but it's time that you let us help you," I said through my tears. "You can't be so stubborn anymore, especially not at a time like this.

"We love you so much, Grandmother, and we want you to be around. Please start eating."

She closed her eyes and nodded. I brought a spoonful of soup to her mouth, and she opened just enough for the edge to slip in. Another spoonful followed, then another. I was heartened to see that she was fighting, and pleased to know that I was helping. Eventually, her strength returned; and with therapy, her speech improved, and she regained the use of her left side.

I had never felt as close to her as I did in that visit. I knew that she needed me as much as I needed her.

———

THAT SUMMER, in 1980, I went to New York to cover my first national political convention. Much of it was a blur of anticipation and excitement as I took in the sights, sounds, and smells of the city and the Democrats' intraparty rancor in Madison Square Garden. But I will never forget hearing the powerful speech by Edward Kennedy, the Massachusetts senator who had led an insurgency only to lose the nomination to the incumbent president, Jimmy Carter. Kennedy's grace in defeat, his eloquent call to the party to unite behind a larger purpose of helping all Americans, his encouragement to reach beyond the bitter battle he had lost to the bigger one ahead, resonated with me as one who identified with underdogs.

The tumultuous events in the Garden, and Kennedy's vow that the "dream shall never die," were overshadowed by my trip uptown, to Harlem, where I went to visit my father. As angry as I had been with him for leaving us, for some reason I felt compelled to see him. I hoped he could offer some wisdom to help me turn my life around. Why would I think that a man I had not seen or spoken to in years would have the words to guide me? When you are desperate for answers, you will seek them in the most unlikely places.

I took the subway and headed to the address that Grandmother had given me. I had no phone number, so I showed up without calling. I had no idea what to expect. Once at his building, I climbed to the top of a darkened staircase and knocked on the door. I was greeted by a shorter, graying version of myself. He was no longer the giant from my childhood, but there was no doubt that he was my father. He looked puzzled.

"Don't look so astonished," I said, unable to control my widening grin. "Don't you recognize your own son?"

He smiled and eagerly motioned for me to come in. We did not embrace or shake hands.

"I can't hardly believe it's you!" he said. "You look well, son. I'm real surprised and happy to see you again."

We sat down on a worn sofa to talk. As we chatted about family members, the conversation moved from awkward to polite.

"How are you doing?" I asked as I glanced around the small apartment. The living room was also the kitchen, and the rear area had a bedroom and the bathroom. I had never seen so many locks on one door. There was the unmistakable odor of roach spray. "Are you taking care of yourself?"

"I've been doing fine, real well," he answered. "Ain't had a drop of liquor in more than two years. I found this AA program downtown, and they got me off the stuff. It can kill you if you let it, and I'm not about to go back. Never again."

"That's good," I said, feeling proud of him for getting that part of his life back. I did not raise the issue of how his leaving affected Gary and me. Past was past.

He talked about life in Harlem. "I don't really go anyplace, except my job and home," he said. "You could when I first got here, but now, somebody will knock you in the head in a minute."

Then he added: "I never told you how glad I am that you and your brother didn't turn out like these thugs. You all are doing well, and I have always been so proud of you." It was the first time I had ever heard him praise Gary and me.

We heard footsteps in the hallway just outside his door. He must have noticed concern on my face. "Oh, it's just the numbers runner," he said, reassuring me. "He comes through twice a day, nearly always at this time. You know, there are all these people in Harlem who would spend their last dime on the numbers." This was my father, practical to a fault, even if it meant leaving his boys in the care of his mother because he knew she could do better by them. "They never win anything," he went on, "but they keep playing. I guess it's OK, but it don't make sense to me. Better to save those dimes and let them add up that way."

He laughed the same easy laugh that I enjoyed as a child. His laughter was rare, and I cherished it. Sitting in his cramped apartment, I felt as if we were back in St. Louis, and he was looking out for me, sheltering me. I felt safe. Even though in many ways now, I was better able to take care of him than he could me.

I missed him. There was so much he did not know about my life— so much that I found impossible to discuss with anybody. But in a few hours that afternoon, the words and emotions flowed.

"I've decided to get a divorce," I said. "It's not really anyone's fault, but just something that hasn't worked out. We still care about other, and we will always be friends, but—"

Rufus stopped me with a look of compassion. "If I learned anything," he said, "it's that you don't have to explain yourself to anyone but yourself. As long as it makes sense to you, that's all that matters. The most important thing in life is that you're happy, and to be happy, you have to do what you see as best for you."

I would see my father several other times over the next few years, but this was the one serious conversation we would have. Shortly after I left his place, I went to my hotel room and wrote down all he said. I wanted something to hold on to, after so many years without him.

———

NOT LONG after that meeting with my father, I decided to take a break from journalism. I looked into fellowships, which would give me a chance to determine what I wanted from my career and time to untangle myself from the web of emotions over Sheila and Anna.

I was still married to Sheila but living with Anna. She had moved to Washington, into my one-bedroom apartment. Anna was a dutiful partner, cooking and helping to keep house. When I got home, she always had a chilled martini ready. She listened and shared and did her best to let me know that she was serious about our relationship.

I applied for the Nieman Fellowship, which provided a year of study at Harvard University, a year with no significant professional obligations. The Nieman program was started through a bequest from Agnes Wahl Nieman in memory of her husband, Lucius, the one-time owner of the *Milwaukee Journal*. It was intended to give journalists a pause from the daily grind and the opportunity to grow intellectually by availing themselves of the fine minds at Harvard.

I sought recommendations from several friends and colleagues, each with knowledge of some period in my life and career. They included Joseph Pulitzer Jr., Dorothy Gardner, Jim Millstone, Richard Dudman, and Roy Fisher, then the dean of the journalism school at Missouri. The latter two were former Niemans. All wrote strong letters on my behalf.

Of all those writing about me, the person I had spent the most time with was Dudman, himself a Nieman more than two decades earlier. Dudman was the Washington reporter I hoped to become. He was successful, and he seemed to have found the balance in his life that I wanted. He and his wife, Helen, who worked at the *Washington Post*, had two wonderful children.

Dick's recommendation was a rave:

> My appraisal of Boyd is that in the reporting trade, it's a lifetime career. I expect him to go far. That is clearly his ambition. And along the way, he seems to be never fully satisfied with his own work, always looking for ways to improve it. He takes direction and criticism, gracefully and profitably.

But as he made his last point, he raised a sticky issue:

> His wife, Sheila Rule, a reporter on the *New York Times*, would be a fine addition to Nieman functions whenever she could make it from New York to Cambridge for short visits.

None of my peers knew of my separation from Sheila or of my relationship with Anna. I worried that if they did, they would think less of me. This lie-by-omission would come back to haunt me.

———

IN JUNE 1980, the Nieman Foundation announced its new class of twelve American journalists. Among those selected were Michael Hill, an assistant Style editor at the *Washington Post*; David Lamb, Nairobi bureau chief at the *Los Angeles Times*; Howard Shapiro, a reporter at the *Philadelphia Inquirer*; Carlos Aguilar, a reporter for KENS-TV in San Antonio; and James Stewart, a reporter at the *Atlanta Constitution*. At twenty-nine, I was one of the youngest Niemans ever selected.

Anna and I arrived in Cambridge in early September. We had a two-bedroom apartment in graduate housing on campus, the only place I could secure at the last moment. We were not alone. We shared the space with swarms of cockroaches that seemed immune to the insecticide bombs we exploded regularly. It was as if I was back on Romaine Place, but worse.

Our roommates were the least of our problems. At the first gathering of fellows and spouses at the Walter Lippmann House, the headquarters for the Nieman program, we arrived and searched for name tags. Of course, since I'd failed to clue anyone in, there was no name tag for Anna Marie Jordan, but there was one for Sheila Rule.

That incident was an omen for the year.

I was making six hundred dollars a week and trying to support Anna as well as myself. Once I covered expenses like getting her settled in Washington and trips back to St. Louis to visit her mother, I had to contend with moving us to Cambridge. The moves quickly depleted my meager savings. At a low point Anna had offered to pawn a piece of jewelry I had given her to raise cash. My pride wouldn't let me allow her to do it. Instead, I took out a loan, sinking into debt.

We soon became a house divided. While we developed some strong and lasting relationships with fellows like Hill, the Lambs, the Aguilars, and the Stewarts, Anna and I pulled in different directions. I was hell-bent on becoming the best Nieman ever. Anna started wondering why she was spending a year of her life at Harvard.

By December she had had enough. She left for St. Louis shortly before Christmas, with no word on whether she would return. Once again, I was alone.

I pined for Anna. It was important to set everything right and to make sure that she knew how much I wanted her in my life. I could not bear the thought of losing her, especially after having lost Sheila. I sent flowers and cards and called repeatedly. Eventually she agreed to return to Cambridge and resume our life together. With my personal life in place, even a precarious place, I could focus on the professional one.

———

IT WAS a heady life, to be sure. Like the other Niemans, I was exposed to some of Harvard's best professors, including Daniel Bell, John Kenneth Galbraith, Marshall Frady, Helen Teichman, and Richard Neustadt, whose course on the American presidency was the one I had chosen to satisfy the Nieman's requirement to complete one course. We took two trips, one in January across Canada and one in the spring to Japan. I took a creative writing course, where I drafted short stories that reflected my thoughts about many subjects, like my father and grandmother. Hill deflated me with the critique of one of my stories about two sick people meeting on a vacation, falling in love, and then dying.

"It reads like an episode of *The Love Boat*," he said, referring to the sappy TV show. In truth, he was right. At heart, I was sappy. Still I soldiered on, trying to put some of my feelings on paper. I always arrived early to Nieman seminars with writers, hoping to pick up a tip or two. We had three of the best visit us: John Irving, John McPhee, and David Halberstam.

I longed for the contentment that I thought my classmates enjoyed. But with money tight, I never felt I could deliver on my promise to take care of Anna. Occasionally, we would visit other fellows or David Fink, a former *Post-Dispatch* reporter who lived in the area. He and his wife, Phyllis, were gracious enough to help us adjust to life in Cambridge. But in a way, those trips only added to my woes. I could see how happy David and Phyllis were. And when Phyllis became pregnant, I knew my partnership with Anna paled compared with what they had.

My classmates all seemed to be accomplishing something. Some were writing books; others were engrossed in classes. Still others embarked on personal growth with goals like trying to quit smoking. I did none of these.

In time, the novelty of the Nieman wore off. I had wanted so much from Harvard, but I found myself spending many of my days sporadically auditing a few classes or curling up in front of the television, watching *All My Children* and *The Young and the Restless*. I had little will for more.

But away from the daily pressures of my job, I was able to begin the difficult process of understanding that only I could make myself happy. I had looked to Sheila and Anna, but clearly, it was up to me. In that cramped, cockroach-infested apartment in Cambridge, I took the first steps in a long journey toward knowing myself, and without the Nieman, I probably would not have budged.

The movers made two stops when we returned to Washington in May 1981. One was the one-bedroom apartment on Fifteenth Street and Rhode Island that I had rented for myself. The other was a studio apartment on Wisconsin that Anna had rented. She was determined to go it alone. I was hurt and angry. Ever since St. Louis, we had been marking time, not moving our relationship forward. It was my fault, and she saw through my hesitation. Though it was painful, this split also felt liberating.

———

BACK AT work in Washington, I reclaimed my passion for journalism and tried to restore my finances. The *Post-Dispatch* became my wife and my mistress. I arrived at work early and stayed late. I stopped moping around on weekends. I made a point of doing something, anything, but sit home and feel lonely. I walked the streets of Washington and visited the District's many museums and landmarks. For the first time, I began to discover what it really meant to *live* in Washington. I accepted any social invitation that came my way, reached out to friends, and hung out on the town, mostly in the invisible black Washington—not among the bureaucrats but those who provided their telephones or clothes or drove them to work. They were blue collar, the backbone of the city.

I also took a part-time teaching job at Howard University, where I engaged young minds about journalism. It all reinvigorated me.

Sheila and I finally had the conversation that we both knew was coming and that I dreaded. It was time to divorce. We had been separated for some five years now, and clearly we would not be a couple again. Fortunately, we were able to remain friends.

I knew that I was on my own, but for the first time, I began to believe that was not so bad.

Because my work had improved, and with my year at Harvard focusing on the American presidency, editors decided to give me a shot covering the White House. Jim Deakin, the reporter who had distinguished himself and the paper on that beat, was approaching retirement. As I began to chronicle the pillars of official Washington, like President Reagan, Jim Baker, Elizabeth Dole, David Gergen, and others, writing about them became the most important thing in my life.

I accompanied Reagan on a trip to South and Central America, where he met with other hemispheric leaders. For other reporters it was not much of a news story and no big deal. But it was my first foreign trip as a reporter, and I tried not to betray my first-timer's enthusiasm as we took in the sights in Brazil and Costa Rica.

The Washington powerbrokers did not need the *Post-Dispatch*—or me—in the way that city hall officials did in St. Louis. But some liked me and even respected my work, so they made themselves available for interviews.

I decided to do a profile of Elizabeth Dole, a fast-rising star in the Republican ranks and quite worthy of a serious article. I went into her office at the White House expecting to ask tough questions, as I always did, but she quickly disarmed me. She greeted me with tea and cookies that she served herself. I returned to my office and looked through my notes and realized that I had not asked her one serious question. When I confessed this to my fellow reporters, they gave me hell. After all the politicians I had covered, how could I be taken in by the charms of a woman bureaucrat?

In Washington, access is everything. Just a quote from a high-ranking administration official can make a story—at least in those days when officials were too savvy to intentionally mislead reporters. For reporters at smaller papers like mine, recognition of any kind by those in power was gold. We sought it constantly, like a drug, knowing that it was how we made names for ourselves.

I let that jones get the better of me. At a time of rising unemployment and homelessness, Reagan was being painted as indifferent to the plight of the poor and minorities. He supported tax cuts for the rich as a way of growing the economy and reducing benefits to the "welfare queens," who, he argued, lacked a desire to work. His counselor Ed Meese did not help matters with the absurd argument that the administration was proper in labeling ketchup as a vegetable to meet the nutritional needs of public-school children who received free lunches.

The White House wanted a way to show a president who was firm in his beliefs but compassionate about Americans who were suffering. They needed someone whom they believed would ask a question for which he had rehearsed a compassionate but firm answer. They found that person in me.

On the day of a scheduled prime-time, nationally televised news conference, I got a call from a White House press aide seeking confirmation that I was attending. Yes, I'll be there, I assured her, not giving the unusual inquiry a second thought, and certainly not considering that as one of a few black reporters covering the White House, I was an easy mark. In fact, I felt as if my stock was going up—they knew who I was!

When I walked into the room at the White House, I noticed that I had been assigned the aisle seat in the second row, up front with the network correspondents and major national newspapers. The *Post-Dispatch* never had this place of prestige. Reagan entered and looked at me and winked. I realized that I would have the chance to ask the president a question before a national audience. My stomach turned and my legs shook.

Reporters volleyed questions, and Reagan answered. I bided my time, thinking of what issue to raise. Toward the end of the news conference, the president turned to me.

"Gerry?" he encouraged, nodding and smiling.

Few people who knew me ever called me Gerry—I hated that name—but here on national TV, where news conferences are as much theater as substance, Reagan wanted people to think we were on a first-name basis—the leader of the free world and the young black reporter from St. Louis.

Of course, in my naivete, I did not realize that I was set up. Two of the three questions I had written and rehearsed, among them what he would do about nuclear proliferation, had already been covered. I turned to my third question and fired away, asking what he planned to do about the rising number of unemployed and homeless. It was an important issue but also a "black" question, gaining legitimacy because it came from the black reporter. Reagan's team could not have choreographed it better.

As if on cue, Reagan produced the classified section from a local paper that he said he had been perusing—just that day! He argued that jobs were available for those who wanted them—the real problem, he implied, was simply that people were unable to find them.

There on national television, I had been served up on a platter by Ronald Reagan. I vowed never to allow myself to be used again. Still, the event worked in my favor. Because the president addressed me not just by my first name but by a nickname, administration officials assumed that he knew me personally. Therefore, they must have reasoned, they should get to know me as well. All of a sudden, my phone calls were returned and my requests for interviews granted much more quickly. To Reagan administration officials, I became known as Gerry.

———

WITH THE national television exposure, my position as White House correspondent, and my Nieman, other publications started to notice me.

I flew to New York to interview with *Time* magazine for a job as a reporter and writer. They rarely combined the two roles, I was told, but they would do it for me. The *Philadelphia Inquirer* called, looking for reporters to place in Delaware, its next circulation growth target. I could do the job, said one of the senior-level editors, Jim Naughton, but in all honesty, he advised candidly, it would be a step down at that point in my career.

Then I heard from Tony Day, editorial page editor of the *Los Angeles Times*. Day was a sharp journalist, a gifted writer, and a kind and patient man. He invited me to Los Angeles to visit the paper and picked me up at the airport the Sunday evening I arrived. We went directly to his home, where we had drinks by his pool. Dinner was fabulous. I was impressed.

I spent the next morning at the paper, talking to editors and editorial writers. They were smart and aggressive, reinforcing my notion that the *L.A. Times* was one of the nation's best news organizations. And the atmosphere was laid-back, not like the constant hustle in Washington. I was thrilled when Day called several days later offering me a job as an editorial writer.

While I had gone on several interviews in recent months, I did so more out of curiosity than anything else. There was never harm in talking about possibilities, as my pragmatic brother, Gary, had drilled in my head. But Day's offer was different. He represented a paper where I actually wanted to work. The thought of moving to Los Angeles troubled me, as I would have to leave Washington just as I was beginning to understand and appreciate it. And I still owed the *Post-Dispatch* about six months. Under the rules of the Nieman program, fellows are supposed to return to their news organizations for at least a year, since employers agree to make up the difference between the reporters' salary and the fellowship stipend. The stipend was about half of my *Post-Dispatch* salary. I felt obliged to honor my commitment to the *P-D.* Day understood.

"I'll wait," he said, after I explained my hesitancy. "You still have the job when your year is up." It was a classy move, and I could not have felt more wanted.

When six months came and went and he had not heard from me, Day knew what was happening. I was wavering, he said, as if he had a window into my mind. I wanted to work at his *Times,* I admitted, but I did not want to write editorials. I was in my early thirties, and the notion of retiring to the rarefied corridors of editorial writers and not being on the ground as a reporter was unsettling. I was years away from editorials, I reasoned. And what I did not share: I had no taste for moving to L.A., alone again, and trying to figure out a new life.

Day was gracious. I declined the offer (without saying so), and he took it off the table (without saying so). There was no need for further discussion.

A short while later, the *New York Times* called. Or rather, Bill Kovach, the Washington bureau chief, asked me to send clips if I wanted to be considered for a job. Moving to the *Times* but remaining in Washington was a better proposition. But doubt crept in. Could I really succeed at the *New York Times?* Over the years, Sheila and I had talked about her experiences at the paper, but it still seemed like foreign territory. I had never wanted to work there and did not know if I could fit in. Journalism is journalism, I know, and you can do good journalism anywhere. But the *Times* had its own storied culture and way of life. I consulted Gary, who helped me see that I really had nothing to lose. I sent my clips.

I met with Kovach and David Jones, the National editor, over separate lunches in Washington. These were just the first steps toward a job at the *Times.* No senior editor has anything to say about who is hired. It is not a democracy and never has been. The only vote that counts is the executive editor's.

Jones, who over fourteen years would become the longest-serving National editor in the paper's history, was a master of *Times* politics. He was, above all, a survivor. He was also a man of enormous intelligence and competency who had been considered as a possible executive editor for the paper. But for whatever reasons, it did not happen.

That was also true of Kovach, a Southerner who had come up in the poorer regions of East Tennessee. Kovach's ancestors had come from Albania and arrived before the Civil War, settling in one of the few regions in the South that opposed slavery. Thus, they were outsiders fighting for a principle, a quality that Kovach embodied at the *Times*. And despite his legendary explosive temper, he was also known for his empathy and compassion.

Both Kovach and Jones were determined to change the face of the *Times*. Not in radical ways—they were both wise enough to know what buttons to push and when. But they wanted the *Times* to be more skeptical of Washington bureaucrats and to use its enormous talent and resources more aggressively.

Sometimes their choice would survive the paper's rigid hiring process, as it did when Howell Raines was hired to work in the Atlanta bureau in 1978. But just as often, it would not—a recruit would get to New York for interviews only to flame out.

Jones and Kovach got me to New York. I had to take it from there. It was the first time I had visited the newsroom, and I could not have been more nervous. Sheila had briefed me on the *Times'* notorious interview process. It is a ritual unlike anything most journalists ever experience. I was given an itinerary with appointments to meet various senior editors. Then came a pause in the schedule. It was then that I would learn if the assessments were positive enough to warrant an audience with the executive editor, Abe Rosenthal. A meeting with Abe was a good sign. No meeting, and I would probably never work at the *Times*. The routine had the feel of the reality shows that would later proliferate on TV. Call it *The Candidate*: hopefuls can be voted off at any turn if an interviewing editor objects.

I cannot remember the editors I talked to, what they asked, or what I answered. But I will never forget the request that I meet with Mr. Rosenthal—if I had the time. Of course, I have the time, I replied.

I had heard about the best and worst of Rosenthal. Many considered him a bully and a tyrant. But he was also known as a brilliant editor— one who made firm decisions about what was best for the *Times* and never looked back. Sheila told me how she became a foreign correspondent for the *Times:* Rosenthal read a feature story she had written about a black family's celebration of Easter. He liked it a lot. He had told her that he couldn't stop thinking about the story, and he decided on the spot to make Sheila a foreign correspondent and to send her to the Caribbean, then Africa. The decision would change her life forever. She would have assignments in Kenya, South Africa, and then London. And she would grow from new experiences and exposure, all because of Rosenthal's reaction to her article.

Still, when I seated myself in his back office, across from this slight but intense man, I did not know what to expect, what to say, or how to win him over. I had never felt more intimidated by any one person.

Rosenthal made it easy. Mercifully, the first words out of his mouth were, "You have the job." So, he continued, just relax and tell me about yourself. "I want to get to know you."

I sighed with relief and prepared to tell my life story. But Rosenthal intervened. He wanted to tell his story first.

For the next hour, we talked about him. His life as an international correspondent in India, Poland, Afghanistan, and Japan. The Pulitzer Prize he won in 1960 for reporting from Poland. His love for the *Times*. He shared how every day he arrived at the paper, he reminded himself how fortunate he was to be the executive editor. I was no longer intimidated but enraptured. I became a sponge, trying to soak up all of his experiences. He had lived a life that meant something, had gone where few journalists had or would. I wanted to hear every bit of what he had to say.

He ended the "interview" far too soon for me. I managed to ask two questions: "What's my salary, and how many weeks' vacation will I get?"

Rosenthal dismissed me with a wave of his hand. "I don't deal with that," he said impatiently. "Talk to Jim," referring to Jimmy Greenfield, then the chief administration officer in the newsroom.

As I was still trying to get my mind around the fact that I'd just been hired by the *New York Times*, Rosenthal escorted me to Greenfield's office at the end of the corridor. Greenfield, a former Foreign editor and confidant of Rosenthal's, was very much old school, not considered to be among the "radicals" pushing the *Times* in new directions. He greeted me with a smile and a vigorous handshake. We were soon alone, and he turned to ask me a question that stung.

"I really enjoyed your clips—they're so well written," he said as I sat there smiling, pleased with myself. Then he added: "Did you write them yourself, or did someone write them for you?"

"Of course I wrote them myself!" I blurted out. I was too surprised to respond any other way.

Later, I thought I should have told him how offensive his question was. I would understand the context: the *Times* was a place where blacks felt they had to convince their white peers that they were good enough to be there. It was my first exposure to the racial culture of the paper, the ugly underside of life at the *Times.*

6

D.C. GRIND

When Gerald and I covered the first Bush White House, I was always amazed at how he could shake out information from the most secretive people in the administration. I was terrible at getting scoops of any kind. On phone calls with sources, I would degenerate into whining, "I'm desperate. Ple-e-e-ease help me."

Gerald would watch me, shaking his head, and then show me how it was done. He would call over to the Republican National Committee and ask for Lee Atwater. When the legendary bad boy of politics got on the phone, Gerald would growl, sounding like a hard-boiled detective on *Law and Order*: "What the *hell* is going on over there?"

He was just fishing, but his tone made Lee and his minions fall into line at once. They would spill their guts, and Gerald would have another great story.

Gerald was a very elegant dresser, and I always gave him ties and pocket squares for Christmas because I knew he had great style. I think he was flummoxed by casual Friday. Sometimes, I'd see him walking down Forty-third Street on a Friday afternoon, without his suit jacket and with his shirt half untucked. That was the best he could do. He was not suddenly going to be wearing checked flannel shirts and pleated khakis. His sense of decorum and formality was too strong for that.

—MAUREEN DOWD

M Y BOSSES at the *Post-Dispatch* had other thoughts about my leaving. David Lipman, the managing editor, insisted that I fly to St. Louis. I owed him and the *Post-Dispatch* a face-to-face meeting, he reasoned. I agreed, although I had already made up my mind.

Lipman, who had edged out Millstone for the top editing position, played me masterfully. As soon as I sat across from him in his office, he reached in his desk drawer and produced a check for several thousand dollars. The money was a bonus for the good work I had done lately, he said, and was mine to keep whether I stayed or left. He then talked about a raise and about putting me in a special bonus program for executives and a very few journalists. Then he asked, "What do you want to do with your career?"

At that moment, I thought about everything—reporting in Washington, city hall, even the lousy consumer beat. I thought about the *Maneater* and *Blackout* at Mizzou. I knew I wanted to run a paper. I told Lipman that I wanted to go into management.

Lipman said the paper would place me in one of the top five editing jobs. Because I was only in my early thirties, he reasoned, I would be in a good position to edit the paper eventually. He then said he would take me under his wing and teach me what I needed to know.

I weakened. He added that if editing was not as rewarding as I'd hoped, he would make me a National correspondent based wherever I wanted. He then led me to the office of Joseph Pulitzer Jr., the publisher. Pulitzer got right to the point.

"This is your home," he said. "You grew up here. I'm not losing you to the *Times* or to anyone else."

It was a simple, passionate declaration, and it worked. At that moment, I switched my allegiance back to the *Post-Dispatch*.

Flying back to Washington, I felt sick with confusion. How could I leave a newspaper that was home? I replayed my interview with the *Times* and second-guessed my decision. The paper was overwhelmingly huge, had an executive editor who was widely feared and a newsroom replete with cronyism, and already I had experienced a racially motivated insult.

I called Kovach, the *New York Times* Washington editor, and told him I changed my mind. "I know what you are feeling," he said, sensing my anguish. "We offered you the moon, and they offered you the universe. But just remember that their offer came after we had made ours."

"Take the weekend and think about it," he said. "If you haven't changed your mind, I'll inform the folks in New York."

I spent the weekend pacing and smoking, smoking and pacing. I reached out to Sheila and Gary, both of whom counseled that there was no wrong decision.

I did not have to make my journalistic mark at the *Times*, I reasoned. As Pulitzer aptly described it, the *Post-Dispatch* was home and family. How could I be disloyal?

Eventually, my ambition won out. I was good, I believed, but as long as stayed at the *Post-Dispatch*, I would never know *how* good.

On Monday, I walked into the office and dialed St. Louis.

Next, I called Kovach, who was delighted with my decision. He repeated his pledge: "We're going to do right by you."

Once I came to know the *Times'* culture, I realized how much Kovach had stuck his neck out for me. Newsroom protocol meant that he should have informed editors in New York immediately when I backtracked. Had he done so, I would have been history. Editors would turn their backs on a young reporter who could not decide between the *Times* and the *Post-Dispatch*.

In the end, I took a pay cut to work at the *Times*. That was probably a first. I did not take the *P-D*'s counteroffer back to the *Times* to see if they would match it. I kept this fact from my brother, the finance guy, who would have been appalled.

At first, I was haunted by my decision. Writing for the *P-D* was never just a job to me; the paper was a place where I was safe and secure.

It did not help that my assignment was amorphous; I was to cover "urban affairs," a euphemism for blacks, poverty, and civil rights. I had tackled those subjects early in my career at the *Post-Dispatch*; I was giving up one of the top assignments at my former paper, the White House, to start over at the *Times*.

I thought about that, along with the pay cut, as I left my apartment and headed to my first day on the job on November 14, 1983. Again and again, I could not help but ask myself, "What on earth were you thinking?"

―――――

THE *TIMES*' Washington bureau was located above a liquor store in a building at Seventeenth and K, in the heart of offices housing powerful lawyers and lobbyists. It was closer to my apartment than the *Post-Dispatch* office, and I could get there in about ten minutes. I got there early.

"Hi, hi!" boomed the voice of John Finney, the main assignment editor and the only other person there. He arrived early each day to organize the daily report.

Finney, a *Times* veteran with a slight paunch, moved through the bureau as if he owned it, handing out assignments, scheduling stories, and rigorously puffing on the pipe that always dangled from his lips. Though he lacked the celebrity status of star reporters, he was invaluable to what the staff produced. Practically everyone in the bureau had a quirk or two, as I soon discovered. Finney's was his greeting: "Hi, hi!"

The bureau had a range of characters. There were those like Finney, who were WASP, Ivy League, and old school. There were the younger, ambitious reporters who had "rabbis"—high-ranking or strategically placed editors who often served as mentors—in New York plotting their careers, often unbeknownst to their supervisors in Washington. Then there were those of different pedigrees, like Kovach, and those like me, who were new and finding their way.

No matter their lineage, few people on staff, like their colleagues in New York, seemed happy—even the stars. Instead, they hung in a state of perpetual neurosis as they struggled to remain on top. In doing so, they cultivated an environment of fear, distrust, and agendas. The twin goals: protecting one's turf and watching one's back. The situation was worsened by a constant shuffle of those in power. A friend or enemy would find his fortune enhanced or diminished by staff changes. Then the dominos would fall, ushering in new bosses and alignments. It felt like a game of musical chairs: no one knew when the music would stop, but everyone was poised to grab a seat when it did.

For my first few days, I observed how the bureau functioned. Stories were assigned in the morning, and by early afternoon, reporters provided summaries of what the stories would ultimately say. Summaries were followed by the daily news conference with senior editors in New York. Often Washington editors would talk a story up, while editors like Rosenthal amplified, challenged, or argued for a different approach. Story meetings occur every day in newsrooms around the country—editors from departments like Local, Business, and Sports "pitch" their best offerings for the front page—but I had never seen a process so brutal. Before the call, the mood in Washington was often tense. Trying to convince Rosenthal of the merits of a story could quickly become verbal warfare. Then—*boom!*—he would render a decision.

On my third day, Finney summoned me to his desk and asked if I was "ready" for an assignment. I assured him I was. I thought it was a strange way of making the request, and I wondered how many new white reporters heard their first assignment preceded by that question. Finney pitched me facts about a legislative breakthrough on Capitol Hill involving subsidized housing. It was similar to hundreds of stories I had covered, although I did not feel it necessary to tell Finney that.

I reported, filed a summary, and then wrote it up. As always, I first asked myself what the legislative maneuvering meant. The answer, of course, formed my lede: "Breaking a legislative stalemate over the Government's role in housing, Congress today moved toward passage of legislation that would authorize new Federal subsidies for 100,000 additional housing units around the country." My first story for the *Times* appeared on page B10, under the byline Gerald M. Boyd.

As a reporter for the next six years, I would write hundreds of stories each year. But that first time, I felt an enormous sense of professional and personal validation. Yes, I was ready.

———

TRUE TO his word, Kovach did everything he could to make me feel welcome. He would stroll by my desk at lunchtime and ask if I had any plans. I rarely did, and we would head off to Duke's Restaurant, often with B. Drummond Ayres, a reporter and editor. Kovach was a complicated man. As editor of a staff numbering near fifty, he was fearless, creative, and passionate. He also had a dark and brooding side, which would surface when he lost some battle with the editors in New York.

He would use those lunches to vent about the stupidity of his bosses. I sat there soaking it in over drinks.

I also learned the unspoken rules of the *Times*. For example, good form meant not knowing just the name of a colleague but also the first name of his or her spouse. Kovach had a cheat sheet listing the home numbers of senior editors. In parentheses was the first name of each spouse or partner. To call Editor X and have his wife answer the phone and not acknowledge her and make nice was considered a faux pas. So was badmouthing colleagues, given the porous environment. No one knew for sure what friend or rabbi that colleague might have.

Whenever Kovach was outraged by some blunder in New York, he would leave the office early with a stomachache. He seemed to have quite a few in those days.

The entire news operation revolved around one person, Abraham Michael Rosenthal, the sixty-one-year-old man who had spent fourteen years as managing and executive editor. Everyone knew his various moods, his likes, and especially his dislikes. They knew when he arrived in the newsroom each morning and when he left each evening. It was then that they collectively exhaled.

Because I was based in Washington, I rarely crossed paths with Rosenthal. But thanks to the newsroom chatter, I was aware of all things Abe. Once I planned a brief trip to New York, which included a quick stop in the office. Before I left, Ferne Horner, the Washington bureau office manager, warned me about whom to avoid. Horner was a woman of mystery. She revealed almost nothing about her life before joining the *Times*. She was single, superstitious, and loved opera, cats, and a drink or two after work along with her cigarettes. We became fast friends. Horner cautioned me not to talk to Rosenthal's assistant, because she would take everything I said back to her boss.

I tried to avoid cliques in the bureau, which was easy to do. I really did not belong to any of them. I had the most in common with younger and newer reporters, but even then, as a black man, I was an outsider.

Fortunately, I made friends outside of the office, and I would see them on weekends. I dated, and among the women I saw were a wealthy white woman and a black woman who worked for the telephone company in the District.

I settled into my beat, chronicling the poor and covering the occasional big urban affairs story, like the 1984 "State of Black America" report published by the National Urban League. The conclusion was dismal, as usual: "While individual achievements by blacks quite rightfully attracted public attention and drew deserved commendation, the plight of black Americans remained strained throughout 1983 with no light apparent at the end of the tunnel." But the beat quickly became more of the same, and once again, I felt as if I were running in place.

————

THE 1984 presidential campaign changed my career path and probably the course of my life. Eight Democrats were seeking the nomination to challenge the incumbent Reagan and his vice president, George H. W. Bush. Covering all the contenders, which the *Times* was committed to do, took enormous labor. The paper had assembled its presidential election team before I arrived in 1983, and by January 1984, many were seeking vacation relief from long days on the road. As Kovach considered replacements, he asked me if I wanted to spend a few days covering Jesse Jackson. Jackson was a long shot for the Democratic nomination but was nevertheless shaking up the political landscape with an electrifying campaign. I jumped at the opportunity.

Kovach and David Jones, the National editor based in New York, supervised the coverage. The other main player was Howell Raines, who was chief national political correspondent. Talented and ambitious, Raines, in his early forties, had already achieved success while working at the *Atlanta Constitution* and *St. Petersburg Times* before joining the *Times'* Atlanta bureau. He had moved to Washington and briefly covered the White House before landing one of the paper's most coveted jobs covering national politics.

While national politics consumed our attention, internal politics were also at play. Rosenthal was four years away from mandatory retirement, and already the staff was preoccupied with who would replace him. Editors and reporters were forming coalitions based on longtime relationships and interpretations of what was best for the paper.

Kovach, Jones, and Raines were comrades in arms as they tried to use the aggressive campaign coverage to make a statement about how *Times* journalism could be improved. They wanted a report that was sharp, sophisticated, and that generated buzz within political circles and beyond.

I was ignorant of all of these issues when I joined the political team. I did not know Raines and had no contact with him outside of my daily telephone calls from the field. Each morning I would check in with him and report what I knew or expected to happen that day. He would suggest how the information should be handled, as a story or as a feed to a story that he or another political reporter was writing. Our conversations were straightforward and professional, and he easily passed on information, hunches, and tips for me to pursue. I sensed that he valued my contributions and that we were working toward a common goal.

In mid-January, I was assigned to write about Jackson's surprisingly strong showing in Virginia's caucuses. He had come in second, thanks in large part to the decisive support he had received from black voters in the Tidewater area. The second-place finish reinforced the view that he could run a decent campaign if he could rally black voters, one of his key objectives. Thanks to the support of preachers in the area, that possibility seemed real.

My reconstruction of how Jackson had succeeded in Virginia was my first front-page story in the *Times*. I could not have been more surprised. As I followed him on the campaign trail, Jackson and I sparred frequently. I saw myself as a kind of truth squad, pressing him for answers whenever he made vague policy pronouncements. As president, he would say, he would create thousands of jobs. How will you pay for them? I would ask. When he sermonized about a rising tide lifting all boats, I challenged him with: Mr. Jackson, what exactly does that mean?

I was always respectful, as I was with most of the politicians I covered, but I was determined not to give him a pass. I felt that some of my black colleagues accepted what he said at face value. Some of them openly championed Jackson's candidacy and felt they would not be covering a national political campaign if the candidate were white. There was truth in that; the number of black reporters covering the campaign at least doubled and possibly tripled as a result of Jackson's candidacy. But I did not feel beholden to Jackson. I had a job to do.

I had never met the reverend before 1984, although I grew up following him in the media. He was one of the most charismatic men of his generation, and certainly one of its most engaging speakers. Yet he was often characterized as an opportunist and a showboat. Traveling with him through the South and Midwest, I came to see him in all his complexity. I regarded him as narcissistic and unpredictable. I saw his raw ambition but also the enormous will that it took to press forward, pulling a nation and its racial baggage along. I saw how his efforts came at tremendous cost to himself and to his family.

One of Jackson's strengths was an ability to know just the right buttons to push with his audience. On a bus trip through Iowa, he sidled up to me.

"You know," he said, "you're not like a lot of these other reporters. You're serious and all business. You are going somewhere in your career. I hope one of my sons grows up to be like you."

I was flattered, and I thanked the reverend. But I suspected that somehow he had deduced I longed for a family and children. At the next opportunity to question him, I was even tougher.

The campaign was already a volatile mixture of race and politics, and then it blew up. Late one night I was awakened by a phone call from New York, asking about a story in the *Washington Post*. Near the bottom of the story, headlined "Peace with American Jews Eludes Jackson," was this bombshell: "In private conversations with reporters, Jackson has referred to Jews as 'Hymies' and to New York as 'Hymietown.'"

The revelation that Jackson, whose candidacy was based on appealing to people of all of religions and ethnicities, used a slur to describe

Jews suggested he was a hypocrite, an anti-Semite, or both. The editor in New York asked if I ever heard Jackson utter those comments. To the best of my memory, I said, I had not.

"OK, we'll use the account in the *Post* and credit them," he said, quickly hanging up.

For the rest of that night, I could not sleep. I lay there recounting all the times I had interviewed Jackson, trying to determine how I could have possibly missed "Hymietown." I could not recall his ever using those words in my presence.

The next day I learned that the source of the information in the *Post* was Milton Coleman, a black reporter whom I respected immensely. If Coleman said Jackson had spoken those words, I had no doubt that he had. I asked Coleman when Jackson made the disparaging remarks. He remembered that it was at the Butler Aviation Terminal at National Airport shortly before Jackson and several reporters boarded a private charter for a campaign appearance. I was one of those reporters.

In fact, as the plane was being fueled that morning, Jackson, Coleman, and I had breakfast. Coleman reminded me that I had left the table a couple of times, once to use the bathroom and again to fill my plate with food. Perhaps Jackson said those incendiary words in my absence.

Even if this was true, it rang hollow. I worried that my colleagues might think that I withheld the bombshell, that I was shilling for Jackson, even though I was among his toughest critics. I was devastated. I asked Coleman if he recalled my being present. He said he could not.

For a while, I was fixated, continuously trying to figure out what happened. And then I got angry, as Coleman became a target of groups like the Nation of Islam that accused him of trying to destroy Jackson's candidacy. At one point, the *Post* had to provide security for Coleman and his family. Even knowing the negative reaction, if I had had what Coleman had, I would have run with it, too.

I could not help but wonder what my *Times* colleagues thought about the "Hymietown" incident. I had been at the paper for several months, but just one incident like this could overshadow all my previous good work. Could they possibly believe that I would cover up for Jackson because he was black?

Kovach answered that question, although I never knew if he was speaking just for himself or for the collective management. He declared without equivocation that if I had heard the slurs, I would have printed them.

"That's the kind of reporter you are," he said. Then he sent me back out on the campaign trail.

———

THE DEMOCRATIC field was flush with candidates, including Mondale, the eventual nominee; Senators John Glenn, Gary Hart, Alan Cranston, and Ernest (Fritz) Hollings; former Senator George McGovern and former Florida governor Reubin Askew. Over the course of the campaign, I spent brief stints with all of them, filling in for reporters who took vacation. As the field narrowed, other fill-in reporters returned to their previous assignments, but I never went back to urban affairs.

I spent considerable time with McGovern and came to admire his courage and convictions, but I hated traveling with him. Most often, he flew around in small propeller planes. The ride felt more like a roller-coaster than an aircraft.

I also came to know Gary Hart, whom I struggled to figure out. The Colorado senator had enormous promise as a politician and a loyal following. But he also seemed to have a penchant for recklessness. Once, he decided, against the advice of the Secret Service, to go whitewater rafting on a river in Colorado. Reporters traveling with the candidates had a choice: we could tag along or be driven to the spot where the rafting ended. I took seriously my role of staying with my candidate, so even though I could not swim, I donned a life jacket and tagged along. But before we pushed off, I turned to Hart and asked, "Why in the world are you doing this, given how dangerous it is?"

"I love danger!" he responded with a sense of glee. The quote made its way into a story I wrote and was recycled four years later when a second Hart bid for the nomination disintegrated after it was discovered that the married senator was allegedly having an affair with the model Donna Rice.

Covering the campaign established me as a political reporter rather than merely a black journalist who had joined the *Times* to cover "black" issues. The transformation was important: I was multifaceted and could take on the big-thought and big-picture stories. This repositioning did wonders for my confidence and ultimately my career.

Still, after my umpteenth plane ride to my umpteenth city, the glamour of a campaign beat began to give way to the drudgery of routine: From the hotel to the bus to the plane to a new city, on the bus to the next event, then back on the bus to the plane and next stop. Hotel rooms looked the same, speeches sounded the same, and one small city morphed into another.

Fortunately, I had connected with Raines, thanks to our frequent conversations, and comparing notes with him was the highlight of many of my days. We often had the same take on developments and seldom disagreed on approaches to stories. Raines was leading a team of reporters who included Phil Gailey and Fay Joyce, and I worked closely with them. The camaraderie kept me going; in fact, I spent weeks on the road at a time, not asking for time off and not putting in for comp time, as was my right.

Another highlight was Jacqueline Adams, a correspondent for CBS. Jackie, who was also covering the campaigns, was smart, polished, and had an air of refined elegance. Boston-bred and Harvard-educated, Jackie was at ease in Washington's professional and social circles. She seemed extremely secure in herself and had clear goals for her life and career, and she let it be known that she wanted a husband or, as she called it, "a kindred spirit." Jackie and I spent long hours talking, first about politics, then about ourselves. By the time the Democratic National Convention headed to San Francisco in July, we were seen as a couple.

On the last night of the convention, Raines hosted a dinner for *Times* reporters and editors who had worked the campaign. He acknowledged the work that Fay Joyce and I had done by giving us each an expensive pen. It was a small gesture, but one not common at the *Times*. It meant that I had met his test of what a political reporter should be.

Further validation came when I got the nod to follow Mondale, the newly minted Democratic nominee, when he left San Francisco for vacation in his home state of Minnesota. Just eight months after I joined the paper as an urban affairs reporter, I was traveling with the man who had a shot at becoming president. In the upcoming general election, I remained on the campaign, covering George Bush.

———

UNLIKE MY work with the Democratic candidates, traveling with Bush brought sanity to life on the road. Aboard *Air Force Two*, there was no waiting on taxiways, no runway delays. No scrambling for a quick bite to eat. When we got on the plane, meals were waiting for us, prepared by air force stewards. They reflected the tastes of the candidates: Bush enjoyed Mexican food; Reagan, meat loaf and apple pie.

Each morning we had baggage call at a civilized hour. When we arrived at the first-class hotel where we would spend our time, our keys would be waiting, our bags already in our rooms. Staff whisked us from one location to the next in a motorcade that never stopped for a light. Anything we needed, a telephone, a phone number, or the help of an aide, was almost immediately available.

This was my introduction to George H. W. Bush—or at least the campaign he was running with Reagan. In all honesty, covering the incumbent vice-presidential candidate was a snore.

The Republicans were in a commanding position from the start, bolstered by Reagan's enormous popularity and a strong sense that the economy was improving. They were also strong on defense, leaving the Democrats with slim chances.

While the president took *Air Force One* to the biggest and best political events, the vice president took *Air Force Two* to whatever was left. Small towns in big states like Pennsylvania, Ohio, and Michigan, or big towns in small states like Wyoming and South Dakota. Bush's role was to attack the Mondale–Geraldine Ferraro ticket but not to make bold policy pronouncements—or news. He did both well. Often, my editors relegated my dispatches from Bush campaign stops into roundups or short stories inside the paper.

With the pressure off, I used the time to get to know the man. It helped that all conversations aboard the presidential and vice-presidential planes were off the record unless otherwise acknowledged. I watched how he ended his days of campaigning with a dry martini or two—followed by a glass of milk. The milk, I knew, was for an ulcer. His Rolodex was as thick as some telephone books, and he turned to it often. His energy and enthusiasm seemed boundless, and he fully embraced the role of Reagan's No. 2. He could be incredibly thin-skinned, especially when his public service credentials were questioned. Although Bush was born to privilege—his father was a onetime senator from Connecticut and he was educated at Yale—he tried mightily to be one of the boys. Joe Six-Pack he wasn't. He valued loyalty and surrounded himself with aides who were more comfortable taking orders than generating ideas. He despised leaks and never forgave those who committed such a sin.

Our relationship was strained at first. Bush avidly resented the mainstream press, and he regarded the *Times* as one of his top enemies. I knew of the tension, but I also knew that, like other politicians, the vice president needed the paper to get his message out and to help shape public opinion about his leadership abilities. For him, this was all the more important since he was considering a run for president in 1988. After a while, it became clear that Bush and his staff were sizing me up, too.

———

BEING IN the air, on the road, often alone with my thoughts, I could not help but reflect on the sad state of my personal life. I was approaching thirty-five and still living in a one-bedroom rental with makeshift furniture. I had no wife, no children, and no clear plan for my future. I wanted a partner and stability as much as I wanted the next big story. I enjoyed my work immensely, but I did not see myself riding planes and writing slight variations of the same political yarn for the next few decades. I wanted more, soon. But even if I came up with answers, I had to put them on hold for the time—everything was devoted to the job. Since I had joined the paper, almost two-thirds of my time was on the road, in hotel rooms, and living out of suitcases.

The only time I stepped away from the campaign was to move Grandmother to a nursing home. The year before, my cousin Walter died. He was not yet forty. He used to check in on Grandmother regularly, and with his absence, she had no one to look after her. She had moved out of the flat on Romaine, and for a while lived with Gary and his wife, Andrea. After some time, she moved in with our cousin Ronald. But at eighty-eight, her body was weakening, and she needed more constant care.

I flew home to talk to her about the decision. The resignation on her face pained me greatly. "But Grandmother, we don't know what else to do," I said. "You just can't take care of yourself anymore."

She patted my hand and looked me in the eye. "If you think this is what's best for me, then I'll do it," she declared. And she said no more.

We found an airy, well-run place in the midtown section of St. Louis and settled her in. I watched as the staff helped her wash and move around and gave her meals and medication. As I left her, I thought of this proud, independent woman, this fierce fighter, stoically surrendering to what the grandchildren she raised thought was best. I realized I might not see her again. And I cried all the way to the airport.

———

SHORTLY AFTER the election, I met with Kovach. Reagan was about to begin a second term, and the *Times* decided to change a number of beats. My new assignment: I would be one of two correspondents assigned to the White House. Under his watch, he liked to announce, the *Times* would never be beaten on a big story the way it had been by the *Washington Post* on the Watergate scandal in 1972. Even on daily developments, he wanted the competition to follow the *Times*, rather than have the bureau chasing everybody else.

He paired me with Bernard Weinraub, a *Times* veteran who had enjoyed a distinguished career covering Vietnam, Northern Ireland, London, and India. Weinraub, whom everyone called Bernie, was well regarded by many editors in New York and a favorite of Rosenthal and the managing editor, Arthur Gelb. In teaming us, Kovach broke with tradition by not making one or the other the senior White House correspondent. Instead, we were equals.

Bernie was the consummate insider, overanxious and easy to anger. I was the outsider, reserved and hard to read. We were like fire and ice. He would blast aides with "That's fucking outrageous!" when he thought they favored our competitors. I focused on getting the aides to favor us. From our first days together, we formed a good team. Bernie was steeped in the ways of the *Times*, from who mattered to whom to ignore. My strength was my knowledge of the White House, since I had had that beat at the *Post-Dispatch*.

Once we covered a media event at Andrews Air Force Base packed with journalists and dignitaries. Ferne Horner, our office manager, sent a car to pick us up, but amid the throngs of people, the driver had trouble spotting us. We jumped in his car and had him call Horner to confirm our identities.

"I have a neurotic white man and a quiet black man," the driver relayed.

"You have our guys!" Horner cheered.

Bernie had his detractors at the *Times*. Some thought he was arrogant, while others believed he had received special treatment because he was so close to the top editors. No matter what others thought, I liked him from the start. Instinctively, I trusted him, one of the few times I did so with a white colleague. He struck me as vulnerable and, like me, worried about how others saw him. But while I tried to hide this concern, he did not. I admired his courage. Despite our obvious differences, in many ways we were quite similar. Bernie was not concerned about status or using the White House as a stepping-stone; he just wanted to do good journalism. We both would do anything to prevent being beaten on a story.

Kovach had maneuvered Finney out of the job as assignment editor and had found a soft landing for him. With New York's approval, he replaced Finney with Raines—known as the journalistic pit bull—as deputy bureau chief. The choice was well received within the bureau. In his role as chief national political correspondent, he had received high marks for managing scores of writers covering politics in 1984, helping the paper produce a smart and sophisticated political section. In his new role, he managed the daily Washington news report. Bernie and I reported to him.

In the *Washington Post*, we faced the formidable team of Lou Cannon and David Hoffman. Cannon, who had covered Reagan from his days as California governor, was later a respected biographer of the president. He knew aides and friends of both Reagan and his wife Nancy. Hoffman was talented, hardworking, and very skilled at intimidating sources into coughing up news. Then there were other *Post* reporters with access to the White House, including Bob Woodward and Ann Devroy.

Plus we confronted the network correspondents, all seasoned, talented, and tough, among them Lesley Stahl of CBS, Sam Donaldson of ABC, and Chris Wallace of NBC. Bernie and I were assigned to cut them down to size. Just getting in the game was hard enough; winning it seemed almost impossible.

Fortunately, we lucked out when Reagan made the highly unusual decision of allowing Jim Baker, the White House chief of staff, and Donald Regan, the Treasury secretary, to switch jobs. Baker was smooth as silk and extremely skilled at manipulating the press. He had his favorites, and they started with the *Washington Post*. Regan was different. Like the president, he was appalled by leaks. But unlike Baker, his newspaper of preference was the *Times*, a result of the years he spent in New York rising through the ranks and becoming chairman of the investment bank Merrill Lynch.

The blunt, sixty-seven-year-old Regan, who always had a joke or two to share with the president, was readily available to meet with reporters from the *Times*, even though he rarely volunteered anything that approached news. Still, the word circulated through the White House that he was willing to talk to the *Times*, so his reluctant aides normally returned our phone calls. They, too, seldom volunteered any information.

Bernie and I realized that his principal aides, such as Thomas Dawson, Dennis Thomas, Al Kingon, and David Chew, were not going to play the leak game easily, so we set out to develop Washington-style friendships with them. We had dinners with them and their spouses—Jackie gamely filled in as my partner—with no set agenda and no discussion of White House business. Our aim was to get to know them and to let them get to know us. Slowly, our approach began to pay off. Instead of a "No comment," we would occasionally get a morsel of helpful information. Even a tip such as whom Regan was meeting with could be valuable, because it pointed us toward something to explore.

Either Bernie or I would attend the daily briefings normally given by Larry Speakes, the president's spokesman. They seldom yielded a story; they were not designed to do so. News came from working the phones. People might respond with an "I can't help you on that" more often than not, but sometimes they hinted that I was on the right track and even suggested other sources. And, of course, occasionally, they "volunteered" information in the hopes of getting a story out that they wanted to be made public.

The challenges of my old job with the *Post-Dispatch* paled compared with what I experienced at the top. While there was more status—key White House aides called back and agreed to meet for the occasional interview—there was also the pressure not to just get the news and get it right but to deliver it filtered through a lens of authority, nuance, and insight. What I reported and wrote could sway political and public opinion, help ease fears, and even lead a nation to or from war. I no longer had the luxury of an excuse for why I might have missed a development or misread a policy pronouncement. I was the *Times'*—and the readers'—first line of defense. I took that charge seriously.

I considered myself fortunate, but I had no doubt that I was worthy of the assignment. I knew that putting an outsider—which I still was— in such a coveted position was anathema to the paper's culture. It was not lost on me, either, that I was the first journalist of color to cover the beat for the *Times*. But I did not feel as if my race had anything to do with my getting the post. Nobody could tell me that I did not earn it. I had not been so excited about my work since my days at the *Post-Dispatch's* City Hall bureau. Which explains why I did not walk into the daily White House briefings; I swaggered.

———

IN THE bureau, Raines was making changes, with Kovach looking over his shoulder to make sure that he did not go too far. On the first day as editor, for example, he ordered Stephen Engelberg, a reporter, to cover a hearing on Capitol Hill. Engelberg reported back that the hearing was over by the time he arrived.

"Either you get me the story or I will find someone who will!" Raines barked. It was a defining moment in how he ran his shop: no alibis, just results.

Nothing seemed to give him more joy than beating our main nemesis, the *Washington Post.* "We might be beaten," he would often say, "but we should never be out-thought or out-hustled."

He was determined to rid the bureau of what he considered dead wood, so he systematically pressured several veteran reporters to leave the paper. His tactics were ugly: he bounced reporters' stories back repeatedly, needled them to produce more, and challenged their basic understanding of their areas of coverage.

Years later, I would come to understand how he saw the bureau staff as made up of an A team and a B team. The former received his encouragement and attention; the latter, he ignored or tried to force off the paper.

For those he deemed worthy, Raines went to the mat. One of his new stars was Maureen Dowd, a quick-witted reporter and writer who had come from *Time* magazine. Dowd tackled a story from all directions. She would profess ignorance of a subject, a ploy to elicit help from knowledgeable sources. Most of the time it worked. Then she would make call after call, connecting the dots. For example, she would set out to learn Bush's favorite color. One person might say it was blue. She would ask the next person, How long has Bush's favorite color been blue? Next, she would ask a source if Bush's mother's favorite color was blue. Thirty calls later, she would report that Bush loved the color blue because his mother had given him a blue blanket when he was five and he still kept it packed neatly in a trunk. And once a year, on his birthday, he would retrieve the blanket, smooth it out, and remember it fondly.

Raines constantly searched for Dowd's kind of story; she had a knack for zeroing in on the nutty way that Washington really worked and delivering with attitude and voice. This kind of writing was unusual for the *Times,* and some editors did not know what to make of Dowd's offerings. Is this too opinionated? Un-*Times*ian? they would ask. Raines would not only convince fellow editors that what Dowd had to say—and how she said it—mattered, but he would argue her stories onto the front page.

Raines advanced other careers, including mine. He was generous with his time and had a gift for recognizing the heart of a story. Once,

I hesitated to draw a particular conclusion in a story even though all of the facts made it obvious. I was worried that my sources would conclude that I was being unfair.

"Why are you pulling your punches?" he asked. "You have this story cold, and the White House knows you do or else they wouldn't have talked to you. They know it and you know it, so what's the problem?"

He was right. He also taught me that anything could be news. While he placed a premium on breaking stories, he also understood that news could be in analytical pieces, profiles, or even feature stories such as who attended a major Washington party and who did not. The secret was to figure out what the story was and decide the best way to tell it.

As he worked his magic, more of us became what I would call Raines disciples. In a way, Raines was the journalistic father we all wanted to please. That meant breaking stories that everybody talked about. When we did, we would get an "attaboy" from Raines, often in the presence of others. Such recognition was priceless for young reporters eager to make a name in Washington journalism.

I had more contact with Raines now, and I studied him carefully. Like others, he had his quirks. To many of us in the bureau, the Engelberg incident was overkill. And there was the annual office picnic where Raines had a Southern friend roast a whole pig, head and all, in a pit so the bureau could experience real barbecue. It was hard to eat and harder to enjoy with the animal's head still attached and its eyes staring at you as you sliced into it.

Our relationship developed slowly, but the man I was getting to know was easy to like. Having grown up in Birmingham, Alabama, he was greatly influenced by the struggle for civil rights. I was intrigued by his life and perspective, and at ease in his presence.

I admired that he was not just driven but that he was centered as well. His wife, Susan, and their two sons, Ben and Jeffrey, seemed to give him a sense of balance that allowed him to not take the *Times* and its daily battles too seriously. He always made time to spend with his family or take off for a weekend of fly-fishing, escaping the madness of the moment and returning recharged and once again ready to wage war.

And Raines was proud of who he was. He was not an Ivy Leaguer like some at the *Times*; he got his B.A. at Birmingham-Southern College and M.A. in English at the University of Alabama. He cut his teeth working for a series of small newspapers, including the *Birmingham Post-Herald*, the *Tuscaloosa News,* and the *Birmingham News.* He wrote books with Southern themes: *My Soul Is Rested,* an oral history of the civil rights movement, and *Whiskey Man,* a novel set in Prohibition-era Alabama.

Despite his deep Southern roots, he had no problem joking about rednecks; and he was not shy about expressing his undying love for the University of Alabama's Crimson Tide and its legendary football coach Bear Bryant. At the same time, he was well read and fond of quoting Yeats. To assemble some men means fitting together one or two pieces. It took considerably more to put Raines together; he had so many parts.

At the end of most days, after the stories were fed to New York, a dozen or so of us would gather in Raines's office to gossip, to talk about challenges that we faced the next day, or simply to carp about editors in New York. Raines, sipping bourbon, held court. We enjoyed being around one another, and our relationships blossomed. Most of those who joined in were considered part of the A team, although he never identified us as such. Those he had issues with wisely stayed out of his way.

————

EACH AUGUST, Reagan would leave Washington and spend the month at his beloved Rancho del Cielo in the mountains above Santa Barbara. It was a dream for journalists traveling with the president, because the White House went into a virtual news blackout. The press office's daily reports routinely included the following: "The President spent the day clearing brush and chopping wood."

Reporters enjoyed the calm. They took their families along and, after filing whatever they could turn into a story, spent their afternoons on the beach or exploring wine country nearby. At night, they treated themselves to fabulous dinners at Santa Barbara's many fine restaurants. If we invited an aide, we could expense the entire meal. As a reporter, initially I never felt so pampered.

The *Washington Post* ended this carefree existence. On this, the first Santa Barbara summer for Bernie and me, the *Post* unleashed a stream of exclusives that other reporters scrambled to follow. We were beaten by the competition almost daily. The *Times* had egg on its face, and Bernie and I, who were trying to establish ourselves on the beat, were humiliated by the run of exclusives.

We spent weeks trying to figure out who was behind the leaks. Reagan had a skeleton crew traveling with him, and most of them were in no position to be the source of the news that the *Post* reported. Finally, only one possibility made sense: *Post* reporters must have interviewed willing White House aides before vacation began and then squirreled away the information until the reporters arrived in Santa Barbara. At that point, they unloaded one story after another.

The next summer we did the same thing. In the weeks leading up to the trip, Bernie and I both conducted a series of interviews with White House aides. Both of us traveled to Santa Barbara, and from the time we landed, we started unloading stories.

Around eight o'clock, just as many reporters were sitting down to dinner at some sumptuous restaurant, beepers would sound off. The *Times* and the *Post* were on the streets back east. Some evenings only one of us had an exclusive. Often both papers did. Newspaper reporters and network correspondents went crazy trying to match our scoops.

At one point, the competition became so intense that Speakes asked for a cease-fire between the *Times* and the *Post*. He wanted us to agree to stop producing exclusives, as we were making everyone's life miserable. Fat chance, we said, and the Santa Barbara summer wars continued for as long as Reagan was president. In the end, I am not sure if we won, but I know for certain that we did not lose.

———

GRANDMOTHER DIED on November 15, 1985. Periodically I had received reports on how she was faring in the nursing home. I had mixed emotions about our decision to move her there. I drew comfort from the fact that she died in peace, surrounded by new friends and people who were fond of her. But I felt guilt too, because while she gave so much of herself to us, in return we uprooted her and abdicated her care to others when she needed us most. When Gary called with the news, I listened in silence as he talked about funeral plans. I had more thoughts than words as I tried to absorb the reality that she was gone. I was spared this sense of loss when my mother died because I was too young to understand it. Now I felt the force of grief.

When I saw her in the casket, I knew I would never be the same. I bent and kissed her forehead and thanked her for all that she had done for me, for us. I did not cry. I could not. We proceeded to a cemetery in a suburb near St. Louis, about five miles from the house she loved on Romaine. There we put her in the ground.

I turned to my way of dealing with death, which was not to deal with it. But I had never felt so alone and empty. Other than Gary, there was no one I really trusted, but Gary did not have my grandmother's gentle hand in helping me hold the pieces of my life together.

Eventually, alone, I went through the stages of grief: from shock to denial to bargaining to guilt to anger and then depression. Acceptance and hope came hard. I thought of her every time I ate rice or smelled a clove of garlic, every time I woke up early to finish a task, every time I ironed a shirt or washed my clothes, every time I ate banana pudding or opened a Christmas present. She had given me everything she had, from her love of simple foods to her acute sense of fairness. She had taught me the importance of family, not by her preaching but by action. In return, I tried to live up to her standards.

If my constitution were different, I would have reached out more to Gary and Ruth. I would have clung to them. I would have found some way to let them both know how much I needed and loved them, and how much we needed to be there for one another now that a huge piece of our lives was gone. But I held my emotions close, probably to avoid the pain of releasing them, giving them voice. And I went back to work.

Five months later, my mother's mother, Georgia, died on April 8, 1986. And just like that, the matrons from Itta Bena, Mississippi, and Camden, Arkansas, the women who had loved and guided my brother, sister, and me, were gone.

———

I WAS tired of waiting to feel safe and secure; I wanted both immediately. I became fixated on success and family, and I saw two ways to get there: continue on my path at the *Times* and surround myself with people who could help me reach my goals. Grandmother would have been shocked by my selfishness. But in Washington, I felt so removed from her; so little in my life seemed connected with her and her values. And I saw what life did to her; for even the most righteous, it can be cruel and stingy. Suddenly what mattered most was how fast I ran and how high I climbed. And in my new world order, Jackie seemed the perfect partner.

On paper, she was a good match for a *New York Times* White House correspondent. Ambitious and wise in the ways of Washington, she was the number two White House correspondent at CBS. Once she set her sights on a goal, she pursued it doggedly. That quality made her an exceptional journalist and helped her climb the ranks at a time when far too few blacks and women saw real opportunities at CBS. And she had hedged her bets, getting an MBA from Harvard, just in case she hit a wall in TV journalism or wanted to pursue another calling.

I had never met anyone like Jackie. I was dazzled by her strategic mind—she seemed to have a solution for every problem—and the way she leveraged her personal and professional connections. She decided I did not dress the part of a *Times* White House reporter and convinced me to make over my wardrobe. We replaced discount shirts and suits with designer clothes at designer prices. She stocked my closet with not just any ties but ties from Hermès, the pricey Parisian brand. When I worried about how to develop sources at the White House, she suggested we throw a series of private dinners. We were not just a couple, but one that represented the heft of the *Times* and CBS. She wanted to use that to our advantage. We hosted intimate gatherings of Washington's elite, and more often than not, they came. Informed gossip was always the subject of conversation. Thanks to her, my circle of contacts expanded fourfold.

I was not in love with Jackie. But she represented security and progress when I felt vulnerable and rudderless. Those are not the qualities that sustain a lasting relationship, but in my state, they mattered greatly. While we shared some goals, we had big differences. She knew herself and what she wanted in a mate, while I did not. She thought of having children as an option, while it was a must for me. She was an extrovert while I was somewhat reclusive. Even so, she stepped into a void in my life, and before I knew it, filled it completely. I felt I needed her, and I started entertaining the possibility of marriage.

In a way, Jackie helped forge my friendship with Raines. Raines, Maureen Dowd, and I were with Reagan when he attended an Association of Southeast Asian Nations ministerial meeting in Bali, Indonesia, in April 1986. One evening as Raines, Dowd, and I strolled along one of Bali's lovely beaches, I floated the subject of marrying Jackie. Initially, Raines and Dowd were reluctant to discuss something so personal with me, but eventually they both advised against marriage. They thought my feelings for Jackie were more deep friendship than love. I appreciated their honesty. In later years, I would return to both of them for personal advice.

The discussion in Bali made me take a closer look at my relationship with Jackie. But eventually, I brushed aside any doubts they raised. That was easy to do because Jackie was working me from her end.

One year we attended the annual White House Christmas Party as a couple. As we walked through the receiving line to greet the president and the first lady, Nancy Reagan asked me point-blank when I planned to marry Jackie.

"Soon," I replied, smiling politely, trying to move on.

She would not let go of my hand. "How soon?" she demanded, with a straight face. For a moment, I was speechless.

We went back and forth with the soon/how soon routine as the president looked on with amusement. Finally, Mrs. Reagan said, "You've waited long enough."

Later I learned that Jackie had put Nancy Reagan up to this game. I was angry and embarrassed. But the incident told me how far she would go to get what she wanted.

———

ON NOVEMBER 3, 1986, the day before the congressional elections, the Arabic language journal *Al Shiraa* printed a story alleging that the United States was supplying military spare parts to Iran. Since 1980,

Iran and Iraq had waged a brutal war. Eventually, more than one million people would be killed in the eight-year conflict. The story also reported that Robert (Bud) McFarlane, the president's national security adviser, and four other Americans had visited Tehran in September to negotiate the release of American hostages held by terrorists in Lebanon.

The story triggered a feeding frenzy in Washington—my first—with information scarce and officials willing to share anything even scarcer. We set out to establish who knew what, who approved what, and, most important, the roles of the president and of the vice president. Like dogs with their teeth in a good piece of meat, journalists obsessively picked apart the administration's explanations and excuses. Often our efforts yielded only incremental follow-up stories. We frantically jostled for anything new.

The suggestion that the administration was trading arms for hostages was explosive enough, but then came the astounding: Attorney General Edwin Meese discovered that only twelve million dollars of the thirty million dollars the Iranians had paid for weapons shipments actually went to the U.S. government. The rest was diverted to a lieutenant colonel named Oliver North, then working on the staff of the National Security Council. The money had gone to fund the military efforts of the contras, anti-Communist rebels fighting the Sandinista government in Nicaragua.

From the "shredding party," in which aides worked late into the night destroying important documents to keep them out of the hands of Congress, to the suicide attempt by McFarlane, we documented an administration of tough, smart, and often arrogant men unraveling at the seams.

Coordinating such a story was a major challenge. It had tentacles all over the world, from Washington to Tel Aviv, from Nicaragua to Iran. Editors pulled together a team that aggressively covered all bases—at least for a while.

Unfortunately, the Iran-Contra Affair, as it became known, could not have broken at a worse time for the paper. The *Times'* publisher, Arthur Sulzberger, had announced that Rosenthal was retiring and that Max Frankel, then the editorial page editor, would replace him as executive editor. Suddenly, there was more concern about newspaper careers than trading arms for hostages. We became consumed with our own internal affairs and watched as the *Los Angeles Times*, the *Washington Post*, and the networks overtook us.

Leadership waned. It was the first time I encountered a dangerous truth about the *Times*. When those in key editing positions become preoccupied with other—internal—matters, news coverage suffers severely. I would watch this occur repeatedly over the next two decades. At that point, though, I felt like a child with only a vague sense of what the grownups were doing. In fact, several reporters pulled together and tried to get back in the game.

One of my assignments was to work my Bush connections, building on the relationships I had established in the 1984 campaign and beyond. I would slink off to the daily White House briefings, where reporters would pounce on exclusives from other news organizations. I was angry that they were not chasing the *Times* and that our preoccupied top management left us in this embarrassing position. In the end, I contributed to the story, although not nearly as much as I wanted to.

Iran-Contra marked a clear break in the relationship between the public and the press. Laws were clearly broken, and some officials went to jail. But the public did not see the press as the good guys, out to expose wrongdoing. This was one of the first signs of such a gap in the public's perception, and it would only grow in the next decades.

In fact, some people regarded the renegade Oliver North as a hero and dismissed the entire affair as another instance in which the liberal media was trying to bring down a hugely popular conservative president. When Reagan said he had not intended to trade arms for hostages, it was difficult for the press to convince the public otherwise, no matter what the facts showed. Reagan ended his presidency in 1989 with the highest approval rating of any president since Franklin Roosevelt.

———

MAX FRANKEL made it clear to all in the newsroom that, more than anything else, he was not Abe Rosenthal. He was determined to infuse the paper with new priorities and less intimidating leadership. His first memo to the staff in October 1986 indicated how he wanted to be different:

> From this moment on, as in my first twenty-five years at the *Times*, I have no editorial opinions and I find the transition no more peculiar or difficult than that of a lawyer appointed to the bench. A passion for fairness dominates even our opinion pages, but partisanship and special pleading have no place in the *Times* newsroom. All else is welcome, most particularly good fun.

Then he turned his staff upside down. He kicked some editors out of positions and gave them the title of senior editor. Few in the newsroom had any idea what those new titles meant or what role the editors performed. Frankel was thinking progressively. He appointed Soma Golden National editor. She was the first woman to head a major department. Later, he would appoint the first female assistant managing editor, Carolyn Lee, and the first black woman to head a major department, Angela Dodson, who became editor of the Style department. Some of those moved out were Rosenthal favorites. Others were simply less equipped, he undoubtedly felt, to manage the kind of journalism he wanted the *Times* to produce.

Frankel also created a centralized leadership structure in which assistant managing editors were dominant. Each controlled a department or section and served as a Frankel lieutenant. While power under Rosenthal was concentrated with a very few editors, the new boss distributed it to about a dozen people. Widening the leadership tent was a seismic shift in newsroom management.

As he changed personnel, Frankel also expanded the definition of news. "News is anything new, anything you didn't know, if knowing it matters," he explained. It was up to the *Times* to define the news based on the perception of readers' needs and interests. In the age of television, he argued, the public already knew the headlines and needed something more from their paper. He wanted reporters to add perspective and analysis, something readers could not get from their TV.

His thinking took some getting used to. The presidential news conferences that routinely led the paper's front page—stories that I often
wrote—no longer held that vaunted position.

Still, there was no arguing with him. For all of his being not Rosenthal, Frankel was not one to trifle with. I did not know him, but I knew
he had a temper and that it could be triggered when he felt he was being
misled or suffering fools. Either way, the discussion abruptly ended as
he made clear what *he* wanted.

Frankel's life could have been from a movie. His family lived in
the German city of Gera until rising anti-Semitism forced them to
flee. After a harrowing journey, he finally landed in America, while his
father ended up in Russia. They were separated for seven years, while
the young Frankel became Americanized and his mother eked out a
living sewing on buttons at a clothing store in Brooklyn. Eventually,
the entire family was reunited and lived in Washington Heights, in
northern Manhattan. As it had been for me, journalism had been his
ticket out of the ghetto.

I was impressed by his first communication to the staff, about the
newsroom as a place that had fun. But my opinion of him was shaped
mostly by those whom I knew and respected, like Kovach and Raines.
When Frankel made his first appearance as executive editor in the
bureau, a kind of victory lap, Kovach rushed to greet him and insisted
on carrying his luggage. It was a small gesture of courtesy, but Kovach
seemed to be according the new executive editor enormous respect. I
had never seen him operate this way around anyone, including Rosenthal, and I did not know what to make of it.

Even Raines was affected by Frankel. For the first time, he appeared
nervous in story meetings with New York. Suddenly, he spent far more
time preparing for the meetings. Before one session that he knew would
be particularly contentious, he scribbled a note and held it up. It was an
old Cheyenne Dog Soldier's war cry: "It is a good day to die." It was the
first time that I saw him use that expression, as if he was summoning up
courage to meet the challenge at hand. It would not be the last.

If Frankel could affect Kovach and Raines in such ways, it was clear
that he was someone I needed to take quite seriously.

He made a brilliant move: he kept Arthur Gelb, perhaps Rosenthal's closest confidant, on as his managing editor. Gelb knew the newsroom, had great judgment about people, and was extremely close to Sulzberger. This gave Frankel time to move more deliberatively as he picked a replacement. This did not resonate well in Washington. Some of us were expecting Kovach to move back to New York, where he would eventually become managing editor. In our plan, Raines would replace him as bureau chief and in time begin his ascent to the top. Frankel had other plans.

Kovach was the first casualty. He, too, had assumed that he would be promoted to a top position. But Frankel took his time as Kovach stewed. Eventually, Kovach left the *Times* to become executive editor of the *Atlanta Journal-Constitution*. One of the paper's most ardent change agents had abandoned ship.

Raines was next. He had expected to succeed Kovach as Washington bureau chief, a job he felt he had earned as deputy. He was prepared, knew Washington and the bureau. Frankel disagreed. In fact, he argued that Raines was not ready for the position, one that Frankel held almost a decade earlier. Instead, he wanted Raines to be London bureau chief, a prized assignment where he could grow and broaden himself as a journalist. It must have been painful for an editor with Raines's ego to have his boss tell him that he needed more experience. He later said that he thought seriously about quitting. In the end, he accepted the assignment and moved his family into the *Times*-owned apartment in London. His run as a foreign correspondent was far from distinguished. He was waiting to see how Frankel's personnel moves would play out.

Frankel brought in Craig Whitney, a fixture in New York, to run the Washington bureau. Whitney had been assistant managing editor for newsroom administration after a lengthy career as a foreign correspondent in Vietnam, Germany, and Russia. He was a dedicated editor. Clearly, he had Frankel's confidence.

But even the smartest and most diligent can falter when it comes to appreciating the subtle ways of Washington. Without contacts, sources, and insight, a bureau chief will struggle to manage the outfit. Whitney lacked knowledge of the routine and rhythm, of who mattered and who did not. Frankel teamed Whitney with R. W. (Johnny) Apple Jr., the chief Washington correspondent. Apple was to serve as a counselor when and if Whitney needed advice. Although they were friends, they were not an effective team. Apple was a diva, not a teacher. And rightly so: he had the breadth of experience, the keen analytical mind, and the writing talent to make him invaluable to the *Times*. I always marveled at how he could produce just the right story to mark an important news event. But Apple's biggest interest was himself and his stories, not helping Whitney learn about Washington.

Frankel also named Judith Miller, a foreign correspondent with postings in the Middle East and no editing experience, as Whitney's deputy. They could not have been more different from the two Southerners who preceded them. Whitney was laid-back and understated, and Miller was volatile, with huge camps of supporters and critics. She was also close to Arthur Sulzberger Jr., who was being groomed to take over as publisher when his father stepped down.

Where Kovach and Raines were approachable, Whitney appeared remote, and Miller heavy-handed. She displayed the same drive as Raines, managing the daily report as if Washington itself depended on it, but she lacked his charm. She also had a nasty habit of rereporting stories to check the accuracy of what reporters filed, showing a lack of confidence and stirring resentment in her troops. In two swift moves, the bureau's high-energy, hard-charging atmosphere disappeared.

These transitions marked my first real lesson in power at the *Times*. With so many talented people to choose from to fill a job, the executive editor usually had several suitable candidates. Who won depended on mastery of office relationships, contacts, history, a bit of dumb luck, but seldom talent alone. Climbing the ladder seemed a daunting exercise that, at that point, I could not fathom.

Frankel's moves left me struggling with the loss of Kovach and Raines. Only two years after I had joined the *Times*, I was on my own, the place I hated to be. As I tried to get my bearings under the paper's new leadership, I considered the jaded candor of one of my colleagues, David Binder, a once-rising reporter whose star had dimmed: "Sooner or later," he would often say, "the *Times* will break your heart."

7

FAST TRACKED

We could have been a funny movie, Gerald and me, covering the
Reagans and the Bushes. Ben Stiller and Chris Rock. You get the
point. I was impatient, easily annoyed, quick to see racial and
ethnic conspiracies against us. If we didn't get the right seats on
the White House plane, I'd tell Gerald those blankety-blank bigots
in the White House travel office were playing their games. Gerald
would just say I was out of my mind, which made me even angrier.
Wasn't he supposed to be the one who was paranoid?

Although I was older and, I suppose, more experienced, we
were genuine equals. I don't know what Gerald learned from me,
but I learned a hell of a lot from him. He was a natural charmer.
All the women at the Reagan and Bush White House adored him.
He would joke with them and treat them with respect. And even
in that sea of conservative Republicans, Gerald dazzled them.
He even charmed people who were, let's face it, charmless. Pat
Buchanan. Gerald could charm anyone.

Essentially every editor on the *New York Times* has one task:
to create the best journalism each day. But Gerald had two: to
represent his race and create the best journalism. That's a hell
of a burden. I have no doubt that Gerald felt a mixture of pride,
anger, resentment, and confusion. How does a sane man represent his race at an institution like the *Times* while doing his job

like everyone else? And I think that may have caused some of Gerald's short temper and abruptness or impatience—things that I never saw when he was simply a colleague and a reporter. And not Jackie Robinson.

Top editors were so desperate to promote him. "You're our Jackie Robinson." What a dumb thing to tell him. It kind of unhinged Gerald. And who could blame him for that?

—BERNARD WEINRAUB

I N ONE of his first acts as the new bureau chief, Craig Whitney replaced Bernie Weinraub with Steve Roberts, the paper's chief congressional correspondent. Roberts offered more depth and experience, Whitney explained. Plus, he was connected to Howard Baker, who had replaced Donald Regan as President Reagan's chief of staff. This would give Roberts enormous access, he argued. I thought he had lost his mind. He was weakening one of the bureau's most important beats.

I was stunned and angry. Bernie and I were a potent team—we had results to show for it. I assumed the relocation had something to do with Bernie being one of Rosenthal's boys. I never knew the motives for sure. Once Whitney broke the news, I reached out to Bernie. I knew he would undoubtedly see any new assignment as a demotion, though he had done nothing to earn such treatment. I argued disingenuously that his new beat—covering the State Department—was better than the White House since Reagan was a lame duck. Even I was shifting my focus from Reagan to Bush's campaign to be the next president, I said. He accepted the post reluctantly.

Roberts and I clashed from the beginning.

He argued that he deserved the designation of chief White House correspondent. That meant writing all the major news stories, making all the major contacts, and taking all the important trips. Although I had been at the White House for considerably longer, he wanted to make me his number two.

"I'm near the end of my career, and you have years and years ahead of you," he reasoned. "I need the title."

I told him he was nuts. We would operate as team, I said, no senior or junior. We were at a stalemate, but Whitney did everything he could to give Roberts the advantage. From that moment, my guard went up. I would snarl at Roberts whenever he suggested I do something that I saw as second tier. I became visibly angry whenever Whitney assigned Roberts a major story, which he did far more regularly than he did me. I grew less interested in the team succeeding and much more concerned with my own success.

On January 25, 1988, the day Reagan was to deliver the State of the Union address, I reviewed the story list with disbelief. Roberts was to write the main piece, and Johnny Apple, the analysis. For the first time since I began covering the White House for the *Times*, I had no role in the State of the Union package.

Starting that morning, Roberts tried to get an advance copy of the text. He made a pest of himself, constantly calling Baker's office. After a while, they told him they had no idea when the text would be available. As the hours passed, New York grew more and more anxious and put more heat on Whitney. Whitney, in turn, practically camped out at Roberts's desk awaiting word. I watched as everyone grew more and more desperate.

Finally, around five that evening, I decided to take one for the team. I called Karen Fuller, an assistant to communications director Tom Griscom. She said to meet her in front of the White House in ten minutes. I took the text back to the office, marched directly into Whitney's office, and slammed it on his desk, startling him from whatever he was reading. Then I turned and walked out of his office and out of the bureau, since I had nothing to write that day. Over the next few months, Roberts made more enemies than friends in Baker's office, and they stopped returning his calls.

———

WHITNEY AND Roberts had me wondering if I had the right stuff for such a prestigious assignment. I knew I had the talent—I had actually done the job—but I still carried around my demons. I felt I lacked the proper pedigree. In Frankel's view, I had surmised, *Times* editors and reporters were more than journalists; they were ambassadors. They could sit around late into the evening talking politics, economics, and world affairs with top government officials, knowing as much about the issues as their sources. I did not think that Frankel saw me that way. I did not know how he saw me, since I had never spoken with him. He had seen enough of my work to know that I was a strong reporter who broke stories. But based on recent events, I thought his prototypical White House reporter was a Roberts type, not a Boyd.

A saving grace was Judith Miller, the deputy bureau chief, who, despite her pushy and combative style, played a strong, supportive role in my coverage of Bush and his impending campaign. As an editor, she did not give everyone equal treatment. Miller had no qualms about dressing down a colleague in public and was not above screaming to get her point across. I once watched as she brought Robert Pear, one of the mildest-mannered, hardest-working reporters I knew, close to tears. It was not long before she returned to reporting.

Had I remained in the bureau, I probably would have driven myself crazy wondering what Frankel and other top editors in New York thought of me. Fortunately, I was spared the angst by the presidential campaign. For the last two years, I had bird-dogged Bush, the Republican Party front-runner. I spent much of my time on the road with him, rather than fretting in Washington.

Looking back, I realize how foolish I was to give Frankel and other editors so much power over how I saw myself as a journalist. But with all the changes, my insecurities were on overdrive. In that sense, I suppose, I had become a true *Times*man.

————

AT THE *Times*, everything seemed to be about status. Who had the largest office, whose byline appeared on the most important story, and how reporters and editors were identified. Perception mattered greatly, and I learned to balance perception with my reality.

Once, when Reagan was flying to Tokyo, Johnny Apple signed up for the trip. On the press charter, one first-class seat was reserved for each news organization that regularly traveled with the president. Others making the trip had to sit in coach. Apple would never accept coach, and even though I was the White House correspondent, he expected me to give up my premium seat. I would not allow him to humiliate me in front of my colleagues, so I suggested to him that we rotate: he could sit in first class during the first leg of the trip, and then we would switch. He accepted the deal. What he did not realize was that the first leg was from Andrews Air Force Base to Detroit, a few hours. The second leg went nonstop to Tokyo, about triple the flying time. I even felt sorry for Apple, a big man, as he endured hours in a coach-sized seat.

For reasons I have forgotten, Maureen Dowd and Robin Toner developed an intense dislike for each other. Dowd clearly was already a star, and the tough, tenacious Toner, after covering the Dukakis campaign, was promoted to co-chief national political correspondent, sharing the job with Michael Oreskes. Neither woman could be underestimated, and both were quite territorial. Because there were so few talented women in the bureau, I am sure their rift naturally attracted more attention than it warranted. Even so, I warned new reporters not to pick sides, and tried to remain neutral. I cared deeply for Maureen, who had become a close friend, and had enormous respect for Robin.

In time, it became clear that the bureau lacked the competitive drive it had under Kovach and Raines. We had fallen embarrassingly behind the competition on the Iran-Contra story, and we were no longer trying to peek around the corner to what was coming next. The *Times* still was the powerful *Times*, but to me, the bureau had shifted to a lower gear.

Editors in New York could see it. They constantly second-guessed Whitney. New York ordered him to spend more time at the bureau's news desk, seated among the staff, and less time in his office. So he had a speaker-phone installed on the news desk to participate in the daily story conferences. Of course, reporters would crowd around the desk just as the meetings began. We could hear every doubt or unpleasant word editors said about our stories. Eventually, Whitney's management role shrank, and he spent more and more time searching for a new office site for the bureau—a necessary task, but it took him away from the news. Frankel would cite the office relocation effort as one of Whitney's primary accomplishments when he named a new bureau chief.

Feeling no sense of direction, common purpose, or team spirit in the bureau, I started looking for a way out. Fortunately, it was looking for me, too.

———

SOMA GOLDEN, the new National editor, wanted to meet for lunch. Golden's appointment was no surprise; she was close to Frankel and had worked on his editorial board. She had also edited the Sunday Business section and had management experience. When we met, Golden spoke glowingly of my talents and pitched to me the idea of joining her National staff as Atlanta bureau chief.

"You are perfect for the job," she said. "You can cover the South as a black man, bringing nuance that no white reporter could." I considered the offer for a few days, then concluded that I did not want to live in Atlanta or cover the South as a black man. Much to my amazement, the next week an announcement was posted that Ronald Smothers, the City Hall bureau chief and urban affairs reporter, who was black, would be the new Atlanta bureau chief. Smothers was a competent reporter, but I had far more status as a White House correspondent. Clearly race had motivated Golden more than talent. I was glad that I had declined her offer.

Next I went to New York to meet with Joe Lelyveld, the Foreign editor. Lelyveld, intense and all business, had already enjoyed a distinguished career at the paper, with assignments to South Africa, India, London, and Hong Kong. He had written a Pulitzer Prize–winning book, *Move Your Shadow: South Africa, Black and White.* He had spent his entire career at the *Times* and knew the institution the way one of my childhood heroes, Lou Brock, knew how to steal bases.

The dynamic between us was awkward from our first meeting. The Harvard-educated Lelyveld was extremely bright but also cagey. It seemed as if everything he did and said had a subtext. Still, when he pitched the idea of joining the Foreign staff, I was eager to be a part of his team. As he described the job of representing the *Times* overseas, it seemed more like a calling than an assignment.

All of the ranking editors had spent time overseas, and since I wanted to become one, I knew I had to punch that ticket. I asked that

Lelyveld assign me to a "hot story": a region in flux. I thought that played to my strengths. Over the next few days, we agreed on the Philippines. President Ferdinand Marcos and opposition leader Corazon Aquino were locked in a brutal struggle for power. Given the fierce battle for democracy, Lelyveld certainly met my request. I accepted with the understanding that I would start my assignment shortly after the 1988 election.

Lelyveld impressed me mightily. I was eager to become a correspondent and glad that he recruited me. He started sending me books on the Philippines, and I began to prepare myself for a foreign tour.

Frankel, too, invited me to New York, saying that he wanted to talk about my future. At first, I was both curious and intimidated. But once I met him, I quickly relaxed. It was the first time I had spent any time with him; he was charming and quite engaging. He came across as a kindhearted uncle, walking around the newsroom puffing on a pipe and chatting people up. He was funny, seemed sincere, and had an uncanny ability to anticipate what I was thinking.

He got to the point, explaining how the paper severely lacked minorities to promote to management and how difficult it was finding suitable candidates. He added that increasing diversity was not just one of his priorities but Sulzberger Jr.'s as well, and that my help toward the effort would mean a lot. Then Frankel put me on the spot. He asked if I was planning to go to the Philippines because I wanted to be a foreign correspondent or because I was hoping the assignment would help me get into management. I confessed that it was the latter.

Frankel made his offer. Instead of sending me overseas as a way into management, he was ready to place me in that role now. I would go on a "fast track," performing a series of editing jobs that would allow me to develop my management skills in the same few years that I would have spent abroad. If I succeeded, I would be promoted.

The deal came with a warning: as a first, like Jackie Robinson, I would face pressure and even challenges from skeptical colleagues, but if I could cope with that, I would enjoy every opportunity to move up the ranks.

I warmed to the offer, even with the caveat. Never could I have anticipated this turn of events, especially when I joined the *Times*, covering urban affairs. My one concern was not overcoming white colleagues' doubts but whether my giving up foreign correspondent experience would be held against me if I went for higher jobs in the future. I asked him about the prerequisite.

Frankel assured me that the lack of an overseas posting would not hold me back. I was passing up the opportunity to help the paper, he reasoned, and would not be penalized for doing so. I concluded that his offer held nothing but promise for the paper and for me. Frankel had nothing to lose. If I succeeded, I could be moved along and the *Times* would have a black editor in senior management. If I failed, he would be under no obligation to promote me.

I would start the job in early 1989. My title would be special assistant to the managing editor. It had no real meaning in the organizational chart. The importance of the job rested with Frankel. I took a leap of faith and accepted.

———

GEORGE H. W. Bush was never the politician that Ronald Reagan was. Reagan was known as the Great Communicator. He could rally a stunned nation, as he did with his heartfelt, eloquent words from the Oval Office after the *Challenger* space shuttle exploded in 1986, taking with it seven adventurous souls. Reagan had a number of smart and effective aides who were well versed in manipulating journalists. While his conservative policies divided the nation, he remained one of the most popular presidents of his generation.

Bush, by contrast, had image problems. He spoke in tortured syntax and repeatedly found his conservative credentials challenged. Reagan was portrayed as a fighter, while Bush was depicted as a coaster. As he began his presidential bid in late 1987, Bush had much to prove. For decades, no sitting vice president had been elected president, and many doubted Bush's chances. He was haunted by his losses: the hard-fought 1964 Texas senate race to Ralph Yarborough; the close 1970 senate race to Lloyd Bentsen; the surprisingly tight 1980 Republican presidential primary to Reagan.

Bush, in Reagan's shadow, lacking Reagan's sense of confidence, and haunted by Iran-Contra, seemed well suited for the job of number two, and a half dozen Republican challengers were betting that he could move no higher. But many underestimated Bush's determination and strategic thinking.

For months, well before the presidential campaign began in earnest, the vice president began to use his office as a springboard for building a political base for enhancing his already formidable reputation as a foreign policy expert. His strategy became a textbook example of how a vice president should run for the top office. He traveled extensively, visiting places in the Middle East such as Israel and Jordan, African countries like Egypt and Niger, and Poland and other parts of Europe. Nearly always, I accompanied him. He would tout these trips later, arguing that his firsthand exposure to world events and leaders made him one of the best-prepared candidates ever to seek the presidency.

I left that assessment to the voters, but in those years on the road, I got an intimate look at Bush.

In some ways, after years of covering candidates seeking the nation's highest elected office, my views of them had become tempered, even jaded. I did not see the president, any president, solving the world's problems, whether it was poverty or conflict or hunger or AIDS, here or abroad. He could raise public awareness and muscle Congress into cutting taxes or increasing spending. And on rare occasions, he could perfectly capture the sorrow of many Americans, as Reagan had done when he described the *Challenger* astronauts as slipping "the surly bonds of Earth."

But the president was only a man. Powerful, yes, but still human, sifting through hundreds of briefings and thousands of facts and praying that his decisions are right. And everyone, from family to friends, from foes to hucksters, wants a piece of him. I certainly did not feel sorry for the president, but I knew that the position had as much bad as good.

In taking stock of the candidates I covered, I always tried to see beyond the speeches, the press releases, and the photo ops to take a measure of the man: Was he decent and fair? Were his priorities in order when it came to himself, his country, and his family? Was he self-absorbed, or did he find the time to care for others?

What I saw in Bush, I liked. He could laugh at himself, and he often did, easily. He did not seem vengeful, although over the years, many had hurt him. Finally, to see him around his wife, children, and grand-children was to see a man whose family came first. He could be most politically incorrect, as when he called a grandson of Latino heritage "the little brown one," but clearly, he had an abiding love for his clan.

On one of our trips in 1986, I sat down with Bush in his private cabin aboard *Air Force Two*. The vice president had discarded his dark business suit for the more personal flight jacket emblazoned with GEORGE BUSH VICE PRESIDENT.

We rehashed much of Bush's past, such as his attack on Reagan's economic policies as "voodoo economics," his support for gun-control legislation while a Texas congressman, and his much-scrutinized record of waffling on abortion. As we talked that night on *Air Force Two*, I think the true man emerged. His politics were as inclusive as they could be under his party's "umbrella," and he wanted to represent everyone, regardless of ideology, if possible.

None of this meant that I gave Bush an easy time of it. In fact, I hounded him repeatedly about his role in Iran-Contra. Each time, he refused to answer my questions. But I persisted, so much so that he came to expect such questioning. In the early stages of the campaign, only a few national reporters traveled with the vice president. But often local reporters who heard my Iran-Contra questions would join the inquisition. Bush enjoyed little peace from the scandal.

Bush despised the *Times*. He believed it would never treat him fairly. This was his view of journalism in general, but he saw the *Times*, especially, as a leading liberal voice and thus a powerful foe. Over time, however, I believe he came to distinguish me, the reporter, from my employer. He told me he saw me as a straight-shooter who covered him fairly, Iran-Contra notwithstanding. But he still believed that the nameless editors who managed my work were out to get him.

———

COVERING BUSH'S strategy demanded a different style of report-ing. I went where he went, occasionally filing stories by way of a West-ern Union teletype operator. I followed closely but not so much for the story, since he rarely made news. Instead I made sure to study the man, his aides, and his positions on issues, and to file my assessments away for later. Each trip opened my eyes to people and world affairs in significant ways.

I joined the Bush party in March 1985 as it set out to visit some of the poorest countries in Africa. Saharan Africa was of no international import to the administration, other than as a stop on Bush's itinerary. But for me the trip was huge. It was the first time that I had been to the land of my ancestors, and although I had no idea what part of Africa was home to my forebears, I did not care. I felt instant kinship with the Sudanese, whose smiling faces and warm welcomes touched me deeply. Several asked me what tribe I was from and suggested that given my features, my ancestors were probably from Sudan. We had trouble communicating because of language differences, but I knew that they were pleased to see me.

The poverty was unlike anything I had ever seen. No television or newspaper image could ever fully convey its breadth and depth and toll on lives. Sudan was in the midst of intense famine caused by civil war and drought. On the sprawling Wad Sherife settlement near Kassala, I saw some of the seven hundred thousand refugees subsisting in the kind of squalor and destitution that made my years in St. Louis seem like fine living. At one feeding center for children, I saw malnourished five year olds weighing less than twenty pounds.

The trips had their lighter moments. Our next visit was to the Western African nation of Niger, where Bush announced that the country had been selected by the administration to receive financing under an experimental program intended to encourage "free market" agricultural practices. Given the severe poverty, the administration's eleven-million-dollar contribution was minuscule, but it was a start.

One night, the traveling party of journalists and aides decided to cut loose at a disco in the basement of our hotel. As we mingled, in walked a stunning black woman followed by an entourage. She sat there alone, with no one talking to her or asking her to dance. This is ridiculous, I thought, and I crossed the room and chatted her up. Actually, her English was pretty good. Before long, we were on the dance floor, one song followed by another. She was enchanting but seemed distant and lonely. As the evening ended, I walked her to her car. I was surprised to see her get into a Mercedes—one of several in her entourage.

As she drove off, the owner of the disco came up to me and with alarm in his eyes informed me that the beautiful woman was the daughter of the country's leader, Seyni Kountche.

"No one talks to her," he said. "It is not allowed."

Suddenly, I was terrified. When I returned to my room, I shoved a dresser and a couple of chairs in front of my door. I thought that would buy me a little time for escape should the security forces try to break in and carry me off to prison. The next morning, after a sleepless night, we said good-bye to Niger. I could not have been more delighted to leave.

Over the next months, I traveled with Bush to the Middle East, where camera crews recorded his visit to the Wailing Wall; Egypt, where he saw the Pyramids and went to Luxor; Jordan, where the proud Jordanian Air Force insisted on flying us to the site of the Dead Sea. The pilots had trouble staying in formation, and repeatedly the copters got too close for comfort.

I accompanied Bush to Poland, where he visited with Lech Walesa, the popular Solidarity founder who later became the country's leader. That stop was also for domestic political purposes, intended to boost Bush's standing in Polish communities in the Northeast and cities with major Polish enclaves, such as Detroit and Chicago. I was most taken when he visited the Birkenau and Auschwitz concentration camps, where millions of Jews—and others—perished. Under a heavy gray sky, Bush laid a wreath at the Wall of Death at Auschwitz, site of twenty thousand Jewish deaths by Nazi firing squad. Like the poverty in Africa, those stark reminders of inhumanity were difficult to comprehend and forget.

———

IT IS hard to know if all of the foreign travel helped Bush; the most lasting legacy of the 1988 presidential campaign was the effectiveness of negative campaigning. All of his political advertisements, all of his speeches and policy statements, meant little compared with the relentless string of attack ads unleashed on his Democratic opponent, Massachusetts governor Michael Dukakis. Bush owed his presidency to the shrewd expertise of several hard-edged operatives, including Roger

Ailes, Mary Matalin, Jim Baker, Marlin Fitzwater, Bob Teeter, and Rich Bond. But few were as skilled at manipulating the media with unflattering rumors and scorching attacks as Lee Atwater, Bush's campaign manager.

I got to know most of the group fairly well but developed a special relationship with Atwater. He had honed his skills playing bareknuckled politics in South Carolina and had become one of the best political minds of his generation. He craved winning. Atwater did not create the controversial Willie Horton ad, but he embraced it to tap into racially motivated fears of whites nationwide. Before the 1988 campaign, few voters outside of Massachusetts had heard of Horton. He was the black murder convict serving a life sentence who, while on furlough in a program supported by then-governor Dukakis, raped and brutalized a young white woman. By November, Willie Horton was almost as well known as Dukakis—and the Democrat's presidential bid sunk.

As much as I detested his methods, I appreciated Atwater's insight. He understood how little the pundits inside Washington knew of the concerns and fears of those living outside the nation's capital. When we spent time together, especially if we were on the road, he insisted on attending some local event like a wrestling match. It was there, he argued, that we could see real people and overhear real concerns. I eventually adopted his strategy. As an editor, I would urge reporters to get outside of New York City and go into the Kmarts and Walmarts in small towns to learn what "real" people were thinking. I would preach this message so much that one editor who lived on New York's Upper West Side challenged me by arguing, "We're real people, too."

But she wasn't. Journalists attend the same colleges, live in the same neighborhoods, eat at the same restaurants, and send their children to the same schools. There is nothing wrong with that, but that lifestyle doesn't allow them to begin to understand the hopes and dreams of those who do not live in their world. That's what Atwater understood.

Perhaps I was reading more into it than was true, but the day after Bush's victory, the president-elect seemed different. For the first time in the five years I covered him, he seemed calm and at peace. At the same time, he seemed humbled, as if he understood that he was about to sail into unpredictable waters that could turn treacherous at any moment. It is one thing to be a heartbeat away from the presidency. It's another to know that the job will be yours in a matter of months.

The media spent this time trying to figure out whom Bush would reward through high-level appointments. I had a series of exclusives, including Bush's decision to nominate John Tower as defense secretary, and his decision to tap William J. Bennett for a newly created position to coordinate the federal government's war on drugs. Once again, my contacts within his inner circle paid off.

The president-elect gave his first interviews to two reporters. One was from his hometown paper, the *Houston Chronicle*. The other was me.

———

ONCE MY political reporting tour ended, as Frankel and I discussed, I started my career as an editor. My first post: assistant editor in the Washington bureau.

I was thrilled because Frankel had shifted Whitney to a European assignment and replaced him with Raines. Frankel saved face by arguing that Raines's time abroad had provided him the seasoning that he needed to run the bureau, just as he had predicted. Few of us in the bureau believed that.

The Howell Raines who returned was not the Howell Raines who had left. I could not pinpoint just how he had changed. In some ways, he was even more driven. But he also seemed more guarded and less confident. I believed he had trouble figuring out whom he could really trust. Frankel had taught Raines a lesson in power, and Raines sought to build support elsewhere. The most significant ally he coveted was Arthur Sulzberger Jr., who was poised to become the *Times'* next publisher.

Raines would sermonize about what it took to succeed as a Washington correspondent. He talked about an A team and a B team and how the A team did not take the train at 7:00 P.M. Instead, they stayed later and worked harder. He also discussed the need to accept one's place. He had always had a crush on the actress Michelle Pfeiffer, he said, but he had given up any hope of acting on it. It was important for others to accept life's limits, he explained.

What few of us knew was that Raines was struggling through what he later described in a book as a midlife crisis. He and his wife, Susan, had decided to divorce, and his world was tossed. Still, he was an able teacher, and I learned a great deal from him as an editor.

I would use many of his lessons repeatedly as I moved up the ranks. One was how to appeal to the vanity of reporters, a powerful tool. The conversation went something like this: "I really need this story, and I know that you can do it better than anyone else. I can find someone else if you'd rather not, but you're the best person I have." Most of the time, such flattery worked.

Another was how to handle direct challenges to my authority. "You know more about this issue than I will ever know," he would respond, "but I didn't get to this position based on *your* knowledge. I got here based on my instincts and my gut. And if I fail, I'd rather fail based on *my* instincts and gut, rather than your knowledge." Almost always, when I responded with those words, the challenge evaporated.

I quickly learned the range of the talent in the bureau. Some reporters whom I had regarded as stars needed enormous help conceptualizing or writing stories. Others, like Robert Pear, ran two steps ahead of the competition and were a dream to edit. The first time I edited one of his stories and suggested a few minor changes, he made a point of thanking me for my help, something few reporters take the time to do. He was a class act.

I also enjoyed the challenges of making the right decision at the right moment. For example, when President Bush nominated Tower to become secretary of defense, and his drinking quickly became a serious obstacle to his confirmation, reporters bombarded Tower with interview requests. We learned that he was staying in the Jefferson Hotel and dispatched a reporter, Susan Rasky, to interview him. Somehow, she learned his room number. As she approached the door, she heard sounds of passion on the other side. Tower had company and clearly was not up studying for his confirmation hearings.

Rasky called and asked if she should interrupt by knocking on the door.

"Susan," I said with all the seriousness I could muster, "we're the *New York Times*. Wait till he finishes, then knock."

As green as I was, I seemed to be doing all of the right things, as Raines's assessments affirmed. In May 1989, he wrote to Frankel about my progress: "Your decision to put him on the fast track toward editing is looking like a very smart one. Please don't punish me for giving you this report by taking him away before Labor Day."

Labor Day, and New York, came all too soon.

———

NEW YORK scared me. There was so much about the city that I did not understand—from life in its far-flung boroughs to the overwhelming alphanumeric jumble of its massive subway system. I believed I could perform as an editor anywhere, but New York represented so much more than my job. Moving there would take me farther from my roots and away from my friends and colleagues in Washington. I would be working alongside many reporters and editors whom I had never met. And I would enter the newsroom with a strange title in a position of authority, although it was not clear what that authority meant.

In hindsight, I was letting those old demons get the best of me. I tapped into long-held worries about status and worth and whether I was really good enough to succeed at what I assumed would be high-stakes management. I did not think I could make it in New York on my own. What I needed, I surmised, was a partner whom I could trust and lean on. Who could help me put those demons to rest.

I finally asked Jackie to marry me, and she said yes. She brought companionship, added financial security, sophistication, and fine judgment. Big brother Gary was ecstatic; he was taken with Jackie's celebrity and considered me lucky for snagging a glamorous network correspondent. Friends were supportive, though like Raines and Dowd, they had their doubts. To my litany of reasons that I thought I should marry, I added Jackie's loyalty. Sheila, in her role as my friend and as one who had already endured my lack of commitment to the institution of marriage, shot back, "But Gerald, dogs are loyal!"

Jackie and I married July 22, 1989, in a small ceremony in Washington. Bernie was my best man and Bill Plante, a colleague from CBS, gave away Jackie, whose father had died years before. Representative

William H. Gray III, the Pennsylvania Democrat who was also an ordained Baptist minister, officiated.

I moved into the house Jackie owned on Capitol Hill. Settling in came easier than I had thought. We connected with neighbors and continued our so-called power dinners with a who's who in media and politics. Jackie was quite fond of entertaining, so I let her take the lead in making our social connections. I really did not know what I had expected from our marriage, but it seemed comforting and reassuring. As a part of such a strong team, I felt more prepared for the rigors of New York.

When the call finally came, Frankel said he was promoting Dan Lewis, then the deputy National editor, to run the Week in Review section. He wanted me to take Lewis's place on the National desk, as number two man to Soma Golden, whom I knew from her attempt to recruit me for the Atlanta job. I had not been a national correspondent, but I certainly understood the nature of national beats from my time in Washington and on the campaign trail.

Jackie and I rented a two-bedroom apartment on the East Side, and she began searching in earnest for a place we could own. We bought a dog, an English springer spaniel that we named Sheba. Our financial outlook improved dramatically, as I participated in a bonus plan and received stock options. None of this meant immediate wealth, since the economy was stalled—there were no bonus checks and the stock options were underwater—but I celebrated my anticipated benefits. Nothing was rough about our new life together.

Work, on the other hand, was rough indeed.

———

FOR THE first time in my career, I came face-to-face with blatant racial tension in the workplace. When I arrived at the *Times* newsroom on West Forty-third Street, the environment reflected sharp divisions. Emotions were raw over the Tawana Brawley case, in which a fifteen-year-old suburban New York black girl alleged that she was abducted by six white men, raped, and smeared with feces. And when a group of black and Latino youths were tried and convicted in the rape of the

Central Park jogger, a white woman, the local media's depiction of the young men as animals deepened the fault lines. These issues hung over the newsroom like polluted air.

I was no stranger to racial differences; I had faced that reality all of my life and still found a way to succeed. I did not think the newsroom would be so difficult. Clearly, I was naive. The hostility I encountered initially, which I can best describe as passive aggression, surprised me. No one ever challenged my authority outright, but I had to repeat my orders frequently and then double back to make sure they were followed.

Most of my colleagues were politically liberal and believed in racial equality. Yet many had never been in a position of having to take orders from a black person, especially one whom they did not know. In fact, few blacks were at the table when editors discussed important issues. Scanning the newsroom, I saw no black editors on the Foreign, Culture, Week in Review, Science, Sports, or Business staffs. Both National and Metro had black editors, but not in leadership positions. There were no natural avenues to discuss issues, so most racial dialogue took place through angry memos or heated conversations that a few blacks risked having. Some of those who spoke out frequently were often seen as militant—not exactly a career-enhancing label. In this highly charged atmosphere, I saw that I needed to tread carefully. I could be both a change agent and a lightning rod for racist views and assumptions.

To some colleagues, the paper's new emphasis on diversity not only opened a door for me but also gave me an unfair edge over the competition in climbing higher. Perhaps they had a point. Still, they had to consider that the newsroom had failed previously to give blacks significant opportunities to work as editors, which was why it was in its current situation. Also, no black editor could remain in a position of authority if he or she could not deliver the goods. The *Times* did not operate that way. He might be demoted or sidetracked, as the *Times* rarely fired anyone, but he would not be in leadership for long. Finally, we blacks assuming power in the upper levels of newsrooms almost needed to have our heads examined, given the strife and isolation that we faced.

I often felt that I had few people with whom to discuss my challenges, other than my wife and Paul Delaney, a former Madrid bureau chief who had been moved from deputy National editor to news administration when management determined that he was not going to rise any further. This was the same man who had once swept through St. Louis as a star reporter for the *Times,* the man whose future seemed limitless. Now Delaney seemed discouraged and bitter. His advice had little to do with succeeding at the *Times.* In fact, he warned me to watch my back.

———

I WAS suspicious of my new boss, Golden, after the Atlanta incident, and we got off to a bad start. Her immediate supervisor, John Lee, an assistant managing editor, briefed me on the role I might play on Golden's desk. He said that despite her strengths, she could be disorganized, and he counseled that I could be an asset because I seemed quite organized. We would make a good team, he reasoned.

As we discussed expectations over breakfast, Golden, far from the enthusiastic editor who had recruited me as a reporter, seemed suspicious as well. She asked me what role I saw myself playing on *her* desk. I innocently mentioned that I had heard that she had difficulty with organization and that was one of my strengths. She stopped me midsentence.

"Who says I have problem with organization?" she demanded to know. "Who says that? I think I'm very organized."

Golden was unlike any editor I had known. She excelled at spotting trends and cultivated ardent loyalty among her troops. She had learned how to succeed in a man's world, and that meant speaking her mind. But she had problems expressing exact concepts. "This story is a look at the Bush administration and that kind of stuff," she would say. Frankel seldom challenged her for more clarity, in the way he would have done with other department heads.

Golden shared how she wanted to operate: National correspondents reported to the assistant National editors, not Golden or her deputy. The system meant that I would not have contact with the correspondents. I saw that as insane. How could I perform as deputy National editor if I could not engage the reporters?

I thought she wanted to marginalize me, or perhaps she did not think that I could do the job. Either way, I stewed, I did not move to

New York to be the spook who sat by her door. So despite her decrees, I still reached out to reporters. That soon brought me into conflict with one of the assistant National editors, Jon Landman, who was incensed that I was talking to *his* reporters. He took his complaints directly to Golden. Not surprisingly, she supported him and insisted that I back off. Once again, I refused. I had been in New York less than a month, and I already had made enemies.

In a way, Frankel contributed to my diplomatic challenges. On my first day, at the daily news meeting, he sat me in a cluster of seats reserved for the top editors. He reinforced that with other moves, such as inviting me into top-level meetings of the masthead, something people in the newsroom noticed. Joe Lelyveld, whom Frankel had tapped to be his managing editor in December 1989, also showered me with attention—so much so that it was clear that I was being groomed. He helped me understand the newsroom, but his actions made me an instant target. No matter how hard I tried to win them over, some colleagues remained leery or outright hostile.

One of those was Landman, who probably felt threatened by this hotshot from Washington whom everyone seemed to be fawning over. Landman, who was born in New York and had graduated from Amherst College and Columbia University Graduate School of Journalism, found himself in an unfortunate position. Traditionally, most of the ranking editors started their careers at the paper as reporters. Landman had worked as reporter at *Newsday*, the Long Island newspaper, and the *Chicago Sun-Times*, but not at the *Times*. Thus, it appeared as though his road to the top was blocked.

We clashed constantly, and it became increasingly difficult for us to work together. Finally, Frankel and Lelyveld alleviated the tension: they shipped Landman to the Metro as an assistant editor with a mandate to shake things up. At the time, *Newsday* was trying to make inroads into the city's market with a New York edition.

With Landman gone, my relationship with Golden blossomed. Most of her suspicions and doubts vanished, and we performed well together on major stories such as the October 1989 San Francisco–Oakland earthquake. I appreciated her leadership and was able to help keep the report on track.

———

I GREW more comfortable as I began to understand life in the newsroom. I was drawn to Frankel, and I wanted to reward his faith in me. He prided himself on managing and became skilled at deciphering the paper's multimillion-dollar budget. When disputes erupted over turf, he would proclaim, "We don't solve our problems at the reader's expense." When the newsroom faced tough budget choices, he would announce: "I'd rather make ten thousand cuts of a hundred dollars than one cut of one million." He was a brilliant editor and seemed to be a good man. But some of his opinions and decisions brought him intense public scrutiny and rebuke.

In response to criticism that other newspapers ran more front-page articles by and about women, Frankel told Eleanor Randolph of the *Washington Post*, "If you are covering local teas, you've got more women than if you're the *Wall Street Journal*." The remark prompted a revolt in the newsroom, with women—and some men—wearing tea bags on their lapels or as earrings. Frankel later apologized for it.

That dustup was tepid compared with the Patricia Bowman affair. Bowman was the twenty-nine-year-old woman who had accused thirty-year-old William Kennedy Smith—a medical student and member of the prominent Kennedy clan—of rape.

Frankel gave us a glimpse of his thinking at one senior editors' meeting, when he launched into a lengthy rationale about a newspaper's responsibility when it came to printing the name of an alleged rape victim. He reasoned that the press was printing volumes about the accused (who was later acquitted), even though he had not been convicted of a crime. Fairness, he suggested, dictated that we give the same attention to the accuser. The discussion went back and forth with predictable arguments. Frankel hit the intellectual high points, but he overlooked the fact that rape was unlike other crimes. To name the accuser exposes her or him to stigma in a way that no other crime does. Although he faced strong disagreement, Frankel made up his mind to break with the *Times* longstanding policy—and the policy of most newspapers.

He ordered the National desk, led by Golden (I had left by then), to begin gathering information on Patricia Bowman's life for a potential profile. The reporting was hurried and hush-hush and focused on less-than-flattering parts of Bowman's life, like an illegitimate child, a tendency to hang out at bars, and "a little wild streak" in her sexual history. It even included a reporter peering through Bowman's daughter's bedroom window to see what books were on the nightstand.

Two days later, on April 16, 1991, what had become a philosophical discussion turned into a policy nightmare. When NBC News broadcast Bowman's name, Frankel felt that his views were validated. He ordered the profile that was still being prepared rushed into the paper that night. Although Golden and some other editors read it, none was comfortable publishing it.

Criticism was swift and universal, so much so that Frankel had to convene a staff meeting in the auditorium to defend his decision. He took to the stage alone; Golden certainly did not agree with his decision to run the story. Lelyveld did not surface once in the entire discussion. In the end, Frankel did little to placate those at the meeting. In fact, his comments offended a number of women, including Golden and Maureen Dowd.

Not surprisingly, the *Times* returned to its policy of not naming alleged rape victims.

Frankel had also shown poor judgment when he suggested in an October 1990 forum on women and the media that he saw a double standard for blacks on staff:

We've reached a critical mass with women. I know that when a woman screws up it is not a political act for me to go fire them. I cannot [easily] say that with some of our blacks. They're still precious, they're still hothouse in management, and if they are less than good, I would probably stay my hand at removing them too quickly. It's still a political act, and it would hurt the organization in a larger sense, so you tolerate a little more in the short term.

Frankel went before an audience—a group of black journalists from throughout the city—to defend and explain himself.

Despite his fumbles, I was convinced that Frankel's intentions were good. The *Times* had serious problems recruiting and retaining blacks and other minorities. It was a recurring theme. To Frankel's credit, while his predecessor, Abe Rosenthal, was largely indifferent to increasing the number of people of color, Frankel made it a priority. But the way he went about achieving "critical mass," as he called it—tying recruitment to senior managers' bonuses, instituting a policy that a black reporter had to be hired for every white reporter hired—led to resentment among editors who believed that they were being denied talented white hires and raised doubts about the abilities of those blacks who were hired.

Frankel kept his word regarding my fast-track education. Six months after I became deputy National editor, I moved again, across the newsroom to be deputy Metro editor.

I brought to my new post several lessons in managing, among them, the need to choose my battles carefully, then determine the best tactics to win. I had also learned that issues of race and gender greatly magnify the attention and response to any change.

Second, while the role of a top editor is to lead, he cannot get too far in front of those who are following him. If he does, he will be less likely to hear—and respond to—dissent. He will also find himself an easy target.

Finally, to rush a story into print, especially one that reflects a shift in policy, is to court danger flagrantly. When such a decision is driven by a deadline, that is all the more reason to step back. There is always tomorrow to get it right.

8

MY *TIMES*

I call it the Look.

Gerald had this remarkable way of projecting profound skepticism yet genuine affection in a gaze that underscored a sense that he knew better than you. He'd tilt his head in your direction. His soulful eyes, sparkling like dampened gems, would find a spot between your nose and forehead. Then he'd let the faintest smile take shape just under his mustache.

Once he affixed the Look, the careful logic of your arguments would melt like glaciers sunning. Without a word, Gerald would implore you to think again—not because he had to be right—because he cared too much for you to be wrong.

I'll never forget the last time Gerald gave me the Look. It was in the mid-1990s, and I had left the *New York Times* to pursue "opportunities" at *Newsweek*. Gerald had told me it was a mistake. I had been writing for the magazine for little less than a year when he invited me to his apartment for a party. We stepped away from the festivities and onto the deck, where we shared a couple of drinks and cigars, and he asked me why I was wasting my time at *Newsweek* when I should be back home at the *Times*.

I uncorked my bottled response. For the longest moment, Gerald offered no words. Only the Look. The next thing I knew I was back at the *Times* and beginning one of the most exhilarating and fruitful periods of my thirty-year journalistic career.

—MICHEL MARRIOTT

I N MY new assignment, I replaced Dennis Stern, the deputy Metro editor. Stern and his boss, John Darnton, were laid-back and extremely popular among reporters. Both were solid journalists and decent men and worked hard to encourage and protect their staff. But the Metro report was not as strong as Frankel and Lelyveld wanted. They had parachuted Jon Landman in from National as the third-ranking editor in the hope of energizing the report.

Landman took their instructions seriously and embraced his role with zeal; on many days, he was all but running Metro. It was an arrangement that both Darnton and Stern seemed to accept. Once I joined the mix as deputy, I became Landman's boss again. Even in a newsroom as large as the *Times*, Landman and I seemed unable to stay out of each other's way.

Landman clearly had a strong relationship with Lelyveld, and like mine, it would change over time. As deputy Metro editor, I was seeing more and more of Lelyveld, who took on the role of a mentor. He genuinely loved New York and was determined to teach me about his city. We would head out to Brooklyn for lunch at Junior's; up to the Bronx to visit Lelyveld's alma mater, the storied Bronx High School of Science; walk over to lunch in Hell's Kitchen; or take the subway downtown to some Chinatown dive.

At the same time, I kept counsel with Raines. His best advice for tackling my new job: *Get out of the office.* Treat it like a reporting assignment, he suggested. Interview people and visit sites that Metro reporters would be covering. An editor needed firsthand knowledge to be successful, he argued. I took his words to heart. After a fire killed eighty-seven people at the Happy Land social club in the Bronx on March 25, 1990, I convinced Darnton that we should visit the site ourselves. Our reporters were astonished; they rarely saw their bosses on the scene of news events.

I went to the press room at city hall and to Albany for dinner with Governor Mario Cuomo. I dined with former mayor Ed Koch, and I spent hours meeting with reporters to find out about their beats and tap their expertise on who and what mattered. I hated being unable to grasp the significance of some news development and hated even more when someone—particularly Landman—had to explain it to me.

Much worse, I knew, was ignorance. So I traveled and read, and I met with almost anyone who seemed worth knowing. It was all part of getting to know and, in my own way, falling in love with the city.

To me, New York works because people mind their own business, at least most of the time, and because anything they need is only a telephone call away, at least in most of Manhattan. Of course, this comes with a price tag, but for those with enough money, the city is a dream. For certain things, I would never compromise: I cared little for the Yankees and hated the Mets because of their rivalry with my beloved Cardinals. But even when I saw the city at its worst, as when a brazen thief reached through the front window of my cab and snatched the driver's money, I found much more to love about New York than to hate.

One day in December 1990, a smiling Lelyveld gave me a heads-up: John Darnton would soon become the new weekend news editor. I saw that as a good move for Darnton, who had been a fine boss. He gave me space to perform as his deputy and eagerly shared his own take on the paper and the staff. He had invited me into his home early after my appointment, and I was fond of his wife, Nina, and their three children.

I did not connect the dots immediately. Metro, the biggest department in the paper, was now without an editor. In short order, Frankel called me into his office and offered me the job. It was the one senior management post I never expected; I had lived in New York for fewer than two years and did not know the A train from the Q. But I leaped at the opportunity—and the challenge. I would manage a staff of more than one hundred reporters who reflected some of the best—and some of the greenest—on the paper. And I would do so with a mandate to make Metro not only more competitive but a first read.

On December 7, 1990, Frankel posted his latest announcement: Adam Clymer was moving from senior weekend editor to become assistant Washington editor in charge of congressional coverage. John Darnton would have control over the entire paper on weekends. Finally, it said:

> Gerald Boyd will become Metropolitan Editor, thus ending his impressive rotation from desk to desk while a Special Assistant to the Managing Editor. We have all recognized a first-rate journalistic mind and a warm manager of staff and now look to Gerald to give us the next big lift in the coverage of both New York City and the surrounding region.

I had left the *Post-Dispatch* in 1983 and the opportunity to become a top editor there, in effect rolling the dice. Now, just seven years later, I came up sevens and elevens.

———

THE FIRST time I addressed the staff, I was honest as I could be. I told them that they all knew more about New York than I did. I told them there was no way I could succeed without their help. I told them that I truly needed them. I was not just making feel-good talk; I really meant it. Plus, I was terrified.

Parts of the job boggled my mind. I was to put together a budget for the new fiscal year that totaled in the millions; I did not tell anyone that I had trouble balancing my checkbook. I learned on the spot about boosting staff morale, identifying priorities, and shifting them as the need arose. I developed a keen sense of how I wanted to operate as a manager. Much of my approach was based on instinct.

In 1987, the year after Frankel had taken over, the stock market crashed, prompting a prolonged advertising drought and stringent cost controls. Deeply embedded in the psyche of the *Times'* leadership is how to protect the core—the integrity of the news operation—in difficult times. An approach common to most businesses is to cut costs. But the *Times*, to the contrary, often tried to grow its way out of financial hardship. Investment in the product, top executives believed, would pay off in the end.

Despite the tough economy, Frankel and Lelyveld successfully argued to Sulzberger and Lance Primis, the paper's general manager, that the company should upgrade its "local" section, the part of the paper that carried regional and sports news. Sulzberger and Primis agreed to add two pages of Metro news and two of Sports, a separate Sunday section for Metro, and a City section for more localized neighborhood coverage. The expansion gave me the opportunity to hire about twenty new reporters. Over the next few years, Metro became the entry point for many who would have stellar careers at the *Times* and beyond, among them Deborah Sontag, James Bennet, Mirta Ojito, Frank Bruni, Diana Jean Schemo, Alessandra Stanley, Evelyn Nieves, Kimberly McLarin, Brett Pulley, Barry Bearak, Jane Fritsch, and Michael Specter. Almost 75 percent of the new hires were women, and minorities were a noticeable portion. We sent a powerful message throughout the industry: the *Times* was shopping for the best journalists available, and they included those of color.

As Frankel explained it, the new Metro section would emphasize those stories that people talk about around the dinner table. It would focus on common concerns such as transportation, education, crime, jobs, homelessness, and taxes. The key was to identify those issues and then find interesting ways to write about them. As I traveled the country recruiting, I would use Frankel's pitch and add that our goal was to beef up coverage in the boroughs, Long Island, and North Jersey. I wanted recruits to cover their regions as if they were foreign countries.

Frankel's aim was not just to spend the company's money. There continued to be genuine worry about the New York edition of Long Island's *Newsday,* which was targeting many of the same upscale New Yorkers who read the *Times.* New York *Newsday* was scrappy and lively, frequently beating our paper. The *Times* was facing one of its most challenging competitive threats in years.

One way I tried to shore myself up was to hire a solid deputy. Again, I relied on my instinct. I passed over Landman, much to his disappointment, I could imagine, and tapped Michael Oreskes, who was in

Washington covering national politics. Oreskes was the quintessential New Yorker. He had graduated from City College, covered labor for the *Daily News* and Albany for the *Times*. He and I had good chemistry, and I was not threatened in the least by his ambition, which was obvious even when he tried to tone it down. I saw that drive as a strength and knew that his success would be mine as well. I also knew that, ultimately, I was in charge.

I needed a strong partnership to help me change the way that Metro approached the news. I wanted a kind of kitchen cabinet in which editors routinely discussed issues and stories, including those we had missed and those we should be doing. This approach was modeled on one that Raines had used in Washington, and I knew it could work if we committed to it. There had to be a sense of trust among the editors. They had to be willing to collaborate—to amplify or refine an idea. And we had to throw out the hierarchy, which was anathema to the way the *Times* typically operated. Oreskes played a significant role in cultivating that more open atmosphere.

I also found myself relying on Suzanne Daley, an assistant Metro editor who had grown up at the paper. She was one of the smartest editors I had come across, and she had incredible instincts.

Daley came up with a most innovative approach to editing to assist a new struggling reporter trainee whom many in management doubted would be hired after his trial period ended. She asked the reporter what subject he was most passionate about. The elderly, he replied, although he was only in his twenties. Daley created a mini-beat for him that focused on the elderly. The reporter produced a series of strong page one articles about the elderly, joined the staff, and went on to a distinguished career. He became a *Times*man because Daley was clever enough to pique his enthusiasm at a time that he needed it most. She had a knack for approaching her job that way.

In time, the company's investment in Metro began to pay off. More often than not, we were ahead of the competition on stories. I loved the unpredictability of the report and took particular pride in the Sunday edition. No story was off-limits; our challenge was to find the smartest way to bring everyday issues to life. It was as if I were back in college, having spirited meetings with the staff of *Blackout*.

I REPORTED to Dave Jones, the editor who had helped recruit me to the *Times* and who by then was an assistant managing editor over Sports as well as Metro. Jones was a micromanager of the first order, and knowing that, I made almost no decision without first running it by him. I resented the *Times'* hierarchical management structure, but I learned to live with it; besides, Jones was far more helpful than not.

While Jones watched over Metro and Sports, John Lee, another assistant managing editor, was in charge of the Washington bureau, the Foreign desk, the National desk, and the Business and Science sections. Warren Hoge was responsible for the Sunday magazine and the Style and features sections. Al Siegal was in command of technology and copy editors.

Frankel relied on his assistant managing editors to carry out his edicts and to be his eyes and ears in the newsroom. They served on committees with military-sounding titles like In-Com and Ex-Com. I forget which had the greater power. In a way, it did not matter, since Frankel and Lelyveld made most key decisions themselves.

At the daily 5:00 P.M. news meetings, a dozen or so editors sat around the conference table discussing stories and pitching those they thought suitable for page one. I would spend thirty minutes or more preparing for the forty-five-minute meeting. I tried to have ready answers for any question that Frankel or Lelyveld might ask. The two of them sat at opposite ends of the long oval table. Editors who were unprepared experienced the sensation of being a human Ping-Pong ball. First Frankel raised questions and challenges: *thwack!* Then Lelyveld raised some more: *whack!* While the hapless editor tried to compose an answer, Frankel would swat with another query. Then Lelyveld would follow up with one of his own. It was painful to watch. Some editors physically shook when they presented. Others sent subordinates, avoiding the meetings at any cost. I learned early that the best way to handle a question that I could not answer was to fess up: I don't know, but I'll find out and get back to you.

I always felt as if I were performing and that the editors, all of whom were white, watched me with particular interest. I believe that occasionally Frankel and Lelyveld took pity on me rather than humiliating me as much as they could. But the few times they did call me out made me a stickler for being prepared.

———

I WAS learning daily what it meant to be one of the highest-ranking black editors at the *Times*. (Angela Dodson, a black woman, was in charge of the Style department.) Often, I was the only black staff member at the daily news meetings, publisher's lunches, and off-the-record affairs with politicians like Governor Cuomo, city comptroller Elizabeth Holtzman, New Jersey governor Jim Florio, and civil rights pioneer and former Atlanta mayor Andrew Young.

Black or not, I was determined to occupy the space, advice I gave to other editors on how to succeed. By that, I meant to bring my whole self to the job, meeting challenges head-on, being visible, accessible, creative, responsive, and direct. I was not there just to double the number of black department heads. It was my job to move the Metro report forward. This effort led to my second clash with Landman.

Under Darnton, he had made many staffing and assigning decisions himself. Darnton was quite comfortable with this approach. I was not. When I learned that Landman had made a major decision without consulting Oreskes or me, I told him that he was out of line. We all had to be on the same page, I explained, and that meant talking decisions through as a leadership team.

Landman bristled at the loss of autonomy, and when it was clear that we were pulling in different directions, Frankel and Lelyveld assigned him to Raines's Washington bureau. By then, it was clear to all the senior editors that Landman and I had a difficult time working together. Even when we tried to be collegial, we clashed.

Landman might have concluded that he was forced out of Metro because of diversity. Arthur Sulzberger Jr., who was close to becoming publisher, continued to make it clear that increasing the number of minorities and women at the paper and in management was a priority. I have no doubt that some whites at the paper believed the effort blocked them and other deserving whites from advancement.

I do not think the institution as a whole was sexist or racist, although some of its editors were one or the other or even both. Mostly, the *Times* suffered from ignorance, indifference, and arrogance, which played out on every level.

I was often confused with other blacks on staff, most frequently Paul Delaney. We looked nothing alike, and unambiguous reminders, it seemed, did nothing to correct my white colleagues' eyesight.

I ranted against giving stories working titles such as "Blacks" as opposed to more descriptive labels that fit the subject. The title "Blacks" did not give a clue, while a title like "Colleges" or "Jobs" or "Poverty" did.

"We would never slug a story 'Whites,'" I argued.

For a while, my tirades worked. But it was never long until the vague labeling returned.

When individuals or organizations like the National Association of Black Journalists (NABJ) called the *Times* on hiring or coverage flaws, the public message was that we could and should do better, while the internal dialogue was often that the paper would address such concerns in its own way and in its own time.

And then there was the bizarre.

Once I attended a publisher's lunch hosted by Arthur Sulzberger Sr., a genuinely decent man who had several African Americans on his senior management team and one among the company's board of directors. After the lunch, with David Dinkins, the city's first black mayor, editors discussed how they were most unimpressed. I had found Dinkins, like most of the publisher's guests, predictable and somewhat boring. Trying to find something good to say about the mayor, someone remarked how no riot had taken place on Dinkins's watch.

"That's why we elected him," the elder Sulzberger replied without missing a beat, "to keep the lid on."

I was equally stunned by comments Lelyveld made in reference to the lack of women on the paper's masthead. Lelyveld lamented the fact that many women chose family over career and were unwilling to sacrifice to move up the ladder. Then, with a mischievous grin, he volunteered how a friend solved the problem at another newspaper.

"He found a lesbian to promote," he said with a laugh.

At an NABJ conference, *Times* executives gathered to discuss company needs for recruiting minorities. A top editor at one of the golf magazines that the company owned at the time chimed in. His publication needed black writers desperately, he said, but there was not much chance of recruiting any.

"As you know," he told the group in the pre–Tiger Woods days, "blacks grow up in inner-city neighborhoods where there are basketball courts, not golf courses. It's impossible to find any blacks interested in golf."

Arthur Sulzberger Jr. happened to be in the room. It was only a matter of time before the senior editor was looking for a new job.

––––––––

ONE OF my biggest challenges was getting the staff to understand that they faced new, higher expectations. I tried to rally my editors by pronouncing that there was no such thing as a slow news day, only slow editors. No doubt, some saw me as an asshole for such remarks, but I meant them in good humor. If reporters had their own stories to do, that was fine. But if not, it was up to editors to come up with assignments for them.

I used every trick I learned in Washington. I would tell a reporter that if he did not get the story, I would find someone who could, or that he was the best person in the world to tackle the subject. I took note when the competition scooped us, and I demanded explanations and prompt responses. My new leadership was in vivid contrast to the *Times*-ian arrogance that something was not news until the *Times* said so.

I walked the room, chatting up the staff. "How was your vacation?" I would ask a reporter whose byline had not appeared for a few days.

At first, they appeared startled—until they got used to my brand of humor. After a while, some reporters would strike first: "So, Gerald, how was your vacation?" they would ask, suggesting that I had been coasting.

I tried to give my staff room to be creative, but I wanted no surprises. When news broke late at night or on weekends, I expected a call. I stressed that my door was always open and that I was available to discuss anything. I knew that people had lives outside of the newsroom, and I tried to show them that I valued them for who they were, not just what they could produce. I was appalled to hear how one previous Metro editor had responded to a reporter's urgent request to meet because his life was falling apart.

"OK," the editor replied, looking at his watch, "you have five minutes."

I wanted to send the opposite message. When one of my reporters was attacked on the subway, I went immediately to the hospital and stayed with her and her husband for hours. These were my people, and I wanted them to know that they mattered. I was a boss, but first I was a cheerleader and, when possible, a friend.

I also tried to shuffle the deck. Most of the reassignments made sense and worked well, but sometimes I fumbled. One of my victims was a veteran education reporter. I thought her writing had a lively, conversational touch that would suit a new column that chronicled the social antics of celebrities and power brokers in New York. When the reporter resisted by arguing that the assignment was beneath her, I lost patience.

"Look, you'll never win a Pulitzer Prize covering education," I said, trying to end the conversation.

I brought her to tears. Every reporter comes to work each day hoping to win the most coveted prize in journalism. Here was her boss telling her that it would never happen. She would still recount the conversation a decade later. I pledged to never again be so arrogant or dismissive.

———

IN EARLY 1991, my father entered St. Luke's Hospital in northern Manhattan. There was no one problem—his body, it seemed, had simply given up. The years of drinking, smoking, and worrying caught up with him. When I went to see him, I was amazed at how small he was, unlike the man who loomed so large when I was a child. Death came quickly and peacefully. He was sixty-six. I did not ask the doctor for the cause. It was as if knowing would have made me feel the loss more keenly.

We held his funeral at the Unity Funeral Chapels in central Harlem. I was touched when a group of colleagues made the trek uptown to pay their respects. Gary and I buried Rufus in a cemetery in Long Island with full military honors under overcast skies. I received the carefully folded flag and the thanks of a grateful nation for his service.

Neither Gary nor I cried, nor did we share our memories about the man we called Daddy. The distance was just too great. We returned from the cemetery in silence, each lost in his own thoughts.

Once again, death led me to take stock of my life. I was forty years old and a professional success. Despite the pressure and craziness of the newsroom, I felt immense joy from my job as Metro editor. In many ways, this should have been the happiest period in my life. But personally, I felt alone, frustrated, and filled with guilt.

My satisfaction with work only reinforced my unhappiness at home. It was not Jackie's fault. She had set out to become the perfect wife of a *Times* editor, in addition to continuing her own career at CBS in New York. She found us a gorgeous duplex condo on East Eighty-fourth Street, where our neighbors were Walter Cronkite and Henry Stern, who once was and would again become the city's park commissioner. Jackie brought in a decorator and made the place elegant and comfortable. The apartment had a huge backyard, where I began many days drinking coffee, smoking, and reading the paper. Occasionally I fired up the grill, which still gave me enormous pleasure.

Jackie had grown close to Lelyveld's wife, Carolyn, and the four of us would get together "to have some fun," as Carolyn would say in her cheery way. Every few weeks we met for dinner, and Jackie and I became regulars in their home whenever they entertained. Each year when the Lelyveld family and friends gathered for Thanksgiving, Jackie and I joined them.

Jackie resumed our Washington practice of power-broker dinners. One December evening we hosted Mayor Dinkins and wife, Joyce, along with the Lelyvelds, Raines, and Sam Roberts, a city-wise veteran Metro reporter, and his wife, Marie Salerno. The most interesting part of the evening was not what the mayor had to say, but watching Lelyveld and Raines trying to one-up each other. On another evening, we hosted Rudy Giuliani, who spent much of the time talking about what he would do if elected mayor. It was clear that he would be a formidable opponent for Dinkins.

For some reason, these social events did not resonate with me anymore. I knew they went with the job, but during each one, I found myself wishing that everybody would go away. The dinners seemed to mean the world to Jackie, a clue that we were drifting apart. I started to resent her for forcing them on me, even though I knew they were the right thing to do.

Jackie and I were living together, but we were not working toward common goals. I was frustrated about children. Jackie said that she could be happy with or without them, although she kept reminding me that her biological clock was ticking. Her take-them-or-leave-them approach troubled me; rearing a child was something that we both needed to want with equal fervor. I also worried that if we had children and our marriage failed, I would be doing what my father and his father had done—walking away. I did not want to repeat that cycle.

I would spend hours at the office, lingering until the last minute, and then reluctantly drag myself home to a place where I felt empty. Weekends were the worst; they meant two forced days away from the office. On Sundays, I parked myself in front the television and watched football. Otherwise, I spent my time thinking about how miserable I was becoming and how helpless I felt to do anything about it.

I came to realize that I had used Jackie as a crutch. The driving force behind our relationship was that I could lean on her. But now that I was happy in my job, comfortable in New York, and making more money that she was, my newfound sense of independence only added to my guilt for having been so selfish. She deserved better. So did I.

Even our yearly August vacations to Nantucket were joyless. Once, we invited Gary and his family. Plans for a pleasant get-together unraveled when Gary and Jackie got into a nasty argument. Jackie accused Gary of being jealous of my success, which he denied, insisting that he was quite proud of me. I left them trading accusations and walked alone on the beach, thinking about how little either of them understood me or my relationships with them.

Despite their differences, Gary believed Jackie was the perfect wife and once had proclaimed that he would die for her. That startled me, because I knew that I would not.

As I struggled, Jackie did what she could to make the marriage work. By appearances, it did. But the more frustrated I became, the more I blamed Jackie. Jackie sensed my disconnection, and true to her nature, she set out to fix the problems. She suggested marriage counseling.

I did not believe in shrinks; I grew up believing that a man had to solve his own problems. But I felt overwhelmed by the emptiness in our relationship and in my personal life. There was no one I felt I could reach out to for answers. I would discuss my feelings with Gary, but he would always see me as his little brother, the one he had guided on Romaine. I had traveled miles from there, something that was hard for him to accept. He no longer knew me, nor did I know him. I thought it was dangerous to share my problems with colleagues. I did not want anyone to conclude that I was weak or to have information that could be used against me.

I began to doubt that I could ever complete the picture of happiness that I had painted for myself back in St. Louis. Just as my father had done for years before he sobered up, I started relying on alcohol—mostly, I reasoned, to help me get through the social events and to manage the weekends. Of course, drink did nothing to fill the emptiness. So, in spite of my reservations about counseling, I agreed. If I was going to be truly happy, I needed help that did not come in a bottle.

––––––––

OVER MORE than a decade, Raines and Lelyveld jockeyed for Arthur Sulzberger Jr.'s favor. Sulzberger benefited from the competition. Instead of having one strong editorial voice in his ear, he had two. The fierce adversaries, each convinced that he had the better vision for leading the *Times*, could hardly have been more different, at least outwardly. Lelyveld was reserved and awkward, although he became less so as he rose in the ranks of the paper. He was happily married to his childhood sweetheart, and they did practically everything together. Raines was outgoing and charismatic and, once he divorced, a man about town.

In less obvious ways, the two men had a lot in common. Both were driven and political, skilled at analyzing a situation and coming up with a creative solution. Within a company that prides itself on structure and order, neither hesitated to challenge conventional thinking. Each knew he was the best man to run the *Times*. Neither saw that possibility as a given, but each was convinced that he was up to the task—if the opportunity came along.

I don't know exactly when Raines and Lelyveld became archenemies, but I can trace the animosity between them to one incident in particular. It began with a routine request from Lelyveld, who in his role as managing editor expressed concern that Raines's Washington bureau was missing some aspect of a story.

Over the telephone, Raines exploded, "We're doing the best we can! If you can do a better job, then come down here and do it. Otherwise leave us the fuck alone!"

"Your Mr. Raines has some temper," Lelyveld said to me, relaying the conversation, which Raines later confirmed.

Lelyveld was well aware of my relationship with Raines, and he clearly shared the exchange for a reason. He said no subordinate had ever addressed him like that. Although Lelyveld shrugged it off, I knew he would never forget such an act of disrespect. For men who were proud and unaccustomed to second-guessing or open defiance, it was a defining moment in their relationship.

Anyone watching closely could detect the competition. Each pursued power in his own way, and they were constantly in each other's sights. In conversations, Raines was always interested in the newsroom gossip, especially if it involved Lelyveld. You could always get Lelyveld's attention with the latest news about Raines.

Sometimes they both took a special interest in mentoring and encouraging talent—as with writers like Maureen Dowd, Alessandra Stanley, and Rick Bragg, and with editors like me. As I grew close to both of them, I often felt like Charlie Sheen's character in the movie *Platoon*, the grunt whose loyalty drifted between his two sergeants before he finally chose one. Whether their competition improved or harmed the *Times* depends on one's loyalty. More than anything else, it defined the paper's journalism.

In 1992, Arthur Sulzberger Jr. was tapped by his father to be publisher. One of his first acts was to make Raines editor of the editorial page. In the pecking order, that meant he ranked above Lelyveld. At least for a while.

———

DOWD AND other Washington colleagues urged me to go for Raines's position as bureau chief. The Washington job had enormous appeal. I knew the players and believed that I could lead the bureau. I sought advice from Raines. He endorsed the move, saying it would make me more attractive when it came to future promotions. Plus, he argued, it would be good to get out from under Lelyveld, whom he saw as stifling and overbearing.

Lelyveld argued the opposite: I was on a fast track and could best remain there by staying put. I had accomplished so much already that I would soon be on the newspaper's masthead, he suggested. He saw Washington as an unnecessary detour.

Finally, I met with Frankel. I highlighted my knowledge of Washington and my ties to the bureau and asked to be considered for the job. If I wanted it, Frankel said, he would have to give it to me. I had earned it.

"But I hope you don't ask for it," he added.

He said there was still enormous work to be done on Metro and that he already had a plan for Washington. He assured me that the bureau would be in good hands.

In the end, it was not much of a decision. I had been recruiting people and reassuring the Metro staff that the department, long considered by many a stepping-stone to roles in more desirable posts, was just as significant as other parts of the paper. I felt I would be a hypocrite if I moved to Washington.

I remained as Metro editor, but I was determined to do more to put my stamp on the report. It was one thing to assert that Metro was as strong as the other departments; it was another to produce journalism that made colleagues—and our readers—take notice.

Late in 1992, I was shocked to learn that the son of a former girlfriend had been arrested for murder after allegedly shooting a rival in a fight. Over the years, I had chronicled the growth and development of this boy; the last update had him doing well in school and hoping to become a musician. Now he was in jail for taking someone's life. *What happened?* I wondered.

That led me to thinking, *Who are these kids, especially those in the inner city? What are their values, their dreams, their influences? And, most significant, how are they falling through the cracks?*

I realized that I did not have a clue, nor did most reporters and editors. We did not live in their world, and even if some of us came from it, few of us looked back. I was certain that the *Times* needed to write about the kids crowded into inadequate public schools, the kids without nannies, the ones growing up poor and struggling to survive. I was equally certain that we were clueless what to write.

This project was not like writing about the presidency or the breakup of the Soviet Union or a war in some faraway place. We had the background and training to handle such subjects. But the subject of inner-city kids, to the staff of the *New York Times* in 1992, was fresh ground.

It was clear that this was more than just a Metro story. I reached out to Soma Golden about how we could tackle the subject together. The more we talked, the more we knew that we needed the input from the kids themselves.

That is how we ended up at a community center in Brooklyn one Saturday morning, about half a dozen *Times* editors and reporters and three times as many young people representing a range of races and ethnicities. For hours, we listened as they talked about their lives. A sad recurring theme emerged. In nearly every case, some social support was failing them: church, school, police, politicians, even parents. Their resulting frustration—the sense that they were on their own—acutely shaped their values and influenced their behaviors. I will never forget the young woman who declared that she did not believe her life would be better than that of her parents, despite the progress of recent decades. The scary part: she did not believe that she needed to play by society's rules.

I was struck by the profound sense of hopelessness in these young people's lives. Golden and I decided the best way to open a window onto their world was to present the stories of ten poor children of different ages, races, ethnicities, and from different parts of the country. Reporters spent months working on the project, each exploring in depth the life of a child, detailing how the children fought against tremendous odds and how institutions failed them at nearly every turn.

In the end, the series "Children of the Shadows" generated enormous public attention. It was one of the most satisfying pieces of journalism I ever helped to edit.

——————

AS WE launched the "Children" project, the Metro staff faced its biggest challenge. Just past noon on Friday, February 26, 1993, a massive car bomb exploded beneath Tower One of the World Trade Center. Details were sketchy, but throughout the rest of the day and the weekend, the staff worked hard to fill in the blanks. Eventually, the *Times* learned that terrorists had driven a Ryder rental van into the parking garage and detonated a 1,500-pound urea-nitrate bomb. Six men were eventually convicted in the crime, which killed six people and wounded more than a thousand.

The *Times* threw its impressive resources and manpower on the Trade Center story and led the pack in reporting. The Metro staff worked with unbelievable drive and energy. We passed along tips, checked and rechecked sources, and pursued each piece of information—how law enforcement officials discovered the van's partially obscured vehicle identification number, which led them to the renter, the apartment where the bomb was built, and information about the life of the alleged mastermind, Ramzi Yousef.

We worked in sync with the Foreign desk, retracing the steps of the terrorists and following their ties to the Middle East.

But I did not want to neglect other news. In my emerging management approach, I was determined that the staff be able to "fight on more than one front." This was more difficult than it should have been. Some reporters lacked hustle or drive. They were content to contribute as little as possible. This became clear when I lectured a veteran reporter, a white man, about his poor production. He sat in my office listening, puffing on his pipe, and nodding, and finally it dawned on me that he was not about to change. I said to him: "I bet you have had this exact conversation with the last five Metro editors. And I bet you're thinking that you survived them and that you will survive me."

He bobbed his head in agreement, and I could only smile. As a department head, I had only so many weapons to use to goose performance. I could reassign, admonish, or simply ignore a lax staffer. If I was lucky, I might be able to pawn him off on another department head. What I could not do was fire him, since the *Times* rarely fired anybody.

Fortunately, there were more than enough strong reporters and editors willing to do good journalism. Two of the best were Dean Baquet and Jane Fritsch. Lelyveld had hired Baquet, a black man, away from the *Chicago Tribune*, where he had won a Pulitzer Prize. I had recruited Fritsch, a white woman, from the *Los Angeles Times*. The two teamed up to examine Empire Blue Cross Blue Shield, one of America's largest not-for-profit health insurers. They found an operation riddled with fraud and mismanagement. I encouraged them to stay on the story and keep digging. And they continued to come back with more.

On April 12, 1994, the Pulitzer board announced that our staff won the coveted prize in the spot news reporting category, the *Times'* first Pulitzer for local reporting in more than two decades. The citation read: "For its comprehensive coverage of the bombing of Manhattan's World Trade Center."

In addition, Isabel Wilkerson, a gifted black writer who worked in Chicago as a national correspondent for the *Times*, won in the feature-writing category for a profile of a fourth grader for the "Children of the Shadows" series and for two stories on the Midwestern flood of 1993.

The paper also won a third Pulitzer for feature photography. Kevin Carter, a freelancer, captured a powerful image of a starving Sudanese girl who collapsed on her way to a feeding center while a vulture waited nearby.

It was a special moment, both personally and professionally. Not only had the *Times* won three Pulitzers, but a black female reporter and a staff led by a black editor had earned two of them.

The *Times* also had two Pulitzer finalists, both from Metro: the Baquet-Fritsch team for their Empire Blue Cross Blue Shield series, in the investigative reporting category, and Robert McFadden, a superb rewrite reporter, in spot news. McFadden would win in that category two years later.

A staff regarded as second-rate only a few years before had won one Pulitzer and nearly captured two others. There was no question that Metro was on the rise.

As Jackie joined me for the newspaper's celebration that night, I was all smiles, but I could not help but think of the gulf between my personal and professional lives. One of my proudest moments as an editor echoed with the emptiness of my life as a man.

———

MARRIAGE COUNSELING is a form of torture. Two people who should be able to communicate on their own turn to a facilitator for help, hoping that answers emerge to questions that are driving them apart. In our case, Jackie found a psychologist who confirmed all of my worst fears. We sat in front of him describing our lack of passion and intimacy and common goals. Most of the time, Jackie did most of the talking, and not surprisingly, she and the therapist developed a strong rapport.

I began to see the sessions as a waste of time because the more we talked the more I realized the real source of my problem. Finally, the psychologist asked to see me separately. As I sat down in his office, he asked what was troubling to me.

"I don't want to be married," I said. Then I ended the session.

Still, I felt paralyzed. I was sure that leaving Jackie would hurt my prospects of rising at the paper, especially given her relationship with Carolyn Lelyveld. I had a crazy notion that everyone would ask: *How could a man who could not manage a marriage manage a staff at the* New York Times?

Maybe you can tough it out, I challenged myself, as I imagined other senior editors were doing. A little sacrifice for the sake of my career.

In all honesty, I wanted to be with someone else.

———

FOR MANY years I had been active in the recruitment of minorities. I saw previous efforts as spotty and disorganized. *Times* staffers would attend minority journalism conventions—prime opportunities to recruit—with no game plan or priorities. They would scatter over the next few days, chatting up potential candidates. The haphazard effort netted few good results.

I pushed for us to meet before the conventions to identify candidates we wanted to pursue. I wanted us to rank those we considered priorities and those worth tracking. The goal was to devote most of our attention and effort to the priorities.

In 1990, as we headed to Los Angeles for the National Association of Black Journalists convention, one of the candidates at the top of our list was a copy editor named Robin Stone. She was working for the *Boston Globe*, after a stint at the *Detroit Free Press*. Bill Connolly, a senior editor and one of the *Times'* most gifted copy editors, came to know Robin while teaching at an editing fellowship run by the Maynard Institute for Journalism Education. She was in her midtwenties—young by *Times* standards—but Connolly raved that she was a must-have candidate.

As I walked through the lobby of the Century Plaza Hotel on the first convention day, I could not help but notice a petite young black woman leaving the phone bank. She was fair-skinned with shoulder-length hair. As she came closer, I was startled to see her name tag: ROBIN STONE. Here was the person we had spent so much time discussing back in New York. Since I felt I already knew her, I approached as I would an old friend.

"Are you *the* Robin Stone?" I asked, with a grin, catching her by surprise.

With a blast of attitude, she snapped, "Who wants to know?"

I read her body language and backed off. I formally introduced myself and shared that she was on the *Times'* short list of potential candidates. She still seemed cautious, but at least she heard me out. I invited her to breakfast the next morning and told her that other editors from the *Times* were eager to talk to her. She agreed to meet with me, and as she walked away, I could only mouth one word: "Wow."

The next morning in the hotel dining room, I gave Robin the pitch that I had given myself in deciding to come to the *Times*. I told her that she was clearly talented, but she would never know how good she was unless she worked at the *Times*. Robin was unimpressed by the status of the *Times*. She challenged me on the opportunities available to editors and on the newsroom environment, especially for minorities. I tried to be honest, telling her that the paper still had a way to go. I shared that the current leadership wanted a newsroom in which minorities could thrive, and I pointed out that she would be working for me.

The breakfast was the start of a lengthy recruiting process. Other senior editors pitched the paper, and eventually she agreed to come to New York to take the editing test and undergo the obligatory multiple interviews with senior editors. She was stellar on both fronts and accepted an offer as an editor trainee. I knew that the *Times* was getting a first-rate copy editor, but I had no idea how much I would become attracted to her. The first time she came into the newsroom, she turned heads, including mine. When I saw her, I walked into a tall trash can, scattering recyclables across the floor, leading some reporters to look up and smile. So much for the unflappable Metro editor.

Robin spent the next few years paying her dues, working the graveyard shift and weekends, and even doing a brief stint as a reporter. She was well liked throughout the newsroom, filling in whenever a desk was shorthanded, in departments like Style, Week in Review, and Foreign. I watched as she blossomed into a strong editor. While many young journalists were consumed with doubts about what it took to succeed, Robin seemed to have none.

As difficult as it was, I kept my distance and our relationship professional. Robin did not seem the type to find herself in a messy situation with her boss. Plus, she planned to marry her college sweetheart.

But Robin appealed to me in so many ways. She grew up in a modest neighborhood in northwest Detroit, the eldest of two daughters whose single mother worked at the post office. She was fifteen when she started her first job, as a cashier at S. S. Kresge, the five-and-dime. She attended public schools and majored in journalism at Michigan State. By her senior year, she was working full time and attending school full time at night. She knew hard work, and her Midwestern pragmatism colored her view of everything she saw.

In 1992 the National Association of Black Journalists held its annual convention in Detroit. Robin invited *Times* colleagues to a barbecue at the home of Allen, her mother's boyfriend, who would become her stepfather. I liked Ora and Allen immediately. They were welcoming and down-to-earth, two of the most decent people I had ever met. Robin's mother, an avid Lions fan, managed to get tickets to a scrimmage, and I left the barbecue with her to catch the game. By the end of that day, I was even more taken with Robin.

By the time the Pulitzers were announced in 1994, I was strongly attracted to her. We had worked together on the "Children of the Shadows" series, and she shone as an editor. She often sounded like a crusty veteran, challenging me and other editors to make the stories better. Throughout the process, I enjoyed just being in her presence.

Of course, this did nothing to help Jackie's efforts to save our marriage. In fact, it only added to my guilt and frustration. I finally rebelled by refusing to attend the Lelyvelds' annual Thanksgiving dinner at their country home upstate. I had no desire to spend the holiday with somebody else's family. I wanted a family and traditions of my own. Jackie rented a car and took Sheba, our dog.

Late that evening when she returned, Jackie and I finally confronted our problems. I confessed that I no longer wanted to be married and was in fact attracted to someone else. I decided then to move out. No matter what the consequence at work, it could not be any worse than the way I was living.

I packed a couple of suitcases and moved to a furnished apartment on the East Side. The separation brought back memories of leaving Sheila, but this time, I knew I was making the right decision.

Jackie and I reached out to another psychologist in a last effort to repair our marriage. This therapist also asked to see us individually, and when I met with her, I shared that I was attracted to another woman. We talked a lot about priorities. Why was I so worried about how a divorce from Jackie would affect my career? the psychologist wondered. Why was I giving the *Times* so much power over my life?

I knew that she was asking the right questions. I could no longer live based on what I thought the *Times* expected of me. From that moment on, I knew I would not return to Jackie. We made no announcement; few people knew that we were separated. I was alone, but for the first time, I did not feel lonely. In fact, I felt at peace. For once, I had taken control of my personal life.

After a meeting one afternoon, I received a handwritten note from Sulzberger Jr. "You seem troubled, my friend," it read. "If I can help, please let me know."

I did not tell the publisher what was troubling me, but I was determined to fix it.

9

SHIFTING PRIORITIES AND ALLIANCES

In the summer of 1992 I'd decided that twenty-three years at the *Times* were enough. I could rise no higher and did not want to start repeating assignments and marking time, which to me would have been akin to waiting for the Grim Reaper.

As I was negotiating with the University of Alabama to take the position of journalism chair, the news leaked to the newsroom. Of all the tears and disbelief of colleagues and friends, none was more touching than the hand extended and emotion expressed by Gerald. When he first heard, he repeated something we had said so many times since our first meeting, in St. Louis in 1974: "Let's have a drink."

We sat and talked about everything but my pending departure. Finally he brought it up. He could not believe there was not some way to keep me on the paper. He wanted to do something. He offered a column. But working on Metro, even for Gerald—as exciting as it might have been—was not for me.

I told him this and added that, in fact, Max Frankel had already raised the idea of a column and other possibilities. Gerald looked even more disappointed. Then he vented, telling me how frustrated he was by my plight as well as that of other blacks at the

Times; he said he realized that they had legitimate complaints about their treatment. It was the first time he'd expressed that kind of frustration to me.

Afterward, we both walked into our separate histories. Our last public event together was as panelists at a symposium on covering race at the University of Michigan in 2001. Off the podium, we did what we always did—continued the discussions over drinks.

—PAUL DELANEY

A FEW weeks before the Pulitzer announcement, Jackie and I joined the Lelyvelds for dinner at the Four Seasons. Lelyveld suggested the two of us arrive early to talk shop. As we waited for our drinks, he shared the news: Frankel was retiring, and he would be the new executive editor. I was delighted for him. I could think of no better successor.

My next, obvious question: who would be his managing editor? There was much speculation about succession—there always is—and some had even mentioned me as a long shot. I did not give the reports much credence. I had been in management for fewer than five years. While I had worked in three of the biggest departments, other editors had far more experience and knew the paper better. Still, I thought I deserved consideration. I had taken the Metro staff and turned it around, burnishing my leadership credentials.

Lelyveld announced with immense pride that he had lured Gene Roberts, former executive editor of the *Philadelphia Inquirer*, out of retirement. Roberts, once a *Times* reporter and National editor, had turned the *Inquirer* into a Pulitzer magnet. I had never worked with him, but I knew that he was one of the best editors of his generation. A choice between the two of us was not much of a contest. But I was surprised that Lelyveld did not give me serious thought. Roberts, after all, represented the past. He was not the person to help Lelyveld take the newsroom into the much-heralded digital age.

Lelyveld must have read the disappointment on my face. He explained that he chose Roberts because he needed him and could learn from him. I could, too, he encouraged. He said that Roberts's contract would be up in three years and that, by then, I would be ready. Lelyveld's words were unambiguous, the kind of commitment I had never heard from him. He assured me that the job was mine the next time around. I could wait three years for such a prize, I responded, if I was certain it would come.

Once our wives arrived, we celebrated Lelyveld's good fortune while Jackie and I struggled to get through our meal.

At the office, Raines gave me his thoughts about Lelyveld's choice: he believed Lelyveld was looking for a father figure. Lelyveld, the son of a prominent but self-absorbed rabbi in Cleveland, had had a distressing childhood.

True or not, Raines's theory seemed logical. I did not know what Lelyveld saw in me, but I knew that he respected my work. His promise bonded me to him. I became a loyal member of his team, a constant cheerleader on his behalf, and I made more of an effort to enrich my own relationship with him. But no matter how much time we spent together, there remained an uneasiness that neither of us could bridge. I rarely saw him unguarded, unless he was with his two daughters or his wife. He bristled when described as shy and awkward or as the last person you wanted to be stuck in an elevator with, though he sometimes gave people that impression. I found him far too complicated for that simple description. Lelyveld always had an agenda, which probably is why I remained guarded, too.

There was reason to be wary. More than once, I watched Lelyveld declare war on subordinates who challenged him, much as he had done with Raines. The issue was never that he was right or wrong but that his authority was tested. He made it quite uncomfortable for those who confronted him.

Even so, I sought his approval. And when I got it, as I frequently did, I sighed with deep satisfaction and relief. Eventually, as I grew comfortable with his demeanor, I let my guard down. I also sought his advice on how to prepare myself for the managing editor's post. Lelyveld suggested that I travel to deepen my understanding of foreign news—to make up for my lack of foreign reporting experience, he stressed. As soon as I could, I scheduled trips to the Middle East, Asia, Europe, and Africa to meet with dignitaries and check in with our correspondents.

———

BEFORE HE passed the baton to Lelyveld, on July 13, 1993, Max Frankel announced the appointments of two new assistant managing editors: Soma Golden and me. I became the first African American editor on the masthead. I was to be the first AME listed, since the names appear alphabetically. But Soma Golden, the ultrafeminist, added her husband's last name to hers. Thus, she became Soma Golden Behr, and her name went before mine. It was a reminder of how at the *Times*, even the smallest detail mattered considerably.

Initially, I assumed the duties of John Lee, who became the director of editorial development. The duties included supervising Foreign, Business, Science, and the Washington bureau. But while Lelyveld continued the journalism that came to define the paper under Frankel, he dismantled his predecessor's management structure, giving more power to department heads and having them report directly to him and Roberts instead of the AMEs. The AMEs had other tasks assigned to them. In the new structure, I assumed a major responsibility: running the daily news report. The job was usually performed by the managing editor, but because Roberts defined his role differently, he had no interest in the task. His decision meant a huge opportunity for me; with the daily news report as a part of my portfolio, I became the third most powerful editor in the newsroom.

The structural change was significant. While I had taken on a major new role, Lelyveld essentially diminished the role of many other AMEs while elevating the status of department heads, who traditionally ranked lower than AMEs. He took steps to lessen the gap between their salaries and made the changes without the knowledge of the AMEs. Where the masthead would once discuss appointments, Lelyveld and Roberts now held those discussions and made their decisions in private. They determined newsroom priorities by consulting with the department heads. The change meant enormous new power and a new way of doing business for many editors. While there was no mass revolt, there were plenty of bruised feelings. I heard from the injured almost daily.

Roberts quickly proved a mixed blessing. I got along well with him, unlike several other AMEs. He had a huge distrust of senior editors, especially AMEs. He believed they were prone to gossip, and he intentionally kept them out of the loop. He did not appreciate others second-guessing his decisions and had little patience for the management tools that Sulzberger Jr. sought to bring to the newsroom. Roberts was a human steamroller when it came to stifling dissent; anyone who disagreed quickly became road kill.

He did not take me under his wing but was readily available for advice, and he left me alone to run the daily newspaper. He and Lelyveld agreed with my plan to have two news meetings each day instead of the one at 5:00 P.M. That gave us an earlier look at developments and allowed us to ask questions and make suggestions without the pressure of the evening deadline. The noon meeting was tame compared with the later one, but the change made us far more productive and efficient later in the day.

———

THE NEWSROOM'S gyrations became less of a concern. With the help of my own therapist, I stopped giving the *Times* so much power over my life and started to focus on how I could make that life more satisfying.

I had never believed in the concept of a soul mate; in fact, I dismissed it as emotional mush. But with Robin Stone in my sights, the phrase made all the sense in the world. I was determined to have this woman, despite our age difference and her fiancé. We had come to know each other as supervisor and employee, as mentor and mentee, and I could tell she was fond of me. Since she was no longer reporting directly to me, I gathered my courage and invited her to dinner one evening not too long after she brought her intended to a *Times* gathering and flashed a diamond ring. That night over dinner, I began my campaign by telling her, "You're not going to marry that man."

Through our lawyers, Jackie and I tried to work out a divorce settlement. She wanted everything, from alimony to the house to my life insurance. I wanted a divorce at almost any cost, but dying for it seemed extreme. After months of haggling, the two of us met at a bar and agreed on the final details over drinks. Essentially, I gave her the East Side duplex, which was valued at over one million dollars. I got my sanity, which was priceless.

When Robin and I first started to date, we worried about being spotted together. But on more than one occasion fellow editors passed us on the street without even noticing, much less recognizing us. We chalked it up to the reality of the world outside the walls of the integrated workplace: if they had no reason to, whites seldom looked into the faces of blacks.

Still, I did not want to hide my relationship. To make the *Times* management aware of our situation, I told Lelyveld. His encouraging words surprised me. He said what was most important was for me to be happy, and if I was happy with Robin, that's what really mattered.

Robin found a three-bedroom rental apartment on the Upper East Side and promised to join me there when her lease ran out. I was too eager to wait. One day while she was at work, I hired movers to pack up her tiny two-bedroom Upper West Side apartment and move her across town. At the end of her shift—she was deputy editor of Living, one of the features sections—I called her and told her to come home to me. Fortunately, she was moved enough by my grand gesture to stay.

Robin, a fitness buff who did not smoke and rarely drank, encouraged me to quit cigarettes and lose weight. She had no problem being in a relationship with a balding older man, but not one who was out of shape as well. I made a halfhearted effort to cut back on smoking and joined a gym. To keep up with her, I took up bike riding and, for a brief moment of madness, in-line skating. Colleagues got a good laugh when I limped into the office after a nasty spill one weekend in Central Park.

I was still seeing my therapist, but the bouts of depression were gone. For once, I was enjoying both my career and my personal life. Robin and I both wanted to start a family, the sooner the better. While career mattered, other things did, too, she reminded me, like family, friends, and giving back. We traveled—from weekend trips to Atlantic City to a week in Rome and Venice—and I adopted her family as my own. As president of the New York Association of Black Journalists, Robin devoted much of her free time to leading the chapter. Our apartment bustled with the energy of meetings and fellowship among officers and members. Robin's enthusiasm for NABJ reminded me of my organizing days back in St. Louis.

Once Robin and I were together, I could not understand why I worried so much before. The *New York Post*'s Page Six included a "blind" gossip item asking what senior editor at the *Times* was sacrificing his career for love of a junior colleague. Although it did not name names, we knew the item referred to us. I even believed their take on the situation could well be true, but I did not care.

———

THE NEWSROOM in the mid-1990s was on the verge of one of its most important undertakings, transferring its content to other media platforms. The effort, which would prove costly and contentious, brought into conflict the current state of journalism and the journalism of the future. Newsroom leaders were slow to grasp the importance of the changing media landscape, and the transformation was slow to gain traction. Sulzberger Jr., who was determined to lead a *Times* revolution on several fronts, also embraced popular business trends of the time, such as leadership and morale seminars and diversity training. Of course, not everyone shared his enthusiasm.

One of the first changes he espoused was teamwork. He stressed a set of business theories based on the teachings of W. Edwards Deming, a professor emeritus at New York University whose ideas helped revitalize Japanese industry after World War II. Sulzberger seized upon two of Deming's tenets: an emphasis on quality first and a management style that relied on collaboration rather than top-down orders.

Editors largely discounted his efforts. They suggested that the Deming strategies could go only so far given the deadlines, the competition, and the need for results. In the *Times*' demanding environment, commitment to excellence often meant bruised feelings, second-guessing, and strong leadership from the top, editors argued.

But Sulzberger pushed forward even when he faced strong opposition. At the time, I did not understand the battle or why it was so
intense. Sulzberger had watched his *Times* under Rosenthal function
as an awesome news machine, but at an enormous price—fear. He had
worked as a reporter in Washington and on the Metro staff, so he knew
the culture firsthand. He was determined to make the environment
more collegial and bearable.

In 1995 Sulzberger brought in Martin Nisenholtz, director of content strategy at Ameritech Corporation in Chicago, to develop and
implement a digital strategy for the *Times*. The rail-thin Nisenholtz
had an easy manner that belied the fire that drove him. He embraced
the newsroom's mantra of creating quality journalism, but he also displayed the spirit of an entrepreneur. The newsroom was the key to the
institution's Web strategy because of its content, but the new business
was seen as a threat to many in the newsroom. Like two seasoned prize-
fighters, Lelyveld and Nisenholtz squared off.

Sulzberger found a measure of success in bringing together key
players in the newsroom and on the business side to agree on the newspaper's priorities in an effort to make the *Times* more nimble. To do so,
he had to overcome journalists' concerns that business-driven strategies would change the nature of how the *Times* made news decisions.
To them, the wall separating the news and business sides was sacred.
Sulzberger did not see his role as the final arbiter of disputes between
the two divisions but preferred they work out their differences.

He directed three editors from the news side and three from the
business side to go off and craft a mission statement reflecting what he
had in mind. It began by reasserting the *Times*' commitment to quality
journalism but acknowledged that it took profits to fund this quality.
The language was usable by both sides when defining their roles: quality journalism from the newsroom that would be paid for by profits
from the business side. The simple statement would guide how the
Times operated for the next decade. It was amended over time, but the
core idea remained.

By the time Lelyveld became executive editor, this new arrangement was formalized though a group known as Mohonk, after the inn

in New Paltz, New York, where Sulzberger held one of the retreats. The Mohonk group included four senior executives from the business side and three senior newsroom editors. Largely because Roberts had no appetite for serving on Mohonk, I was appointed to the committee, along with editors Dave Jones and Al Siegal.

The committee became one of the newspaper's leading vehicles for strategic planning. It explored ways the *Times* could transfer its brand from the newspaper to other platforms, as well as growth opportunities, such as how to expand the paper's national edition, and it took on specific challenges, like strengthening the paper's Internet presence and responding to the *Wall Street Journal*'s plans to create a weekend section. One of its earliest efforts was inspired and spearheaded by a committee member, Janet Robinson, who at the time was senior vice president of advertising.

Robinson was deceptive. She was dedicated, compassionate, and understated, qualities that were consistent with a former public-school teacher from Newport, Rhode Island, and Somerset, Massachusetts. She was also tough as steel and had smarts to match.

Robinson had joined the Times Company in 1983 as an account executive at *Tennis* magazine. By the mid-1990s, she was leading a push to grow the paper through national advertising, which complemented the paper's national circulation expansion. She became a powerful force in a male-dominated company that was slow to push women to the top.

———

SULZBERGER JR., who completed Harvard Business School's program for management development in 1985, also encouraged editors to broaden their management experience. Unlike in other fields, newspaper editors are often promoted because they excel in producing good journalism, not necessarily in managing or leading people. At Sulzberger's insistence, I attended a program known as Leadership at the Peak. The weeklong session, in Colorado Springs, Colorado, was intended to help top executives assess and improve their leadership style and effectiveness. Participants from various professions were required to complete a form that helped identify their strengths and weaknesses, hopes and fears. We also brought in assessments from about a dozen colleagues with ranks above, below, and at the same level.

I was shocked at the gaps between how I saw myself and how others saw me. My colleagues described me as a leader who cared about those whom I managed. But they also said I could be a bully. They saw me as guarded and selfish, and concerned primarily about rising to the top. I could not believe that people considered me to be so arrogant.

It was difficult to go under a microscope and be subjected to such harsh scrutiny. I left Colorado understanding that I had enormous capital in the bank among my colleagues, but that I had to start spending some of it so that they could get to know me better. The assessment was humbling.

I was also struck by how almost everyone in my group of about a dozen was struggling to live a more fulfilling life. I could certainly relate. As a final act, we wrote letters to ourselves describing how we wanted to reorder our priorities. I promised myself I would keep it sealed until I achieved my goals. They included being happily married, having a child, owning a house, and stopping smoking. Not one goal on my list had anything to do with my career.

I returned to the *Times* determined to use what I had learned. I saw the program as a kind of emotional preparation for executives and suggested that all senior editors attend. Not surprisingly, my view was not shared in the newsroom. Some editors, Lelyveld included, derided the experience as "charm school." Still, I worked to make myself more accessible and pledged to make good on my personal promises.

———

ONE OF Sulzberger Jr.'s most confounding efforts was improving newsroom coverage and culture through increased diversity. To his credit, he tried to tackle the issue head-on by forcing the newsroom to engage in mandatory diversity training. But as with some other management schemes early in his tenure as publisher, he faced resistance.

Sulzberger seized on the work of a so-called diversity expert in Chicago named Thomas Kochman. He was considering Kochman to provide training for the entire newsroom, a contract potentially worth several million dollars. Lelyveld responded to the request in his trade-mark passive-aggressive way. He did not reject the idea outright, but he insisted that a group of senior editors first meet with Kochman and assess his sessions before accepting the proposal. Lelyveld took Dennis Stern, who was by then in newsroom administration, and me. Kochman pulled out all the stops for us.

We arrived in Chicago late one evening after a long flight delay and rushed straight from the airport to dinner with Kochman and a top aide. I was tired and grumpy and started to resent that Lelyveld had dragged me along. My being there reminded me of what many blacks on staff often complained about: blacks had credibility in the news-room as long as the topic was race, but for other matters of importance, whites typically turned to other whites. No matter how much I fought this way of thinking, no matter how much my own career contradicted it, it would resurface.

From the beginning, Kochman misread me. Surely, he must have thought, the black man supported diversity training for his staff. As we talked at dinner, he told me that he knew I had grown up in the South. When I asked why he believed that, he said it was because I was reluctant to look him squarely in the eyes.

"That's a trait all blacks from the South have," he said.

Actually, I told him, surprised that he was so far off base, I was from St. Louis. I was not making eye contact because I was exhausted and I wanted to sleep.

The next morning we audited one of Kochman's workshops, which was attended by a dozen or so executives from other companies. In the name of diversity, Kochman embraced and justified stereotype after stereotype: all Asians were quiet and loyal, all Hispanics were patriotic, and all blacks were late to meetings. Kochman tried to help the white participants understand. Blacks, for example, cared about time, but they had other priorities. If a black person confronted a choice between listening to a colleague's problem or getting to a meeting on time, he or she would choose the former.

Kochman then asked, if we were stuck in a paid parking lot with no money, what lot attendant would be more sympathetic: a black man or woman, a white man or woman, an Asian man or woman, or a Hispanic man or woman. The black woman, he answered, explaining that they are the most compassionate of any race or gender.

I could not help but laugh. I had just gone through a divorce with Jackie, a black woman who tried to take me to the cleaners. I saw not one ounce of compassion in how she had dealt with me. By that point, I had given up on Mr. Kochman.

The next day, Kochman asked the group how many of us knew a Hispanic person. Several volunteered that they had Hispanic nannies or housekeepers. I decided to humor him.

I raised my hand and said I knew Hispanics quite well from the time I spent in Central America.

"That's fascinating," Kochman said. "What were you doing?"

"I was working for the government," I said conspiratorially. "I can't talk about what I was doing."

"Fascinating," he repeated, as if he had never before seen a specimen like me.

I left him to wonder if I was some kind of covert operative for the CIA.

Lelyveld, Stern, and I returned to New York and reported to Sulzberger that the *Times* had nothing to learn from Kochman. We did need to improve diversity, but it was up to us to figure out the best way to do it. I argued that if we took the money we were willing to pay Kochman and used it to hire more minorities, that expenditure would go a long way toward our goal.

Lelyveld had used me. He knew that despite my commitment to diversity, I was not about to buy into such a program. He also knew that having a black man criticize Kochman was the perfect way to drive a stake through the heart of the effort. Unfortunately, neither Sulzberger nor Lelyveld embraced my suggestion to commit the money that would have gone to Kochman to hire more minorities. Still, I believe it was wise for the *Times* to take a pass on the diversity guru.

––––––––

DESPITE THE increasing demands on my time as an AME, I made sure to travel abroad, especially since Lelyveld made clear that he saw my lack of a foreign posting as a deficit. Also at Lelyveld's invitation, I joined the International Press Institute, a group that promotes press freedom around the world. The IPI typically holds its annual conventions outside of the United States, so attending them gave me the opportunity to visit *Times* troops in various regions.

Once I went from Israel to Egypt to Frankfurt to Berlin to Paris and finally to Rome. As I boarded an El Al plane in Tel Aviv, a security agent reviewed my passport and travel documents suspiciously. She asked if I had been to the West Bank. "Yes," I replied. And Gaza? "Yes," I said again. And now you're headed to Cairo, Frankfurt, and Berlin? "Yes," I said for the third time. She summoned her supervisor, who summoned his supervisor. After much discussion, they let me go. But they upgraded me to first class, where a young, earnest man sat next to me. I had no doubt he was Mossad or some other type of security agent.

In 1994 I made an even more ambitious trip, first to Paris and then to Abidjan, Nairobi, Johannesburg, and Cape Town, for the IPI convention.

I was delighted to be in South Africa when the national leaders were implementing a new constitution and paving the way for elections. As I traveled the country, nearly everyone passionately debated what kind of justice or education or commerce system South Africa should create. I had never encountered the South Africans' level of engagement and excitement anywhere. I also heard a few whites share their fears about what would happen to them under majority rule.

Lelyveld and Sheila had given me a list of friends and acquaintances from their days as correspondents, and I spent much of my time in Johannesburg and Soweto hearing many of them describe their lives under apartheid. Their tales made my struggles at the University of Missouri seem infinitely smaller.

Cape Town reminded me of Santa Barbara, with mountains on one side and the ocean on the other. Nearly every place I went, people asked if I knew Michael Jackson. I took time out from the convention to attend a campaign rally held by Mandela's African National Congress, which reminded me of my old days on the campaign trail in the States.

I envied the *Times'* Johannesburg bureau chief, Bill Keller, whom I thought had a wonderful job. Keller had long been a foreign correspondent and won a Pulitzer when he was Moscow bureau chief. When we met, I suggested that he consider management one day. I argued that the newsroom needed someone with his leadership skills and that he could be helpful in changing the paper's culture. Journalists with his talents should not sit on the sidelines with so much happening in management.

Keller seemed disinterested and showed no real reaction. Little did I know.

10

JOY AND HEARTBREAK

In the mid-1990s, the National Association of Black Journalists was meeting in Nashville, and one evening Gerald convened a group of people to join him for dinner at a soul food place in the city. I was standing in the cafeteria line with my tray when this big voice somewhere behind me booms out angrily, for the whole restaurant to hear: "What are you doing serving that white man in here?!?"

I froze, and so did everyone else in the restaurant. When I finally turned around, there was Gerald, bent double at the waist and laughing so hard he was crying. The one person who did not get the joke was the woman behind the counter, who put her hand on her hip and fixed Gerald with a steely stare and said: "You shut up! He's a human being like everyone else and can eat here if he wants!"

—WILLIAM SCHMIDT

On June 29, 1996, I did something I doubted I would ever do again. Under a searing sun at high noon in the suburbs of Detroit, I got married.

Robin and I exchanged vows in the sprawling backyard of her mother and stepfather. A huge delegation came from the *Times*, led by Joe and Carolyn Lelyveld, and including Maureen Dowd; Bernie Weinraub and his wife-to-be, Amy Pascal; Soma Golden Behr and her husband, Bill; Al Siegal and his wife, Gretchen Leefmans; Mike Oreskes and his wife, Geraldine Baum; and Felicia Lee and her husband, Adolfo Profumo. I was surprised and touched that so many flew in and braved the heat.

Many of Robin's NABJ colleagues came, and some of those who could not afford the expense of an airline ticket carpooled for the ten-hour drive from New York. That meant the world to her. The guest list numbered more than 150 and included journalists from around the country.

Gary served as the best man, and Robin's sister Terri was maid of honor. Robin was radiant, and I marveled at how far we had come. Nothing in our relationship came easy, especially when I think of how I almost lost her earlier because I worried about newsroom perceptions. Unlike at my first two weddings, this time I had no doubts, no second thoughts.

We honeymooned at a quaint bed-and-breakfast on Mackinac Island, the historic landmark tucked between Michigan's Upper and Lower Peninsulas. Robin did not want to venture outside the country on some exotic excursion because she was five months pregnant. Since our first attempt ended in miscarriage the previous year, we could not be careful enough.

I admired my wife's attitude of "to hell with them" regarding those who gossiped about our private life. Our goal was three children—two biological and one adopted. I drew the line, however, when Robin wanted to wait until after the birth so she would have the proper profile in her wedding dress. I pushed her to move the ceremony before instead of after her due date of October 31. There was no way she was going to have my child without being married to me.

I also admired my wife's free-agent spirit. To her the *Times* was a job—not a way of being. I envied how she left her work at the office and found time for other pursuits, like outings with her friends and NABJ. And there were sides of Robin that she revealed to few, like how she was sexually abused by an uncle when she was a young girl, and how she managed to thrive in spite of the hideous psychological and emotional aftereffects. Few people knew that she was a Big Sister while living and working in Boston and remained close to Ghana, the young woman she mentored. Ghana was a bridesmaid in our wedding.

Having failed at two marriages, I was the last person to give advice on the subject. But failure taught me a couple of lessons. First, the relationship has to be natural. Second, you must truly enjoy each other's company. For once, I could not wait to get home from work. I wanted to see Robin, share our experiences of each day. Whenever she traveled, I was not myself until she came home. I was amazed at how often we saw a situation the same way, whether it was what takeout to order for dinner, what career move to make next, or how many children to have.

The first time I saw the sonogram image, I cried. At forty-five, finally, I was about to become a father. I had no idea what it really took to be a parent—or a husband, for that matter. My primary role, I thought, was providing for my family financially. I had a lot to learn, like putting the family first and making time to spend together, even when there did not seem to be enough, and drawing strength from each other no matter the challenge.

The August before Zachary was born, Robin and I took our third trip together to Martha's Vineyard, Massachusetts. We looked forward to the late-August ritual of loading up a rental car for the five-hour drive, then riding the ferry over from Cape Cod. We would rent a rambling house near the Atlantic or a Vineyard lagoon and invite family or friends to join us for a while. They came in shifts, and our two to three weeks were filled with languid days on the beach, long walks and bike rides, and nights with margaritas, grilled seafood, and movies or raucous card games. I cherished those trips; they more than made up for the Augusts of my childhood.

This particular year, a wild storm barreled up the East Coast, disrupting ferry service. Our departure was pushed back for two days after the lease ran out on our rental. Robin and I had encouraged our guests to leave before the storm, and we rode it out in the basement of the rental. Afterward, I ran around like a madman, searching for a bed-and-breakfast vacancy along with everyone else who was stuck on the island, while Robin, seven months pregnant and showing every bit of it, took it all in stride. In a way, the 1996 Vineyard trip was an omen of the life we were about to share: truly joyous experiences interrupted by nasty bumps.

———

WE NEEDED a name. We were never told but somehow knew it was a boy. I wanted the name to reflect my mother's maiden name and that of Tom Morgan, my fellow alumnus from the University of Missouri, who over the years had become a close friend. Tom, a respected newsman and a former president of the National Association of Black Journalists, was gay and had been battling HIV for years. I admired his strength and courage and his measured approach to life. Robin wanted her namesake, Robert, an uncle who died before she was born. I liked "Robert" too, because of my uncle in Harlem who had supported Gary and me through the years. We settled on Robert Thomas Boyd. But one day, Robin asked, "What about Zachary?" She argued that it conveyed energy and spirit, and fit a baby that at one time seemed to do backflips in her belly. Thomas and Robert were strong, she said, but almost too serious and sober. I dismissed her, partly joking: "I don't know any black people named Zachary." True to form, she did not press. Once she put it out there, she let it rest.

On November 4, the day before the presidential election and four days past Robin's due date, we went to the doctor's office to check in. The doctor saw that Robin was losing amniotic fluid and decided to induce labor. We headed to St. Luke's Hospital in Upper Manhattan, where we put into practice the weeks of Lamaze classes. Robin, determined to have the baby naturally, struggled through the night. Finally, the doctor grew worried about the baby's heart rate, and just after five in the morning, we were whisked into an operating room for an emergency cesarean.

My first view of our six-pound, eleven-ounce son came as he was pulled from his mother's womb. I cut the cord and held him gingerly. He wailed loudly while Robin and I wept silently, and I thanked her for bringing our child into the world. I then went into the waiting room and started dialing the twenty people on Robin's list of must-call family members and friends, and my brother and sister. I also put a call in to Lelyveld at the *Times*, where I heard that many colleagues were betting that I would find it impossible to stay away from the office on an Election Day. How wrong they were.

As voters went to the polls to send Bill Clinton to a second term, Robin and I took turns holding our boy. When the nurse asked what to put on the birth certificate, Robin gave me a sly grin and offered Zachary. She knew she had me. At that moment, I would have been happy to call him Godzilla. Our son became Zachary Robert Thomas Boyd.

———

ZACHARY RIGHTED my life. I never felt as much of a reason for being as I did once he arrived. Like all newborns, he changed everything drastically, and not just in obvious ways like the absence of a full night's sleep. More often than not, what a journalist sees or encounters inspires stories. In that sense, Zachary opened up a universe of coverage that I had paid scant attention to. Becoming a father meant discovering a world of cribs, strollers, and the extraordinary Diaper Genie. There were issues such as finding a pediatrician, securing a nanny, and when and how to think about preschool, which, in New York, starts almost immediately after birth. I became engrossed in subjects such as how children develop, pediatric medicine, education, and children's toys and television programming. In the process, I became a better editor.

I spoiled Zachary, trying to make up for what I thought my Christmases and birthdays lacked. Robin did her best to counter me. While I went crazy buying Zach far too much—for instance, at three, a telescope that could practically see Pluto—and suggesting elaborate birthday parties where the gifts piled high, she would stash many of the new toys away, doling them out over the course of the year.

While Zachary was still playing with building blocks and Legos, Robin and I were completing college-length applications and submitting ourselves to interviews to convince private preschool administrators that we were terrific parents with a brilliant son. Eventually we chose a private school on the Upper East Side, where Zachary quickly developed a rep as a smart, independent boy. He spent two years there.

I did not contact Harvard for an application, but I was as proud as any other parent who is convinced that his child is special.

Even at four, Zachary was precocious. He could argue with the best of them. Once he and I headed to the neighborhood pizza parlor for lunch, but Zachary wanted pizza from a different place, a few blocks farther away. When I told him that the nearest parlor was his only choice, he refused to eat. We returned home, and the debate began.

"You don't have to eat lunch," I proclaimed, recalling a childhood where that meal was a luxury.

"But parents have a responsibility to feed their children—and that includes lunch!" he countered.

I could only laugh. I do not remember how we resolved the standoff, but I was impressed with his argument and thought that he would make a great lawyer someday.

But his passion was clearly in the area of science, especially computers. By five, he knew the names of all the planets and that a nebula was a cloud of dust and gas. He was a master at strategy games like chess and played Monopoly as if he were Donald Trump. When I had a word processing or Internet problem, I would turn to him for help.

I carefully crafted a strategy for making our son a lifelong St. Louis Cardinals fan, like me. The key, I believed, was for him to become enchanted by the first ball game he experienced in person. So I waited for St. Louis to come to town, and we took the subway to Shea Stadium to see my hometown team play the Mets. Zachary was thrilled to be in the stadium, with his hot dog and cup of soda that was as huge as his head. But instead of rooting St. Louis, he cheered for the Mets. Of course he would, he explained, he was a New Yorker. St. Louis was some city out in the sticks; New York was a real city. He reminded me of when I was a child, reacting to my father's hailing from Itta Bena.

I never imagined just how difficult it could be to raise a child. I had fantasized that Zachary and I would solve our problems with thoughtful father-son discussions. I would impart knowledge, and he would listen and thank me for my wisdom. I quickly abandoned this whimsy. Once when we were in the grocery checkout line, Zachary kept picking up a piece of candy, and I kept telling him to put it back. But why couldn't he have it? he asked. *Why? Why? Why?*

"Because I said so!" I bellowed, ending the discussion. I had become my grandmother, stern and firm. I also used Grandmother's method of discipline, delivering a much-needed spanking on occasion. But the look of fear in his eyes and in Robin's reminded me that we could not teach our son not to use violence if we ourselves were violent. Besides, spankings did not seem to be effective anyway.

Despite the trials and occasional moments of terror, I loved being a father. Not long after Zachary was born, Robin and I talked about having more children. It was just a matter of when.

———

AFTER ABOUT a year of learning the institutional quirks, Martin Nisenholtz, the *Times*' digital czar, launched his own startup by publishing, updating, and enhancing the newspaper on the Web. His team's responsibility was to create a structure that could feed the site around the clock. That was the continuous news desk, made up of reporters and editors who worked only for the Web.

Lelyveld did not help the new venture; he reminded Sulzberger Jr. frequently that no Web operation was making money. But launching the newspaper onto the Internet was the publisher's passion as much as taking the paper national had been his father's.

It was not so important whether the public received the news from the paper or the Web, the publisher frequently said, as long as they received it from the *Times*. But even so, he did not want the institution to forge blindly into the Internet, given the costs and uncertainty of success. He favored an incremental approach. The company took small, "chewable" bites instead of large gulps as it had in 1993 when it forked over more than a billion dollars to an ill-fated purchase of the *Boston Globe*.

Lelyveld and Nisenholtz were old versus new at a time when the media landscape was rapidly changing. When the company began plans to offer a separate tracking stock tied to the value of Internet properties, a process that made many Internet startup executives wealthy, Lelyveld fought against a plan to award shares to senior editors. He wanted the shares kept in a common pool that he would distribute as he saw fit. He lobbied Sulzberger incessantly, but the publisher eventually said no. Editors would receive the shares, like other top executives.

Lelyveld could not hide his frustration as he announced the decision at a meeting of top editors: "For the first time in my career as executive editor, I have lost a fight with the publisher," he said. "He has decided that you will receive the options."

We all tried to appear as crushed as he was. But as we left the meeting, a senior editor turned to me in feigned pain and lamented how he would have to call his wife and tell her about Lelyveld's defeat.

"She'll be crushed that we now have money for a new kitchen," he deadpanned.

Nisenholtz soon became persona non grata in the newsroom, but I had grown fond of him and his efforts to get us to see a media landscape broader than newspapers. Robin and I had him over for Sunday brunch once, but I could not escape feeling like a traitor, knowing how much Lelyveld resented him.

In 1999 Nisenholtz was promoted to the post of chief executive officer of the new-media venture, formally called New York Times Digital. His rank and salary were a reflection of his growing importance within the company. He no longer reported to Lelyveld and had in fact become an equal. This only added to their strain.

As most newspapers did, Nisenholtz created a business model that gave customers free use of the site but required them to register to receive the content. By contrast, the *Wall Street Journal* charged users, generating instant income from its site. In the first nine months of 2000, New York Times Digital, which included www.nytimes.com and the *Boston Globe*'s www.boston.com, posted a loss of $46.2 million, while the *Journal*'s owner, Dow Jones and Company, posted a $37 million profit. But the *Times* had fourteen million users compared with the *Journal*'s five hundred thousand paid subscribers.

Nisenholtz's model needed time to work, and that meant the company would have to continue to carry his unit. But that October, as executives haggled about the best way to proceed, the stock market plunged. Investors lost interest in Internet IPOs, including the *Times*'. As Nisenholtz explained in announcing the pullback, "It went from irrational exuberance to unqualified pessimism." Like many other media companies, the *Times* and its Internet operation faced a grim financial future.

Eventually, Lelyveld began to come around. At a retreat of top executives, after a morning of discussing the *Times'* potential across various platforms, he finally offered his views. Speaking for the newsroom, he said he felt that others saw it and him as a fragile old man without the wherewithal to adapt to a new media landscape. He assured that crowd that he could adapt and exhorted everyone to challenge him and the newsroom to do so. The publisher was thrilled. Clearly, Lelyveld had become a worry, even if Sulzberger had not expressed it publicly. Lelyveld, in the presence of all, acknowledged that he was on board. Everyone heard the message and understood what it meant.

But Lelyveld had his limits. Sulzberger had given the executive editor the authority to block from the Web any content that he opposed, hoping that would appease him. Until election night 2000, Lelyveld never used it. On that night, however, when Lelyveld believed the site was declaring George W. Bush over Al Gore too hastily, he ordered the results removed. Accuracy mattered more than speed, he argued. In Nisenholtz's world, speed was everything. After that incident, the two men hardly spoke.

———

AT TIMES, I admitted it to myself: no matter how much we tried, I really did not know Lelyveld that well, and he did not know me. Although we spent countless hours together at the paper, and more time strategizing over meals and drinks or socializing outside the office, we did not forge what I would consider a friendship. I enjoyed his company, especially when we included his wife, Carolyn, a passionate spirit who wrapped herself around noble causes such as helping children with AIDS and improving public schools. Unlike her husband, she was always warm and at ease. I was not troubled, though; I thought Lelyveld respected me and valued my contributions enough to make up for any lack of warm and fuzzy feelings between us.

Early in 1997, I realized the depth of that respect. Gene Roberts was to end his three-year run as managing editor in September, and rumors started about his likely replacement. Lelyveld had begun a formal selection process, a news report said, which identified a short list of candidates that included me and Bill Keller, the Pulitzer Prize–winning Johannesburg bureau chief with whom I had met on my South Africa trip in 1994. Keller had left reporting and become the paper's Foreign editor, the same position Lelyveld held before being named managing editor. Naively, I did not regard him as a threat. I considered myself a seasoned manager who played a lead role in producing some of the paper's most impressive journalism. Beyond that, I had Lelyveld's commitment from three years earlier to make me his next managing editor. I found it hard to believe he would renege.

As the public guessing game ensued, I got a call from Mike Oreskes, my former deputy, who was now Metropolitan editor. Oreskes described a campaign to discredit my candidacy. Some colleagues were questioning my abilities as they tried to build a case for Keller. I dismissed the gossip but found myself taking stock of my standing in the newsroom. I thought about how much I had changed since the Colorado leadership program.

I realized that Oreskes's call had another purpose: to determine if I knew whether Lelyveld had reached a decision. If not, Oreskes still had time to throw his hat in the ring. That's how he operated. He was one of the most political people in the newsroom, something that I actually liked about him. I told him what I thought to be true: that Lelyveld had not made a decision and that I did not know when he would.

Oreskes's call made me crazy, though. I had had enough of speculation and decided to confront Lelyveld directly. In his office, I said that if there was a contest involving Keller and me or anyone else, I wanted him to give me the opportunity to share my vision and make my case. Lelyveld responded that he knew me well enough to make a decision without hearing me out. His words did not reassure me; he had already decided.

For weeks, speculation continued, and I became defensive and bitter. Finally, as we sat down for dinner in a pricey Midtown restaurant whose name I quickly released from memory, he delivered the news.

He confirmed that the contest had indeed come down to Keller and me. He had concluded that either one of us could do the job, which made the decision difficult. But he gave Keller a slight edge because of his experience as a foreign correspondent. Of course, I thought of Max Frankel's pledge that my lack of a foreign assignment would not be held against me, but this was no longer Frankel's paper. I heard Lelyveld out. He listed the many strengths of Keller and me before ending the suspense.

"So in the final analysis, I asked myself who I would name to take my place if I got hit by a bus," he said. "Whose name would be on my lips as I lay there dying? And the name that I heard myself speaking was Bill Keller."

The name felt like a dagger thrust into my gut. My emotions swirled together: hurt, betrayal, embarrassment, abandonment. But bitterness—bitterness reigned.

"I hope you don't get hit by a bus," I replied. And I rose to leave.

Lelyveld grabbed my arm and asked me to stay. If my performance did not warrant the promotion, I responded, I did not have much of a future at the *Times*. I surprised myself. Not once did I consider the consequences of what I was saying, only what was in my heart. At that moment, resignation made the most sense.

"So you mean that the only job that you would take at the *Times* is managing editor?" he asked. He was using an old management trick, one that he had perfected. He put the issue in my lap. I should be able to find another job at the *Times* that would make me happy, he reasoned. I explained that my reaction stemmed not only from being passed over for the job but also the embarrassing way the entire process unfolded, his commitment years before, and how I saw him as someone I could trust.

Lelyveld launched into his vision for a new management structure that gave more people beyond the top two editors real power. He wanted to name two deputy managing editors, a first. I would be one, in charge of news, and the other would be John Geddes, then the Business and Financial editor. Geddes would be in charge of operations. I said I needed time to think. Lelyveld welcomed that as a positive development.

On the way home, my mind reeled. I blamed myself for not getting the job. Surely, there was something in my DNA that made me unworthy. Obviously, I should not have assumed Lelyved would honor his commitment; maybe I should have threatened to resign if he chose anyone else. Maybe I should retaliate by claiming discrimination. I thought I had a strong case.

I was finally sobering up after bingeing on Lelyveld for almost a decade. Like most former drunks, I was not pleasant to be around. For the next few days, I stayed home in a funk, avoiding anyone from the *Times*. Adding to my disappointment was the feeling that I had failed Robin. Not just because she was my wife but because she believed me when I said that she too would reap rewards from her hard work at the *Times*. She tried to comfort me, but I knew the decision confirmed her worst thinking about the paper, especially regarding how it treated people of color.

I often wondered what path I might have taken had I left. But I buckled after a full-court press from Sulzberger, Lelyveld, and Keller. With the new title came enhanced responsibilities, the ability to oversee my own projects, and more financial security, or what some refer to as "golden handcuffs" that keep you shackled to a job that is not the job you want. In the end, I stayed primarily because I did not want to leave the emotional protection of the paper. I became one of the walking wounded, living out David Binder's prophecy: the *Times* had indeed broken my heart.

I sought out Raines for comfort. Over drinks, he offered his analysis: In selecting Gene Roberts as managing editor, Lelyveld wanted a father figure. In choosing Bill Keller, he wanted a brother. No matter how good I was, Raines reasoned, Keller met the definition of a brother more than I did. We were just too different. Raines's interpretation made as much sense as any, and I consoled myself by turning inward and to my family.

———

NO DECISION can be more liberating than the one to engage life on your own terms. That fueled my new sense of freedom, an unexpected consequence of Lelyveld's choosing Keller over me. For once, I was not preoccupied with office politics or climbing the ranks. Sure, my new title was in effect a consolation prize, and I was certain that I had gone as far as I could at the paper. But the clarity gave me a sense of relief. Journalism was still my calling, but what I did was not as important as who I was. More than anything, I saw myself first as a husband and father.

In their own ways, both Robin and Zachary taught me about balance, something I had never appreciated. Now there was more to my life than just work. When I came home from work, Zachary really did not care what kind of day I had. He wanted attention, and so I would manage to fold myself onto the floor to play a game or watch one of his TV shows. At night, Robin and I would alternate reading to him. I cherished those moments that I never had with my parents.

Robin and I worried about Zachary. He would come home from his exclusive preschool telling of how his classmates summered in Greece and enjoyed birthday parties with live animals and acrobats that must have run into the thousands of dollars. "Where do we summer, Mommy?" he asked. "Detroit" was her response. Another time, as Robin's mother struggled with a reluctant seatbelt to buckle Zachary into her SUV, Zachary suggested, "Grammy, just get a new car." We were horrified. His experiences did not reflect our values or what we wanted him to learn. We started searching for a school that did.

From the day Zachary was born, Robin and I entered the complicated world of affluent black parents who had grown up in black communities steeped in traditional black experiences. That world was one we knew and valued and regarded as vital in defining who we were as adults, including our success.

By contrast, Zachary did not know that world. In his Upper East Side neighborhood, where few African Americans live, he was one of only a handful of black children in his entire private preschool. Nearly all of his classmates were white, and all of his playdates were with white children. We did not push him to befriend the few children of color in his class; we did not want to force relationships on him.

Once as I tucked him into bed, Zachary surprised me by declaring that his hair was ugly.

"What do you mean?" I asked.

"You need long, straight hair to be pretty," my four-year-old said. "And I don't have long, straight hair."

His remarks shook me. He was already influenced by Madison Avenue's view of beauty. We had to do something. We bought books about African American heroes and made sure that a trip to Atlanta included a visit to the Reverend Dr. Martin Luther King Jr.'s old neighborhood and museum. The two of us spent a father-son weekend in Washington, D.C., where we lingered on the steps of the Lincoln Memorial and I tried to explain in terms he could understand the 1963 March on Washington and what it meant to be black in segregated America. At home, Robin and I made a conscious effort to offset the negative messages he received about blacks. I never expected this would be a part of my parenting so soon, but I saw that no matter how young, no matter how innocent, children could not escape the disturbing aspects of race relations in our country.

We began looking at schools with two primary concerns: that Zachary receive a solid education and that he experience a diverse student body. He did not need exclusivity; he needed to feel a part of the real world.

We visited a public school for gifted children in our neighborhood. Robin and I were both products of public education, and we believed in it greatly. But passing though metal detectors and having security guards wand us dampened our enthusiasm. We tried to imagine how our son would feel entering the security gauntlet each day. And we asked ourselves: even at a school for the gifted, would he get the best education possible in a class of twenty-eight with two teachers, no matter how hard the teachers tried?

Robin visited a top East Side public school outside our district, where administrators were nonetheless eager to make room for the child of a senior *New York Times* editor. But she made an alarming discovery. She saw few black and brown children in the main classrooms, but disproportionately more in a special education class, in a tiny room with few windows and dim lighting. We wanted no part of such a segregated system.

We settled on a private school a few blocks away that satisfied our concerns. It was founded in the mid-1960s on the principles espoused by Dr. King. Its class sizes were small by public school standards—sixteen to twenty students—with a teacher and a teacher's assistant. What impressed us most was its diversity—about 40 percent of the student body was minority and at least 75 percent of the students received financial aid to help pay the annual tuition of fifteen thousand dollars.

Although we cringed at paying more for a year of elementary school than the cost of attending many state universities, we felt comfortable with our choice.

Still, the school was far from perfect. It defined diversity in terms of race, gender, and ethnicity but not in terms of thought. Zachary learned in atypical ways. And he constantly debated his teachers, asking why something had to be done precisely as requested. He was a challenge. We began to get negative reports—can't stay in his seat, interrupts the teachers, disrupts the classroom, won't wait his turn—regularly.

In some ways, though, we were heartened by the influences of his new school. When Zachary was around six, we held a book party for a friend in our house. As the evening wore down, Zachary announced that he wanted to sing a song he had learned at school. The crowd encouraged him, and Robin helped him up onto the bench at our kitchen table. Zachary closed his eyes, and with all the force he could muster, belted out the Negro spiritual "O Freedom":

And before I'll be a slave
I'll be buried in my grave
and go home
to my Lord
and be free.

For a moment, everyone stood in silence. Eventually our awestruck guests gave Zachary an ovation. I fought back tears. Not only was my son unafraid to express himself but he also knew who he was.

————

MY FINAL break with Lelyveld came over Robin. She was deputy food editor when Lelyveld decided to remake the feature sections. She and her boss, Trish Hall, threw themselves into the project, and after Hall left the newspaper, Robin filled in as section editor with her sights set on the job. After about six months, Lelyveld decided to name as section editor Rick Flaste, a longtime friend and former *Times* colleague who had helped redesign Science *Times* and other sections. Lelyveld brought Flaste, who was white, back with the mandate to oversee the redesign project that Robin had helped develop.

Robin decided that she would rather not be deputy to a new boss to implement her ideas. At the same time, she received an offer to become a senior editor at *Essence*, the popular black women's magazine. She knew she had a lot to contribute, and the idea of working for the top magazine in its genre appealed to her greatly.

She met with Lelyveld as she considered the offer. He said that if she wanted to work for a magazine, she could join the *Times*' Sunday magazine, where he would make her a junior editor. He said he had not heard of *Essence*, and at lunchtime, he went out and bought a copy. He then tried to convince her that she was too talented to work for such a publication. The more he talked, the more determined Robin became to leave.

He missed the point entirely. *Essence* spoke to two issues she cared deeply about: blacks and women. There was no need for further conversation. To Lelyveld's amazement, Robin left the *Times* for *Essence*.

———

IN 1998 we decided to stop renting and buy a brownstone in Harlem, which was sputtering back to life as people priced out of better neighborhoods in Manhattan sought more spacious and affordable housing farther uptown. Robin was enchanted with the idea of living in the historic epicenter of black American culture. I was leery of being a pioneer at age forty-seven. Harlem had come far since the crack epidemic had subsided, but it still lacked many services—such as good grocery stores and taxis available right at your street corner—that we took for granted.

After months of searching, we could not find a place in Harlem that we could agree on. Our broker pointed us instead to a rundown brownstone on the Upper East Side. The price was far more than Harlem houses but a fraction of what other homes in the neighborhood cost.

Our new home, a former rooming house two doors down from the estate of Andy Warhol on Lexington Avenue, was four stories of padlocked doors, 1960s appliances, flaking, lead-based paint, and threadbare carpets. It had termites, asbestos, ancient plumbing, shoddy wiring, holes in the ceilings and floors, and forty years of stuff that the seller had piled in every corner and crevice. It also reeked of urine from the seller's many cats—we counted at least six. Its sorry state was the only reason we could afford it.

We hired a well-known architecture firm, fumigated the place, and plunged into a gut renovation. Each week we visited the "dirty house," as Zachary proclaimed it, to follow the contractors' progress. Over two years we watched as our bank account was depleted but our eyesore gave way to an elegant home that was a reflection of the life I had always wanted.

Lelyveld was eager to see the place, and despite my reservations, I invited him and his wife, Carolyn, to visit a few months before we were to move in. Robin suggested we make an afternoon of it: first a tour, then brunch at our apartment, which was nearby. On a pleasant spring day, the Lelyvelds met us at the house, where they had to enter from the back alley because the front entrance was still boarded up. Just as Robin opened the door for them, the handle fell off. We carefully led them through the dusty interior, past sawhorses and piles of construction material. It was clear that much work still needed to be done, but Robin gamely described plans for colors and how each room would be used.

Carolyn Lelyveld graciously asked questions, but Lelyveld seemed completely uninterested. After we finished, as we stood outside on Lexington Avenue hailing a taxi, he finally shared his impression.

"Well," he pronounced, "it's a dump."

"Yes, but it's our dump," I responded, trying not to show how much I resented his thoughtless comment.

Much to my amazement, the next day, he shared his assessment with others in the newsroom. I would never again invite him into my home.

11

THE OUTSIDERS

It was spring 1998. I was summoned to Gerald's office for what I assumed would be a career-crumbling experience. A day earlier, I had spoken up in a brainstorming meeting for the race series about a story idea that I thought was uninteresting. Absentmindedly, I asked, "Who's brilliant idea is this?" The answer: "Mine," Gerald said.

Most pitches were fascinating, except for a few, including Gerald's, about two bureaucrats, one black and one white, and how their worlds did or did not intersect along racial lines. I thought the idea was boring and said as much. Less than twenty-four hours later, I was asked to see him in his office. I was prepared to dust off my resume. But the opposite happened.

Gerald said he liked the way I had spoken up in the story meeting and thought I had a lot of terrific ideas. I was astonished. "I can't speak for all black people," he said. Then, "How would you like to be an editor on the project?" I had been on the paper for less than two years, and only as a reporter. No matter, Gerald said. He had confidence that I could both write the story I had been assigned and be an editor on the project. He loved thoughtful discussions and did not mind being challenged. And he believed in giving people big opportunities to push themselves and to succeed.

That was not the only time that Gerald believed I could do something before I was sure. Even without assigning himself as a mentor, Gerald had a way of mentoring anyway.

—DANA CANEDY

I'd always thought that it took more courage for Gerald to do the race series than for me. There are plenty of white editors at the *Times* but very few black editors. And Gerald was the one black editor who had climbed the ladder the highest.

Failure was not an option for him on a project about race. But it was a threat. Often we would retreat to my office and wonder if we would ever get through the series successfully. Tough editing problems stretched as far as we could see. With fifteen reporters, fifteen photographers, and a half dozen editors spending precious time on this story, we knew the *Times* was making a huge commitment, and we were out on a limb that could come crashing down before we finished.

Gerald set a tone of openness that was remarkable for him. We knew from the start that we would have to use ourselves to show our writers and editors the kind of detail and depth we sought. He talked about his childhood, and his days at college, when he wore a big afro and a dashiki. Many on the team were quite surprised by that. At the *Times*, he did not seem to be a rebel, even though he was a pioneer.

He was not always easy to work with. He liked to zig and zag: sweet Gerald on Monday, combative Gerald on Tuesday. Some times both Geralds in one day or even one hour. That kept people off balance, which some found unpleasant. He once tried to explain this behavior to me: "What do you expect from a black man who grew up poor on the streets of St. Louis?" I took that to mean that he couldn't really trust a lot of people, especially white people.

We were lucky. I don't think any other two editors, black and white, would have had the power, experience, and trust at the paper to do what we did. Neither one of us alone could have done a great series about race, and we both knew that.

—SOMA GOLDEN BEHR

"I FIND you intimidating," declared Jane Gross, a diminutive veteran reporter.

We were gathered in Soma Golden Behr's Upper West Side brownstone, a group of black and white reporters and editors, discussing racial attitudes. I had asked Gross to share her thoughts about me as they related to race. This was not a request that I had ever made of a white person, much less a member of my staff.

Her jolt of honesty came as our team spent a day mulling over how the newspaper could shed light on race in America. A candid answer was risky: it could offend not only a boss but colleagues as well. When Gross saw me, she said, she saw an intense-looking black man. She found that vision intimidating.

I applauded her openness even as my heart sank. As a ranking editor and newsroom leader for ten years, I prided myself on being open and available. Those lessons from the Colorado "charm school" were not lost on me. I insisted on having a desk in the newsroom, close to staff, as well as the one in my office. I made a point to walk the room, exchanging ideas with reporters and editors. But Gross painted a strikingly different picture. Each time I played back the conversation, I thought, *When does a black editor become just an editor?*

That was just one of the questions I struggled with as we sought to tell how people live, cooperate, and negotiate conflict through the prism of race. It was one of our most challenging ventures ever. While the paper produced some of the best journalism in the world, examining corporations, governments, and other powerful institutions, it was not nearly as effective in covering race. No matter what their race or background, most reporters and editors simply don't know the subject well enough. One time, senior editors grappled with the significance of hip-hop, a major artistic, social, and economic force. The discussion was so naive that we dropped the subject. When the megastar Selena was killed in 1995, white senior editors, ignorant of her significance, had to be convinced by a minority journalist to move her obituary to page one.

Emboldened by the success of "Children of the Shadows," Soma Golden Behr and I had begun a search for another big idea to explore. Lelyveld was encouraging, promising us some of the paper's best reporters, photographers, and editors once we had a solid idea. I wanted to focus on race, but I knew it was difficult to explore; because it weaves through issues like education, employment, justice, and religion, getting sidetracked is easy. Other news organizations had tackled the issue, some quite well. In fact, the same year that the *Times*' Metro staff won a Pulitzer for coverage of the 1993 World Trade Center bombing, the *Akron Beacon Journal* won the award for examining racial attitudes in its community. For the *Times* to engage the issue, we had to be original.

As Golden Behr and I started meeting with reporters and editors, we asked them a basic question: what should the *Times* be writing about race? Ideas ranged from looking at the criminal justice system to an examination of whether America was evolving into a country where racial identity no longer mattered.

On the day of the O. J. Simpson verdict in 1995, as public reaction divided almost universally along racial lines, I took note of the parade of lawyers, academics, politicians, and others debating the outcome on television and in print. These kinds of race-related dialogues— How could blacks be celebrating? Why were whites outraged?—were missing in everyday settings. Really, the Simpson verdict had little to do with the story of race in America. He had wealth and fame and could ignore the wounds that other African Americans felt. I knew the story of race in America would be found in the silence about race in America.

W. E. B. Dubois had said a hundred years ago that the problem of twentieth-century America was that of the color line. That still held true in the late 1990s. Sure, more blacks had climbed into the middle class, thanks to the courts, higher education, and a general shift in societal norms. Still, a gap as wide as an ocean persisted, with nearly one in three black men between the ages of twenty and twenty-nine in the country's criminal justice system and with the ranks of the poor still swollen, disproportionately, with black single mothers and their children. At the same time, people of color had become tired of trying to explain themselves to whites, and whites were increasingly tired of listening to what many considered whining. We were at a racial stand-off. We had to coexist, and so we did, silent but assuming and misunderstanding one another. This was at the core of the interracial struggle that described the story of race in America. I wanted to capture that struggle, to show how and why people rarely share their true feelings across racial lines, and the costs of that silence.

The concept seemed simple, but it would take hard work to deliver. First, we had to delve into our own racial hang-ups. We had to be honest with ourselves and with one another. None of us had ever done this kind of work before. We decided to host "off-site" meetings, where nearly two dozen of our best reporters and editors gathered to determine what stories to tell and how to tell them. I knew that Golden Behr and I would have to take an active role in getting the discussion started, as the project leaders. If we opened up, we hoped, others would follow suit.

For the first time ever, I told colleagues about my experiences with race, starting with working at Cooper's Market. I told about racial incidents in college and throughout my career. I felt vulnerable sharing what I considered racial slights, such as when *Times* colleagues called me by the name of another black person, or how I always scanned the room when I entered, in search of another person of color. I did not care if whites considered me overly sensitive. I wanted them to understand why blacks think about race so often. Whether they are discriminated against or ignored or feared, they know the reaction is probably triggered by race.

Fortunately, our strategy worked. Slowly, colleagues began to open up as well.

Jane Gross was one of the first to speak. She mentioned how little journalists interacted across racial lines and shared her delight in having dinner with a black reporter new to the staff, Ginger Thompson. Gross described the evening as quite special because it was one of the few opportunities she had to engage a black colleague. I asked Thompson to share how she regarded the dinner. She said she had thought little of it; she had wanted to learn about the *Times*, not necessarily to connect with a white reporter. In fact, she considered it work and was glad when it ended. I thought the exchange was priceless.

I returned to explore Gross's other point, that she found me intimidating, even though I rarely dealt with her. Was it my voice? My expressions? My skin tone? I asked if she felt that way about other black editors, singling out Dean Baquet, then the National editor, whose skin was lighter than mine. Gross said she felt more comfortable around him. The words stung. But we were there to be honest. I could not help but wonder if her honesty reflected a pattern. Was this how whites saw blacks in authority? Blacks in general?

Janny Scott, another white reporter, told how she was raised in a life of privilege in which she was cared for by black nannies, both facts she was uncomfortable sharing with her black colleagues.

Don Terry, from the Chicago bureau, was one of the most militant reporters on the staff, a feisty black rabble-rouser who seemed to see everything through the lens of race. Terry, who argued vehemently that Tawana Brawley was indeed assaulted, stunned everyone in the room when he shared that his mother was white and that he had two white half-brothers.

Terry's father, an actor and a labor organizer, had met his mother during the civil rights era. In their own ways, both had instilled in him the importance of fairness. His interactions in the newsroom were often driven by this notion, much more than by race. In his mind, for example, Brawley should have received the same benefit of the doubt from the grand jury that she would have if she were white.

The exercise exhausted nearly all of us. But we were convinced that we were on the right track. Next came the harder work: figuring out how to say what we wanted to say.

We did not want to replicate what had been done before; no polls of public attitudes or comparing opinions and "expert" voices. We decided to tell the stories of real people and to let their finite experiences, woven together, give a bigger picture of the problem. The approach is known as narrative journalism. We would focus on a minority and a white in a similar situation and then explore their lives, assumptions, and attitudes across racial lines.

The key to this approach was access and trust. We spent weeks and, in some cases, months searching for subjects who would cooperate. We needed people who felt comfortable opening their lives to a reporter for as long as we needed. More than a few times, after weeks of work, people would back out abruptly. Finally, we had to avoid judging our subjects, no matter what we heard or saw. We knew that the reporters and editors involved had their own biases. We had to find a way to ensure that those biases did not interfere with the narratives.

We identified potential areas, such as corporate America, the military, the church, politics, education, and journalism, and then sought access to people with viable stories. We soon added less obvious areas, such as Hollywood, a former plantation run by a black female manager in the Federal Parks Service, and hip-hop. At the last minute, we added a story at the urging of Mireya Navarro, a Latina writer on the project. We explored how blacks were interacting with Latinos, the fastest-growing minority group, through a federal set-aside program.

We conceded that we all had racial bias. To identify them and filter them out of our stories, we established a new structure for editing, starting with a biracial team of editors who queried and guided reporters. One black reporter, Dana Canedy, proved so insightful that I assigned her to edit as well. Instead of having reporters simply conduct interviews and then write their stories, we asked them to pause repeatedly. After each round of interviews, the editors quizzed the reporters not just about what they were finding but what they were feeling and why.

Editors challenged reporters who were quick to judge their subjects. One black reporter, Steven Holmes, suggested that the black army sergeant he was writing about cared little about his family or the value of education. Holmes described the sergeant's white counterpart in glowing terms. In interviews with the editors, Holmes made it clear that he did not like the black sergeant. He explained why: the black sergeant told Holmes he did not like to read books other than comics. When Holmes arrived for an interview, he said, the sergeant sternly ordered his wife and children out of the room. Holmes was shocked to see the man treat his family that way.

Only when Holmes delved deeper into both sergeants' backgrounds did he gain a richer picture of the men. In the end, we showed them warts and all, full of the insight that comes only from months of reporting and thinking.

Another reporter refused to go back to his subjects. He insisted that his first draft was a complete portrait, and he challenged my professionalism for demanding more. I removed him from the project. He was the exception.

After two years of planning, reporting, photographing, and editing, the series of fifteen stories, "How Race Is Lived in America," ran from June 4 to July 16, 2000. One, "A Limited Partnership," resonated with me the most. Amy Harmon, a business reporter, wrote about two men, one black, one white, launching an Internet company. They were good friends and cookie-cutter images of each other. They were both married, with two sons each, similar educations, and similar careers. They were both driven.

The two men were once partners in a new Internet company that they sold in the late 1990s, making them both multimillionaires. To raise money for the business, one of them had to become the CEO, the face they presented to potential investors. They agreed without discussion that the white partner would take the title, despite the fact that it was the black man's idea that had launched the business. The black man went along with it, but he struggled with the decision. After the partners sold the company, the black entrepreneur charged into a new Internet venture in which he could be CEO. It was as if he still had something to prove.

Of all the stories in the series, this one made me cry. I saw the black man's experience as a tragedy that garnered far less attention than our racial differences: the impact on everyone when no one talks honestly about race. I knew of other minorities who sold themselves short by making decisions that seemed expedient. I had done the same thing myself. But the success always comes at a price.

I had also seen how many minorities still believed that they could not be true to their heritage and succeed. "Don't make that mistake," I would often tell young journalists of color. "You are not simply a darker version of your white colleagues." If they were afraid to lend their insight on topics that they knew more about because they were ashamed of their background, I would tell them, they were of no use to me or to journalism in general.

I knew from whence I spoke. For years, I saw the struggles of my forebears as a source of embarrassment rather than strength. There is no need to be arrogant about it, but people of color who have overcome incredible odds should ask themselves how many of their white colleagues could have succeeded if they had been raised by a single parent or had grown up on welfare or attended schools with large classrooms and overwhelmed teachers. How many could have made it with no one looking out for them, pushing them forward whether they were ready or not, and helping them look beyond failures to something more?

After her story ran, Harmon and I talked repeatedly about the enormous pressures that blacks in power felt. She said she had never considered those experiences before she began the project. I hoped her work had the same effect on her readers.

———

REACTION TO the series was widespread and overwhelmingly positive. Invitations poured in for reporters and editors to appear in public and talk about race. Golden Behr and I and other team members went on the Charlie Rose show and traveled to Cambridge, England, to discuss race relations in the United Kingdom. We also attended a gathering hosted by the South African ambassador to the United States and participated in more than a dozen discussions at universities and with civic groups across the country.

The most meaningful event was our appearance before colleagues in the *Times*' auditorium, which was filled to capacity. For two hours, we frankly discussed our experiences with the project and some of the paper's failures to deal with race. I would never forget the gathering's candor. I left believing, perhaps naively, that part of the answer to racial misunderstandings was something as simple as honesty.

Personally, I took that answer to heart. The project greatly enhanced my relationship with Golden Behr, my partner and the woman who had once been my boss. We had much in common as trailblazers, the first black and the first woman to lead major departments. We were promoted to the masthead on the same day. We had worked together on major projects that received wide acclaim. I knew her family, and she knew mine. But until the race series, we had never had a straightforward discussion about race. As the project progressed, the middle-aged Jewish woman and middle-aged black man repeatedly shared their attitudes, fears, and concerns, and even the occasional non-PC joke. She revealed, for example, how seeing a group of black teenagers approaching her on a dark street made her apprehensive. I could make the same claim, I told her. I shared the isolation and pressures I often felt as a first black editor, and the issues she raised were not much different from mine. Over common ground, a relationship built on professional admiration and respect deepened into a genuine friendship.

As we received congratulations and, in April 2001, a Pulitzer Prize in national reporting for our work, it was not lost on me that my own experience in journalism and at the *Times* could have easily been a part of the series.

———

IN MY thirty years in newsrooms, no one ever called me a nigger. I know that some of my white colleagues saw me that way, especially in the heat of anger. That muzzled anger represents the troubling side of race in our country. Far more often than not, honesty across racial lines disappears in a vacuum between open-minded, civil discourse and smoldering rage rooted in uninformed assumptions. The causes go deep into the tortured history of a country that has been built on the backs of people of color who were tolerated and not embraced.

The institution of journalism also bears a responsibility. Knowledge of other cultures should be a prerequisite for anyone entering the business. Any decent journalist starts with a core of general knowledge. In newsrooms, that core assures that we all have enough smarts to produce a newspaper. Everyone knows not just who is serving as president but governor and mayor as well. In New York, they know that the city has five boroughs and that the least populous is Staten Island. Knowing the basics unites those in the profession, permitting a verbal shorthand when they discuss stories as well as the importance of one story over another.

Yet there are no penalties for ignorance about race and ethnicity, about blacks, Latinos, Asians, or Native Americans, their histories, and their cultures. And journalism provides little incentive to learn; that knowledge is not considered a necessary part of the job. The ignorance produces misunderstandings, often from assumptions made by whites with the best of intentions, but assumptions nevertheless.

I first saw this in the newsroom at the *Post-Dispatch*. Because the paper had a scholarship program for blacks at the University of Missouri, many whites on staff assumed that Sheila, my first wife, who had graduated from the university, was a scholarship recipient, like me. She had to correct that perception repeatedly. To Sheila, it was not a slight to be lumped in with the scholarship group, but doing so ignored the story of her father, who often worked two or three jobs, and her mother, who worked as well, to send their daughters to college. It ignored the fact that she got there just as most white people did. Assumptions that ignore the whole story are at the root of one of journalism's ultimate sins: a lack of intellectual curiosity.

African Americans' journey into the nation's newsrooms mirrors that of their forebears in the country: they have been tolerated but rarely embraced. In the 1960s, when riots erupted in major cities across the country, news organizations faced a critical shortage of blacks on their staffs. White reporters were attacked by rioting blacks who saw them not as detached observers doing their jobs but as part of the oppressive establishment. So newspapers recruited practically anyone black who worked for them, including janitors, copyboys, and receptionists, to go into troubled areas and report the news. Oftentimes, the black reporters turned their notes over to whites, who then wrote the stories and got the bylines.

The 1970s marked a turning point. Once in the profession, blacks wanted to do more than turn over their notes. Those were the days for celebrating firsts. When the *Post-Dispatch* sent Bob Joiner to an out-of-town assignment, blacks at the paper took enormous pride in the show of trust in him. When Charlayne Hunter-Gault went north to open a Harlem bureau for the *Times*, the move attracted national attention.

The few blacks who moved beyond local staffs to become national and foreign correspondents—among them Judith Cummings, Paul

Delaney, Les Payne, and Tom Johnson—were applauded throughout black journalism circles. The final hurdle that journalists of color faced was management. In those days, news organizations recognized that they needed to have minorities for fair, more balanced coverage, and getting and keeping them meant devoting attention to them. White managers did not go overboard by any stretch, but some provided support to let blacks know that they were wanted. Those blacks who showed real talent were coveted like precious art or real estate; someone was always offering them better or more rewarding jobs.

While the *Times* hired blacks as reporters and gave a few prized assignments, there was no clarity of approach or sense of urgency to promote them or to hire enough of them to reflect the growing diversity of the city or country. Few blacks on staff seemed happy as they adjusted to a climate of fierce competition and fear, one in which career-making decisions were unpredictable at best. One day Sheila worked for Metro; the next, she was named to the Foreign staff, all because Abe Rosenthal enjoyed one of her stories. One day the paper celebrated the appointment of Paul Delaney as the first black deputy National editor; the next, it passed him over and gave the job of National editor to someone else.

In 1995 Angela Dodson, the paper's ranking female black editor, left the paper. In the winter of 1996, she filed a discrimination complaint with the city's human rights commission against her bosses. The allegations of racial and gender bias damaged the paper's reputation among minority journalists and sucked time and energy from top editors as we spent countless hours preparing to testify. I was shocked and saddened that Dodson's lawsuit named me as one of those who discriminated against her. Eventually she settled out of court as management embarked on repairing the paper's image.

The paper could be highly defensive when criticized for the lack of minorities in coveted reporting slots and other positions of power—"The *Times* is racially blind," "We make our decisions based on merit"—but was agonizingly slow to respond with solutions. The message from the top was to diversify, but without a plan, diversity remained a concept rather than an executable strategy. And editors had their pet justifications for blocking hiring and promotions; when challenged they often responded with the paper's typical arrogance: "We need to do what's best for the paper," they would argue, as if hiring or promoting a person of color could not possibly be what was best for the paper.

I pushed against the waves of indifference or outright defiance by focusing on two goals: incremental advances, one person at a time, and long-term strategies, such as a more thoughtful approach to recruiting. Success came in spurts, two steps forward and one back.

By the time I became a manager, I could look back and see progress, reflected in numbers and assignments, even though not always in attitudes. Not only were there some journalists of color in management but others held coveted assignments in Washington, on the National staff, or abroad. The latter was especially important, because that had been the career path of whites who became top editors.

Even so, by the early nineties, the paper was far from achieving the kind of diversity that Max Frankel once described as critical mass. Across the country, veteran journalists of color were leaving newsrooms, no longer having the drive or energy to push for change. Some abandoned mainstream news organizations altogether, like my former *Post-Dispatch* colleague George Curry, who left the *Chicago Tribune* in 1993 to edit a short-lived but provocative general-interest black magazine called *Emerge*. Some threw their efforts into teaching or writing, or reinvented themselves in foundations, public relations firms, or the government.

Real progress at the *Times* came by the mid-1990s, once top editors became more imaginative in their approach toward minorities. The paper stepped up its presence at minority conventions, sending scores of high-level recruiters, including Sulzberger Jr., to mingle with potential talent. Then Lelyveld instructed the paper to create an internal mechanism for developing its own minority talent. The paper, like other news organizations, would grow its own crop of *Times*men and -women by establishing a reporter-trainee program, followed by an internship program. Both programs gave young minority journalists a chance to show they could succeed. When prized staffers considered other offers, the *Times* countered with a decent raise, a bonus, assurances from top editors, or other incentives. Lelyveld made commitments to some minority staffers that if they remained they would receive choice assignments or promotions.

The efforts improved diversity and the morale of many at the paper. But they probably added to the smoldering anger of whites on staff who believed that minorities received special treatment. It was a ridiculous argument, since far more white journalists were handled in precisely the same way because of favoritism.

Addressing the racial imbalance was one of the paper's most profound struggles. I was no expert, and nothing had prepared me—not Cooper's or college or even twenty years in the business—for the battle to bring diverse backgrounds and perspectives to the paper, to make a diverse group of people feel welcome and valued. But in its own way, each of those experiences made me aware of injustices and the need to address them. I never backed away from this fight. In fact, I stepped to it whenever I saw the opportunity, as if I were Uganda X, tempered by time.

———

PERSONALLY, I always felt that my colleagues never judged me on merit alone. I accepted this fact, but it hurt, deeply at times. I wanted them to understand that I was motivated by the same desires and fears that motivated them. But I did not believe that being a journalist meant abandoning my blackness.

I often found myself in no-win situations. People projected their best and worst experiences on me. If their career was going up, I was an inspiration. If it was headed down, I was a jerk, or worse. If the unhappy person was black, I was an Uncle Tom, a sellout, unwilling to help a brother or sister out. The truth is, I believe I encouraged and supported all good journalists who worked hard, regardless of race, ethnicity, or sexual persuasion. Anybody who wanted a free ride knew not to look to me for help.

And for those who wanted to indict the *Times* on issues of race, I was an easy target. For example, columnists and pundits accused me, the black Metro editor, of sanitizing the paper's coverage of the 1991 riots in Brooklyn's Crown Heights, in which blacks attacked Hasidic Jews after the death of a black boy. One problem with this account: at the time the stories ran, a white editor made the calls. I was vacationing on Nantucket and had nothing to do with the coverage.

On another occasion, I participated in a journalism panel with Gay Talese, the former *Times* reporter and noted author. I was quite honored to join the dapper writer and told him so, explaining that reading his book *The Kingdom and the Power* in high school helped inspire my interest in journalism. As the event wore on, Talese blasted the *Times* newsroom for what he described as liberal bias in covering racial issues. Then, oddly enough, he accused me of killing a front-page picture of a black-and-white couple exchanging vows in Selma, Alabama, because it championed interracial marriage. I responded that as Metro editor I lacked the authority to make such a call. But for the record, I said, the photo did not merit the front page because interracial marriages were no longer so unusual.

Later, the writer Jim Sleeper recounted Talese's story, identifying me by name, in a book he wrote about liberal bias in media. It was one of my first experiences of being attacked unfairly and inaccurately in print, and it would certainly not be my last. If a white person was spreading a falsehood about a black person, the assumption seemed to be, white was right and there was no need to verify the story with me. I asked a *Times* lawyer to let Sleeper know he got the story wrong. To my knowledge, the writer never corrected the record.

Over the years, I became less surprised and more hardened by the accounts that attributed racially motivated decisions to me, most of which could never have happened because the *Times*' hierarchy would not have allowed them. Yet because the subject involved race, the accusers—usually white—could take leaps of logic with impunity.

———

ON A pleasant March morning in 2001, I joined Arthur Sulzberger Jr. for a private breakfast. So much was happening at the newspaper and the Times Company that it was difficult to determine the purpose of our meeting. I knew that Lelyveld had already told Sulzberger that he planned to step down as executive editor in September. At the same time, Matt Storin, the editor of the *Boston Globe*, also owned by the *Times*, had announced his retirement plans, and a search was under way for a replacement. Two key editing jobs had to be filled, as well as other top positions, once the dominoes started to fall. I sensed that something good would come my way.

As we ate oatmeal and sipped coffee, Sulzberger came to the point. He was speaking to me wearing two hats: the publisher of the *Times* and the chairman of the Times Company. As publisher, he led the search to replace Lelyveld. As chairman, he would help find a new editor for the *Globe*. He wanted to know if I was interested in becoming the next editor of the *Globe* or if I preferred to remain in New York to pursue the managing editor position, the logical next step up from my post as deputy managing editor. While offering nothing officially, he dangled two highly attractive options. I could hardly contain my joy.

After all my struggles and hard work, after all of the uncertainty about my future, I had a realistic chance of either running a major newspaper or being in one of the top two positions at the *Times*. For years, little else had mattered.

But now I had accepted that I could do great journalism regardless of whether I ran a newspaper or not. With my life so much richer because of Robin and Zachary, I was finally having the conversation I always imagined having. It was a shock to realize that I was within arm's reach of a prize that I had stopped coveting.

I thought about how little I cared for Boston, the city where I had lived as a Nieman fellow two decades earlier. I could not go there even if that decision would mean missing a chance to run a good newspaper. I could not see myself leaving New York, I told Sulzberger. And after a decade in senior newsroom management at the *Times*, I said, I knew where the bodies were buried. I could identify problems and help fix them.

By staying in New York, I was taking a big risk. Replacing Lelyveld had become a contest between Howell Raines, now editorial page editor, and Bill Keller, Lelyveld's managing editor. While I was considerably closer to Raines than to Keller, I had no assurance that Raines would choose me as his managing editor. As for Keller, I had no clue about how he felt about me or my abilities. He had always been a difficult read.

Keller enjoyed Lelyveld's unflinching support, and Lelyveld was acting as a kind of campaign manager, leading an intense and continuous lobbying effort with journalists, executives, and others arguing on Keller's behalf. Meanwhile, Raines was hard at work on his own campaign. The debate was not about who was the better editor, since both were highly competent, Sulzberger said. He had to consider other important factors, among them management style, what direction they wanted to take the newsroom in, and whom they would appoint to their senior management teams. As I saw it, the paper had never had such a fierce competition for the top post.

Sulzberger sought my assessment of both men. I told him that I was much closer to Raines but that I respected Keller. When he asked who would make a better executive editor, I immediately said Raines. I felt that Raines was a stronger leader and would bring more passion and energy to the newsroom. Moreover, the newsroom needed a shot in the arm, I told him, and that could best come from new leadership. Over the last decade, it was led by Frankel and then by Lelyveld, who carried on Frankel's vision, just as Keller would undoubtedly carry on Lelyveld's. This pattern stifled new thinking. While Keller would make a fine executive editor, compared with Raines, it really wasn't a contest, I said.

It seemed the publisher had already reached the same conclusion.

———

AT 4:00 P.M. on May 21, the staff assembled to hear Lelyveld praise his replacement as a wonderful journalist and leader, as well as a wonderful writer.

"I feel very easy about the future of this newsroom," he said as a beaming Raines looked on. He had kind words to say about Keller, but they hardly registered. Everyone was consumed by the upcoming transition.

I heard from my friend immediately. No sooner than I had sent a congratulatory note, Raines wrote back that he wanted to talk to me. Two days later, we walked to a restaurant near Times Square, where we had a heart-to-heart. As always, the conversation came easily, especially when he said that I was at the top of his short list of candidates to replace Keller as managing editor.

Although he was a highly visible presence at the newspaper as editor of the editorial page, Raines had not worked in the newsroom for almost a decade. He was on a steep learning curve, and he sought my thoughts about the challenges he faced. I did not sugarcoat my concerns. I said the newsroom was adrift without clear lines of authority. Many well-paid senior editors felt out of the loop and were not contributing. My biggest concern was that I saw some staffers as complacent. Despite some aggressive reporters, many seemed to tread lightly. I recalled how the paper responded to the death of Korey Stringer, the Minnesota Vikings offensive tackle who collapsed of heat stroke at a practice. While *USA Today* dispatched a reporter to the scene immediately, the *Times* did not. No one saw the need to pounce on a story, and far too often we were chasing rather than leading our rivals.

I added that there seemed to be a disconnect between the paper's strategic goals and its journalism. For example, the Web site had not received nearly as much support as it needed from the newsroom. While the paper's readership had become increasingly national, publications like *USA Today*, the *Wall Street Journal,* and the *Washington Post* had improved their presence with national sections such as Sports, Business, and National news. This threatened our franchise. Raines seemed to hang on my every word.

Raines drew me into the thick of the change that he wanted to bring. Every few days, he invited me to his office on the tenth floor to answer more questions or hear his latest strategies for shaping the paper. Lelyveld and Keller were now lame ducks. It was jarring to see how quickly their power dissipated.

About a month after announcing Raines's appointment, Sulzberger made history by naming Gail Collins, a sharp-witted columnist on the *Times'* op-ed page, the new editorial page editor—the paper's first woman in that position. Her selection surprised many because she had been at the paper for only six years. Raines had lobbied strongly for her; the appointment was another sign of his growing influence with Sulzberger.

Nearly two months after Raines's appointment, he called again, inviting me to dinner. I eagerly accepted. On the evening of July 25, a Wednesday, I smiled broadly as we greeted each other in the lobby. We climbed into a town car and headed across town to the Four Seasons restaurant. Clearly there was to be more to this dinner than usual.

In private, Raines can be quite sentimental. He said he had chosen the Four Seasons because it was where Abe Rosenthal had taken him to offer him a major promotion years ago. He wanted me to enjoy a similar memory, he said. Once we were seated with a round of martinis—his vodka, mine gin—he began with an apology. He was sorry he had taken so long to reach a decision, but he had to consider other candidates. He said that I shouldn't have read anything into the delay, because he never had any doubt about his first choice.

That said, he offered me the position of managing editor.

Reaching across the table, he placed a blue Tiffany box in front of me. Inside was a silver key ring with the clasp in the form of a fish, in keeping with his hobby of fly-fishing. He showed me that he had an identical key ring, and said they should represent our connection. We would operate as a team, he said, and there should be no air between us.

The cab ride home took forever as I eagerly looked forward to sharing the news with Robin. I arrived at our newly renovated and decorated brownstone and could only smile.

"We got there," I finally managed to say.

As always, Robin kept me grounded. "Honey, I love you, and I'm so proud of you," she said after we embraced. "You really deserve it, and I know you're going to be a great managing editor. Now please take out the garbage."

———

ON THURSDAY, July 26, Robin and I arrived at the *Times* building and proceeded directly to Raines's office on the tenth floor, where the publisher joined us. As we all rode down to the third floor where the staff was assembled, I held Robin's hand to steady myself. I knew I was becoming not just the paper's managing editor but its first black managing editor. I had thought about how to acknowledge the moment in history, along with what I saw as my obligation to the paper and the staff.

Raines's remarks touched me.

"Gerald has strength," he said. "He has spine. He has gentleness. He has a deep, deep commitment to the ideals and values of the *New York Times*. And I know he will be a worthy steward of those values. I believe Gerald will be a strong link in that timeless chain of *New York Times* quality, integrity, and commitment."

We embraced to strong applause. As I prepared to speak, I spotted a group of *Times* Scholars, college students who had overcome disadvantages and obstacles and won four-year scholarships from the

company. I had helped start the program a few years before and had
been actively involved during the first years. I looked in their faces and
saw my story all over again. I fought back tears as I found Robin's face
and composed myself.

I spoke of my loyalty to the *Times* readers, to the staff, and to Raines.
Then I noted the significance of my appointment. "I hope tomorrow,
when some kid of color picks up the *New York Times* and reads about
the new managing editor, that kid will smile a little and maybe dream
a little bigger dream," I said, ending my remarks. "That's all I'll say
about first-ness."

I had a piece of unfinished business. A few weeks after the announcement, I had dinner with Lelyveld. Once again, the evening was awkward.
I told him how I believed that his contest with Raines had created a
Times culture war with two distinct camps that forced people to choose.
It was tough for me to choose, I admitted. While I owed Raines more
than I could ever describe, I also appreciated what Lelyveld had done
for me. No matter what had happened between us, I said, I wanted him
to know how I felt. It was my way of saying good-bye.

Less than a week later, Raines and I made our first trip together as
the new top editors-in-waiting. We went to Atlanta to meet with about
a half dozen national correspondents. The trip started as an occasion to
glad-hand, but it became much more. We had not even begun our new
jobs, but our first meeting was a harbinger of what we would encounter.
It was not good.

We left New York on a Friday morning with Rick Bragg, a national
correspondent, and Katy Roberts, the National editor and Bragg's
supervisor. At a dinner, Raines set the tone. He expected a more energetic National staff, with correspondents traveling more throughout
the region. He also railed against excuses, arguing that the work came
first. I sat there with a sense of déjà vu. The old Raines who had shaken
up the D.C. staff as deputy bureau chief seemed to have emerged from
a long respite in the ivory tower of the editorial department. Before the
evening ended, it was clear that his goal would be easier to articulate
than to achieve.

When he talked about the need to travel, some reporters raised
family issues. Others saw his comments as an attack on the staff and

became defensive. When Raines singled out Bragg as his model national correspondent, some bristled. They saw Bragg as arrogant and self-promoting. He was the last person they wanted to emulate.

We did not realize it then, but the disconnect went to the heart of the problems that we would soon encounter. Journalism was no longer the rough-and-tumble profession that it had been when I started, when a city editor could shove me around. Instead, like other occupations, it had become a profession in which the staff insisted on balancing their careers with their personal lives. Granted, these were veterans who did their jobs impeccably. We knew they would be warmly welcomed at other newspapers if they were not happy at the *Times*. The shift made the job of managing them far more demanding because reporters would say no to assignments as often as they said yes.

Roving national correspondent? Why? challenged one reporter, arguing that using the Internet instead was often more efficient.

That would be difficult, said another, a recently divorced father, because of his duties as a dad. His editors would just have to accept his terms.

The dinner was the first time I experienced a feeling that would revisit me throughout my tenure as managing editor. I felt caught between Raines's vision, which I shared, and how he went about making it a reality. We both wanted the paper to change, but on this occasion, and many others, he would be so hard charging and heavy-handed that his message would get lost in the force of the delivery. So the next morning, I fell into a new role: the peacemaker, the fixer, the person who would circle back to repair the damage. In one-on-one follow-up sessions, I tried to smooth some of the sharp edges that the dinner created. I assured the correspondents that they mattered, despite the tough talk. In private, I began to caution Raines when I felt he was pushing too hard. Sometimes he listened; sometimes he did not.

Neither of our approaches netted the results we wanted. Over the next six months, nearly a third of the correspondents would leave the paper. Raines was sanguine about the departures, reasoning that they gave us room to hire replacements to our liking.

———

IN LATE August, two weeks after the Atlanta trip, I traveled to Orlando for the annual convention of the National Association of Black Journalists. For us, the event was a family affair. Each year Robin and I would go with separate agendas: she as a chapter president, national officer, and committee member—even once as an expectant mother— and I as one of the *Times'* top recruiters.

But this trip was different. I was to receive the association's Journalist of the Year award for my work leading the race project. And in a few weeks I would take the helm of the *Times* as managing editor. When Robin and I walked into Disney World's Dolphin Hotel to check in, the black journalists who mingled in the crowded lobby broke into spontaneous applause. Those I knew and some I had never seen before showered me with handshakes, congratulations, and good wishes. I had never experienced anything like it, and I was touched.

The looks from many whites at the conference reflected the usual curiosity. I could tell they wanted me to show right away why I was the highest-ranking African American in the *Times'* news department. In other words, they expected me to prove why I got the job. Over the years, I had become skilled in meeting this expectation. At this point, I ignored the probing looks. I had nothing to prove.

At the awards ceremony, I was introduced by Dana Canedy, the sharp editor from the race project who had become a dear friend to Robin and me. I accepted the NABJ's Journalist of the Year award on behalf of my colleagues at the *Times*, and also acknowledged Sulzberger Jr., Lelyveld, and Golden Behr for her work with me on "How Race Is Lived in America." I also cited Raines for having the "good sense" and courage to choose me as his managing editor.

After the ceremony ended, Raines pushed through the crowd that surrounded me, and we embraced warmly. Words were spoken, but they were unnecessary. In the background, I saw Lelyveld, standing with other colleagues, smiling. He was on the outside looking in at what we represented, a new era at the *Times*.

12

THE GREATEST STORY

A true story: Sometime in the early 1990s, I was surprised to see the mythic and enigmatic Gerald Boyd listed as a panelist at a New York Association of Black Journalists seminar. The topic? Fellowships. I had never met him and was eager to hear what he had to say. Everyone on the panel was polished, professional, prepared, their credentials impeccable.

When it was time for Gerald to speak about his time at Harvard, one of our most revered academies, he cleared his throat and in his St. Louis lilt he shared: "Well, during my time with the Nieman, I mainly became addicted to *All My Children.*" There were uncomfortable chuckles and one laugh from the gut. That was mine. The remark, I would learn as I came to know him, was quintessential Gerald. Then he quickly shifted gears and silenced the room with his candor about what it took to get to the Nieman and to the *New York Times.* He implored us all to love what we do, to identify a great story, and to hone the skills to execute it.

Since that time, I came to know him better through my enduring friendship with his wife, over warm gatherings at their home, and when I read an early draft of this book. But that NYABJ panel remained with me because he never changed. He knew that what mattered more than anything else in journalism was the truth, regardless of the subject, audience, or time.

—PATRIK HENRY BASS

W E SHOULD not have been leading the newsroom that day. Raines and I were supposed to take charge in mid-September. But like so many issues, even the transition was caught up in the culture wars. As Raines explained to me, Lelyveld sped up his departure by a week to underscore his disappointment that Sulzberger had rejected Keller as executive editor. So Lelyveld made his last day September 3, 2001. The newspaper hosted a huge sendoff in his honor at the New York Public Library on September 5, and Raines and I began our new jobs on September 6, a week ahead of schedule.

Five days later, on the morning of September 11, I was sitting in a barber's chair on Amsterdam Avenue about sixty blocks north of the office. It was a gorgeous day, with the kind of weather that leads people to play hooky and head to the beach for one last taste of summer vacation. The sky seemed infinite, winds were calm, and the temperature was in the low eighties. At eight thirty, the barbershop was not crowded, so I got a seat right away.

I had already dropped off Zachary at school that Tuesday before I headed across town. Arthur and Gail Sulzberger were throwing a dinner party that night in honor of Raines and Gail Collins, the new editorial page editor. Robin and I were among the invited guests. For me, haircuts always preceded important events, so I was sticking to my routine, getting my hair cut before I headed to the office.

This morning, I sat back and let the Haitian barber do his work. If not for the dinner plans, I thought, it would have been a good day to slip out of the office early, head home, and throw a couple of thick steaks on the grill for dinner. Around eight forty-five, the barber was about halfway through my cut when a man stuck his head through the doorway and shouted, "Hey! Did y'all hear about the plane that crashed at the World Trade Center?"

I bolted from my seat.

"What are you doing?" my startled barber shouted as I fished in my pocket for money to pay him. "I not finish!"

"Man, I gotta get out of here," I said as I shoved a crinkled twenty at him and strode toward the door. I was still wearing the smock.

"I not finish! I not finish!" he kept repeating. I was out the door, and he was on my heels, clippers in hand, still trying to get me to come back. I snatched off the smock and tossed it at him and ran toward the subway stop at 103rd and Broadway.

I figured I could make it to Midtown at rush hour faster by subway than by taxi. My mind raced as I descended the stairs, trying to calculate how many minutes it would take for the train to get to Forty-second Street. Seconds felt like hours. Passengers filled the station trading rumors about what was happening downtown. After a few minutes, it was clear that no train was coming. As I headed back upstairs, I heard a voice on the public-address system announcing that all service was suspended. I was desperate.

I frantically searched for a taxi. It was not more than ten minutes since I had first heard the news in the barbershop, but it felt like days. I just had to get to the *Times*.

I saw a gypsy cab coming—a sedan that picks up passengers primarily in poorer neighborhoods or where few taxis go. I took a deep breath and stepped in front of it, holding up my palm for him to stop. The driver screeched to a halt, cursing at me out the window.

"You gotta take me to Times Square!" I shouted.

Before he could respond, I reached in my pocket and waved forty dollars in his face. He snatched the money and told me to get in, calculating, I'm sure, that it was almost four times the normal fare.

I pleaded with him to get there as quickly as he could and promised to pay any speeding tickets. As he raced down Broadway, I asked him to put the news on the radio. I also asked his permission to light up. I avoided smoking in cars because it made my clothes reek. But at that moment, I needed a cigarette badly.

Fifteen minutes and one harrowing ride later, I was in the newsroom.

———

I REMEMBERED February 1993, when a bomb exploded in the north tower at the World Trade Center, killing six people and wounding scores more. Even before I got to the newsroom on September 11, I knew the damage this time would be much more severe and the casualties much, much higher. I switched into gear, bringing all my instincts and experiences into play.

No matter what else we did that day, I wanted to make sure that I kept the newsroom focused and that we did not publish anything that would prove to be false. In the chaos of covering a breaking news story, I knew, the opportunity for errors soared.

In the 1993 attack, false speculation marred some of the initial coverage from other news organizations. Two years after that, when a truck bomb destroyed the federal building in Oklahoma City, the initial assumption was that the explosion was the work of Islamic extremists. That proved false when Timothy J. McVeigh and Terry L. Nichols, Americans who by no stretch of the imagination were Islamic extremists, were charged and convicted of the crime.

I did not want us to leap to conclusions about the nature of these attacks. I did not want mistakes to blemish our report.

As I arrived in the newsroom, reporters were already being dispatched to cover the disaster, even though the nature of the story was still a mystery. Raines was not in yet. I assumed he was on his way. Several senior editors gathered in my office, and we watched television in disbelief as United Airlines Flight 175 crashed into the south tower. When the second plane hit, we knew this story would be different from any that we had ever covered. First, American Airlines Flight 11 and now, eighteen minutes later, United's 175. This was no accident but an orchestrated attack. Somebody was using jumbo jets as missiles. But who and why were question marks.

At 9:08 A.M. the Federal Aviation Administration banned all take-offs and landings through New York City airspace. The Port Authority announced that all bridges and tunnels into Manhattan were closed.

The borough was isolated, with no traffic allowed to come or go. At 9:17 A.M. the FAA announced the grounding of all commercial airline flights.

At 9:30 A.M. President Bush announced that terrorists had attacked the United States, the first official clue to the kind of story we were covering. But his words told us little. As we batted theories around, we already faced the first of several important decisions. Many reporters and photographers were already scheduled to report to points around the city in preparation for the primary election that day. But with this huge story growing bigger by the minute, something had to give. We scrapped the primary coverage and decided to devote the entire A-, or first, section to the breaking story.

The decision meant two things: the *Times* was all but abandoning coverage of elections in a year when the city was voting for a new mayor, and the news would displace premium advertising at a cost of one hundred thousand dollars per page, or two million dollars a day. For years, the *Times* had given the executive editor, and in his absence the managing editor, the authority to throw out advertising to accommodate news when a major story broke. It was part of the paper's culture, dating at least back to World War II. If a plane crashed or the Berlin Wall came down or a president was shot, advertising made way for news. Every editor moved up the management ranks with some version of that history embedded in his or her mind. That philosophy of putting news first is part of what separates the *Times* from other newspapers.

The business calculation was that part of the losses from ad sales would be offset by gains in circulation. Typically, the *Times* gains readers during a major news event. Later, we would learn that the newspaper sold an astounding one hundred thousand additional copies each day in the first week after the attacks.

Raines arrived just after the second plane hit. He came to my office and asked for a briefing. We had lots of information to share, but few real facts. The next decision—how many reporters and photographers to assign to the story—was easy. Everyone available.

We needed time to sort things out, but the story did not give us a chance to pause. Next, an American Airlines flight from Washington to Los Angeles crashed into the Pentagon. The scope shifted from local to national.

Around 10:05 A.M., as we watched the television sets in horror, the south tower of the World Trade Center collapsed. The story grew exponentially. On a given weekday, about fifty thousand people worked in the towers, and hundreds of thousands of visitors passed through. We knew that thousands of fire, police, and emergency service workers were also on the scene. And our staff was directly affected. Some lived in lower Manhattan, some near the Trade Center. We had no way to know where our staffers were or if they were safe.

We were no longer detached witnesses to breaking news. Sarah Slobin, a graphics editor, was at the scene and raced to escape as the first tower fell. Barry Meier, a Business reporter who lived downtown, walked into the office covered with ash. I instinctively reached out and embraced him and asked if he and his family were all right. Then he headed off to tell the Metro editors what he saw.

Several reporters and editors were so disturbed that they joined the human exodus leaving Manhattan across the Brooklyn Bridge that morning and did not return to work, some for several days. But no one suffered physical injuries, a minor miracle considering the dozens of staffers living and working in lower Manhattan.

My insides were churning. President Bush had begun the day at a school in Florida and was now aboard *Air Force One,* zigzagging across the country with no announced destination. I recalled the times I had flown on *Air Force One,* with its elaborate security and communications gear. It always seemed invincible. If the president's security detail feared for his safety, I thought, then no one was safe.

I went to the phone to call home. I had only half listened that morning when Robin told me her schedule for the day. She too worked in Times Square, running *Essence* magazine's Web site. But did she go directly to the office? Zachary was in school far uptown, but was he safe? Was he aware of the terror gripping the city? The line was busy. Initially I took that as a sign that Robin was home, on the phone. But each time I called, I got a busy signal. I felt I had to do something.

For a reason I can't explain, I felt compelled to leave the office and dash around the corner to the Chase ATM. I withdrew several hundred dollars from our checking account. I had no plans for the money, but somehow I felt reassured that the cash would help me take care of my family in an emergency.

It was madness. While ash rained on thousands of dazed New Yorkers escaping lower Manhattan, the White House and the Congress were being evacuated to "secured" locations, as one report said. Then came a report of a fourth plane crashing in a field in Pennsylvania's Somerset County, about eighty miles southeast of Pittsburgh.

By the time the north tower crumpled at 10:28 A.M., elements of the story were obvious. The United States was a target of terrorism. There was an unquantifiable loss of life. The attacks paralyzed the nation, grounding airlines and closing Wall Street. Fear and grief hung like heavy clouds. Television made us relive the tragedies, repeating the breathtaking images of crumbling towers, horrified onlookers, employees leaping to their deaths. Over and over and over.

It was time to put out a newspaper, to tell a wounded nation the significance of the attacks and the extent of the damage.

Shortly after 11:00 A.M., senior editors assembled in a windowless conference room on the fourth floor to begin shaping the coverage. Nearly every major news desk—Metro, National, Washington, Foreign, Science, and Business—was involved in some aspect of the story. For me, the biggest challenge was how to coordinate this unwieldy report.

I led the meeting in two stages. First, I asked desk heads to convey what they had learned. One by one, they went around the table briefing everyone. Editors in the Washington bureau, vital to the coverage, reported over the speakerphone. Then I went around again and asked editors what specific stories they had to offer.

I scheduled the meeting in two parts to avoid getting bogged down in discussions about individual stories before we were clear about the overall picture. It was important to make sure that the editors were seeing the same forest while their reporters focused on the trees. I followed that routine whenever the *Times* faced a major news event, trying to make sure we always saw the forest first.

When it came to the trees, I wrote down the "slugs," the titles of stories, on a yellow notepad, along with the names of the reporters writing them. Typically, there are about three stories to a page, along with illustrations or graphics or pictures. We had enough slugs that day for at least twenty pages of stories. In effect, the *Times* was producing the regular *New York Times* and a special paper within the regular paper. All by a deadline of about 10:30 that evening. Fewer than twelve hours to go.

Most of the slugs were obvious stories. There is always the "lead-all," the main story in the upper-right-hand corner of page one. In a major news event, the lead-all is where a reader can get the gist of what happened and what it meant, just from reading one story. The front page might have more interesting or entertaining stories, but the lead story was the most important news of the day in the view of the executive editor. This particular lead-all would have a "banner" headline stretching across all six columns.

Both Washington and New York were shaken—those were stories. So was the human toll, including the victims and the survivors, and the loved ones desperately searching for answers. So were the president's day and the reason the towers collapsed. And the airlines—would anybody ever get on a plane again? The nation's transportation system and business infrastructure were in turmoil. All important stories.

I kept turning back to an editing exercise that I had learned from my earliest days in management. I wanted us to examine everything we had and then ask a basic question: what could the *Times* do to provide additional value to its readers? There should be something in our newspaper that readers could not find anywhere else.

The exercise always led to several important questions: Had the paper assigned its most polished and sophisticated writers to the major stories? Were all the angles covered and adequately staffed by the best reporters? Would readers find a well-reasoned analysis of what happened? What had we missed? Was the package compelling not just in words but also in images? Were there better ways to tell some stories graphically?

That morning gathering was the first of a half dozen similar meetings over the next few hours. We assembled again and again to discuss stories and to see pictures and graphics and page designs. No issue was too small. Somebody ordered lunch and dinner. For weeks afterward, the newsroom would provide meals to the staff.

With the city closed to incoming and outgoing traffic, it was impossible for many reporters and editors to get to the *Times* building on West Forty-third, so we labored without several key members of our senior leadership team. One was Andrew Rosenthal, who had just started his new job as assistant managing editor. In that position, his responsibility was to help shape the daily news report. Looking across the Hudson River to the Manhattan skyline from New Jersey, Rosenthal could see the smoke and ashes from the towers. But when he raced up the turnpike, he found the tunnels and the George Washington Bridge closed. Another key editor, Al Siegal, the dean of assistant managing editors, tried to hitch a ride across the Hudson with the Coast Guard, to no avail.

As the hours raced by, it was as if we were in two worlds: one of the trained professional, trying to perform under incredibly trying conditions, and the other, the same frightening and confusing place inhabited by every other terrorized American.

In both worlds, rumors flowed nonstop. At one point, speculation sped through the newsroom that Times Square was the next terrorist target. One of the most obvious hits in Times Square would be the *New York Times* building, but we would not evacuate the paper solely because of rumors. Everyone soldiered on as if there were nothing to fear.

I knew that Raines was leaning on me. Despite his years preparing for the job, until five days ago he had not been in the newsroom in nearly a decade. There were nuts-and-bolts realities that were new to him, including production issues and what reporter or editor or photographer was best for a particular assignment. Raines filled the role of commander-in-chief but relied on my judgment and let me do my job. Instead of barking orders, he listened and asked questions, then shared his views. We settled into a comfortable dynamic in which I managed the details while he focused on the big picture.

The staff was magnificent. More than a hundred reporters were working the story in New York and Washington. Other reporters fanned out across the country in places like Boston, Chicago, Atlanta, and Shanksville, Pennsylvania. Foreign dispatches came from places like Cairo, Jerusalem, Kabul, Berlin, and Moscow. Editors stayed in constant contact, exchanging information and relaying new developments up the chain.

Just before 4:30 P.M., I finally reached Robin. She had been trying to call me, too, but the thousands of calls into and out of New York overwhelmed the telephone systems. She had sent me an e-mail—our cable Internet was still working—but I had not thought to check there.

Robin explained that she had never made it to work that morning. After learning of the attacks, she went to Zachary's school to pick him up, just as other parents did throughout the city. Zachary's school let out early, around noon, and the two of them spent the day at home, where she listened to the radio with the volume on low. She did not turn on the television, to spare Zachary the frightening images.

Once I heard her voice and knew that she and Zach were OK, I turned my full attention to the report. By four thirty, when the senior editors again assembled in the conference room to review the stories and choose those for page one, the major news event was fewer than eight hours old. Throughout the day, thousands of words were written and filed, dozens of stories edited, and twenty-five pages designed and paginated. The photos—hundreds of them—were riveting. A freelance photographer, Kelly Guenther, was near the World Trade Center and managed to capture United Flight 175 moments before it crashed into the south tower. We saw flames shooting out of the tower just as the jet slammed into it. There were images of stunned and bloodied survivors and ordinary people staring upward in disbelief, victims leaping from the towers in desperate attempts to live, and dazed pedestrians wandering ghostlike through the streets.

Around 8:00 P.M., two and a half hours before deadline, Paul Winfield, a deputy news editor, sat at his computer and typed the lead-all banner headline: "U.S. Attacked." It was simple but powerful. Raines approved it right away. Headline writing is one of the most underappreciated aspects of newspaper work. It is an art form, governed by rules that take years to master. Good headlines, for example, should not duplicate the first or last paragraphs of a story. They must fit into whatever space is allocated. Writing a head is like putting together a puzzle of words, tone, and nuance, often with minutes or seconds to spare. At the *Times*, editors who write the headlines for the stories on page one are some of the most experienced and talented at the paper. Because I had started out as a reporter, headline writing was never one of my responsibilities. And despite my rank, it was not a job I could perform without years of training. Even then, I would have not been as skillful as Winfield. He was one of the best.

The next couple of hours raced by as the first edition deadline approached. Shortly after 11:00 P.M., as Raines and I inspected a copy of the A-section, it was obvious that we had produced a paper for the ages. We had faced the biggest challenge in our lifetime as journalists, and we had met it.

Even so, we still had to get the *Times* to our readers. The eight hundred thousand newspapers distributed in the New York region are printed at plants in College Point, Queens, and Edison, New Jersey. Since Manhattan was closed to incoming traffic, Sulzberger Jr. and others on the business side of the paper brokered special arrangements through state and local officials to allow the delivery trucks into the city. Their deal brought the *Times* and other local newspapers in by police escort sometime after midnight.

Now it was time to turn our attention to tomorrow. We were all mentally and physically exhausted, but the paper dated September 12 was behind us. Raines and I rounded up those editors still in the office to discuss next steps.

It was after 2:00 A.M. when I finally left the *Times* building, along with Raines, Soma Golden Behr, and other masthead editors Carolyn Lee and Tom Bodkin. The streets, normally bustling with traffic and pedestrians at any hour, were almost deserted, except for the occasional occupied taxi and National Guard troops with their automatic rifles. The Guardsmen stood in front of a military-recruiting post on an island between Seventh Avenue and Broadway. The scene was unnerving.

With the subway still closed, for a moment I thought I would have to walk the fifty or so blocks home. Raines walked south in search of a taxi downtown, and the rest of us, who all lived uptown, stood on the corner where revelers gather on New Year's Eve, trying to decide what to do. Fortunately, we spotted an unoccupied cab, and after promising the driver a huge tip, we all piled in for the trip uptown. He dropped each of us off, one by one. I was his last passenger.

When I opened my door around 3:00 A.M., I realized that it had been almost twenty hours since I left home. I had always felt a high from finishing a job, an experience that most journalists can relate to. Completing an assignment on deadline was invigorating, no matter how much the work exhausted me. But not this time. I simply wanted to see my wife and kiss my son and sleep.

Robin was waiting for me in the doorway. We embraced in silence. It seemed no words could do justice to the day or our emotions. So we just stood there, holding on to each other for I don't know how long. Then we went upstairs to check on Zachary. I slept hard for those precious few hours; at 7:00 A.M., I was up and ready to go again.

For days afterward, during quiet times in the office or lying in bed late at night, I would dwell on one unanswerable question: what was the last second like for those who perished? What had the firefighters, police officers, and rescue workers thought as they realized that their attempts to save lives had brought their own deaths? What were the thoughts of the passengers and crews on the hijacked planes, especially those who fought valiantly on the plane that crashed in Pennsylvania? And what about the hundreds of other victims trapped in the burning Twin Towers? What did they think and feel in their final moments?

Clues surfaced in descriptions of last-minute telephone calls between victims and loved ones. I lingered on their final words, near tears.

––––––

WE WERE prepared to cover this story like no other paper. The terrorists struck primarily in our backyard. We had hundreds of reporters available for duty. The Washington bureau, about forty-five reporters strong, followed developments in D.C. We had staff members with the highest expertise covering every aspect of the story, from the impact on Wall Street and Broadway to the physics behind the collapse of the towers.

The paper was fortunate in other ways. In January 2001, the *Times* had published a three-part series, "Holy Warriors," that combined the work of Stephen Engelberg, the head of investigations, and reporters Judith Miller and Craig Pyes. The articles were prescient about the terror network of al Qaeda, its leaders, and Osama bin Laden, including his desire to attack the United States. The earlier knowledge gave the paper a huge advantage in writing with authority about the terrorist group. The paper was also one of a few with a reporter, Barry Bearak, in Kabul, Afghanistan. That was invaluable because of the close ties between that country's ruling Taliban and al Qaeda.

Raines challenged the staff to produce a special type of story for the section. The idea was refined by masthead editors into the kind of overview typically found in newsmagazines. The articles, known as "All Known Thought," were at Raines's insistence reported, written, and edited in just a few days or less and often ran a page or longer.

At a meeting several days after the attacks, senior editors struggled with how to package the voluminous terrorism report. Keeping the report in the A-section meant keeping premium advertising out to create open pages. It was a costly decision.

Fortunately, Tom Bodkin, an associate managing editor in charge of design, provided an answer. By combining two other reports into one section, the paper could make room for the terrorism package to have its own section. The A-section could return to its normal configuration of foreign and national news and expensive ads. Bodkin also suggested that the combined reports, Metro and Sports, each have its own front page. If we printed one of the reports upside down, readers could then flip the section and find the other with its own front page. It was ingenious. Raines immediately embraced Bodkin's ideas, and Sulzberger Jr. nearly fell out of his seat when he heard the "flip" proposal. It was bold, clever, and solution-oriented, three characteristics that appealed to him.

The new section, called "A Nation Challenged," debuted on September 18, one week after the attacks. The section, with its title supplied by Al Siegal, perfectly captured how the country had transformed itself and chronicled how it continued to change over the next few months. But what anchored the section, what gave it its humanity, was the feature in which we profiled the victims, known as "Portraits of Grief."

The portraits stemmed from conflict and ingenuity. One morning after the attacks, Janny Scott, a Metro reporter who had contributed to the acclaimed race series, argued with her editors to give more space to stories about the victims. Scott, one of the most unassuming yet talented reporters on the paper, was interviewing families of victims. She was convinced that they wanted to tell more about their missing relatives. As they talked, Christine Kay, an assistant Metro editor, refined the idea. The team would write about each victim, they agreed, but instead of covering the arc of lives from start to finish as traditional obituaries do, they would focus on one revealing anecdote about each person. The result was more than 1,800 vignettes that appeared over several months and attracted a huge public following. This simple concept produced some of the most powerful journalism ever to appear in the *New York Times*.

The new section represented the best of what the newspaper could be when everyone pulled together. "Portraits of Grief" was perhaps the most popular feature in the section, but it was just one of many smart efforts from all parts of the paper.

———

SHORTLY AFTER the attacks, Sulzberger, Raines, and I visited Ground Zero. It was a ghost town, barricaded, and deserted except for police officers, Guardsmen, and construction crews. We wandered around the site where time stood still. Cars sat where they had been crushed on that Tuesday, and heaps of ash and dust still coated everything. On the front of one building was a hand-painted sign with a single, chilling word: MORGUE.

But it was the papers that left the most powerful impression on me. Thousands of pieces of paper strewn about the ground, snippets of real lives, work, and daily routines that were no more. It was not just what we saw that was so painful but what we knew no longer remained. In so many cases, the scraps were the only signs that people in those buildings and on those planes existed.

In the days ahead, I worked eighteen- to nineteen-hour days, seven days a week. Robin adjusted her schedule to spend more time at home with Zachary. We called on our lawyer and drafted our first wills, discussing the difficult issue of who would raise Zachary if something happened to both of us. On Sundays, I tried to get home by four thirty so the three of us could at least eat dinner together. It was a little thing, but it mattered a lot. Sundays were family days, and our Sunday dinners were the one constant in our lives. On the first Saturday after the attacks, as I was leaving for the office, I apologized to Zachary for not spending more time with him. He rushed over, embraced me, and gave me a big kiss.

"Put out a good newspaper, Daddy," my four year old said with a smile. It was the best encouragement I could get.

As much as we tried to shield Zachary from the news, it rattled him, although it was not until later that we appreciated just how much. He watched his father go off to work each morning, but for weeks did not see him come home. He caught bits of information and glimpses of pictures in the many newspapers on the kitchen table and counters. He saw worry on the faces of those he loved. His babysitter, an immigrant from Paraguay, initially spent several frantic hours after the attacks searching for her husband, who worked at a shoe repair shop near the Twin Towers. He turned up unharmed, but Zachary soaked up all of her anxiety. A few days after the attacks, he innocently asked us about good people and bad people and where people go when they die.

One wall in his bedroom featured a colorful mural of the New York City skyline, with World Trade Center towering in the distance. He cried when he realized that he would never see the real Twin Towers again. Then Zachary, who had always been fearless about life, became too afraid to sleep in his bedroom.

One night several days after the attacks, as he finished his prayers, he added this: "And Lord, please take care of the people who died at the World Trade Center."

It was a moment that I will never forget, a child forced to come to grips with a world that he could not begin to understand. The scary thing was, I felt the same way.

13

MANAGING UP,
MANAGING DOWN

Mischief.

It had to be just the right moment, and you had to be watching very closely to catch what poker players call the "tell." The sparkle in his left eye. The slightest of grins curling the corners of his mouth. And then, the earnest "no-kidding—I'm-really-asking-you-this" game face was locked down, betrayed nothing, and the trap was sprung.

Mischief.

"Do you really think that story is any good?" he'd ask the reporter.

"Do you serve people like him?" he'd ask the black hostess, pointing to the white man who walked with him into the rib joint.

"Why on earth would we do that?" he'd ask executives swollen with their idea.

Mischief.

As a quality it can be underrated, easily dismissed as a Dennis-the-Menace trait best left to kids. But used by a pro, it can be the equivalent of a bump under the basket in the NBA—something intended to throw the player just a bit off balance. The resulting scramble to regain equilibrium would speak volumes about confidence and character and who was in the game.

You'd gush. You'd bluster. And then you'd see the game face crack and the smile begin to peek out. And you'd laugh. And he'd laugh with you. And you'd feel embarrassed that you were caught out but relieved to realize it was laughter shared that mattered to him. Oh. And by the way, you'd take another look at what you were championing to see if it couldn't be better.

—JOHN GEDDES

"YOU ARE such a great partner," Raines said as he greeted me in his office on the morning after 9/11. "I'm so glad I picked you."

Like all journalists, I was susceptible to flattery, and his words were working on me. I did not respond, because no response was needed. I just smiled and began to meet a new day of challenges.

But several days later, Raines repeated the words as we relaxed in his back office, where he nursed Jack Daniel's and water, and I had a glass of gin. This time, I looked puzzled. I wondered why he felt he had to make the same point.

"The reason I say that is because of what Keller told Sulzberger," he continued. "He said that no matter whom Sulzberger picked as executive editor, under no circumstances should you become managing editor. Under no circumstances."

The words stung. They combined my worst fears about the paper with my strongest doubts about myself. I thought about the times that Keller and I spent in the newsroom, the smiles we exchanged and how we talked with ease about our children, our wives, mortgages, and the need for balance in our lives. We never had a deep connection, but there was no indication that he had a problem with me.

I could understand if I was not his choice for managing editor, just as he was not my choice for executive editor. But to tell Sulzberger that under no circumstances should I be promoted to managing editor was not only petty but also disrespectful. I could never imagine operating that way.

"Who cares what Bill thinks?" I shrugged it off.

But I could not stop thinking about it. I wondered whether Lelyveld shared that view and whether the publisher had heard similar concerns from others. I thought about Raines and how he regarded me. Why did he feel the need to share Keller's comment? Did he have his own doubts?

It was part of a long-running scenario in my career. Far too often, I heard white colleagues raise issues about journalists of color who were candidates for promotion or choice assignments. They never seemed quite ready or worthy of risk. In my mind, I had floated above this ground, a proven commodity with talent and experience. I had held more senior jobs than practically anyone on the paper and played a major role in work that garnered two Pulitzer Prizes. I did not believe I was a shoe-in for the job—every top editor had enemies—but *under no circumstances*? That was far different, far more sinister, than merely favoring another candidate.

I pressed my memory for other examples of this view. At my meeting with Sulzberger shortly before I became managing editor, he worried aloud about whether I could lead the paper in Raines's absence. The question sent me searching for words to reassure him. He accepted what I said, and we moved on, but I left the meeting angry. I could not believe that at this point I still needed to prove myself.

Raines also described how Keller had told Sulzberger that if he were named executive editor, he would choose Jon Landman as managing editor.

Landman, now Metro editor, had never worked as a reporter at the paper and was a constant critic of the paper's commitment to foreign news. Even his friends regarded him as temperamental, and he lacked an appreciation for the paper's business side. Metro had few minorities among its top editors, and many journalists of color found him impossible to stomach.

Did Keller really feel that Landman was better for the job than me or the ten other assistant managing editors and deputy managing editors with more experience and depth? At that moment, I hated Keller and Landman and even Raines for telling me the story.

The day before, we had faced the greatest challenge we could experience as editors. We relied on each other, much like soldiers in combat, an experience that bonds. The revelation was a defining moment in how I decided to perform as managing editor. I determined that I would ignore those who questioned my abilities, those I saw as enemies, and help Raines realize his vision for the paper. Clearly, I told myself, he wanted to gain my loyalty by reminding me that he wanted me when no one else did. For a while, it worked.

———

DESPITE MY unease after learning about Keller's comment, I eagerly looked forward to producing the paper. I began each morning by chairing a ten-thirty meeting of the masthead that focused on planning for the next day's paper. A larger meeting of masthead and department heads followed. Then came the daily news meeting at noon, and a second daily news meeting at four thirty. After that, I read stories and weighed in on packaging and design.

Raines seemed comfortable relying on me. As he prepared to depart each evening, normally before I did, he pretended to request permission. "Is it OK if I leave?" he'd asked, as if my response mattered. Sure, I always said.

Raines came to the newsroom determined to do journalism the way the uncompromising General George Patton fought World War II: aggressively and ardently. He spoke of the newsroom's need to function at a "higher metabolism": to run faster and push harder. But because the newsroom had changed in the nearly nine years that he was away, much like Patton he seemed out of touch with the current alliances and larger considerations that now guided the paper.

To Raines, it was imperative that we keep up with the high-tech evolution of newspapers and media consolidations. Less important was the new standard of managing employees—a compassionate approach that would have made old-time editors spin in their graves. The *Times* reaffirmed this shift by distributing to everyone at the paper a code of con-

Odessa Thomas Boyd,
Gerald's mother.

Gerald Michael Boyd, high school
graduation, 1969.

Newlyweds Gerald and Sheila Rule with Rufus, Gerald's father, and Evie, Gerald's
grandmother, in 1973. Rufus had made a rare return trip to St. Louis just after Gerald
and Sheila were married.

RIGHT: Uganda X finds domestic life in St. Louis, November 1975.

BELOW: On the campaign trail with Jesse Jackson, 1984. Gerald's friend George Curry is to the right of Jackson.

Greeting the Reagans with Jacqueline Adams, December 1986. "Nancy Reagan asked me when I planned to marry Jackie," Gerald writes. "Soon," he replied. "How soon?" she demanded.

ABOVE: Traveling with the Bushes, October 1987.

LEFT: Covering George H. W. Bush, July 1988. Bush despised the *Times*, Gerald writes, but "over time, I believe he came to distinguish me, the reporter, from my employer."

BELOW: Max Frankel's management team: from left, Soma Golden Behr, Warren Hoge, Dave Jones, Joe Lelyveld, Al Siegal, Carolyn Lee, Max Frankel, Jack Rosenthal, Gerald Boyd. 1994.

RIGHT: With Robin Stone
at Soldan High class reunion,
St. Louis, 1994.

BELOW: Gerald, Robin, and Zachary:
first family portrait, May 1997.

At the Central Park Zoo, 1998.

LEFT: Computer lessons, 1999.
BELOW: In Central Park, July 1999.

Surprise fiftieth birthday celebration. Gerald later remarked that it was the first "real" birthday party he ever had. Lenox Lounge, Harlem, October 2000.

Sister-in-law Andrea and brother Gary with Gerald and Robin at Gerald's fiftieth birthday party. Lenox Lounge, Harlem, October 2000.

Gerald took his haircutting duties seriously, spring 2001.

Choosing photos with Howell Raines, left of Gerald, for the *Times'* 9/11 coverage.

RIGHT:
A welcome respite at
Martha's Vineyard,
summer 2002.

LEFT: Man to man. In Grand Rapids,
Michigan, for the wedding of Robin's
sister, Brandy, October 2005.

RIGHT: Gerald, Ruth, and Gary Boyd
in Birmingham, Alabama, for the
wedding of Gary's daughter, Cassandra,
November 2005.

Taking a break
from horseback
riding. Last family
vacation, Aruba,
August 2006.

duct called "Rules of the Road." The guide spelled out proper behavior for the staff and senior management, such as treating one another with respect and civility. In the new world, editors had to handle staffers with care, even if staffers gave their personal lives far higher priority than they did the institution. In this new world, five reporters turned down an assignment to work in Detroit, a ticket that might lead to promotions. It was not about Detroit; five also said no to the position of San Francisco bureau chief. In this new world, managing meant results, but it also meant being more accommodating to your staff.

I don't recall ever discussing "Rules" with Raines, who promptly adorned his wall with a picture of Bear Bryant, the legendary University of Alabama football coach, and who espoused military and sports metaphors such as "flooding the zone." Raines expected the staff to leave everything they had on the field.

"I want to hunt big game, not rabbits," he often said, describing the kind of stories the staff should pursue. In one meeting with Sulzberger Jr., Janet Robinson, then the company's senior vice president for newspaper operations, Gail Collins, and me, an animated Raines described how he wanted not only to lead the competition but to descend from the mountains like Attila the Hun and pillage the rival papers, raping their women and daughters. The remarks reflected the verve that helped Raines beat out Keller. We all laughed awkwardly, but we were also glad when Sulzberger admonished him to use less offensive imagery.

Raines, like other editors, had no magic bullet for reversing the steady decline in circulation that was afflicting most of the nation's publications. As with other newspapers, many of the *Times*' traditional readers were growing old and dying off. Younger readers were turning to other news sources, most often the Web.

But Raines had two strengths: he was flexible and pragmatic. To him, almost any idea to grow circulation and boost profits was worth considering. Unlike Lelyveld, he saw the Web and other media platforms as directly tied to the financial well-being of the paper. This attitude was no doubt one of the many factors endearing him to Sulzberger. Raines believed that the *Times* had to remain the best print paper in the world while building a Web site ready for a broader future in digital, broadcast, and cable. One of our first moves was to welcome Martin Nisenholtz, head of digital operations, back into the newsroom and pledge to do all we could to help him.

At the same time, Raines argued that the paper continue to meet the needs of a very sophisticated audience and also attract new readers in the region and around the country. The *Times* had to become as indispensable to the history professor in Kansas as it was to the cultural executive or financier in New York, he argued. He saw the coverage of sports, culture, and business as portals to a broader national audience. We agreed on this point. Papers like *USA Today*, the *Wall Street Journal*, and the *Financial Times* were growing their national audience and capturing our potential readers. We could not ignore the threat they posed. Raines believed, for example, that the Sunday Arts and Leisure section had become too exclusive and highbrow, emphasizing cultural events such as the Stuttgart Arts Festival instead of pop culture. He challenged the paper's culture coverage, a realignment I believed was overdue. To grow, the paper had to reach younger and more diverse readers.

He constantly repeated this powerful example: When Aaliyah, the twenty-two-year-old singer and actress, died in a plane crash in the Bahamas in August 2001, the *Times* barely noticed the story. Our critics thought little of her work. National editors did not regard the longtime Detroiter as a national figure. The *Times* dispatched no reporters on the brief plane ride from Florida to the Bahamas. Just as they'd underestimated the impact of the 1995 death of the Latina superstar Selena, *Times* editors were largely ignorant of Aaliyah's significance to her fans. The *Times* looked out of touch when a huge public outpouring of grief swept through parts of New York and cities like Detroit.

Raines's manifesto for change was discussed and debated throughout the newsroom. But among reporters and editors, achieving his goals became secondary to his bare-knuckled management style. Raines seemed to think that success centered on him, not the staff. And he had grown petty, a trait I had never seen in him before. For months, a group of editors had been working on designing a new typeface for the front page. The facelift would be Lelyveld's parting gift, making the page airier and more accessible. The redesign was not finished before Lelyveld left, and when it was presented to Raines in his first days on the job, he scrapped it. He would not have the former editor dictating a decision that was now his to make.

Raines's biggest challenge was that our staff did not know him. For nearly a decade, I had been in the newsroom in New York, and friends and foes alike knew what to expect from me. He, on the other hand, had been away, in Atlanta, Washington, London, and then seven floors above, in the editorial department. If they knew him better, I thought, he would have had more goodwill to trade on; they would respond differently to his messages and the way he delivered them. But almost from the beginning, the newsroom reeled. And I found myself in an unexpected position: I had to accept the dictates of my new boss or fight them. I often did both.

———

IN OUR first days, we tried to cultivate a constituency. We reached out to senior editors at the *Times*, especially those on the masthead, who were most marginalized by Lelyveld. Giving them new power and prominence would make them loyal followers, we believed, and as such, they would play an active role in conveying the message of change. But giving them power meant removing power from the editors the level below, the department heads.

Of course, every action brings a reaction. The department heads, who had operated under Lelyveld with virtual autonomy, were now being second-guessed by assistant managing editors. They bristled at the new system, arguing that it limited their roles. To some extent, they were right. And they rebelled.

Several months after the transition, Soma Golden Behr warned Raines that his repeated sermons on change were harming his efforts to transform the paper. They emphasized what was wrong rather than what was right, she said. A backlash was brewing. I appreciated that Golden Behr took seriously her responsibility to share concerns she heard from the staff, regardless of how severe those reports were. Raines encouraged her at first, but after a while, he began to regard her as disloyal.

Another complaint surfaced: Raines's meetings came to be seen as bawdy and offensive to women. His brand of humor raised eyebrows, although everyone laughed. I knew he was not sexist, but his jokes, about Alabama or poor white trash or the Civil War or fishing, were remote to many on staff. They were out of sync, like a comedian doing a monologue at a funeral. Some of his habits also became problematic. When certain reporters sought him out, Raines was unavailable. E-mails from those outside his constellation of stars went unanswered or were answered slowly. Raines ordered a television for his office, a state-of-the-art, flat-screen model that cost a bundle. That drew chuckles but also condemnation from those who saw it as the mark of a self-centered and ostentatious man.

The criticisms surfaced at an unfortunate time, and Raines and I struggled to get our bearings as the newsroom lurched from one crisis to another. First, the terrorist attacks, then George W. Bush's war in Afghanistan. The news was piling on for a new leadership team that had been in place fewer than five weeks. One minute, I was worrying about how well the paper was covering the effects of the attacks on children in New York. The next, it was whether the *Times* was doing enough reporting on al Qaeda or the Saudis who turned the commercial airliners into guided missiles. Almost overnight, we deployed about a dozen reporters and photographers to Afghanistan. Some made their way into the country from Pakistan in the south, while others came from the north through Uzbekistan. There was danger and constant concern in both instances.

Producing "A Nation Challenged," the special section that centered on 9/11 and its aftermath, put enormous strains on everyone. It also led to battles over power and authority, fights that would intensify over time. Editors were ordered to produce stories for the section in days, when they wanted weeks. Some rebelled at story suggestions, arguing that their own ideas were more important. And the newly empowered masthead, led by Raines and me, pushed back. The section became a source of daily creative tension.

As I watched this process play out, I could see the strife it caused. It was just what I hoped to avoid. Department heads were particularly incensed over the stream of mandates, which they saw as micromanaging by the masthead. Some, like Jon Landman, were openly defiant, as he ranted about "you guys" issuing such orders. Others, like Jill Abramson, the Washington bureau chief, reacted with stone-cold silence.

———

I WAS worried about our Washington bureau. It played a major and stellar role in the 9/11 coverage, and I felt it needed more firepower. It had talented reporters on the story, such as David Johnston, Phil Shenon, Todd Purdum, Eric Schmitt, and Thom Shanker. But they were being stretched as never before. I had watched the *Times* get clobbered on the Iran-Contra story. We could not allow it to happen again.

Raines and I shored the bureau up by adding the services of Judith Miller, who had worked in the Middle East; Michael Gordon, the paper's best military reporter; and Pat Tyler, a well-sourced investigative reporter who was stationed in Moscow. Miller and Tyler were concerns from the beginning. They were lightning rods, with as many detractors as supporters. Tyler was also a longtime friend of Raines.

These were small steps, but they added experienced bodies to a taxed bureau. I was sure that the decision sent the right message to the staff: we were going to do everything possible to be competitive. But the move only heightened the tension between the staff and editors in New York, I came to realize. While Raines was installing his friend Tyler in the bureau, other reporters like David Sanger and Todd Purdum were experiencing bruising encounters with the new executive editor.

There was also Raines's view of Abramson, the bureau's top editor. Lelyveld had promoted her in January 2001. It was clearly an appointment that Raines would have rejected. I thought I could read Raines well, but I could not understand why he had a problem with her. He complained that she was not dynamic enough and lacked glitz. She certainly was no Kovach, the inspiring editor who led the bureau when Raines and I were there, and definitely no Raines. I wondered if Raines's impressions were gender related. Abramson was conscientious, but like many women editors, she was more understated than her male colleagues. She did not strut or shout. But she was tough and firm when she needed to be. I soon dismissed the notion of sexism. I knew that as a manager, Raines was comfortable with women.

But with this woman, he was not. In private meetings, he second-guessed her, making it clear that he was unhappy with her performance. I soon came to believe that Raines's doubts had little to do with Abramson's talents and more to do with his friendship with Tyler. It was obvious that he wanted Tyler in the position, and by constantly complaining, he was trying to lay the groundwork to get Abramson out. I saw no need to force her out and told him so.

Of course, if Raines wanted Abramson out over my objections, he had the authority to make it happen. But for some reason he was unwilling to pull the trigger. Instead, he kept her in place and made her life miserable.

I did not know Abramson, other than through our daily phone conferences. She had never worked in New York and had come to *Times* from the *Wall Street Journal* long after I had left the bureau. I decided to go to Washington to get to know our bureau chief better. As I flew to D.C., my first trip since 9/11, I thought with displeasure about how colleagues already referred to us as "Howell and Gerald." Sooner or later, the executive and managing editors merge into one person, identified by the first name of each: Max and Joe, Joe and Gene, and Joe and Bill. I worried about that linkage; I did not want to be seen as Raines's appendage, nor did I want to be in his shadow. Yet I knew that our partnership after 9/11, as we handled one crisis after another, left me little choice in the matter.

———

I HAD agreed to talk to the staff at a brown bag lunch and to have dinner with a smaller group that evening. But my main agenda was to get to know Abramson. I was not sure of what I would find, but on the eve of the trip, I received a chilling tip from Andrew Rosenthal, whom Raines and I had installed as an assistant managing editor for news. The Washington staff had adopted a nickname for their inflexible top editors in New York: the Taliban. Washington always had choice words for New York—Raines and I had dubbed our bosses "the Flying Wallendas." But our moniker was far more sobering.

We gathered in a conference room in the lower level of the two-story bureau, and I sat across from reporters such as Adam Clymer,

Robin Toner, David Rosenbaum, David Johnston, and Rick Berke, all of whom I considered friends from having worked with them before. I started by telling them how much they were appreciated and valued. They attacked immediately, saying that top editors were heavy-handed and micromanaging the bureau.

I had no problem being righted by friends who shared my goals. I thought this group knew me, what I was about, and how I managed. We had shared countless evenings together as well as frustrations and hopes.

But they peppered me with questions: Who decided which stories bureau reporters wrote? Why did we use this reporter or that one more than others? Why couldn't the bureau determine its own priorities?

I felt they were not questioning me, a colleague, but challenging me as if I were a distant outsider about whom they were reporting. They all knew that New York determined the direction of the paper, not one of its bureaus. I felt sandbagged, cornered, and disrespected. I pushed my sandwich to the side and fought back.

"We decide!" I exploded. I had had enough.

Later, after I calmed down, I began to see that the issue was larger than stories. It was about perceived slights not only of reporters but of the bureau's leaders.

That became clearer as Abramson and I talked in private. We took advantage of the gorgeous fall day by heading outside, where we walked along Sixteenth Street to Lafayette Park. There we sat on a bench that faced the White House, and Abramson spoke candidly.

She said she felt snubbed by New York. She found it not just insulting but sexist. Instead of listening to what she believed was important, she said, New York editors simply gave orders. That undermined her ability to lead. Alternating between rage and disappointment, she spoke about leaving the paper if we did not do better by her. Each word felt like a punch in the gut. When she was appointed the first female Washington bureau chief in the paper's history, I was disappointed that Lelyveld and Keller did not make more of the occasion. Instead of hosting a big Washington social event that drew politicians and dignitaries, they led a quiet celebration. I thought she received shoddy treatment then, and now she was painting us with that charge.

This was not how I wanted to lead the newsroom. I began to understand Abramson and the challenges she faced. I found that I liked her a great deal, and I left looking to make amends.

Back in New York, I told Raines that we had to change how we dealt with Abramson. We needed to listen more and order less. And we needed to make sure that she was consulted on all decisions related to the bureau. Fortunately, Raines got the message. He apologized to Abramson. He assured her that he had confidence in her as a bureau chief. I was determined to show Abramson—and the bureau—that I was serious about changing. I insisted that Abramson speak first in telephone conferences so she could describe what the bureau was doing rather than being told what to do. I also started more one-on-one conversations, where we could precook decisions before other senior editors intervened. Almost immediately, Abramson responded with new confidence. Once, when an assistant managing editor interrupted her in a meeting, she yelled: "I'm not finished!" Our bureau chief was being heard.

The trip to Washington would later be described by some as a "debacle." But far from a disaster, it served to release some pent-up tension and to change how we were dealing with Washington. It also allowed me to connect with a critical member of our management team. For a time, it brought a cease-fire between New York and the Washington bureau.

————

THAT DECEMBER, we held our second meeting with reporters on the National staff. The session quickly erupted into a nasty debate. Some reporters argued that Raines's "higher metabolism" plan was wrong, and they wanted him to back off. Two of the most vocal argued in a lengthy memo that contrary to running and gunning more, as Raines wanted, the National staff should focus on thematic stories that took time to report and write.

At that point, I became less of a peacemaker. Both types of stories were necessary; it was a constant juggle to get the mix right, but that's what good department heads did. But the executive editor, not a reporter, was responsible for setting priorities. If the reporters did not want to follow his edicts, they could find other jobs on the paper. I was not guided by blind loyalty to Raines, but by another, larger principle. The paper could have only one executive editor. Still, I knew that he could be wrong and a bully. I heard the reporters all out and then arranged for new assignments for several. One quit to teach at a university.

Not long after that, the simmering feud between Landman and me finally erupted.

Sulzberger Jr. triggered the flare-up by questioning how long the paper planned to run "Portraits of Grief," the vignettes featuring victims of the attack on the World Trade Center. It was a reasonable query. Despite its large following, producing the portraits was labor intensive. They ate up huge amounts of space at a time when the paper was devoting big chunks of newsprint to other parts of the section "A Nation Challenged."

The *Times* newsroom was spending several hundred thousand dollars extra each month to cover the aftermath of 9/11, including the war in Afghanistan. And like other newspapers and businesses, the *Times* was grappling with the economy, which crawled to a halt after 9/11. Hiring was all but frozen on the business side of the paper, while the newsroom was allowed only to replace staffers who left. So everyone was being asked to give a little.

Sulzberger wanted to set a date for ending "Portraits of Grief," a plan that Raines and I endorsed. I was instructed to inform Landman, and we quickly locked horns. Landman argued that the newsroom had a commitment to readers to do portraits on every victim who was identified, no matter how long it took. I told him to appeal to Raines, which he did. Raines backed down.

Landman's unwillingness to see broader concerns or to find a way to bridge them only added to the tension between the two of us. What began as an annoyance soon grew into behavior that was untenable.

Raines reacted with concern and amusement. He had worked with Landman briefly when he led the Washington bureau, so he had a sense of how Landman operated. Raines considered him talented but moody and immature. But he felt he could rein Landman in when necessary.

I told him I doubted his assessment. Landman was too brash, too opportunistic. He would not be pleased with one victory, but emboldened by it. He could not derail what Raines and I wanted to do at the *Times*, I said; he was not that powerful. But he could huff and puff and do everything possible to blow the house down.

———

IN EARLY January 2002, Raines and I took stock of the newsroom. The paper had recently ended "A Nation Challenged," telling readers that we would no longer combine all terrorist-related news into one section. Finally, for the first time since we took on our new jobs, we felt that we were getting our opportunity for a fresh start. The newsroom was filled with stark contrasts. Some aspects were going quite well, while others were in need of severe overhaul. Despite our repeated proclamations about change, we were nowhere near getting the staff to buy in. We pushed hard, but almost alone.

But some things were working. A month earlier, Texas-based Enron rocked the financial world by announcing that it was filing for bankruptcy. The huge story had tentacles that stretched far and wide. Enron was one of the nation's largest companies, and Wall Street regarded Kenneth Lay, its chairman, as a model corporate leader. Millions of retirees and investors had their life savings invested in Enron stock.

We put into play our new philosophy, throwing dozens of reporters and editors onto the story. My role was to focus and coordinate those bodies, much as I had done during 9/11. We had reporters from the National staff and the Washington bureau helping the small army of Business reporters working the story. At one point, we sent a New York editor to Houston, Enron's headquarters, to direct reporters. The extra attention paid off. Instead of chasing our most serious competition, the *Wall Street Journal*, we often led them. It was a huge morale boost for the newsroom, and it validated the new leadership.

Not everything ran so smoothly, however. Several weeks later, we met with Neil Amdur, the Sports editor, and his team to review plans for covering the upcoming Winter Olympics. This, too, would be a big story in which the *Times* would be competing with several national papers. But the proposal had nothing special, nothing that would distinguish the *Times*. Raines exploded, berating Amdur in what amounted to a public spanking. He had every right to punch holes in Amdur's presentation, but his behavior violated a basic rule of leadership: praise in public and criticize in private. Amdur and his team returned to the drawing board and developed a terrific plan that they later executed. But the end did not justify the means.

I felt that Raines needed to follow Frankel's model of putting editors more to his liking in place, but even now, when we had a chance to regroup, Raines seemed to lack the will, or perhaps stomach, to do the reshuffling that he had pledged to improve the paper. Without his team in place, I told him constantly, we were spinning our wheels.

As Raines struggled to gain his footing in the newsroom, his lack of understanding of the staff created an unfortunate reality: some editors who were out of step with his expectations, unaware of what he wanted, became his targets. He would beat up on them and then back off. It was management by torture.

I pushed to break this pattern. Whenever we reached an impasse, as we did more and more frequently, we compromised. He agreed to reach out more to the top editors. I saw this as a small step forward. In mid-January, the paper's most senior editors gathered at Eleven Madison Park on Madison Avenue. The evening was a trial run, the first time we had brought the masthead together for a dinner. Only one real issue was on the agenda: gaining their support. I figured that the more the staff interacted with Raines, the more they would appreciate him and his goals. He performed retail politicking as well as anyone.

While political pundit James Carville held court with several acquaintances in the main dining room downstairs, Raines and I courted top editors in a private space on the second floor. As the evening wore on, Raines opened up, and editors saw a different side of him.

He reminisced about his father, W. S. Raines, who had owned a store-fixture company in Birmingham. The elder Raines was instrumental in shaping many of his son's thoughts on work and leadership. Raines recalled when, as a child playing baseball, he had prepared to meet a team from the other side of the tracks and how W.S. had warned him not to take the opposition lightly. That surprised young Raines because his team had superior equipment and seemed destined to win.

"But they're hungrier than you are," his father had said. The incident helped explain why, to Raines, the biggest newsroom sin was complacency, and his biggest newsroom fear was being outhustled.

The group sat mesmerized as he told another story. One summer, when working at his father's business in segregated Birmingham, Raines developed a friendship with a black employee. As he looked on, the black worker came to blows with a racist white worker. Raines's father separated the men. The white worker challenged his father's authority, demanding that the black worker be fired. But W.S. would have none of it. No one told him how to run his business, he told the white man. Raines sought to emulate this toughness.

Raines and I had been friends for almost two decades, but I had never heard that tale before. It made me wonder how well I really knew him, a question that would surface repeatedly as we confronted one challenge after another.

I thought the dinner was just the kind of connection that we needed. Our next step: including the department heads. With almost two dozen editors later assembled at a restaurant near Times Square, that evening was anything but intimate. Some department heads responded well as Raines told his stories and pitched his vision of change. But others did not. Although the gathering helped to ease some tensions, it was clear that the newsroom's leadership remained divided.

———

AS WE began our outreach efforts, Raines told me that he was considering a request from the *New Yorker* magazine to do a feature story on him. The magazine guaranteed that the piece would run more than twenty thousand words. I advised against it, saying that it would be nearly impossible to gain support and push through changes with a reporter watching our every move. And did we really want a reporter watching our every move? The newsroom had always been a place of secrets. Despite proclamations from top executives about nothing to hide, plenty of information was kept private. It was just the kind of information a reporter would seek.

Raines argued that the reporter, Ken Auletta, a well-known media writer whom he knew personally, would have so much access to Raines and others such as Sulzberger Jr. and Janet Robinson that some of what he wrote would have to be positive. I could not understand his logic. Although I knew Auletta only in passing, I thought he would go the extra mile to be tough on Raines because of their friendship. He had a reputation to protect. David Remnick, the New Yorker's editor, was a good man, but he was a close friend of Bill Keller's, so I could not imagine that "positive" would be a part of the agenda. Plus Remnick was married to Esther Fein, a Times reporter. Auletta would have no trouble knowing which rocks to turn over and what might rest under them.

The profile was not to appear until June, but it affected the newsroom almost immediately.

In early February, I traveled to California to further shake up the National staff, as Raines had ordered. I wanted to deliver the "higher metabolism" directive myself and in person. I thought I could temper the sting of the message to correspondents.

My first official meeting was with the paper's San Francisco bureau chief, whom I had hired when I was Metro editor. She was a gifted reporter and writer. The dinner was pleasant, but there was an edge to our conversation. I told her about editors' concerns that she was reluctant to travel, while at the same time, she criticized her supervisors. In the end, we both agreed that the best solution for everyone was for her to return to New York. That had been my goal: to find another assignment in which she could flourish.

The next morning, I had a similar conversation with a veteran reporter who responded defensively and angrily. Then he shocked me by telling me that he did not know the other West Coast correspondents. Referring to the San Francisco bureau chief, he said, "I wouldn't know her if she walked into this room." The disconnection was a clear sign of the problems we faced. The correspondent agreed to consider a reassignment, and we scheduled a visit to New York to continue our discussion.

As I prepared to meet with a third correspondent, I received an urgent call from Raines. He had decided to go forward with the magazine profile. He was worried that my discussions out west would give critics ammunition to attack him. He wanted me to put the notion of reporters returning to New York on the table, but not in a way that caused resentment. We would wait until the article appeared before moving decisively, he said.

I wanted to scrap the final meeting; he was asking me to do the impossible. My talk with the last reporter, whom I had admired from the days that he reported to me while covering Albany, defied all logic and might have seemed comical if it did not involve his life and livelihood: "We really want you to return to New York, but stay on the West Coast until you are ready..." "Yes, we want you to move, but no, we don't want you to be upset..." "Think about what you really want, and let's talk."

I stewed as the United Airlines 767 brought me back to Kennedy Airport the next day. Our goals for the newsroom were first redirected by the attacks on 9/11 and the war in Afghanistan, and now by Ken Auletta. It was no way to run a newsroom.

Staring out the window at some point on the five-hour flight home, I whispered what I was feeling: "I hate this job." Over the next months, I would say those words repeatedly.

———

BACK IN New York, Auletta became privy to the inner workings of the newsroom, including the daily meetings and private discussions. He sat in on strategic deliberations with the paper's business side. In my nearly twenty years at the *Times*, he was the only writer I had ever seen afforded such access to newsroom decisions.

His timing was perfect, since a staff revolt was under way. John Darnton, the Culture editor, had just challenged a harsh performance evaluation—a particularly stinging review by Raines—with a screed attacking his boss's judgment. The response by Darnton, a longtime *Times*man who won a Pulitzer Prize in 1982 for his coverage of Poland, was a direct test of Raines's authority and the second salvo from the Culture department. Several weeks earlier, John Rockwell, editor of the Sunday Arts and Leisure section, resigned abruptly. Rockwell, a cerebral editor who was for years the *Times*' classical music critic, had resented Raines's demands to change the section. Raines took the departure in stride. Darnton's missive was far more worrisome; he had declared war. Raines had no choice but to counterattack. But with the *New Yorker* writer hovering, Raines decided not to respond. I told him I could not believe that important decisions were being directed by a magazine article.

Next came an eruption on Landman's Metro desk, and Auletta witnessed the whole ugly battle.

In mid-March, Landman offered a story for page one that centered on the politically charged issue of racial profiling in New Jersey. The subject had already received enormous media attention and was the focus of a federal civil rights probe. A Metro reporter received information from a source that a commission working for state authorities had found that African Americans were more likely to speed than Hispanics and whites. The fact that they were stopped more had nothing to do with profiling, the authorities concluded. Several masthead editors, including me, saw the obvious problems with the story: it was funded by the state authorities and was thus self-serving; the reporter had not read the study but was relying on a description from sources; and conclusions were based on researchers clocking and photographing drivers as they sped along the New Jersey Turnpike, sometimes at night. How they could distinguish between blacks and Hispanics, or Hispanics and whites, as they drove by was clearly problematic.

Even so, the story became the subject of a test of wills. Raines insisted that it not run until the concerns of senior editors were satisfied. He asked me to make sure that happened, as Auletta looked on. Landman accused Raines and me of censorship, bowing to political correctness. It was as if the paper were being edited in public, which in fact it was. Once again, gross insubordination was tolerated. Raines headed back into his office, where he would spend the next few hours, over drinks, being interviewed by Auletta.

I made several suggestions to Landman about what the story needed, such as the reporter and editors actually reading the study and including caveats that reflected a possible motivation of those presenting the conclusions. Landman resisted and vented, as he always did, but eventually agreed to think about the suggestions. My interaction with Landman was part of an emerging pattern, one that I came to resent. Raines would tend to other matters, such as his interviews, while I would be instructed to fix a problem. And increasingly the problems had to do with Landman. The racial profiling story eventually appeared, but the findings were appropriately qualified.

After years of fighting, I had learned to live with my Landman battles. I knew we were dealing with issues of power and authority. I was not Rodney King, lamenting "Can't we all just get along?" But I wondered how much we could actually achieve if we stopped fighting and worked together. I was determined to do the best job I could, with or without his support. But that effort was about to become more difficult, and it had nothing to do with Landman.

———

IN MID-MARCH, we learned that the *Times* had twelve Pulitzer finalists—a record number and a remarkable achievement. Just the high number seemed to validate Raines's aggressive style of editing. Like Patton in war, he was leading the paper to victory.

In the first week in April, when the Pulitzer Board met in New York to select the winners, Sulzberger Jr., Raines, and I were like children on Christmas Eve as we waited for news. Late Friday afternoon, Raines and I were summoned to the publisher's fourteenth-floor office, where Janet Robinson joined us. The official announcement would come on Monday, but Sulzberger had received word: the *Times* won seven Pulitzers Prizes, more than twice the number any newspaper had ever won in a single year.

We all embraced. Actually, the staff—the reporters, editors, and photographers—won the prizes, not the two of us, but we led the newsroom. The awards acknowledged journalistic excellence during one of our most demanding periods ever. I could not stop smiling. While the *Times* had won eighty Pulitzers over the years, more than any other newspaper, everyone considered it a good year if it won two and a great year if it won three. There were no words to describe how it felt to win seven.

Raines invited Joe Lelyveld, Max Frankel, and Abe Rosenthal, all former executive editors, to join us in the newsroom as the winners were announced on Monday. It was as if each of his predecessors had run a leg of a marathon and passed the baton, and now it was Raines's turn. To me, the invitations were a gracious gesture. But to critics, they were more like grandstanding. Some also saw the gesture as self-serving, because Auletta was on hand, recording Raines's moment of triumph.

Self-serving or not, the record number of Pulitzers meant that the publisher could not doubt that he had made the right choice in Raines. And that night, as the newsroom celebrated at a nightclub near the paper, Sulzberger led the party, promising to drink a martini for each prize won. At the insistence of his wife, Gail, he stopped at three.

In hindsight, the prizes were as much a curse as a blessing. While they validated Raines's hard-charging style of leadership and further bonded him to Sulzberger, they seemed to lead Raines to believe he had no more mountains to climb. In addition to the Pulitzers, he had been recognized as editor of the year by *Editor & Publisher,* a prestigious industry trade magazine. Not even a year had passed since he was named executive editor, and within the industry, the *Times* was the talk of journalism.

Ignoring the buzz would be hard even for a humble person. Raines, it seemed, started to believe that he could now succeed without building the newsroom support we still sorely needed. It was a major miscalculation, one we would both realize only when it was too late.

14

THE MAKINGS OF A SCANDAL

Watching Gerald cover Reagan inspired me to up my game and imagine one day running a newspaper. But I also learned from him how to handle severe disappointment.

Gerald could have sulked when he was passed over for managing editor and Gene Roberts was brought in. Instead, he adapted. Indeed, he said, how one handles adversity is key to proving readiness to lead.

When I didn't get the editorship of the *Boston Globe* after nearly eight years as managing editor, the first call I received was from Gerald. "I'm calling to be sure you're OK and to let you know we [the New York Times company, which owned the *Globe*] don't want you to leave." It was July 2001, and he had been named managing editor of the *Times*. "Keep holding your head high," he said. "Good things can still happen."

He called back later to ask if I would meet with the company chairman, Arthur Sulzberger Jr., at the National Association of Black Journalists convention in Orlando. He said Arthur wanted to assure me I was valued. In Florida, when Arthur and I headed out for a walk and cigars, there was Gerald at the door with that knowing smile. He had helped orchestrate an important gesture for me. I already knew how I was going to handle this situation because I had seen Gerald do it. And I appreciated Gerald's knack for knowing how to be there for you when you most needed it.

Being present and accessible was hugely important to him. So in 2003, it was an honor for me to be there for him. Making his first public comments about the Blair tragedy at the NABJ convention in Dallas, he asked me to introduce him and stand by his side. As we embraced after his address, he whispered: "Thanks for being a friend." I clutched him and whispered back, "There is no place I'd rather be." He was that kind of a guy.

—GREGORY MOORE

A FTER A seven-month delay, Sulzberger Jr. and his wife, Gail Gregg, finally held the party they had planned for Raines and Gail Collins. The event, which had been scheduled for September 11, 2001, took place at their Upper West Side duplex on a pleasant evening in April 2002. By this time, it was more of a celebration than a welcome to the job. Raines gave a warm toast in which he praised several in attendance, including me. I returned the compliment, applauding his efforts to lead the newsroom.

But I was worried. Despite the cheery facade, I knew, as well as everyone in the room, that we had serious problems.

We had settled into a routine. On many nights, Raines would leave by seven, just as the deadline crunch started. He delegated many responsibilities, from improving morale to budgeting to staffing. He would sit in weekly meetings on those topics and, looking bored, ask a question or two, such as "Are we on budget?" and then leave. Neither Frankel nor Lelyveld had ever been so disengaged. Raines had become so delinquent in responding to his e-mails that even Sulzberger admonished him. A backup system was set up so that Raines's secretary could flag the most urgent ones.

I did not know what preoccupied Raines. Perhaps a reality that strikes many successful leaders: what happens when there are no more mountains to climb? Raines had led the newsroom as it won a record

seven Pulitzer Prizes. There was no encore, only the day-to-day same-
ness. It was a different challenge, minus the rush of a big story.

I also knew that he was concerned about his elderly parents, and
that he was in love and sharing his townhouse with his girlfriend, Krystyna Stachowiak. The two were busy renovating a weekend home in
the Poconos. He also busied himself trying to decide between buying
a pickup truck, which would be practical, or a BMW, which was the
kind of car he believed he should drive. He bought both.

But an important newsroom dynamic was at play: Raines was still
the outsider, the absentee parent who had been away from his newsroom family for years. The family had thrived without him. Now he was
back trying to reassert control. Newsroom management still seemed
adrift, with Raines unwilling to execute staffing changes that we had
discussed ad nauseum. I tried to manage each day's problems as best as
I could. We talked, but we rarely had closure on any issue.

One of the few things that excited me those days was another major
project that I was planning with Soma Golden Behr. It would be on
the scale of "How Race Is Lived in America" and would explore one of
the most common questions that persisted after 9/11: why so much of
the world hated the United States and what it stood for. While America
was strongly supported in the days after the terrorist attacks, the Bush
administration came under more and more criticism for a foreign policy
that many saw as arrogant and preemptive. The articles represented a
significant and timely body of work.

It was good to have my hands on a specific project; it brought a measure of relief to the endless back and forth of the rest of my job. I felt as
if I was engaging in journalism again. Still, the daily hassles persisted.

Landman and his editors on Metro were clashing with Felicia Lee,
a black veteran columnist. Landman wanted to replace Lee, the one
minority columnist on Metro, with a white male, a friend of his.

Lee, a talented writer and friend of mine, sought me out for guidance. I knew that if Landman had concerns about her work, it would be
impossible to appease him. I urged her to consider moving to another
department, where she would be better appreciated, and I promised
to help make that happen. This suited Landman fine. Lee left for the
Culture department, where she thrived.

I told Landman that it was unacceptable for the Metro staff, which covered an increasingly multiethnic city, not to have at least one minority columnist. He had to find one, I said. We spent about an hour reviewing candidates inside and outside the paper without reaching a conclusion. He promised he would keep trying.

It was not lost on me that once again I was caught up in another matter involving race and Landman. It was tiresome, but it also seemed unavoidable.

———

IN JUNE the long-awaited *New Yorker* piece crash-landed right into what little order we had managed to establish. The feature story was almost eighteen thousand words. And it was tough.

Auletta was not snowed by Raines's "enormous access" to sources. Instead, like any good reporter, he soaked it all in and wrote the story he wanted to write. It recycled previous criticisms, such as Raines's star system and his habit of favoring newsroom buddies like Rick Bragg and Pat Tyler. It described in detail scrapes with editors like Landman, Abramson, and Rockwell, and reversals of some of Joe Lelyveld's dictates. It also explored the intense animus between Raines and Lelyveld. It was not good at all.

Auletta, a respected media writer, presented a newsroom at war with itself. His analysis would be picked up and repeated by other writers. Raines's friend also portrayed him as a tyrant, a claim backed by editors who spoke on the record.

I thought the assessment was unfair; it was far too early in the life of the new administration to be meaningful. I shared my concerns with Raines, who acknowledged that the article was not what he had hoped. He said that "maybe" I was right in advising him not to participate. But it was out there, he said, and we were stuck with it.

However, the article was not about "we," it was about him. Except when I was described as "an imposing figure"—which I read as big, menacing black man—there was little reference to my role in the newsroom. The "imposing" description was typical of the unflattering way that mainstream media described minorities, black men in particular. And in Auletta's view, it was as if Raines had been running the newsroom alone. I knew the piece was about Raines and did not expect to be central to it. Still, I found it quite a feat to be both imposing and invisible. This was more than unfair and misleading, and other journalists picked it up and repeated it. Again, the message was clear: if a white man wrote it, it must have been true.

―――――

SUMMER APPROACHED, and with it came a lull in action and decisions. Come fall, I hoped, we would finally take on problems that needed fixing—from morale to personnel. That meant staying focused and not losing heart. I still believed that we could achieve the goals that were eluding the newsroom and us. I was still committed to that course.

My commitment had less and less to do with loyalty to Raines. The Auletta piece was a wake-up call. Raines was in search of a place in history. I was at a different point in my career and my life. What mattered to me was that we move forward. I began to distance myself from Raines; I was troubled that many of my colleagues assumed that we walked in lockstep. At the same time, I pushed him to focus on making the changes we had discussed.

One of my first moves was to lobby Raines to recruit Adam Moss, who ran the Sunday magazine, to become Culture editor. Raines had moved John Darnton out, almost six months after his outburst, and we needed a strong replacement. I had worked with Moss in my days on Metro, and I knew he was extremely talented. I thought he would push the Culture department to broaden and deepen its coverage. Actually, I argued for Moss to become the czar for "soft" news, supervising all the features sections. Raines warmed to the suggestion. Moss was interested but reluctant without offering a compelling explanation. He seemed uncomfortable with the notion of taking on more responsibilities under Raines.

Moss's reaction was telling; it underscored just how difficult it would be to assemble the kind of leadership team we wanted. Raines took Moss's rejection in stride.

We had several other important vacancies to fill.

Stephen Engelberg had resigned as investigations editor in June 2002 to take a job as managing editor of the *Oregonian* in Portland.

He left under a cloud of confusion. He told Raines and me that his decision was based on a reassessment of priorities post 9/11, something that I identified with. Yet media accounts asserted that he was leaving because he was frustrated with our heavy-handed management. Engelberg did not dispute that impression.

There was also the job of weekend editor. It was a high-ranking position—an associate managing editor—that had been filled by Nick Kristof, a talented writer who had been a favorite of Lelyveld's. Kristof had won a Pulitzer Prize with his wife, Sheryl WuDunn, in 1990 for their Tiananmen Square coverage in China. Lelyveld had given Kristof a much freer hand in running the weekend operation, something that Raines and I were not prepared to do in the weeks after 9/11. Kristof wanted out.

Sulzberger Jr., Raines, and Gail Collins worked out a deal to give Kristof a yearlong stint as a columnist on the op-ed page, with the likes of Tom Friedman, Maureen Dowd, and William Safire. If all went well, the job could become permanent. If not, he could return to the newsroom. This was exactly how such personnel decisions should be handled. Kristof had served the paper well. He had worked effectively in Lelyveld's management but less so under Raines. This was not a reflection of his abilities but of the expectations of the executive editor. So the best way to handle the situation was to find him a new position that he was excited to fill. It turned out there was no need for the trial; Kristof became a strong op-ed presence.

We appointed Kathleen McElroy, a black woman, to associate managing editor, in charge of news coverage for weekends. She was the next-highest-ranking black editor after me. Although she was well liked by her colleagues, she would soon develop enemies who questioned whether she was ready for the job. Despite the predictable challenges, I believe she performed well.

There was no doubt that our biggest challenge was personnel. I continuously spoke of how the best personnel moves were best for the paper and also best for people's lives. In Raines's view, underperformers should be moved out—or at least ignored. But despite his tough talk and hard demeanor, he could show real understanding and compassion. After the 9/11 attacks, we were both deeply concerned about the emotional state of the staff, especially those who had gone downtown to report or who lived in the area. Raines had addressed the staff, praising their performance and urging anyone who needed it to seek help. He was equally thoughtful several weeks later as we searched for a way to acknowledge the exemplary work of many on the staff. Raines awarded one-time bonuses to several reporters and editors, including Landman, Abramson, and Engelberg.

There was one huge roadblock in the personnel shuffle: finding a place for Katy Roberts, the National editor. She had become bitter about second-guessing from higher-ups and made no secret of wanting out. I worried about her. She was a perfectionist and willing to work a twenty-four-hour day to achieve flawlessness. Yet she was seldom praised and more often criticized. At times, the stress showed.

Raines and Roberts had history; she had worked as the editor of the op-ed page while he was the editorial page editor. Roberts wanted to edit the Week in Review section, and Raines had declared war on the current editor, Susan Chira. I was a huge fan of Chira's. We had worked together at one point, and I respected her skill and dedication. I also admired how she was committed to balancing her career goals with her family's needs, especially as Robin and I struggled with similar concerns once Zachary was born.

Chira was also close to Bill Keller. Raines would criticize her section almost weekly without giving her suggestions to improve it. She would come to me, and I would try to interpret what Raines wanted. But I knew Raines would not be satisfied; he was trying to force Chira out to make room for Katy Roberts.

We came up with the best solutions for everyone involved. As Week in Review editor, Roberts would receive the kind of support she deserved from Raines. We put Chira in charge of a Sulzberger and Raines priority, a newsroom unit to reestablish the *Times'* presence in the book world. In her new role, editorial director of book development, she would serve as an agent for the staff, searching out book projects. It allowed her to work with executives on the paper's business side. That exposure would help her get to the next level.

The final piece of the puzzle: Jim Roberts, the deputy National editor and no relation to Katy, became the new National editor.

We had already brought Suzanne Daley back from a correspondent tour in Paris to become Education editor. There was no one in the newsroom I respected or trusted more. I saw the post as a stepping-stone to higher ones, including the masthead.

The search for a new investigations editor was most difficult. Raines interviewed candidates inside and outside the paper, and none was quite the right fit. It was embarrassing that the *Times* could not find anyone to take such an important job.

I turned to an in-house candidate, Doug Frantz, a strong investigative journalist who had sought to broaden himself with a foreign assignment to Turkey. Frantz had never worked as a manager in the newsroom, but I respected his judgment and thought he would be a great addition to the management team.

The summer ended abruptly and sadly. As Robin, Zachary, and I again spent the last weeks of August on Martha's Vineyard, I learned that one of our editors, Allen Myerson, killed himself by leaping off the *Times* building. I flew back to New York the next day, despite Raines's suggestion that I continue my vacation. I wanted to be in the newsroom with my staff and offer comfort where I could.

By fall, Raines and I announced the series of appointments and the dominoes fell. We had strengthened the leadership of the National desk and investigations. We posted people in the jobs they wanted but also in the right places for the paper. We were sending a strong message to the staff about what kind of leaders we wanted.

———

THERE SEEMED to be only one newsroom issue that excited Raines. For months, senior executives had discussed the need to broaden the *Times'* reach by expanding into foreign markets. The company had already launched several minor initiatives in Russia, Europe, and Asia, but Sulzberger Jr. wanted more.

He decided on a bold move: he wanted to become sole owner of the *International Herald Tribune*, or *IHT*, the Paris-based paper that the *Times* owned jointly with the *Washington Post*. Even in good years, the

IHT, with a readership of slightly more than 250,000, lost money. But it was a beachhead into foreign markets. Sulzberger informed Donald Graham, the chairman of the Washington Post Company and a longtime friend of his, of two options: Graham could buy out the *Times*' interest or sell his own. Sulzberger was both pained and ecstatic when Graham decided to sell the *Post*'s interest for sixty-five million dollars.

The move was radical, risky, and unpleasant.

The *Post* had brought the *Times* in as a partner several decades ago, and the Sulzberger and Graham families were close as two of the last remaining newspaper dynasties. At worst, the move would fail financially. But even if it succeeded, the deal would almost certainly sour the friendship between Graham and Sulzberger.

Even so, we all celebrated as the deal closed on the first of January, 2003. Sulzberger wanted to proceed cautiously. He wanted the senior executives in New York to become familiar with the operations and to allay fears among the *IHT* staff. As he often said: "Change sucks."

Shortly before the deal closed, senior editors and executives from the *IHT* flew to New York to meet their counterparts. At one point during the get-acquainted session, David Ignatius, the *IHT* executive editor and Raines's counterpart, said something that angered Raines. When Ignatius, Raines, and I met for dinner at the Four Seasons that evening, Raines said he was deeply troubled by Ignatius's earlier comments. When a bewildered Ignatius said he did not remember his remarks, Raines exploded: "Either you're a liar or not much of a journalist, since you can't remember what you said a few hours ago!"

Ignatius was speechless. I tried to shift the discussion, but to no avail. Finally, Ignatius acknowledged that perhaps he had made a mistake, and we were able to have a dinner that none of us wanted.

I thought that Raines had begun to understand that he needed to change his bullying ways. But after his outburst, I felt as if I could no longer predict his behavior. The next morning, Ignatius stopped by my office to talk about how he should proceed with Raines. I could only share what I had heard in countless meetings: that the *Times* was comfortable with the leadership team in Paris and wanted to move slowly. But after Raines's display, I knew better. I think Ignatius did, too. A short time later, he resigned and became a columnist at the *Washington Post*.

Actually, I began to feel sorry for Raines. He was at the height of his power but had so little support from those he managed. I believe this made him even more detached from the staff. He was starting to resemble Captain Bligh in the movie *Mutiny on the Bounty*, and the more I saw of this, the more I tried to shore him up. That is, until he blindsided me.

Months of work on our special project were beginning to pay off. Golden Behr had come up with a compelling way to tell the stories of how much the world hated America, and we had a strong team to deliver the goods. As 2002 drew to a close, I felt that we were only a few months away from delivering a superb series.

I had briefed Raines along the way, but it was my project. Just after Thanksgiving, we met for drinks; he said he wanted to catch up on office business before I returned from vacation. As we sat down for martinis at the Millennium Hotel, he made his agenda clear: he wanted to shut down the series. He was worried about committing resources, about a dozen reporters and editors, when the Bush administration was preparing for war against Iraq. I argued that the timing for the series could not be more appropriate. It was clear he had made up his mind, but I argued that we had already invested considerable time and effort on the project and that abandoning it would send a terrible signal to the staff. Raines added he was concerned about whether I could adequately supervise the project given my other responsibilities.

I read Raines well enough to know that he had already decided. It was a painful moment of truth about our relationship. Despite all the talk about partners, we both knew where we stood. He was exercising his authority. My options were to convince him to change his position, appeal to Sulzberger as publisher, or pout. None made sense to me. So I tried to keep the project alive, at least in theory, by getting Raines to agree to allow me to revive it when there were fewer demands on the newsroom.

It was not much of a consolation. As I went through the newsroom informing reporters and editors that we were abandoning months of work, I tried to put a positive spin on the news: it would be revived in time, I said. But I was deeply embarrassed. And I could not shake a suspicion that Raines scuttled the project to remind me who was boss.

SEVERAL WEEKS later, the rift between us widened.

Neil Amdur, the Sports editor, casually mentioned at a news meeting that he was running a controversial column related to the Masters tournament at the Augusta National Golf Club, which Raines had ordered the *Times* to follow closely. Raines wanted the staff to focus on the feminist activist Martha Burk's unexpected protest against the Georgia country club for its men-only membership policies. Raines had seized upon the idea of a modern-day discrimination story and argued that Augusta mattered because the PGA tournaments received major corporate funding and were broadcast by a major network, CBS. Where other news organizations relegated the event to their sports pages, Raines saw Augusta as front-page news. I felt the executive editor had a right to set the paper's news agenda. But as I told him, Augusta was a story, not a cause.

Amdur explained that the Sports column criticized Burk. The writer, Harvey Araton, argued that while Burk was attacking discrimination at Augusta, she was ignoring the difficulties that women encountered in other sports. Several editors, women in particular, had challenged his premise, creating a divide in the newsroom. Although I rarely read columns before they appeared in the paper, I asked to see this one. Araton wrote that Burk's position was generating a backlash among some women, a point I found newsworthy in and of itself. With more reporting, I suggested to Amdur, the piece could be elevated to a page one news story. I later called Araton to make the same point. He agreed to do additional reporting and resubmit the piece.

Meanwhile, Raines was preparing to leave for Paris to visit the *IHT*. He was taking his girlfriend, Krystyna, along with an engagement ring. Before Raines left, Amdur and his deputy, Bill Brink, were back in my office. This time, they had a column written by Dave Anderson, who argued that critics should stop giving Tiger Woods, the black golf phenomenon, a hard time about refusing to boycott the Masters tournament because of the Augusta officials' stance on women.

The *Times'* editorial page had argued that as a minority, Woods should speak up on behalf of women. I had disagreed with the editorial.

African Americans could pick their battles, I believed, which was the
point Anderson was making. I had not asked to see this piece, but the
Sports editor brought it to me. It was similar to a recent column in the
Washington Post by Michael Wilbon, a black columnist. I told Amdur
that I did not think the *Times* should follow the *Post* with a similar
column a week later; that made our paper appear redundant and late.
Since Raines was so into Augusta, I showed him the column for a second opinion. He killed it on the spot. His reason: it was at odds with
the editorial.

I relayed his decision to the Sports editors and told them they could
appeal it to Raines if they disagreed.

While Raines was in Paris asking Krystyna to marry him, a furor
brewed, first in the *Times* newsroom and, with the help of e-mail and
bloggers, among journalists around the country. Critics universally
accused Raines and me of censorship. The "news" among the most
uninformed was that I killed two Sports columns. I was surprised by
the ferocity of the attacks and that none of the journalists criticizing
the paper's leadership contacted me for perspective or clarification. It
was the start of a deeply distressing pattern.

What angered me most was the assumption that the columns were
kept out of the paper because they ran counter to the paper's previous
tough coverage. The suggestion was that decisions were ideologically
based, which could not have been further from the truth. I was also
annoyed that outside journalists expected to have a say in how the
paper was edited.

I was eager to defend our actions. I prepared a memo to the staff,
which Sulzberger Jr. and Raines, from Paris, approved and a team of
senior editors endorsed.

The memo said that I was against censorship—as if my thirty years
in journalism meant nothing. I also reminded staff that the top editors had the right to determine what appeared in the paper, and that
included not running articles that were found to be lacking. The statement also reflected Raines's comments about spiking the Anderson
column because it took issue with the paper's editorials. "Intramural
quarreling of that kind is unseemly and self-absorbed," it said.

When Raines returned the following week—Krystyna said yes—he had a change of heart. He argued that the most important consideration was to end the ruckus, not to stand behind decisions that were clear just a week ago. He said that he had read both columns again and now saw nothing wrong with them. I argued again that the Araton piece should be a news story, but he said he did not think that pushing that argument was worth the effort. Over my strong objections, he ordered that both columns be published. They were, without reference to the paper's editorials. I was beside myself with anger.

I knew that I had been hung out to dry, and I thought the damage went well beyond me: by caving in to the critics, we emboldened them and gave them a way to fight back. Whenever someone questioned our decisions, it took only a phone call to another media organization to have the issue aired and debated in public. This was a defining moment in our tenure as newsroom leaders. And the start of another distressing pattern.

———

RAINES AND I moved on, but after Augusta, our relationship was tenuous.

I decided I needed my own support system, so I first created a kind of kitchen cabinet, a group of senior editors I considered friends whom I would consult regularly. They included Suzanne Daley, Adam Moss, Soma Golden Behr, Bill Schmidt, Jill Abramson, and John Geddes. I sought them out often, and depending on their reaction, I would then consult Raines.

I became obsessed with getting more of our own team in place and lobbied Raines incessantly. I set my sights on finding a new Sports editor. We wanted to bring a fresh perspective to the coverage.

We had identified a ranking Sports editor at the *Washington Post*. Along with Dave Jones, who, as a *Times* consultant, was helping us recruit, Raines met him for dinner. According to the editor, the evening was a disaster. At one point, he said, Raines asked him why he wanted to work for Leonard Downie Jr., the *Post*'s low-key executive editor. According to the editor, Raines asked him whether Downie was the kind of person who could make a newsroom orgasmic by entering it, like Raines could.

Once again, I tried to straighten out the mess. I asked the editor if we could start over. I explained that Raines had probably had one too many to drink that night, which the editor had already concluded. I talked about where we wanted to take the Sports department, the compensation he could expect, and how I thought he could benefit the Sports report. I asked him to come to New York and bring his wife—I knew we had to win her over as well. They were both concerned about living in New York. I suggested that they tour the city with a real estate expert. The editor would have a chance to meet key people, including Sulzberger Jr. They could catch a Broadway show and have a fabulous dinner, on us. I was pulling out all the stops.

For days, we tried to arrange a time for his visit. But clearly the *Post* learned of our overtures. In short order, the sitting Sports editor retired, and our prospect was appointed to replace him. Eventually, we held an internal contest between three candidates, and selected one of them, Tom Jolly. Neil Amdur became a senior editor, focusing on recruiting. In the process, we passed over Joe Sexton, a deputy Metro editor who was close to Jon Landman.

We had lost Doug Frantz to the *Los Angeles Times*, where Dean Baquet had gone in 2000 to become managing editor. Frantz's departure meant the *Times* was short an investigations editor, a serious gap. Masthead editors all recommended Glenn Kramon, the Business editor. When we took our new posts, Raines initially disliked the business coverage and wanted Kramon out. But with the department's strong performance after 9/11 and on Enron, Raines became a big fan. Kramon wanted the position, but the deal unraveled in negotiations.

Raines was unable to contain his joy when he told me Jill Abramson might give up the job of Washington bureau chief. The two had talked about the *Book Review*, he said. That surprised me. I thought the position would be a digression from other news departments such as Metro, National, Business, or Foreign, which were more likely to lead to a steady climb up the masthead, where I could see her landing sooner than later. But I also saw the pluses: It would bring her to New York and broaden her range as an editor, making her even more appealing down the road. It would also end the constant battles with Raines, whom she had managed to checkmate. When I followed up with her, she was not as definitive as Raines.

I knew Raines still wanted to move Pat Tyler in as Washington bureau chief, and I stressed again that doing so would be a serious mistake. Tyler did not have the loyalty of the department. "It will create a backlash just when things seem to be calming down," I said. "And it will not be fair to Pat to come into the job with so much opposition."

We did not discuss it further; succession was hypothetical as long as Abramson remained in the job.

Whether Abramson stayed in Washington or came to New York did not matter to me as much as removing Jon Landman as Metro editor.

Landman ran Metro as his private fiefdom. Using his reporters for non-Metro assignments required his approval, and such requests were seldom collegial discussions. Landman would resist or offer his own choices, and the ensuing debate would escalate into a pitched battle. I was tired of fighting. As a former Metro editor, I was also troubled that my relationships with many people on his staff, some of whom had worked for me, had become distant.

And then Landman simply went too far. About a year after I became managing editor, he stood in my office accusing Raines and me of slanting the news and sacrificing news judgment for ideology. He said this was especially true of Raines, but that I too was at fault since I was Raines's number two and had done nothing to stop him.

Landman had frequently complained to me about Raines's decisions, behind closed doors. Sometimes I listened; sometimes I challenged him. Often, I told him that if he really believed what he was saying, he should tell Raines himself. He seldom did.

But as I listened to him attack my professionalism, I exploded.

"I know we've disagreed, Jon, but I can't believe you would accuse us of slanting the news," I said, my voice rising. "That's the most serious charge you can make against a colleague! How could you say such a thing?"

Landman dug up previous disagreements, such as the New Jersey racial profiling article.

I did not get angry often, but when I did, it showed in my expression and the pitch of my voice. Landman saw that I was angry. He sought to end the conversation, but I insisted we continue.

"No matter how many times I have disagreed with you, I would never, ever question your motives," I said. "I can't believe that you're questioning mine!"

He smiled meekly and backed down, quickly leaving my office. This reinforced my view of him: he was a typical bully, willing to say or do anything to get his way, but ready to retreat if someone stood up to him. The conversation proved a turning point.

I went to Raines and recounted Landman's attack. I told Raines the situation was untenable between Landman and me. One of us had to go. For days, we considered several options before coming up with a plan that would send him to London as the *Times'* bureau chief. Sulzberger Jr. offered to make the request himself over a dinner with Landman. I do not know if the dinner was ever held.

In early March 2003, Howell Raines and Krystyna Stachowiak married in a small, private affair at the one-hundred-year-old Trinity Episcopal Church in Mount Pocono, Pennsylvania. Robin and I were among a handful of *Times* executives and their spouses present. We shared a ride to Pennsylvania with Sulzberger and his wife, Gail, marking the first time that we had socialized with them. The wedding was also attended by Raines's two boys, Ben and Jeffrey, and Grady Williams Hutchinson, the black woman who cared for Raines when he was a child and who was the focus of Raines's *New York Times Magazine* essay that won a Pulitzer Prize in 1992. The event was tender, and I had never seen Raines so happy. It was as if he was finally at peace. If only his colleagues could see this Howell Raines, I thought. They never would.

———

On the evening of Wednesday, April 30, 2003, I sat at my kitchen table trying to understand a young *Times* reporter named Jayson Blair. Two days before, Macarena Hernandez, a reporter at the *San Antonio*

Express-News and a former *Times* intern, contacted a senior editor at the *Times* and accused Blair of plagiarizing her story about the distress of a Texas mother over her missing son, a U.S. Army mechanic serving in Iraq.

Plagiarism, or stealing from previously published material, is one of journalism's highest sins and violates a basic trust between the writer and reader. To assume the veracity of another writer without checking the information firsthand is an unacceptable leap of faith. To use material without attributing it is deceitful and unethical. Both are fireable offenses.

The allegation rattled senior editors, but not because a reporter was under attack—complaints about journalists, including those at the *Times*, are much more frequent than readers might imagine. It is rare that complaints point to a dereliction of duty. But in the two days since Hernandez's alert, evidence was mounting that the plagiarism charge was true. This prompted a larger concern: was this an isolated incident or part of a pattern of fraud?

I first ordered an investigation to learn the facts. Several senior editors began to comb through Blair's previous articles, personnel file, and expense reports. Editors searched cell phone statements, e-mail logs, notes, and memos. They questioned almost everyone who had crossed his path at the paper. I also alerted Raines, who was vacationing in the Poconos. He seemed comfortable with my plan of action.

Investigations in most newsrooms are messy. There is no subpoena power, and those under investigation are not required to testify under oath. Unless they are willing to acknowledge wrongdoing, the entire affair becomes more like a police inquiry.

The summary of Blair's finances was troublesome. On a trip to Washington, D.C., several months earlier, he could not pay his hotel bill. Blair had worked as a reporter for several years yet had no credit cards. His supervising editor had to use his own charge card to cover the tab. Blair took assignments that involved travel; I wondered how he paid. Plus he never sought reimbursement, a new piece of the puzzle.

Initially, I thought his plagiarizing stemmed from financial problems. Perhaps he was unable to pay for the trip to Los Fresnos, the location of the story and, too proud to expose his financial straits to his editors, turned to the Internet. It was unethical, but it made sense. Desperate people do desperate things.

As more information became known, though, it was clear that Blair's problems stretched over several years and numerous supervisors.

In the summer of 1998, Hernandez became a *Times* intern after completing the graduate journalism program with an emphasis in documentary filmmaking at the University of California at Berkeley. She was one of four summer interns. Another was Blair. At the end of the summer, I had taken Hernandez, who had grown up in Texas's Rio Grande Valley in a small town called La Joya, to lunch. I was a deputy managing editor, and my aim was to convince her to remain at the *Times* rather than return home with no promise of a job.

As we ate at Joe Allen, she explained how she really wanted to work at the *Times* but that she needed to be near her mother. Only a few weeks earlier, her father, a sixty-one-year-old construction worker, had been killed in a traffic accident.

She talked about the death of her father, and I talked about the death of my mother. She was making the right decision, I said. I promised that the *Times* would always have a place for her if I had anything to say about it.

By contrast, I had not singled out Blair or connected with him as I did with Hernandez. I knew he had attended the University of Maryland at College Park and had interned at a couple of papers, including the *Boston Globe*, small papers in Centreville and Fairfax, Virginia, and the Maryland bureau of the *Washington Post*. Reading his file later, I saw what had appealed to *Times'* recruiters. An editor from one of his previous posts described him as energetic, hardworking, and willing to go anywhere, anytime. These were just the qualities recruiters prized in interns.

Almost every day in the summer of 1998, I would see Blair at his desk when I came to work. Because I arrived early, the fact that he was already there impressed me.

"Don't you ever go home?" I started teasing him.

By all accounts, he had a stellar summer, praised for his demeanor and his drive. His initial success explained why he remained at the

Times. He received an invitation to extend his internship at summer's end, but he requested a delay to return to Maryland and finish his senior year (which he did not, it was later determined). When he returned to the paper the following summer, he did so as an extended intern.

That summer in 1999, when I would steal away to the "smoking room" on the fifth floor, I occasionally encountered Blair, and we talked. He asked about my career and the careers of other senior executives. He wanted to know how the *Times* had covered some news events. He seemed enthralled.

He shared details of a middle-class upbringing. His father had worked at the Smithsonian, and his mother was a teacher. He told me how much he loved being a journalist and how much he wanted to succeed.

I also knew that in a newsroom full of gossips, Blair led the pack. He attracted people seeking information and repelled those who found his "scoops" unseemly. In January 2000, as we did each New Year, Robin and I opened our home to friends and *Times* colleagues, including young reporters who were stuck in New York working for the holidays. As we considered whom to invite, I mentioned Blair. Robin vetoed him. She, too, had heard he was a gossip and was not comfortable with him in our home.

Blair's path to a full-time reporter position at the *Times* was clear. His hiring was indeed a part of affirmative action efforts but not in the way such programs typically work. At one point, many young reporters started as news clerks and, after a lengthy period, moved up to internships. This nontraditional route to joining the staff was exploited mostly by white men and women. Young journalists of color skipped this path, most often because they were in demand at other newspapers and insisted on joining the reporting ranks directly. This put the *Times* at a disadvantage in recruiting young minorities. Lelyveld sought to address the situation by creating a program in which candidates could work the summer as interns, and if they succeeded, their internships would be extended. If they continued to thrive in the internships, they would move up to interim positions as reporter-trainees. Trainees would be on probation for up to three years, after which they would become full-time reporters or be let go. To head off legal challenges, the trainee program was expanded to include all young journalists, not just minorities.

Interns and trainees skipped the rigorous interview process that I and most staff reporters and editors had undergone during hiring; summer interns were selected by senior editors running the internship program, and department heads decided who became reporter-trainees, with the choices blessed by the executive and managing editors.

The first editor to reach Blair about the plagiarism allegation was Jim Roberts, the National editor. Blair, who was on loan to the National desk from Sports, was in Fairfax, Virginia, covering a court hearing in the case involving the Washington-area snipers. On Monday, April 28, the day Hernandez complained, Blair told Roberts that he had downloaded several articles about the twenty-four-year-old army mechanic and his family before going to Texas, and that he did not recall reading Hernandez's story. But almost immediately after he hung up with Roberts, he called Hernandez and attacked her for raising concerns about his story. On Tuesday, April 29, the internal matter became public. The *Washington City Paper* and the *Washington Post* Web site carried brief stories raising questions about whether Blair had plagiarized. "It's pretty damning, I think," Robert Rivard, editor of the *San Antonio Express-News*, told the *Post*.

I was communicating by e-mail with Rivard. I had assured him we would get to the truth and take appropriate action. He wrote a second, angry e-mail after Blair called Hernandez. I told him that I shared his anger and would ensure that Blair never bothered her again.

Roberts ordered Blair back to New York. Tuesday morning, Blair again denied stealing from the *Express-News* story. We had to put all of his work under a microscope. And since Blair was facing a fireable offense, we summoned company lawyers.

We had already informed Catherine Mathis, the *Times'* head of PR, of the internal review to make sure she was positioned to answer press inquiries. To the PR staff, based on what we had told them so far, the Blair situation amounted to a blip.

On Wednesday, April 30, Blair was to be grilled by company lawyers and senior editors. They asked me to meet with him beforehand as the ranking editor to stress the need for honesty with the investigators.

I tried to emphasize to Blair the seriousness of the charges. There was no small talk. I was firm and direct.

"Jayson, the most important thing you can do is to tell us everything that happened," I said.

"I know, and I will," he answered.

He launched into an explanation of how he had not done anything wrong, and I interrupted him. He was about to give me the same story that he had given Roberts.

"Just be honest and tell everything," I said.

"I will," he promised. As he walked out of my office, he turned and said, "Thanks for everything."

I repeated: "Just be honest."

That was the last time I saw Jayson Blair.

15

INQUISITION

My introduction to Gerald M. Boyd was when I interviewed to be his assistant. One of his many questions was, "What do you think about or know about me?" I remember feeling so unprepared, not being able to rattle off all that he had accomplished to become an assistant managing editor. With great apprehension, I told him I had not done any research on him but I was a dedicated employee who understood hard work and commitment. Surprisingly, I hit a home run. After getting to know Gerald, I realized that he appreciated my honesty—and my having no misconceptions about him or the newsroom.

Several coworkers forewarned me about his temperament. In the early days, they would stop by and ask, "Do you need a shoulder to lean on?" I always told them things were good, and they were. Believe me, there were times when he pushed me to my limits, but he was never negative. He had high expectations, and there was no room for mistakes, although I made plenty. I would retreat, and to make up, he would place a treat from the cafeteria—a peace offering—on my desk. He knew I had a sweet tooth. With that, he would give me that boy-like smile that said, "Can we be friends?" I would smile back, and we would move forward, just like family.

At a training session at the *Times*, I was told to never get coffee for the executives because it would set a precedent. Initially I followed the rule, but Gerald, as assistant managing editor, deputy managing editor, and managing editor, always offered to get me coffee. So whenever he needed coffee, I made sure he had his, milk, no sugar.

—CHRISTINE MOORE

B Y THURSDAY morning, May 1, 2003, it was clear that Blair's plagiarism extended far beyond the Texas story. Roberts found evidence that Blair did not visit several other communities that he wrote about. After Wednesday's intense grilling by company lawyers and Bill Schmidt, the associate managing editor for personnel and newsroom administration, Blair sent word that he would resign. Once he did, I knew, we would lose what little leverage we had to get him to cooperate. We would have to depend on documents, records, and his computer files to get to the truth. We had to move quickly. All of his work, including notebooks and personal information in his desk, was confiscated and secured.

Blair had apparently told friends that he had considered hanging himself the previous night. I did not know whether he was truly despondent or whether this was another lie. Even so, I reached out to several of his newsroom friends to make sure they knew he was leaving the paper so they could offer him support.

I called Sulzberger Jr. to tell him that it was all but certain that Blair plagiarized the Texas story and others, and that he was going to resign. When I finished, he was silent for a moment. Finally, he said, "The most important thing is leveling with our reader. Just remember, it is not the crime but the cover-up." It was the lesson every journalist and corporate officer took from the Watergate scandal that toppled Nixon. Characteristically, he ended the call with a quip: "Good luck," he said with a laugh.

Next, I reached Raines at his weekend home in the Poconos. He was out fishing, and it was several hours before he called back. When he did, he said he was pleased with how we had handled the situation. I said I would keep him informed.

On Thursday afternoon, Blair resigned in a one-paragraph note to Raines and me. PR issued a statement under Raines's name: "The *Times* apologizes to its readers for a grave breach of its journalistic standards," it began. It pledged to review the Texas story along with Blair's other work to "be sure the record is kept straight."

Raines had committed the paper to examine Blair's articles over his five-year *Times* career, hundreds of stories. We needed to figure out how to keep that pledge. To me, it made sense to start with an examination of his most recent story and then work backward, looking for patterns of lifting quotes or information.

On Friday morning, May 2, I assembled two groups of editors: one to focus on finding fraud and another to explore Blair's personal life in search of a motivation for his crimes. They sifted through e-mail and cell phone records and interviewed his friends. Unfortunately, we had no plan to handle the media, and by now that need loomed large.

That morning, a story by Howard Kurtz, the *Washington Post*'s media reporter, said that Blair had "been involved in a number of controversies and the paper had run fifty corrections on his stories." The number fifty surprised me and other senior editors as well. Clearly, someone in the *Times* had drawn Kurtz's attention to the fact. But without context, the number did not explain much. How many stories did Blair write over that five-year stretch? Were the corrections minor or major? Were they mistakes based on faulty information? Changes by an editor? Kurtz addressed none of these issues.

As I considered the holes in the article, Raines appeared at my office door. I was surprised to see him, since he was supposed to be on vacation. He had returned to take command; he wanted an immediate briefing. He listened as I described what we had done, but only with slight interest. He had his own plan, and now I was doing the listening.

He wanted us to assemble a reporting team to investigate and write about Blair's fraud.

"I learned a long time ago that the antidote for bad journalism is good journalism," he sloganeered. He talked about the need to share everything we knew with our readers and to be mindful that it was not the crime but the cover-up. Obviously, he had talked to Sulzberger.

I agreed with his goal of correcting the record and being straight with readers. But I disputed the means. We did not know how wide or deep the fraud went. There were rumors about drug use and drinking binges and that Blair had rifled through the computer files of newsroom colleagues. What was true of the gossip, and what was its significance? I did not want the responsibility of finding the answers to those questions placed in the hands of reporters. The issue was the accountability of the newsroom's senior management. As managers, we had an obligation to ferret out the facts and not just delegate the task to others, I argued. "A handoff is a dereliction of duty."

"But they work for us," Raines reasoned. "They're our reporters."

"But it should be management, not reporters, finding out what Blair did," I responded. "That's our responsibility."

Around and around we went without getting anywhere and losing time. Finally, Raines became irritated and barked his decision: "It's my editorship that's riding on this! I have to go with my gut!"

His remarks were the same as those he had coached me to use in management conflicts with others. Now he was turning them on me. This made me angry.

"But it's my responsibility," I shot back, "to give you the best advice I can. That's why I'm here."

He settled down and sighed, and then he asked me not to criticize his decision in public. His words stung. Never in our twenty-year relationship had he expressed doubts about my loyalty. As managing editor, I had never criticized his actions publicly, no matter how much I disagreed and challenged him in private. Still, he made it clear that he no longer trusted me.

In the next few hours, we shut down one investigation and revved up another. Raines selected three reporters, David Barstow, Adam Liptak, and Jacques Steinberg, for the team. When Al Siegal, an assistant managing editor, noted the absence of a black reporter, Raines added Jonathan Glater, who worked in the Business section.

Raines then asked his longtime friend Phil Taubman, the deputy editor of the editorial page, to manage the probe. Taubman declined. Conferring quickly with several top editors, he went to Glenn Kramon, the Business editor. Kramon was an odd choice; Raines had been one of his harshest critics until Kramon's staff performed so well on the Enron scandal. Even so, Raines did not regard Kramon as a force, only a good soldier who would follow orders. Kramon agreed to lead the investigation. Media editor Lorne Manly assisted him.

As we met with Kramon and Manly, Raines described the investigation as an effort to determine what Blair had done wrong. He added that both he and Sulzberger felt strongly that the team should avoid "demonizing" Blair. He obviously was a troubled man; the institution would not pounce on someone when he was down. I only listened, convinced that Raines was making another mistake. There was no way to fully appreciate Blair's crimes or to understand why he committed them without a complete and unvarnished picture of him. Whatever his demons, they were a big and important piece of the puzzle.

The newsroom was now preoccupied with Blair. Reporters clustered and passed on the latest gossip. They were talking with journalists at other publications and closely following media blogs.

With no preparation, Raines decided to launch a media blitz defending the paper and its top management. That afternoon he sat for interviews with several journalists and immediately created new problems. When reporters asked him about the corrections that the paper had to print as follow-up to Blair's errors, Raines tried to minimize the issue by arguing that some reporters had even more corrections than Blair. The remark ricocheted through the newsroom, creating an instant backlash.

Despite what our years in Washington had taught Raines and me about the importance of defining a problem and facing it head-on, Raines focused on countering criticism of the number of corrections connected to Blair's reporting; he was not interested in examining the context, the whys and hows of a troubled reporter going over a cliff.

We also were not prepared to address another issue that was already gaining traction: Blair survived despite earlier problems because of affirmative action, which had led to special treatment. Records showed that Blair had been one of forty-eight people to go through the reporter-trainee program since Lelyveld started it. Of those, thirty-seven trainees were promoted, while the paper rejected seven, three of whom were journalists of color. (One quit, and three were still active trainees.)

Now, sitting at my desk, I stared at what amounted to a subpoena from the reporting team that Raines had assembled. In fewer than three hours, they had put together a massive demand for information. "Please consider this a formal request for the following materials in connection with our review of articles written by Blair," it said. "Should you decline to provide us with any of these documents, we would appreciate a full explanation of your reasoning."

They wanted everything: copies of all articles written by Blair, including those written during his summer internship; copies of articles he wrote for other news organizations; copies of any letters or other communication originating inside or outside the newspaper concerning Blair's work; copies of his employment application; all evaluations of his performance as an intern, reporter-trainee, and reporter; his personnel files; all reimbursement requests for travel, cell phone use, and other expenses; copies of any internal memos generated by Metro or National tracking corrections to his articles.

I had none of the requested materials. Some items were in the newsroom administration office, some in the departments where Blair had worked. But the team seemed to assume that I had in my possession every piece of information on Blair. The letter was clear. We had lost control of the investigation. I could only shake my head as I recalled Raines's remarks about the reporting team working for us.

Kramon also insisted on adding another reporter, Dan Barry, to the team. Barry was the white reporter whom Landman had offered and I had vetoed to replace Felicia Lee as a Metro columnist. He was close to many of Blair's biggest critics.

At the end of the day, I stopped by Raines's office to say good night. Our relationship was clearly strained. The next morning, Saturday, May 3, we talked briefly by phone, still at odds over his decision. We agreed to continue the conversation over breakfast after the weekend. On Monday, May 5, as I ate oatmeal and Raines devoured poached eggs on white toast at the Millennium Hotel, we both struggled to understand why we had such different approaches to this challenge and what we failed to appreciate about the other's views. Together and apart, we had faced other crises in our career. We were both used to problem solving.

To him, the most important remedy was to get the facts to the public quickly. We could not appear to be stalling, and we had to make the disclosures in a way that brought integrity to the process. My counter was simple: We were managers, already accused of failing to manage Blair properly. By not taking control of the situation, we were further damaging our ability to lead the newsroom.

We got nowhere.

Finally, I asked him how bad he thought the situation was. He was optimistic, saying he was sure that it would pass once the investigation was finished and we told readers all we knew about Blair's deceptions.

I wanted so much to believe him. But I had too many doubts.

"I hope you're right," I responded. "I really hope you're right."

———

BACK IN the newsroom that Monday, Raines and I both went to our offices to read Blair's personnel files. This was the first time either of us had seen the entire contents.

As I sifted through the information, two patterns emerged. One was that Blair was a master at gaming the system. He had skillfully conned some of those who directly supervised him, not just once but repeatedly, as his remorseful responses to critical performance evaluation showed. At the same time, he had exploited cracks in the management structure, made possible by the sheer size of the newsroom with dozens of departments and 1,100 staff members. No one had a complete picture of Blair, only snippets of his five-year career.

The other pattern was that Blair's rate of errors ebbed and flowed. Mistakes are not unusual given the deadline pressure of reporting and writing for a daily paper, and correction counts are just one measure of a journalist's skills. Blair's correction rate actually was within acceptable limits, the reporters' analysis would find. But editors had attributed the mistakes to a young, overeager reporter, not a habitual liar.

During one five-month stretch while he was an extended intern, he wrote more than one hundred stories with only one correction. The production was astounding for a young reporter. The corrections increased slightly when he was promoted to reporter-trainee. Then the bottom fell out.

Beginning in September 2001, his rate of errors escalated sharply. Blair cited as a reason his struggle to cope with the death of a close cousin who died at the Pentagon on 9/11. He supplied a name and took time off to attend the funeral. Friends in the newsroom rallied around him. But the investigative team found that he had lied; while someone from his hometown named Blair died at the Pentagon, the person was of no relation.

On Metro, some attributed the spate of corrections to "reporter exhaustion." Later I learned the language was code for speculation that Blair had been drunk. This information would have helped top management understand the situation better, but at the time, none of Blair's immediate supervisors made us aware of those concerns. Nor did we know of a series of corrective meetings between Blair and his supervisors, including Jon Landman; Nancy Sharkey, who was in charge of reporter-trainees; and Jeanne Pinder, Blair's immediate supervisor. This was not unusual; in *Times* hierarchy, as in most large companies, lower-level employees are managed by their immediate supervisors. It is up to those supervisors to report serious concerns. In any event, documents showed that their sessions with Blair appeared to be working. In late October, after the meetings, Blair wrote to Landman expressing regret for his offenses.

In the one meaningful conversation that I had about Blair before the plagiarism came to light, Landman let me know about a tough end-of-the-year evaluation dated January 2002. He said he would cc it to me and asked that I meet with Blair to echo his concerns, something that department heads often did to emphasize the gravity of their remarks. I agreed immediately.

Landman's review, which he sent to me and Bill Schmidt, the editor in charge of personnel and newsroom administration, began, "There's big trouble I want you both to be aware of."

Attached was an evaluation with compliments and caveats. It praised Blair's energy and enthusiasm, then attributed to him a correction rate that was "extraordinarily high by the standards of the paper." Finally, it demanded that he improve.

When I met with Blair in my office to discuss the review, he attributed his problems to substance abuse, saying that he had started to abuse drugs and alcohol following his cousin's death on 9/11. I chose my words carefully before responding.

"I don't want to sound unsympathetic," I said, "but the only thing I really care about is your performance. Everyone has problems. Only you can decide if you want to get help. You have enormous promise and potential, but your career is your hands. I don't want to hear about what you're doing—drugs or what. I don't care. The issue is your performance, and unless you change, you are blowing a big opportunity."

I encouraged Blair to seek counseling, saying that to do so was not a sign of weakness. Blair said he would get help. Later, I learned that he had contacted the head of the paper's Employee Assistance Program, which helps employees cope with mental and emotional problems that interfere with work, and that they had developed a course of action. Because of confidentiality rules, I did not learn more.

That conversation in my office was the only time Blair and I talked about his performance other than the day before he resigned.

In early April 2002, Landman received an e-mail from one of his editors about another Blair correction. He then fired his own e-mail to Bill Schmidt and Nancy Sharkey, an e-mail that he later claimed he had also sent to me. He never did. It said:

"We have to stop Jayson from writing for the *Times*. Right now."

As Blair's supervisor, Landman had the authority to do just that, to stop Blair from writing for the *Times* by not assigning him stories. More draconian measures, like firing him, could not be done without following prescribed dismissal procedures, since Blair had the protection of the Newspaper Guild. Newsroom administration was developing a case against him with warnings and documenting Blair's failure to respond. That was Schmidt's plan of attack, which I endorsed. Blair was put on notice by Schmidt, who tied Blair's future to his performance. Over the next six months, just one correction out of seventy of his stories was attributed to Blair. Landman and Sharkey praised the improvement.

There was so much in Blair's file, so many up and downs, so much that needed context, I again wondered about Raines's decision to have the team of reporters conduct the investigation and to do it in only a week. It was important to explore each turn to understand what had happened. I went to him to renew our debate over who should lead the investigation, reporters or managers. His reaction floored me.

"Is there anything involving you and Jayson that you need to tell me?" he asked.

"Of course not," I answered. "I hardly knew Jayson."

I was furious. I decided then that if Raines wanted to walk away from my advice, I would not try to save him. I had a feeling it was too late anyway.

———

JAYSON BLAIR quickly became a well-known name in and out of journalism. What was emerging was a portrait of a young black reporter brought along too fast or given too many chances in a misguided attempt at diversity. Others saw him as an example of a breakdown in the *Times'* vaunted system of checks, which could only have come from a serious management failure. I kept hoping the focus would turn to what I saw as the real issue: a man whose sickness made it all but impossible to prevent his crimes.

In the newsroom, Raines and I barely spoke. He spent much of his time in his office on the telephone. I could only imagine that he was seeking advice on how to react. I tried to function as always, attending news meetings, walking the newsroom and engaging reporters and editors, and answering e-mails. Several days after Blair resigned, I kept a previously scheduled lunch with a group of young reporters and news clerks. I was prepared to wax poetic about the rigors and ideals of journalism, but the Blair scandal hung in the air like an offensive whiff from New York City's sewers.

The young journalists were all worried that their senior colleagues viewed them as potential Blairs, capable of fraud and other crimes. My heart sank as I saw their sadness and searched for words to assure them that they were wrong. I walked them through what we knew about Blair's deceptions and told them that it was not a result of age, race, or experience. I said it was important to see Blair's crimes as an aberration and not to condemn a generation of young reporters, especially young reporters of color. My voice cracked as I tried to reassure them.

Raines had also launched a newsroom offensive to meet with reporters and editors in groups and individually. Together we met with National editors, with whom Blair was working when his plagiarism was discovered. They were competent professionals, and their colleagues were asking them how Blair had gotten away with what he did. They wanted someone to blame, and they seized on Raines and me.

Such images from the newsroom were still fresh when I went to the Sheraton New York Hotel the night of Thursday, May 8, to receive the Frederick Douglass Award from the New York Urban League. The annual fundraising event celebrates diversity and equal opportunity, tenets the Blair fiasco had brought under fire.

The *Times* had bought a table, and seated there were Raines and his wife, Krystyna; Russ Lewis, the New York Times Company president and chief executive officer; Michael Golden, vice chairman; Sol Watson, the chief counsel; and several other colleagues from the newsroom. Sulzberger Jr. was visiting Times Company broadcast properties in Memphis and Des Moines. Still, it was a high-powered turnout from the company, one that sent a strong message of support. Robin was in Brazil on a health journalism fellowship.

I had not expected to make remarks, so I came unprepared. But when I was asked to speak, I seized on the matter of diversity:

> When I started in journalism before many of you were born, it was a time in which the story of the day was race. It was a good story, a great story, of the noble struggle by blacks to attain civil rights.
>
> Today the story of race is a paradox. And to cover it, as is our journalistic mission, we must have diversity. We must embrace it and give it a chance to work. And I'm not talking about diversity of race, gender, ethnicity, or sexual orientation, but diversity of age, of thought and background. That is what Frederick Douglass would have wanted. And I'm glad the *Times* is committed to it.

One of the first to greet me after the speech was Raines. As we shook hands, for a moment it seemed as if our relationship was mended a bit.

"Thanks for stiffening my spine," he said. We both needed our spines stiffened.

Earlier Thursday, Raines and I had completed our first round of interviews with the Blair investigative team. The story was to run on Sunday. That the reporters met with us so close to publication time was a bad sign. It's an approach journalists take when they go after investigation targets: develop your conclusions from others and save the prime suspects for last. The team had already interviewed dozens of colleagues and by now had already started to write. They merely looked to us to explain or defend what we had done.

I was not worried about the reporters discovering some unknown secret; I felt I had nothing to hide. But I did feel I was a target as two of the reporters, Adam Liptak and Jonathan Glater, fired questions at me in my office. Afterward, I shared as much with Raines, who had met with David Barstow, Jacques Steinberg, and Dan Barry. He dismissed my concerns.

"Glenn works for us," he said, referring to Kramon, the editor leading the investigation. "If he doesn't do it right, I'll fire his ass and find someone who will."

I knew this was a hollow threat. The train had left the station, and there was no way to slow it down. We were at the mercy of Kramon and the reporters.

———

LIPTAK AND Glater, both trained as lawyers, made an interesting team. Both were polite but purposeful in their questioning. They knew where they were going and were in no hurry to get there.

Liptak, who had spent his *Times* career in the newspaper's legal department, had shown an interest in reporting. When Raines and I took over, we brought him to the newsroom, where he thrived. Glater, on staff since 2000, was seen by some as a diversity hire since he had joined the paper as a reporter-trainee. He was green but a quick study. He had done well as part of the team of reporters covering the Enron scandal, where his intelligence and hard work stood out. Afterward, he had begun to seek me out for career counseling, and I readily offered advice.

From their first question, the interview headed south. They asked about events from Blair's earliest days at the *Times*, events I knew nothing about or had forgotten. On my desk was a copy of the report the management team had assembled. I did not want to refer to it before answering their questions; to do so would suggest I was following a script rather than speaking candidly.

Two questions seemed crucial. One was why Blair had been promoted from reporter-trainee to a full-time reporter in 2001. They suggested that I had played a role. I told them that I did not remember how Blair was promoted and assumed it was based on the recommendation of his immediate supervisor and the approval of the executive editor and managing editor. At the time, I held none of those jobs.

They offered a different take. Blair, they told me, was not included on an initial list of trainees whom department heads wanted promoted that January. The recruitment committee, which I led, had added Blair's name to the list. Several committee members had argued that Blair's promotion was equally deserved because he had been a trainee longer, had written more stories, and had received positive evaluations. I did not have a horse in the race, and I knew that Jon Landman, his boss, would make Blair's life impossible if he did not want him on the staff. But the implication was that I had pushed Blair's promotion to full-time reporter.

I told the reporters that in the end it was Landman who decided to hire Blair. Later, Landman said he consented to Blair's hiring because he believed that Sulzberger and I wanted it because of our commitment to diversity. At that moment, I lost all respect for Landman as a man of decency and integrity.

The other question was for me to prove that I had not provided Blair special treatment. In Blair's five-year career, outside of small talk in the smoking room, I had met with him only twice. In both instances, he was in trouble, and in both instances, I told him he needed to straighten up. The lawyers' evidence: *Didn't Blair suggest that I be nominated for the National Association of Black Journalists' Journalist of the Year*

Award in 2001? Later, I learned that my friend Soma Golden Behr had nominated me based on Blair's recommendation. *Didn't Blair write the feature story on my appointment to managing editor that was published by the* Times' *internal newsletter?* Yes, he did, but he was the choice of the newsletter editor, not me. These were cited as examples of our special relationship.

I began to understand that someone was peddling a story that linked the two of us to imply that I gave Blair special treatment. The story had credence only because Blair and I were both black. Blair was a favorite of mine, they suggested. No, he was not, I insisted. I felt silly trying to prove a negative and, in spite of my efforts to remain composed, became hostile. I know it did not help matters, but by then I did not care.

I told the reporters what I knew about Blair's problems and how I had instructed those supervising him to focus on his performance. I told them that I did not know of Landman's "stop Jayson from writing" e-mail; he had not sent me a copy, nor had he told me about it. This came as a surprise; they were sure I had seen it.

After several hours on Thursday, the questioning picked up again on Friday, May 9: *Why was Blair transferred to Sports despite his rocky history on Metro?* Both Schmidt and Landman wanted the change, as did Neil Amdur, who was Sports editor at the time. Thus, I approved it. Before that, I said, I had vetoed two e-mail requests from Blair to leave Metro. I insisted that he first clear it with Landman. The reporters seemed unaware of or uninterested in that action; it ran counter to their script.

The two wanted to know why Blair joined the National staff temporarily, a month after his move to Sports, given his troubled history. It was a fair question and highlighted my one management mistake related to Blair.

I thought back to the morning in October 2002 when I had arrived in the office after reading the *Washington Post*'s coverage of sniper shootings in the D.C. area. It was stronger, as was the *Baltimore Sun*'s, than what the *Times* had. The *Times* had already committed fifteen reporters in Washington and around the country to the story. Still, we were getting whipped. We had to do more.

We needed to station reporters full-time at various law-enforcement headquarters in Maryland and Virginia in order to develop relationships with law-enforcement officials who might provide tips. Thus, we had to find five reporters, which was difficult. All of the departments were strained, especially the Washington bureau and the National staff. Even reporters in other departments were unlikely to leap at such a routine assignment. They wanted bigger fish to fry.

Meeting with Jim Roberts, the National editor, and Andrew Rosenthal, the assistant managing editor for news, we sought to share the pain: we assigned reporters from Metro, National, and Washington. Assigning Blair made sense to me; he had only recently moved to Sports, where he was working as a general assignment reporter. He was from Maryland so he knew the territory. He had covered police as a reporter, so he knew something about law enforcement. And in the previous six months, I had heard of no complaints about his recent work.

My mistake, which I acknowledged: I did not inform Roberts, his supervisor on the National desk, of what I knew about concerns Blair's supervisors had raised in performance reviews. We had not discussed the history of any reporters joining the team. I did not think it was necessary in a temporary assignment. As I answered the reporters, I silently berated myself. My failure to disclose Blair's history was a huge oversight. I could have told Roberts to talk to Landman, who knew of Blair's talents and work habits. But there was nothing I could do about it now. The lack of a warning was lumped in with the list of evidence that I was Blair's benefactor.

Several weeks after Blair had moved to National, Roberts, who was desperate for more reporters, raised the idea of making Blair a permanent national correspondent. I argued that Blair needed more time to prove that he could handle such an assignment, a view that Roberts quickly endorsed. Even so, in early March 2003, Blair talked to Raines about continuing to cover the sniper trial, which Raines approved. Roberts then seized on that opportunity to use Blair for other assignments.

I did not know how clear any of this history or context was to the reporters by the time my interview ended. So many editors were involved in various aspects of Blair's career that it was impossible to apportion blame. But the team was working a story line, and by their questioning, it ran through Raines and me. The jury had reached a verdict, and we were guilty.

After the interviews on Friday, I strolled into Raines's office. He did not look up as he clipped a fingernail over his desk. For a moment, we stood without speaking. There was not much to say. We both knew how this would end. The *Times* would print a story detailing Blair's misconduct and indicting our management of the newsroom.

I was still bewildered about his and Sulzberger Jr.'s decision not to "demonize" Blair, and once again, I raised the option of presenting a fuller picture of the extent of his lying and deception, which were not just job related but seemed a way of life. Exposing him could help explain why it had been so difficult for the editors to detect his fraud.

Two incidents convinced me of that. One was correspondence that the editors found among Blair's papers. It was an exchange with his parents in which he wrote about being diagnosed with cancer. He asked for money to help pay for treatment, even though all *Times* employees receive health benefits. Once he had apparently received the money, he wrote back thanking them and informing them that the diagnosis was false.

The other was even more disturbing to me personally. From August 2002 until his resignation, Blair's e-mails showed, he had spied on his colleagues for Sridhar Pappu, the media writer for the *New York Observer*. Pappu would request information about staffing decisions, newsroom strategies, and disputes, and Blair would provide steady answers. The string of e-mails revealed a friendly relationship between the two.

In March 2003, Blair supplied Pappu with a list of the fifty reporters who were assigned to cover the Iraq War or the region, including names, locations, phone numbers, dates they were to travel, and other comments. The information was confidential and competitive, and its release was potentially life-threatening.

Reading their exchanges, I felt deeply betrayed. I considered how some staffers described Blair as my favorite while he was doing everything he could to undermine my reporters and my leadership. Raines thought about sharing the information with the investigative team and said he would discuss the possibility with Sulzberger. Either he decided against doing so, the publisher vetoed him, or the reporters chose not to include it in their story.

Nothing was going right. Just before we left the office on Friday, Raines appeared on the *NewsHour with Jim Lehrer* to discuss the article that would appear in Sunday's paper. It was a strange bit of promotion, considering how the article would condemn our leadership. The stress of the last week showed. As reporters and editors stared at television sets throughout the newsroom, they saw the normally confident and articulate executive editor all but gone. Instead, answering the questions of Terence Smith, who once worked at the *Times*, Raines seemed confused and timid. He looked exhausted. The interview was torture, and I was glad when it ended.

We still had one other issue to address. The team Raines had assembled had insisted on independence and wanted neither of us to read the story before it appeared in the paper. Raines agreed and strongly suggested that I do the same. I thought this was madness. The most important story in decades was running that weekend, and the two top editors had no idea what it said. This was counter to everything I believed in as a manager. But to break ranks would pose even more problems, since he had already decided.

Late Friday, I remembered a piece of information about the discussion that led to Blair's joining the team covering the sniper shootings. I rushed upstairs to the office where the investigative team was holed up writing the Sunday piece.

As soon as I walked in, reporters with whom I had been friends for years and whom I believed respected my professionalism responded as if I were the enemy. I suppose to them I was. They quickly covered up files and closed windows on their computer screens as Lorne Manly tried to head me off. He escorted me out of the room, where I delivered my tidbit. For me, this was one of the lowest moments in the entire affair. I felt that I had entered a secret room at the *Washington Post* where reporters were crashing an exclusive. I could not believe that my own would treat me this way.

Back downstairs, I made one request of Raines. I wanted the two of us to address the staff on Monday. At least we could present our case and immediately answer any questions the story generated. Raines agreed and asked that I try to find a location outside the building. He wanted to avoid the upstairs auditorium, where other executive editors had gone to defend their editorial decisions. Then he busied himself preparing a statement to distribute to the staff:

> Jayson's problems are unique to him. While wishing to respect and preserve his personal privacy, we want to make clear that his misfeasance cannot be laid at the feet of our intermediate reporter program or young reporters in general or of programs for renewing and diversifying the talent that makes up the *Times*. Those programs retain our full confidence.
>
> We have been telling outsiders that the best antidote to bad journalism is more and better journalism. None of us can take pride in the episode that is unfolding, but I hope we will all be able to take pride in the honest and open way in which the *Times* responds.

I hated it. It said nothing that meant anything.

On Saturday afternoon, May 10, I took Zachary to a birthday party for one of his schoolmates on the Upper East Side. Watching a group of rambunctious boys racing through the apartment playing balloon games and clubbing a piñata was a brief diversion, but the crisis lingered in the back of my mind.

I took a break from the party and went to the street below to check in with Robin, who was returning from Brazil the next morning. Then I called Raines at his weekend place.

"I'm just taking your temperature," I began.

For about twenty minutes, we talked about how strange we felt and how difficult it was to be in the dark about such an important story. We were powerless, exhausted, and without authority. No matter what happened next, our future was linked to the story that would be on the newsstands in a matter of hours. It was a story that would consume four pages in the paper's front section, a vast amount of space that was typically used to explain war or disaster. It was a story neither of us had read.

16

FREE FALL

The proposition was simple enough. I would put him to work as my principle editorial consultant and he, in turn, would help me rescue and reengineer a powerful but troubled Canadian newspaper chain. First assignment: Ottawa.

Gerald's analysis of the problems plaguing the bureau was deep, wide, and succinct. His solutions were clear. In one memo, he laid the groundwork for what was to become the most competitive and effective multimedia news team in Canada. He then left with his family for Martha's Vineyard, feeling guilty that perhaps he had not done enough. I left the office that day thinking, "I'm glad he's taking vacation. There's enough work here to last me three years!"

Next, I sent him to the Middle East. Our senior editors had organized a trip to Jerusalem, to better understand the issues in Israel, they said. I was afraid a boondoggle was about to occur. Gerald said, "I know some people. Let me take a look." The resulting itinerary led the editors through Egypt, Jordan, the West Bank, Gaza, and Jerusalem. He felt that you couldn't really cover Israel unless you understood the surrounding region. Again, seeing all angles.

As thoughtful as he was, he was also as cynical as they come. At a business review in Saskatchewan, the Gordon First Nation tribe presented to me a "war stick" for our successful new youth publication, distributed for the first time on their reservations. Gerald proclaimed the ceremony "the oldest trick in the book" and told me he was "going for a cigarette break" and that I should "find out what they really want" by the time he got back. When I announced that my grandmother was full Shawnee, Gerald was dumbfounded. He couldn't figure out whether I was telling the truth or pulling a trick myself. In the end he thought it was a fair exchange. "OK, tit for tat, I guess," he said.

—MICHAEL G. WILLIAMS

EARLY EVENING, Saturday, May 10, 2003, a white SUV with the *Times'* logo doubled-parked in front of my home, and the driver dropped off an early edition of the Sunday newspaper that changed my life. Usually, I looked to the early edition to raise questions or suggest improvements before the final edition of the paper's largest issue of the week is printed. It seemed that editing the *Times* never stopped. Sulzberger Jr. once summarized this process with the quip, "You can read the paper or you can edit the paper, but you can't do both."

This time as I pulled away the string that bound the sections, I did so as a reader. My eyes quickly found the story, above the fold, in the upper-left corner of the front page:

"*Times* Reporter Who Resigned Leaves Long Trail of Deception," the headline proclaimed.

The article said an investigation by *Times* journalists found that the twenty-seven-year-old Blair committed "frequent acts of journalistic fraud" while covering major news events in recent months. It described how Blair made up facts and sources and submitted reports that were assumed to be from Maryland, Texas, and other states where he was dispatched, when instead he was often in New York, stealing material from other news organizations and using details from photographs to suggest that he was on the scene. It said his fabrication and plagiarism represented "a profound betrayal of trust and a low point" in the paper's 152-year history.

In news parlance, the piece was a bombshell, the sort of story that I had written or edited countless times. But this bombshell was personal. I wanted to tuck the paper away, as if doing so would make everything it revealed vanish. At the same time, I wanted to read every word and then read each one again.

Robin would be home from Brazil the next morning, so Zachary and I were there alone. The moment felt surreal. Zach went about his business with no care in the world, while ten feet away, his father wore a look of immense pain as he devoured the newspaper spread across the kitchen table.

I braced myself as I turned to the jump page. To hear that a story is running four pages can be jarring, but to see it was misery. I turned back to the front and kept reading. Paragraphs, sentences, and words leaped off the page. Some I agreed with, and some I disputed. Some information I was learning for the first time, which made me even angrier about having reporters conduct the investigation instead of managers and editors, as I'd suggested.

The article described how various editors and reporters had expressed concern about errors and unprofessional behavior during the span of Blair's five-year *Times* career from intern to reporter on the National desk, so much so that Landman was compelled to send his "stop Jayson from writing for the *Times*" e-mail. It said that after Blair had been "sternly warned" that his job was in jeopardy and after he returned from a leave of absence for personal problems, Raines and I "guided" him to the National desk, where he was assigned to the high-profile Washington, D.C., sniper case. It then quoted Sulzberger Jr., who called the damage to the paper and its employees "a huge black eye."

I did not need to read further. The thousands of words could be reduced to those salient facts. Blair had always been a problem, one editor had sounded a desperate warning, and the publisher was outraged. The rest was background noise.

My editing instincts kicked in. If the mistakes were so routine and his behavior so over-the-top, why was there no push to fire him?

Similarly, if Landman wanted Blair to stop writing, why did that not happen? He had the authority.

The story succeeded in its goal of detailing Blair's fraud. But it tried to assess blame and culprits with equal clarity. That effort took more time and demanded more thoroughness than quickness. There was no way to research the five-year career of a troubled reporter in days without sacrificing something. The investigative team had no time to explore and present the motives of their sources. The story lacked nuance and reflection and in some instances presented conjecture as fact. Surely, something so complex as a breakdown in the newsroom of the nation's best newspaper had numerous causes. Whatever the factors, they went beyond heroes and villains, enablers and resisters. Had the *Times* been writing about anyone or anything else, it would have delved more deeply before it ran the article.

I was alone with my thoughts about Jayson Blair and the *Times* that evening after putting Zachary to bed. There were no calls from Raines or Sulzberger, no messages from friends or colleagues. Robin called before she boarded her plane, and I told her the article was brutal. She tried to console me by reminding me that it was not me who committed fraud. She would see me first thing in the morning.

As I waited for my wife, I spent the early Sunday hours in a mental fog. I watched television as the article became the biggest news of the day. Uninformed speculation had already settled in by the time I heard *Newsweek*'s Seth Mnookin on Howard Kurtz's CNN program *Reliable Sources.*

"Well, I think one of the interesting things that has yet to come out is Jayson's sort of mentoring relationship with some people very high up at the *Times*, including Gerald Boyd, the managing editor," he said, adding that the story "sort of" suggested such a relationship.

I had been indicted by a journalist and was about to be convicted. There was never a mentoring relationship. But once again, because a white man was both my judge and jury, nobody doubted his assertions. Before the week was over, thanks to the power of the Internet and the laziness of many reporters, Mnookin's lies were recycled repeatedly.

Robin read the article with the same pained expression as I had had several hours earlier. Like me, she was astonished and angered at Blair and at the huge leaps of logic in the story. As we talked about what next, we knew only that it marked a beginning rather than an ending.

————

BACK AT the office on Monday, Sulzberger Jr., Raines, and I met first thing. The worst was over, both men seemed to believe. Considering what had happened, the session was calm as we discussed how to control the damage. The publisher raised two concerns. He wanted us to make sure there were no other embarrassing situations involving *Times* reporters and to take concrete steps to address the management shortfalls that the story had highlighted. That was how we could get ahead of the scandal, he said.

As the meeting ended, Sulzberger asked Raines and me to return in an hour to discuss other matters. I left Raines standing in Sulzberger's doorway as I went back to the third floor. The newsroom was coming to life; and as I walked to my office, I could see the stares and feel the anger, but no one said anything. Eventually Raines followed, carrying a message from Sulzberger summoning me back to the fourteenth floor. As I traveled back to Sulzberger's office, I wondered what had changed. Raines and I had met him initially as a team. Now we seemed to be flying solo. When I got there, Sulzberger immediately launched into criticism.

"You have not served Howell well," he said.

His words were like daggers, and I struggled to make sense of them. Was he parroting Raines's view or blaming me directly for the Blair scandal? One fact was certain: he was taking me to the woodshed, as was his right, but I could not understand why. Not once had he taken issue with any of my decisions. I had to challenge Raines more, he said. I had to work harder to make sure that Raines listened, not only to me but also to all of the top newsroom editors. I had to make sure that we built a senior management team. That was my job as managing editor.

My nature is to react carefully and cautiously, after considering all sides in a situation. That approach had served me well—until this point. Anger, even when appropriate, usually serves no purpose and can get in the way of a solution. But for the last nineteen months, as we worked to remake the *Times*, my job had been to give Raines my best advice, to troubleshoot where I could, and to help manage the newsroom. I challenged Raines when I disagreed, often in front of the publisher in our regular Monday lunches. I did not take the job to make sure the executive editor played well with others. That was Sulzberger's responsibility.

Despite my ingrained caution, I could not help but get angry. I could not see how any managing editor could force an executive editor to do something if the executive editor was unwilling. Raines was strong-willed and often acted unilaterally. Sulzberger's assessment was ludicrous. I was seething, and I let him know it.

"If you feel that way," I said, "why don't you just make a change?"

Pointing to a picture of his great-grandfather, Sulzberger recalled how Adolph Ochs had refused to do wholesale housecleaning when he first purchased a financially troubled *New York Times*.

"He said the people most capable of getting us out of this mess are the people who put us in it," he told me solemnly "That's what we will do now."

Returning to the third floor, I once again clashed with Raines. He had decided to call off the staff meeting that I had been organizing since Friday. He said it was a bad idea.

"I'm not very good in such settings, and frankly, you're not very good either."

First, there was the publisher's rebuke, and now Raines's disapproval. This was a new low in my professional life. Raines said that we would conduct a series of smaller meetings over the next few weeks, eventually speaking to the entire staff. That approach would take forever, I countered, and would undermine his pledge to communicate immediately with the staff. The article had raised too many questions to wait.

He ignored my comments. Just when it mattered most, Raines and I no longer had faith in each other. I still believed that the crisis, like others, would pass, but I did not see how I could recapture Raines's trust, and really, I had no desire to do so. I did not think much of Sulzberger either.

It is hard to explain my sense of loneliness at that time. It was not hopelessness, because there is always hope. But I realized that I was fighting to preserve a reputation that had taken a lifetime to amass—

while friends remained quiet and foes offered lies—and that brought a feeling of isolation that I had never before felt.

The next morning, I went to see Sulzberger. I told him how much I disagreed with his comments the previous day. I reminded him of the many times I had raised concerns about Raines's actions and behavior. Raines was my boss, I said, and I thought we would get nowhere if we were constantly warring or if I was repeatedly going over his head to the publisher. The *Times* had never before operated that way; it was counterproductive and dangerous. I had always believed that it was best to fight in private; otherwise everyone would take a side and the common vision would be lost. But if Sulzberger wanted a fight, that's what he would get. I no longer cared.

Nothing made sense anymore. Later that morning, I hosted a meeting in the *Times*' boardroom as one of the two national cochairmen of the University of Missouri School of Journalism's major fundraising drive. Those assembled were prominent j-school graduates, some of the most successful names in journalism.

When I had agreed to serve as a cochair, I expressed concern about having time to meet the demands of such a role. Yet over the months, I warmed to it and developed a strong relationship with Dean Mills, the j-school's dean, and others in the development office.

Weeks before, I had eagerly volunteered the *Times* as a place that could draw a good crowd. Now I was welcoming the group to the paper two days after it raised questions about my abilities as a manager. I felt embarrassed and uncomfortable. Perhaps that explained my comments when the session started. Participants were asked to share with the group what a j-school education meant to them and their careers. When my turn came, I fought back tears.

I recalled how I took the Greyhound bus to Columbia with almost everything I owned and how the years on campus changed my life. The road I traveled would not have been possible without Missouri, and I would always be grateful. By then, others in the room appeared near tears. It was the kind of bonding moment that comes from stark nakedness when there is nothing to hide.

I ended with the words of a professor that had stayed with me through my career.

"A journalist should only write what he knows in his heart to be true," I said. "Maybe if Jayson Blair would have gone to Missouri... maybe he would have learned that."

As the development gathering proceeded, in a separate meeting Sulzberger and Raines switched gears and decided that a town hall meeting with the staff was essential. Raines explained his shift by describing a dinner he had held the night before with three *Times* columnists, Floyd Norris, Joyce Purnick, and Clyde Haberman, in which they all urged Raines to communicate with the staff. He said they also challenged Raines's leadership style as arrogant, isolated, and autocratic.

We would hold the meeting the next day, Wednesday, at the Loews Astor Plaza Theater, the movie house on West Forty-fourth behind the *Times*. I greeted the latest decision with ambivalence. It would be three days since the Blair opus appeared, three days of silence from Raines and me. Emotions in the newsroom had already calcified; the staff had already chosen sides. I was sure that our opponents would try to turn the meeting into a show of no confidence. If we had gathered on Monday, we would have been going on the offensive. Instead, we were playing defense. It was not a good place to be.

They shared the plan: The three of us would sit on the stage, although only Sulzberger and Raines would deliver prepared remarks. I would be available to answer questions. They argued that there was no need for me to give opening remarks because, as Sulzberger explained, Raines was speaking for the two of us. We would be contrite and, above all, not defensive. No working press would be allowed, including— absurd as it was—the *Times'* media reporter, Jacques Steinberg.

On Wednesday morning, May 14, we assembled in the boardroom to prepare for the meeting. About a dozen other senior executives and newsroom editors joined us to rehearse comments and fine-tune answers to possible questions. We did not want to respond in a way that would create new problems. The group reviewed the statements and peppered us with questions.

The prep session went reasonably well, although there were several tricky issues. One was the part of Raines's statement in which he suggested that growing up in the segregated South might have influenced his decision to give Blair a second chance. Some in the group thought the remark humanized Raines. Others, like me, found it patronizing and said it would create a backlash. After debate, Raines decided to leave the passage as it was.

In answering a question, Raines said he was convinced that Blair had straightened up because he recognized positive signs from his dealings with other reporters who were recovering addicts. No one bought the explanation, and he cut it.

Sulzberger was asked if he would seek our resignations. He answered immediately that he would not ask for our resignations and would not accept them if offered. No one took issue with his response.

There was a gaping hole in our plan, the group concluded: my lack of initial remarks. Sulzberger argued that the focus should be on Raines, since it was his editorship that was at risk. He was the one who needed to reassure the staff. Remarks from me could distract from that, he said. Of course I felt marginalized; I wanted to defend my reputation. But there was no way of doing that without criticizing the story as well as those whom I saw as detractors. That was not the message that Sulzberger and Raines wanted to deliver. Thus, for the larger good, they wanted me to be ready to answer questions but not to jeopardize their approach.

I deferred to them. We were contending with enough problems, I figured, without my becoming one myself. I still wanted to believe that most of my colleagues were as outraged as I was about suggestions in the story that I gave Blair special treatment. They knew me, and they knew better.

But the issue of my speaking became moot. The group pushed for me to make remarks, and Sulzberger and Raines reversed course. They had had an evening to think about what they would say; I had a few hours.

I was willing to be contrite if it would help the newsroom move beyond the current mess. I would not attack my critics or sound defensive. But I was unwilling to let stand the lies about my relationship with Blair. From my first days as a reporter, I had mentored scores of deserving young journalists. That gave me as much professional pride as any promotion or prize. Blair was not a part of that group, and I would resist any attempt to make him so.

We broke for lunch and prepared ourselves for the event, which had taken on a make-or-break quality. Raines hid away outside of the building with his wife. I spent my time writing and rehearsing my remarks.

At 2:15 P.M., Sulzberger, Raines, and I reassembled in Raines's office to begin our descent into madness. We were united, at least in appearance. Sulzberger carried a stuffed moose, a prop that he frequently used in senior staff meetings to underscore the need for honesty. The moose was supposed to be a symbol for the issues that concerned everyone but that they were afraid to discuss. I carried a card with a capitalized admonition from Raines: "LISTEN DON'T DEFEND." Clearly, he was concerned about how I would respond. It was surreal.

Because the event took place outside our building, the three of us had to navigate a gauntlet of media cameras at the theater. We strolled as if we were on our way to a premiere. At best, pictures of the three of us resembled a perp walk. At worst, we looked like dead men walking. The photos would be recycled repeatedly.

Inside, the publisher plopped the moose on the podium and tried to make the point that the discussion we were about to have would be candid and perhaps even painful. Few in the audience understood what the moose symbolized, and some were offended, later accusing the publisher of making light of a serious situation. Sulzberger presented an ambitious course for the future. He would appoint a committee of people inside and outside the *Times* to make recommendations to protect the paper from another Jayson Blair. He pledged to "rebuild the sense of community that unites us" and to do everything possible to make everyone feel "valued and fulfilled" and to make sure that we treated one another in an "honest, respectful, and fair manner."

I heard the publisher redefine the scandal into a need for a major newsroom makeover. It was as if the *Times* were a deplorable place, where the staff was abused and marginalized.

Raines also painted a devastating picture of his newsroom. He described it as one where hierarchy, favoritism, and fear ran rampant. He promised to change. Never once did he tie such changes to his goal of moving the paper in a direction that was vital to its future.

Over the last nineteen months, the newsroom certainly had been a demanding place, but we faced enormous challenges. We were trying to change the course of the paper while responding to the challenge of 9/11 and its aftermath. More recently, Sulzberger had declared a moratorium on hiring. As a result, we were pushing an ambitious agenda with limited resources. Neither man acknowledged this reality. In fact, they were asking for forgiveness and all but acknowledging that our previous efforts were a mistake. I listened not in anger but in sadness. It was as if they were selling their souls to get beyond this time. But who in the world would want to buy?

Raines delivered the line about giving Blair a second chance because, as a Southerner, he believed that African Americans deserved opportunities. As I watched the faces of my colleagues, I realized that if he had that view of Blair, he probably felt the same way about me. Could his decision to name me managing editor be rooted in nothing more than white guilt over four centuries of oppression?

It was my turn to speak. I had not shared my statement with the planning group and had no idea how it would play. I just spoke from my heart. I did not think I could change opinions, but I thought I had a measure of goodwill. I hoped for the best.

"I would like to apologize to each of you for the failures that brought us here today," I began. "I've spent most of my career in management trying to be effective, and that's one of the reasons this is so painful. We made mistakes. I made mistakes, such as not passing on more information about Jayson's background to editors on the National desk. I will do everything in my power to make sure that doesn't happen again."

Unlike Sulzberger and Raines, I argued that we needed to move forward. And I warned my colleagues against using the situation to back away from diversity, one of my biggest fears.

"This is not about the failure of a minority journalist that reflects on other minority journalists. . . . Let's not make this about race or youth or anything else that divides this most talented newsroom in the world."

I do not remember the response, although I am sure no one applauded. I did get a look of approval and relief from Sulzberger and Raines. I had stayed on message.

Now for the questions. We were at the mercy of the audience. Most of the sharpest attacks came from the Metro desk—particularly from those close to the editor, Jon Landman. Susan Edgerley and Joe Sexton, both Landman deputies, criticized our leadership. Sexton delivered a profanity-laced tirade, asserting that the staff had lost confidence in us and that we should resign. He would later apologize to both of us in a weird e-mail in which he talked about still trusting our leadership.

Landman spoke. He tried to make the point that the decision to reassign Blair, which he had sought, was proper, but only to a point. He said he had no problem moving Blair to Sports, because jobs there were not as taxing as on the National desk. In other words, it was OK for Blair to work for Metro or Sports but a mistake to unload him on National. To his credit, Neil Amdur, the former Sports editor, challenged him. A damaged Blair should not be writing for the *Times*, and Landman should not have wanted him shipped to Sports. Landman was being disingenuous, Amdur said. No one seemed to care.

I kept waiting for supporters to rise in my defense, but none did. I could only listen, not respond, because I did not want to sound defensive. Inside, I felt like exploding.

I was glad and saddened when the session was over. We had kept to the script, but in no way did we have an open and honest discussion. Instead, we served as punching bags, and did so with smiles on our faces.

The meeting accomplished one other goal: retiring the toy moose.

———

I WENT home to Robin, who told me that as an outside observer, she thought the news coverage piled much of the blame on me by falsely linking me to Blair. By Thursday, May 15, I was in an emotional tailspin. As Sulzberger, Raines, and I assembled early in the day, they could see my pain. Both tried to buck me up, quoting Churchill and citing the need for courage. We had gotten through the worst, they both reasoned. I was not as optimistic.

Most painful to me was the lack of public support both during the meeting and in the comments to news media later. In private, I received a fair amount. "Thanks for the time and show of genuine concern about staff morale today," wrote one colleague.

But I knew we had created an environment in which critics felt they had safety in numbers and could attack with impunity. I kept hoping that others who saw the situation differently would begin to speak out.

I was not faint of heart or spirit. I was trying to cope with the reality of watching colleagues I worked with for years, whom I had recruited and helped hire and worked to promote, turn against me. I had been there for them, and now they were my fiercest critics. Their e-mails, sent to Sulzberger and forwarded to me, were devastating. A particularly absurd one suggested that I supported Blair because he reminded me of myself. Hearing me deny the obvious, the critic wrote, was "distasteful."

In the newsroom, Landman, as the author of the "stop Jayson from writing" memo, was a hero. He was benefiting from revisionist history that I had seen his note and ignored it. No one disputed the falsehood, especially not Landman.

Outside the newsroom, the story line had changed. It was no longer about a troubled young reporter but about larger issues involving race, diversity, and newsroom management. Everyone had a view. Tim Rutten of the *Los Angeles Times* wrote that while the *New York Times* was candid about editors' complaints about Blair, it was "less forthcoming" about "the close mentor-protégé relationship that apparently existed" between Blair and me.

The scandal had become everything that it was not. It was an opportunity for some in the newsroom to settle scores. It gave activists on both sides of the diversity debate an opportunity to weigh in, and they did, facts be damned.

––––––

WE HAD no public relations strategy. The less said, the better, everyone reasoned. I vehemently disagreed. We were in the midst of a crisis, and unless we responded, it would only grow. Shortly after the Blair story broke, Raines and I had a silly argument over whether we were actually experiencing a crisis. He said we weren't; a crisis carried an air of desperation, and we were not desperate. We were in damage-control mode, he said. I responded that he was splitting hairs. Whatever it was then, it was definitely a crisis now.

Suddenly the publisher was everywhere. The day after the town hall meeting, he convened a committee of high-level editors and executives to plot the next steps. The committee would meet almost daily. Sulzberger also led the first of several masthead meetings. I had never seen him so engaged, so blunt, so determined. Gone were the irreverence and easy-going spirit. He acted as if his job depended on it, and perhaps it did. He started a series of lunches with top editors, intent on finding ways to address concerns over hierarchy, internal communications, training, performance management, and morale. He pushed for the creation of what would become the Siegal Committee, the group led by Al Siegal, the dean of assistant managing editors, to examine why the Blair fraud occurred and offer recommendations to make sure it did not happen again.

He also established a crisis-management team of top company executives, lamenting that he had not done so sooner. The group included the three of us, along with Janet Robinson; Russ Lewis; Gail Collins; Sol Watson, the general counsel of the *Times*; Cindy Augustine, the senior vice president for human resources; Catherine Mathis; Bill Schmidt; and Michael Golden. Golden, a cousin of Sulzberger's and the company's vice chairman, had long been regarded as a potential rival. His inclusion could only mean that Sulzberger was trying to bring him under the tent.

Sulzberger's intense involvement had mixed results. While it reinforced his promise to change the atmosphere, it also raised doubts about who was running the newsroom. He had always argued that no manager could lead effectively with his boss looking over his shoulder. Yet that was what he was doing.

The first lunch for the masthead quickly turned into a shouting match. Almost from the beginning, Raines went on the offensive. Unlike his deferential tone at the town hall event, this time he attributed his problems to a group of newsroom malcontents led by Landman, whom he said were working to undermine his editorship. Landman had a single concern, Raines said: opposition to my appointment as managing editor. Had Raines chosen someone else, he argued, newsroom morale would be great.

I could not believe what I heard. I wanted to walk out of the lunch, yet I sat there, quietly, feeling mortally wounded. I was astonished that Raines would make such an explosive remark without warning me. Later, when I asked him why he made the statement, he said he had decided on the spot to "shoot for the moon." He felt the tide was turning against him, and unless he did something dramatic, he would lose. I only listened. I was sure that my silence spoke volumes.

Raines's attack prompted a rebuttal from Soma Golden Behr, the assistant managing editor whom I considered a close friend. She chided Raines for criticizing Landman and added that he was entertaining an offer from the *Washington Post*. It would be a disaster if he left at that time. She said nothing about how Landman was trying to exploit a difficult moment for the paper. Golden Behr and I had worked together for more than a decade. We shared secrets and lunches and dinners in each other's homes. We argued and made up and watched each other's back. She was someone I confided in and trusted completely. For months, Raines had mulled kicking her off the masthead to make way for someone of his own choosing. He did not trust her and felt that she encouraged his critics rather than defending him. Each time he raised the idea, I pushed back. When he persisted, I finally let her know his thinking.

I was not upset that she did not defend me. But it pained me deeply to hear her praise Landman. I no longer knew whom I could trust and saw nearly everyone as suspect.

After the lunch, Sulzberger decided to broker a cease-fire between Raines and Landman. I was not invited. Even if the newsroom returned to normal, I thought, how could I manage Landman? I felt humiliated. After the three met, I asked Raines and Sulzberger what they discussed. I never got a full briefing, only that the talk was "full and frank," parlance that I knew from my days in Washington meant nothing. I was certain of one thing: I was on my own.

———

MANAGEMENT MEETINGS were now continual and becoming absurd. Sulzberger had counseled me to challenge Raines more in public. Force was the only way to get him to change his management style, he said. Our disagreements had always been in private. But at a meeting in late May, I openly criticized Raines, telling the senior editors assembled how difficult it was to get Raines to listen. It was like a confession at an Alcoholics Anonymous meeting, and it worked. As Sulzberger looked on with a smile, other editors began to assail the executive editor.

One of the first was Michael Oreskes, now an assistant managing editor, who called Raines a control freak who paradoxically did not like details. It was a clear attack, but Raines roared with laughter. The masthead was encouraged to bring him down a notch or two, and it seemed he was a willing participant in the game.

Increasingly, I relied on my family and my faith. Nothing else made sense. Robin had suspended work on a book she was writing, devoting most of her time to helping me however she could. I relied on her keen perception; she was able to look around the curve and predict what was next. She would monitor news coverage of the scandal, passing along comments of interest. She would advise me when I had to respond to some ridiculous charge and when I should stay silent.

As much as possible, Robin and I shielded Zachary from the *Times* turmoil. But we had our own turmoil at home. The school year was nearly over, and it was rocky. Zachary's teachers had increasingly complained about our son's inability to remain in his seat, wait his turn, and follow directions, symptoms of a diagnosis of attention deficit hyperactivity disorder. Robin found us a lawyer with expertise in the board of education's byzantine special education process, scheduled Zachary for evaluation, and began leading us through the maze of testing, placement, and financing. The school suggested that it might no longer be able to "meet Zachary's needs," so she also began to research other schools. As we weathered the *Times* crisis, Robin also responded to the one with our son. When we finally came together at the end of each day, we traded updates, strategy, and encouragement.

In a strange way, I felt liberated. I was learning whom I could count on and whom I could not. I was hurt when friends and colleagues did not step forward, but I accepted their silence. I took solace in words of support from those who reached out, and silently cheered in one meeting when a courageous deputy design director, Charles Blow, a black man, defended me and criticized Landman.

I had always believed in God as a Supreme Being. But I had also taken pains not to use God as a crutch. In my prayers, I did not ask God to make the scandal go away; I asked for strength to allow me to withstand whatever he had in store for me and to help me endure it with dignity and truthfulness.

For me, there were no more demons to exorcise. I felt I had nothing to lose anymore. When a black colleague and friend told me that a white senior editor expressed doubt that I was "smart enough" to lead the newsroom—speculation that was meaningless but that I resented nonetheless—I called the editor into my office, and I asked him directly if he felt that way. I wanted him to tell me to my face, I said. I deserved to hear it from him since I had done everything I could to support his success. He denied making the comment, and I let the matter drop. Still he got the point: he knew that I knew what he was thinking.

———

THE CRISIS worsened. On the same afternoon of the town hall meeting, the paper received a letter challenging a story written by Rick Bragg, one of Raines's favorites. The letter writer accused Bragg of a misdeed similar to Blair's, filing a story from Apalachicola, Florida, without visiting the town.

Meanwhile, the Internet columnist Matt Drudge reported that at least two *Times* reporters were under investigation for fraud, prompting a new round of media calls. They wanted to know whether the report was true and, if so, who the reporters were.

Sulzberger did not mince words when he spoke with Raines and me. If another reporter was found to have committed fraud, we were finished, he said, referring to the three of us. This time, Raines allowed the investigation to be conducted by managers rather than reporters. I led the inquiry. The aim was the same as in Blair's case: to determine what had happened and why.

Over the next few weeks, the newsroom became a three-ring circus. We conducted the investigation into charges against Bragg, formed committees to create reforms, attended lunches with masthead editors and other top executives, and somehow managed to put out a newspaper each day. Media coverage shifted noticeably. The issue was no longer Blair but which reporters were favorites of Raines, like Bragg. Both had worked at the *Birmingham News* and the *St. Petersburg Times*, and they had been friends for years. I had no doubt that a campaign was under way to force Raines out. Each time there was a blessed lull and we could return to doing journalism, a new allegation surfaced. When we met with Sulzberger to relay what we had learned about Bragg, we were joined by several top company executives. Their presence only highlighted how serious the situation had become.

The findings were good and bad. Bragg had not plagiarized or fabricated facts, and he had actually visited Apalachicola. But he had made generous use of freelance reporters, known as stringers. In fact, Bragg used stringers much more than other correspondents. The previous weekend, I spoke with Bragg several times about the need for him to cooperate with the internal investigation. He could save a lot of time and angst by telling us exactly what work the stringers had performed. But he refused. Finally I was frank: Raines's detractors were using Bragg to bring Raines down, I said, and Raines needed his friend's help. Bragg agreed to provide the information. Checking his expense records and payments to stringers, we were able to understand what happened.

In the process, I learned that Bragg had special permission from Raines to hire whatever stringers he wanted and as often as he needed them. No one knew of this other than Jim Roberts, his supervisor. I was livid. Here I was working to counter the impression that Raines played favorites, and I did not even know the facts. For the first time, I felt that Raines had misled me.

As we discussed possible sanctions on Bragg, Raines took an odd position. He warned that Bragg would probably retaliate by implicating fellow national correspondents. The implied threat angered me. I wanted Bragg fired, and said so. He had abused his position as a national correspondent by having stringers do the bulk of his reporting. That was not how the *Times* operated. Unlike Blair, Bragg was an "excluded employee," which was true of most senior-level editors and National, Foreign, and Washington reporters. He did not have the protection of the Newspaper Guild but served at the pleasure of the publisher, as did I.

Sulzberger listened to all of our recommendations and decided that Bragg would receive a two-week paid suspension and a letter of reprimand. The *Times* would also publish an editor's note explaining that Bragg had violated the paper's policy regarding the use of stringers. That was as far as he wanted to go.

The focus shifted to another of Raines's friends, Pat Tyler, whom Raines had sent to Kuwait to run the *Times* bureau during the war in Iraq. The move had made sense because of Tyler's experiences as a war and foreign correspondent.

For a couple of days, a rumor circulated in the newsroom that Tyler had hired the niece of Ahmad Chalabi, an Iraqi opposition leader, as the office manager in Kuwait, where Tyler had first set up shop before moving on to Baghdad. The rumor alleged that the niece, Sarah Khalil, had transported hundreds of thousands in cash to Baghdad for her uncle.

If she worked for the *Times* it was bad enough, since Chalabi was closely tied to the Bush administration and its efforts to topple Saddam Hussein. Chalabi would later be widely discredited for providing questionable information about weapons of mass destruction to U.S. intelligence sources. If Sarah Khalil had ferried money, the paper was in an indefensible position. Fortunately that allegation proved false.

Howard Kurtz of the *Washington Post* questioned whether Khalil had worked for the *Times*. Clearly he was being fed information by someone inside the paper. As Tyler and I discussed the inquiry, he stunned me by saying it was true. The niece, whom Tyler had known for almost twenty years, had been working for the *Times* since January. She was no longer performing any official duties for the paper, Tyler said, but would be on the payroll through the end of May. Immediately I told Sulzberger, who was as shocked as I was. It was not the first time Tyler had displayed a significant lapse in judgment. The previous Christmas, he told me that he and his family were spending the holiday skiing in Aspen with Prince Bandar bin Sultan, the Saudi ambassador to the United States, and his family. I quickly ordered him to decline the invitation, asking him if he was nuts.

Tyler was a target, but he was being used to get to Raines; and Raines seemed immobile. Now Tyler was adding to the problems. Although he had assured me that Chalabi's niece was removed from the *Times* payroll, he wanted me to know that her car was attacked by gunmen as she traveled from Kuwait to Baghdad. The car took two rounds, he described in an e-mail. I wrote back that as long as she was not in our employ and not escorting *Times* property her situation was not a *Times* matter. "Let me know if you hear anybody writing about this or linking her to the *Times*," I added. He responded that my lack of humanity left him speechless.

I was fed up. I was fighting Raines, his critics, and his friends. We needed to put out fires, yet Raines's favorites were not helping. I showed Raines the e-mail exchange, and he feigned ignorance of Sarah Khalil and her history with the *Times*. I was sure he had already seen the e-mails, since I knew that Tyler copied him on everything.

"Where is she now?" Raines asked. "Is she safe? Do we have any further obligation from a policy or humanitarian standpoint?" I did not answer. If he wanted to pursue those matters, he could. I would not. She was no longer working for the *Times*.

I could not understand his attitude. We were in a fight for our lives, and his friends were being used as weapons. Instead of picking up the phone and asking for their cooperation, he was missing in action.

I wanted to believe that if we could get through this new round of attacks we would be OK. Blair was history, and so were his crimes. The latest arrows did not amount to much. To accuse an executive editor of favoritism is much ado about nothing. It was not news that Raines had reporters that he trusted or liked more than others. Even so, the challenges continued. Several days later, Bragg informed me that he had spoken to *New York* magazine, which was doing an article on "Howell's Favorites." He would not reveal what he had said.

The publisher's response to the latest news was ominous. We were in trouble, he said in an e-mail, and we had only days to turn this thing around. I did not know why our situation suddenly had become so desperate. I knew the publisher was regularly briefing company board members, and I wondered if they had given him a deadline or ultimatum. Maybe he was simply weary from the constant pounding. I certainly was.

I started "negotiations" with Bragg to bring him to New York for a face-to-face conversation. He was a loose cannon, and we needed to get him under control. Bragg was adamantly against the trip, arguing that he would never set foot in the city again. Sulzberger felt a face-to-face was nonnegotiable.

Sulzberger also wanted Raines to mend fences with Abramson, the Washington bureau chief. That could not happen because Raines's steadfast support of Tyler stood between them. Sulzberger once again served as a referee to broker a cease-fire. And as in the case of the Landman meeting, I was not invited.

Events had to break exactly right: Bragg and Tyler would have to show their support for Raines by remaining silent and staying out of the media. Abramson would have to offer her support to Raines. And the constant media attention would have to ease. So far, there was no reason to believe that anyone would cooperate.

There was a new worry. The *Wall Street Journal* was working a story about the turmoil in the *Times* newsroom. Despite all of the recent media attention, advertising had continued to pour into the paper in May, and revenue projections were up. But a damaging piece in the *Journal* could hurt the company's bottom line, given its business-minded audience. Sulzberger wanted to make sure that Abramson did not contribute to the piece.

Abramson and I had become closer since my first visit to the Washington bureau as managing editor. I did not think that she saw me as a friend, but I was sure that she regarded me as a supporter. I had told her that numerous times and had been her "date" to a White House Christmas party. Whenever she had concerns about Raines, she sought me out, and I readily offered advice in confidence. But in the weeks after the Blair scandal erupted, she never offered me encouragement or support.

At the meeting, I later learned, she assured Sulzberger and Raines that she would not cooperate with the *Journal* article. But when she walked into the newsroom after their cease-fire, she appeared more triumphant than a member of Raines's team. I walked over to give her a heartfelt hug, but she was distant and remote. Despite Sulzberger's efforts to make nice, I knew we had lost her.

————

BRAGG HAD accepted his reprimand, but he wanted promises that no one from the paper would disclose the details. Sulzberger assured him that would be the case in a telephone call outlining the sanctions. But shortly after their conversation, on Friday, May 23, an exclusive appeared on the Web site of the *Columbia Journalism Review*: "Rick Bragg, a Pulitzer-Prize-winning reporter for the *New York Times*, has been suspended for two weeks from writing for the paper," it reported. Someone had leaked the news.

Bragg was bombarded with inquiries. His reputation was being tarnished as well as his livelihood, he said. He had a book deal in the works and was worried that it could be withdrawn over the flap. He wanted to go public, accusing other correspondents of excessive use of stringers and revealing phone conversations he had with Sulzberger and me.

My job was now to calm Bragg down, which was impossible. We talked Friday night, Saturday morning, and Sunday morning. He understood that the leak came from someone who wished him and Raines harm and wanted to trigger the very reaction he was having. He would remain silent, he said. Then he called back, vowing to go public, saying he refused to have his reputation damaged just to save Raines. Then he calmed down, and then he started up again.

It was too much. I called Raines and told him that he needed to talk to Bragg. He had recused himself, saying he did not want to get involved because of their friendship.

"But this is the whole ball game," I said. "It's come down to this."

Reluctantly, he agreed.

He reported back with good news. He had talked to Bragg for nearly an hour, and the reporter agreed to remain silent and accept his suspension. He planned to resign from the paper after the furor blew over. What he really wanted to do anyway was write books.

We had survived the latest crisis. *New York* magazine was not doing the piece on Howell's favorites, at least not the next week. Bragg was on board.

But I really could not exhale. Young minority reporters were complaining of mistreatment by supervisors. Raines's favorites were fair game for attack. About a dozen reporters and editors were convening as part of the Siegal Committee's investigation into the Blair scandal and were summoning colleagues to "testify." I was scheduled to appear the following week.

On Sunday, May 25, reporter Judith Miller became the focus. First colleagues traded rumors that she had received a special "security clearance" while covering the weapons of mass destruction in Iraq. It was a charge that we had investigated and dismissed several weeks before, but now it resurfaced. So did another attack. On Monday, Howard Kurtz of the *Washington Post* wrote about a dustup between Miller and Baghdad bureau chief John Burns, based on a copy of an e-mail exchange between the two. Someone at the paper had actually leaked the e-mail. I was appalled that staffers were using outside media to attack their colleagues. It was as if everyone was for him- or herself; all civility had disappeared.

When I told the publisher that Miller, a longtime friend of his, had threatened to resign because of what she perceived as backstabbing by some on the staff, he suggested that it might be good for the paper. Everyone had become fair game. Raines did not help matters. He seemed to be oblivious to the problems at hand, content to engage matters that solved little. In fact, his latest decision, one I had resisted, created new problems.

In a staff announcement showing his commitment to change, he floated the idea of ceding authority, something no executive editor had ever done. It was a Hail Mary that surprised even me. He wrote:

Gerald and I expressed our absolute determination to change the way this newsroom works. The first change, which we are executing immediately, is to push authority of news coverage and staff assignments down to the department heads and to work with them in a consultative way on matters of news judgment and deployment of resources.

Gerald and I will not, of course, duck our responsibility to manage the newspaper and to participate in the most important news and personnel decisions, but the keyword here is "participate."

I resented the announcement enormously. I believed that Raines was throwing in the towel. I began to think seriously that we should resign. If we went on the course that he announced, we would spend the rest of our careers being contrite rather than learning from our mistakes and moving on. After all, we were deeply wounded, and as I learned from a colleague, the department heads in the group that Raines wanted to transfer power to had held their own meeting. Several had vowed not to take orders from Raines or me. I could not see how anyone could lead a newsroom in revolt. We had crossed a line, and it seemed impossible to go back.

On Tuesday, May 27, Kurtz had a new exclusive: Rick Bragg. Despite his pledge not to talk, Bragg had told the *Washington Post* reporter that his use of stringers was nothing out of the ordinary. Most national correspondents did exactly what he had been suspended for, he said.

I demanded of Raines that we fire Bragg on the spot and issue a statement immediately, supporting the National staff and disavowing Bragg's charges.

He disagreed on both counts. He did not want to further enrage Bragg, still worried about what else he would say to the media. "It doesn't matter what he says," I shot back. "Nothing can be worse than not defending our staff."

Sulzberger, who had once been actively involved, now refused to intervene. This was a newsroom problem—our problem—and we had to solve it ourselves, he said. He seemed to be washing his hands of us. Raines and I spent all of Tuesday debating what to do, a full day in which there was no response.

Bragg's comments ignited a wildfire. On Wednesday, May 28, Seth Mnookin published on *Newsweek*'s Web site e-mail exchanges with several national correspondents denying Bragg's claims and defending the *Times*. Why weren't the top editors doing the same, everyone, including Mnookin, wondered. It was maddening. Raines finally agreed to provide Mnookin with a response, but not in his name. It came from Jim Roberts, the National editor. There was still no word from either of us.

Bragg had clearly worn out his welcome. Later that day, he called Raines and raised the issue of resigning. I said it needed to happen immediately or we should issue a statement challenging his remarks. Raines spent the next few hours negotiating with Bragg. Finally at 7:30 P.M., a statement went to the staff:

> Rick Bragg has offered his resignation, and I have accepted it. We know this has been a difficult period. We have full confidence in our staff and will be talking with you more in short order.
>
> Howell

It would take yet another day before Raines would agree to a more extensive statement defending the staff. On Thursday, May 29, he circulated a memo carrying both our names:

> In the last couple of days, we have all been hearing some fanciful accounts that purport to describe the work of our great corps of correspondents, especially on the National staff. It is time for us to step up and say that we don't recognize ourselves or you in that picture.

The six-paragraph statement ended: "For now, we just want to thank our staff for being worthy of our confidence and our readers' trust, and for showing up the fanciful rumors for what they are."

Finally, he had spoken up for our troops. But the statement rang hollow. I was no longer angry with Raines, only weary from the constant fighting. Since the first days of the Blair scandal, Raines had gone with his gut. And at each turn, he made the wrong decision. I knew instinctively that a leader had to defend his staff when it was under attack in public, no matter who made the claims. There was no alternative.

I had come to see Raines as the executive editor who had given me a chance to be managing editor. But I also saw him as a man of extremes that were never before so pronounced and of weaknesses that had never loomed so large, especially over the last few weeks. That was his problem. My problem was my inability to change his actions and my refusal to publicly assail his decisions, especially in the midst of a crisis. Loyalty mattered, and, too late, I wondered if it mattered too much.

Sitting at our kitchen table a few days later, Robin and I reviewed the latest events. Her assessments throughout the ordeal had been flawless. Now she issued her newest: "I don't think you guys are gonna make it," she said simply. Too much had happened, most of it bad. We had made too many mistakes, we had lost the support of the staff, and now, it seemed, we had lost the support of Sulzberger. Every word rang like thunder in my head. I did not want to believe her take, but I found it impossible to challenge. There was no need. On Wednesday, June 4, Christine, my assistant, reminded me, "The publisher wants to see you at six."

17

A TIME FOR GOOD-BYES

He's flashing that lopsided grin. Chest puffed, head cocked to the side. Imitating a pimp's stroll, dangling a knife from his right hand and tracking my steps through the Upper East Side penthouse. "Y'all got four bathrooms in this joint, and one of 'em got a bidet in it!" I exclaim. "Ain't this a look-how-far-we-done-come moment?"

"Girl, don't you take nuthin' out of our house!" Gerald says, drawing the knife higher and completely cutting the fool. He lets out a big fat laugh, then, "What can I get you to drink?" He slices some lemons, pours me a glass of wine.

I am welcomed on this evening of kicking back with the Stone-Boyds. Here, a person cannot help but reveal his innermost parts. Gerald's conversation veers toward story, craft, the news. He dishes advice on moving up, or an unsolicited chastisement about lingering in a lower-level gig. Blacks folks can't afford to tarry, he says—with humor and profanities—to young Connie on this night.

Mostly, though, there is food and drink and laughter. There is Gerald talking smack about how good he is at bid whist and, though he loses, how no one will trump him. When we guests prepare to leave, Gerald hugs me: "Come over more often. Robin really needs family in New York."

In crisis, family, whatever its iteration, shows up in the flesh. Family administers presence. Gerald barely indulges this expectation in his last days. When Tom, his longtime friend, insists on visiting Gerald in the hospital, I drive Tom, also seriously ailing, to Memorial Sloan-Kettering. Resigned to a seat outside the guarded door of the wing where Gerald is being treated, I read scripture, waiting for Tom to finish. Suddenly, Robin opens the door. "He wants to see you," she says. I am glad that he grants me this.

I reach Gerald, who is so very lean now. He can barely lift his head. I kneel in front of his wheelchair. He locks his eyes on mine. "What's up, Black?" I ask, grinning. He smiles that smile. "Girl," he says, chuckling, "you are so crazy."

—KATTI GRAY

THE MONTHS ahead were hard, but still there were moments of laughter. One day after I left the paper, the homeless man who often camped near my house, to whom I contributed regularly, wrinkled his brow in concern and asked if I would be OK. Of course, he was worried that I would become less charitable. I told him I would be fine and pressed a dollar bill in his hand. The usually detached Latina at my dry cleaners became animated when I dropped off a load of clothes. She had seen me on Spanish-language TV, and to her, I was a celebrity. If she only knew what I had gone through to warrant the story, she might have understood why I preferred to avoid the spotlight.

Such was my life just after I left the *Times*: periodic chuckles that broke up stretches of numbing sadness. The first time a cabdriver asked me what I did for a living, I froze. I no longer held the job that had come to define me. Finally, I told him simply that I had retired.

Robin and I had to tell Zachary. Stories about me were front-page news, and for a while, television crews were ringing our bell. We knew that eventually our six year old would hear about it from a classmate or the media. We wanted the information to come from us. So we strategized on what to say, giving it a positive spin by focusing on how I would have more time for him.

No sooner than I uttered the words, he erupted in tears. How can you just leave the *Times*! he demanded to know.

"I want to do other things," I said with as much conviction as I could show. "Maybe I'll work at another newspaper someday."

"But the *Times* is not just a newspaper; it's a public trust," he said, parroting what he had heard me say repeatedly. Then he surprised us by asking to talk to me alone. After Robin left the room, he seemed to be searching for reassurance that I was OK. Somehow I found the words to convince him. Later, he would occasionally talk about missing the *Times*, but in the next breath, he would offer that "my daddy is retired." That talk with my son was one of the most difficult conversations of my life.

————

I RECEIVED letters and calls from many of my former *Times* colleagues eager to get together. I hesitated, in part because it would be impossible for me to let go if I kept reliving the nightmare, which would be central to any conversation.

But something more troubled me. Throughout the ordeal, few colleagues came to my defense, not in the newsroom or in public statements or at the disastrous town hall meeting. I understood how confusing everything was, but their silence left me bitter.

In those early days, I became determined to repair my image. I agreed to testify before Sulzberger's so-called Siegal Committee, offering my take on how the Blair fiasco happened and recommending ways to prevent a similar disaster in the future. I was the last witness. I left the two-hour session believing that my account of events was not heard or appreciated. Clearly, the committee thought I was responsible for Blair's survival at the paper. No matter. I was moving on.

I secured a public relations firm, something I wished the newspaper had done at the start of the Blair crisis. Friends led me to a small company in Texas, Public Strategies, whose New York office was helmed by Ann Richards, the feisty former Texas governor who had endured her own share of setbacks in a highly successful political career. Although the firm normally advised corporations, it eagerly took me on, arguing that I had been mistreated by my paper and other media. Once Robin and I met with Richards, it felt good to have her team on my side.

I worked closely with two of their top strategists, Terry McDevitt, a white woman, and Eddie Reeves, a black man. Trying to repair my image would not be easy. They suggested that I continue to avoid the media until I had a clearer sense of what I wanted to say and was better prepared, because it seemed every word I had spoken was used against me. Just having them around to discuss my situation gave me hope.

Working together, we set our sights on the National Association of Black Journalists convention in Dallas that August, two months after I had left the *Times*. We all agreed that it was the perfect venue for me to deliver a speech and answer questions. Two years earlier, in 2001, I had appeared before the same group as its Journalist of the Year. Now I was returning to defend my thirty-year career. I was eager to state my case publicly for the first time.

Robin and I arrived in Dallas the night before my scheduled appearance and went directly to my suite. I avoided the crowds, including longtime friends.

As I stood before my colleagues at the convention, I felt many emotions. The introduction by Greg Moore, a longtime friend and the editor of the *Denver Post*, brought a lump in my throat as he proudly recounted the highlights of my career.

While I prepared to speak, I looked into the audience. In the front row was Robin, sending strength and courage my way. Next to her sat Sheila, who was still a dear friend. Together they represented bookends of my life and career. I felt blessed to have their support. Off to the right was a section of former *Times* colleagues including Sulzberger Jr. Nearly every seat in the giant ballroom was filled.

The time had come for me to be heard.

On June 5, nine weeks ago to the day, I walked out of the *New York Times* for the last time after resigning as managing editor. You've seen and heard from a lot of people about the whole sad episode.

You've heard from people who were involved, and you've heard from a lot more who were not involved yet ironically seemed to know so much more about it. About the only person you haven't heard from is me.

So let me answer one of the questions that's probably on your minds: How did it feel?

Well, it hurt. And you know what? It still hurts.

I am still grappling with feelings of sadness, disbelief, betrayal, regret, and, yes, anger.

But throughout all of this I have resolved to take the high road, and as I go forward, I will continue on that path. The reason is simple: I would never try to do anything that would harm the *New York Times* or the journalism profession that I hold so dear.

I owe a lot to the *Times* and to so many of my extraordinary colleagues there, including the publisher, Arthur Sulzberger Jr.

It was at the *Times* that I traveled the world as a White House and political correspondent.

It was there that I began my career in management.

It was there, as Metro editor, that I led the staff to its first Pulitzer for local reporting in more than two decades for coverage of the 1993 bombing of the World Trade Center.

It was there that we did the groundbreaking series "How Race Is Lived in America," which also earned a Pulitzer.

And it was there, five days after I became managing editor, that I managed the staff as we covered the tragic events of 9/11, for which the paper won most of its seven Pulitzer Prizes last year.

In my twenty years at the *Times*, I was fortunate to work with gifted women and men who represent the best that journalism has to offer: from editors to reporters, from graphics editors to photographers. To be in the trenches with these professionals as we covered 9/11 and the aftermath, to see their talent, dedication, and hard work, is something that I will never forget.

Yet for me it's time to move on.

We've all seen the damage to our industry by what will go down in history as the Jayson Blair scandal. *The Jayson Blair scandal.* That description has become shorthand in our industry for everything ranging from a lack of credibility to mismanagement to diversity run amok.

Now that the *Times'* internal investigation is complete, and we are no longer mired in media hysteria and finger-pointing, it is time to take a hard look at why this happened and what lessons we can draw from it.

Let me talk first about why I believe this happened.

In a nutshell, we didn't realize until it was too late that we were dealing with something far worse than a reporter whose work had lapsed into frequent error and sloppiness. Obviously, if we had known how deeply troubled he really was at the time, Jayson Blair simply would not have been writing for the *New York Times.*

Let me be clear: I am not saying that I don't share some blame in the scandal. At the end of the day, as the second-highest-ranking name on the masthead and the person directly responsible for the daily gathering of news, of course, a good share of the responsibility is mine.

But those who know me know that I—like my former colleagues at the *Times*—have always stood for integrity. That's one of the main reasons this is so painful. Some have suggested that I looked the other way because Jayson is black. That is, quite frankly, absolutely untrue.

I have neither the time nor inclination to go into the intricate details of this young man's career at the *Times.* Suffice it to say that he received substantial management attention and correction by people much closer to his day-to-day work than I. And many of those who had more direct management of him had ample opportunity to take more direct action over the course of his career.

And while I had no direct oversight of his work, I did have knowledge of some of his faults. And there is no question that I could have and in retrospect should have shared more information about his track record as he moved from desk to desk. That I did not was clearly a mistake.

Once his performance improved—and his performance did ebb and flow—we editors never came together to reevaluate where he was and what should come next. Instead, we were pulled in different directions by the demands of the news and a severe need for bodies to cover it.

There is a lesson there that we would all do well to heed: no matter how caught up we become in covering an ever more complex world, we must never lose sight of the fact that as we work hard to communicate with our audiences, we must take the time to make sure we're communicating with each other.

Now on to the factor of the scandal that many people are not comfortable acknowledging: race.

At least one editor evidently found it difficult to talk to me about Jayson because I am black.

While I have always been proud of my heritage as an African American and have proudly—and successfully—worked to promote all kinds of diversity, absolutely no one can peg me as some newsroom racial revolutionary.

So what does it say about the state of race relations in the newsroom when seasoned management colleagues felt they could not come to me—the managing editor—with concerns about a young reporter simply because both the reporter and I are black?

This is all the more curious given that I have personally broken the news to numerous aspiring young would-be *Times* reporters—including people of color—that they simply weren't ready to work for the *Times*.

This impulse—to fail to even talk to me, to simply assume that I could only see through the prism of race—is the same misguided impulse that led some to assume that I was a mentor to Jayson when that was never the case. The truth is I never knew him well, nor did I have much direct contact with him.

I treated Jayson no differently than any other person on the staff.

It is disturbing—and sad—that people would read more into this because of race. And I would be lying if I didn't say that I can't help but wonder why, after all these years of struggle to establish our worth and credibility in newsrooms, to be seen as top-notch journalists by any measure, as soon as controversy arises concerning an African American reporter, the senior African American is automatically viewed as suspect.

Most people will freely acknowledge that refusing to hire or promote a deserving person because of race, ethnicity, gender, orientation, religion, or physical challenge not only harms that person but diminishes us all. Yet it is just as harmful to fail to correct, discipline, or, if need be, dismiss an underperforming person for the same reasons.

Perhaps naively, I didn't believe that point needed to be made at the *New York Times*. I really believed that the *Times* understood this after publishing the groundbreaking series "How Race Is Lived in America." But racial differences—and differing expectations and attitudes based on race—are still alive and well. Even at the *New York Times*.

———

SOME TIME after that, I flew to Washington, D.C., for the annual convention of the American Society of Newspaper Editors, the industry group that two years before had elected me to its board of directors. In the past, I had attended the meetings with supreme confidence. But on this trip, I was unnerved. I had lost my job because of a scandal, and I knew that many of those in attendance believed that I left the *Times* in disgrace.

The experience was wrenching. For several days, I roamed the J. W. Marriott and the Omni Shoreham hotels wearing a badge with a red tag proclaiming me a director, the title given to board members. Yet I was an editor without a newspaper. And without an editing job, I could not stand for reelection and would have to surrender my seat on the board.

At dinner one night, Valarie Zeeck, the wife of David Zeeck, the executive editor of the *News Tribune* in Tacoma, Washington, offered me her support and then added, "You did wrong, but there were a lot more who did more wrong."

I appreciated her courage to express what others were probably afraid to say to me.

Back in my hotel room, I could not sleep. I replayed her remarks over and over. Maybe I needed to hear what she was saying. It was not easy.

As a child, whenever I was troubled, I would try to escape by going to sleep, as if everything would be better by the time I awoke. Over the years, I found another remedy: denial. I always had a hard time recognizing my shortcomings, especially as others saw them. All too often, my pride got in the way. The reaction was instilled in me from childhood, when I came to believe that there was no room for failure. My life had not been a quest for perfection but an exercise in survival. And mistakes of any kind put that mission at risk.

So at first I bristled when Robin challenged me about my actions in the Blair scandal, and especially when her response made it clear that I had not handled some matters was well as I should have. Now Valarie Zeeck had made a similar point. I had acknowledged my mistakes to the world; now I needed to do so to myself.

I forced myself to confront the truth, attending a standing-room-only session on newsroom ethics where Sulzberger was a panelist. Most of the audience had come to hear about what the *Times* had done wrong, and they hammered the period that I served as managing editor. Even so, I remained in my seat, taking in one painful remark after another. I needed to hear their criticisms, whether I agreed or not.

Oddly, this was therapeutic. I was beginning to see that whatever happened at the *Times* was larger than me. Few situations so grave, intense, and complex are about one person. There was a clash of powerful forces that in the end brought disaster. There were those who performed with dignity, and those who were despicable. As far as I was concerned, there were no heroes.

Whatever my failures, I believed I was the man I had always hoped to be. I was the man whom Zachary would respect when he understood more about how I faced this ordeal. I wanted him to believe, as I did, that I met it with honesty and with a devotion to my profession as well as the institution and those who worked for it.

As I was leaving the convention, I was nearly reduced to tears when Seymour Topping approached me. Top, as everyone called him, was a role model from my earliest days at the *Times*. We had both attended the University of Missouri and were among its journalism school's most distinguished alumni. We had both been on the board of the American Society of Newspaper Editors, and Top was at one time its president. And we both had been managing editor of the *Times*. Now he was at Columbia University, teaching journalism and administering the Pulitzer Prizes.

As we stood in the Marriott lobby, he shared his compassion in his deep baritone.

"I know how hard it has been for you to be here, and I've heard a lot of talk about how well you have handled yourself with such grace and dignity," he said. "I just want you to know how much I admire the class and dignity you have shown throughout all of this. God bless you."

I had no real response. I could not tell him how troubled I was from living with the past or how much I was still hurting. How I still woke up each morning in an emotional fog and how I still avoided former colleagues. I just thanked him for his kindness and left before he could see my emotions get the better of me.

———

ON A crisp, sunny morning in late January 2004, I picked up the mail and noticed a pale vanilla envelope. The return address, embossed on the back, read Henryville, Pennsylvania.

I pulled out a single handwritten sheet of paper. At the top was the name Howell Raines. It was seven months after I left the *New York Times*. I had not heard from my former boss until then.

Dear Gerald,

I was in Florida when I heard the exciting news of your agreement with Columbia. You'll be a terrific asset for the J School. Congratulations to you and to them. I still believe you will wind up running an important newspaper. Meanwhile, I hope your book project goes well. I hope also that Robin and Zachary are thriving. I think of you often and would love to meet for a drink sometime.

All best,
Howell

Reading his words brought it all back.

I was at the Four Seasons when he offered me the managing editor's position. I could still see his look of joy and bewilderment that day in Sulzberger's office when we learned the *Times* won a record number of Pulitzers. I could picture his boys, Jeffrey and Ben, one a musician and the other a journalist, watching with pride at his wedding, and the smile on his face as he paraded through the reception with his new bride, Krystyna.

I saw his stoic expression on the day we left the paper and heard the last words he spoke to me just before we addressed the staff. I looked him in his eyes and said softly, "Thanks for believing in me."

He replied, "I love you."

It was time to call him. Despite all the tumult, we shared an incredible experience.

But a friend from the *Times* faxed to me a preview copy of a twenty-thousand-word article that Raines had written for the *Atlantic Monthly*. In it, Raines blasted my former colleagues, Sulzberger, and me. He portrayed the staff as largely mediocre, the publisher as lacking backbone. He was equally harsh in his comments about me.

"I also wanted to see, as Arthur himself needed to, what Gerald Boyd could do in a high-demand situation," he revealed, reducing my selection to a question mark. My career at the *Times* was one of measurable accomplishments that no one could deny. Yet Raines's depiction was of a managing editor trainee.

This was even more painful than the dozens of inaccurate descriptions of me as Jayson Blair's mentor. Those who trafficked that lie did not know me. But Raines and I had a twenty-year history.

In the piece, Raines all but blamed me for the Blair fiasco. I thought he had blamed me almost from the earliest days, when he marched into the newsroom to take charge. But like a lawyer, I avoided asking a question to which I did not want to know the answer. If he would have said yes, it would have destroyed any chance we had of working through the crisis together.

Here was his answer in the *Atlantic Monthly*.

I never responded to his letter. I was tired of being betrayed, tired of the *Times*, tired of him.

It was clear that Raines was still in denial about what had led to his downfall. In his rant, there was very little self-examination or intro-spection. There had been true believers and unrelenting cynics on the staff, but the vast majority was agnostic. In the end, he lost them. Even he acknowledged that, writing that he "had no reservoir of good will" from which to draw once the crisis hit.

He had also allowed his opponents to define him and what he stood for as an editor, rather than defining himself. Much-needed innovations such as "flooding the zone" on a major story with ample reporting resources or making the staff more competitive were lampooned as excessive and unnecessary. Even the edge he had over Bill Keller as a leader became a liability as he was caricatured as pompous and remote. While he wanted to change everything around him, he never sought to change himself—until it was too late.

In the end, Raines regarded himself as invincible. Leading the paper to seven Pulitzers certainly encouraged that view. Once when we were talking, he made the point that we were the only two editors who were irreplaceable. "The only way they will get rid of us is if we're caught in bed with a dead girl or a live boy," he said, recalling the well-worn Edwin Edwards line.

I finished the article with sadness. Here was my old friend Howell, once again, presenting some legitimate issues but drowning them out with unnecessary static. Tone deaf till the end.

———

I WAS keeping a low profile, writing this book, working at Columbia University developing case studies for journalism students, but when anyone asked for my response to Raines's article, I spoke out in defense of the staff.

At a speech at the University of South Carolina in March 2004, I challenged him directly:

> Howell, my former colleague and friend of many years, offered his personal assessment of many things in the piece. I do not agree with many of his characterizations, including his unfair attack on the staff of the *Times*.

For the past year, my former colleagues at the *Times* have been on a roller coaster where their professionalism has been attacked and maligned. This has to stop.

Whenever I was asked about my relationship with Raines, I would describe it as a marriage, saying that what had happened between us was private. I knew that I would not have become managing editor had he not offered me the job. But my loyalty was long gone. I thought he was being incredibly selfish. The *Times* was still trying to climb back from the calamity of the previous summer, and he knew his article would open old wounds and create new ones.

I finally understood the years of battles I witnessed between Raines and Lelyveld. For years, I had viewed their war as a power struggle between two determined foes, but it was about much more than power. It was a fight for the heart and soul of America's most respected newspaper. That the *Times* was the crown jewel of American journalism made the fight so intense. It was never personal, this contest to control that which is most sacred at the newspaper, its journalism.

Raines and I were amateurs when it came to fighting a war of this magnitude. He had relied on Sulzberger, and I had relied on him. We had no army of true believers willing to stand up for our beliefs inside and outside the *Times,* and we never developed one. Raines succeeded Lelyveld and declared the contest over when it was only beginning.

I had learned much from Raines and Lelyveld, each of whom was vital to my career. Even so, we failed each other at critical moments, and in the end, I was collateral damage in their war. I had only myself to blame. I should have relied less on each of them and more on myself. As Raines's deputy, I should have found a way to force him to engage the problems in the newsroom more wisely. But how? Several former colleagues reasoned later that I should have threatened to resign unless Raines changed. I never thought I would have to go to such an extreme.

Despite the miscalculations and missed opportunities, I believed that I responded as an honorable man—from the beginning of my tenure as managing editor until the day I walked out the door, and afterward. In spite of everything, that brought me peace.

———

I AGREED to meet with Joe Lelyveld, Raines's nemesis and my one-time friend. On the day that Raines and I resigned, Lelyveld triumphantly returned to the newsroom as the interim executive editor. He was expected to restore calm and to hand over the leadership to Bill Keller, his protégé, several weeks later. He reached out, inviting me to a meal. He had not changed in the least. As we planned our meeting over the phone, he said he knew how I was feeling because he had gone through the same thing when he retired from the paper. *The same thing?* I thought in astonishment. He was celebrated when he left the *Times*. I was given hours to leave, with everything I had worked for over thirty years in tatters.

Those were my thoughts when we finally sat for lunch shortly before Christmas 2003. Even so, I wanted to see him. Not for reconciliation. I still wanted to know why Sulzberger had ousted me, and I hoped he could provide some answers. I was living without closure, and it was fueling my pain.

As we sat at an Upper East Side cafe, Lelyveld described his experience in the events that led to my dismissal.

He said he was on the treadmill the day before, when he started to receive urgent e-mails from Sulzberger's assistant to call the publisher. Soon there were eight such requests. When they finally talked, Sulzberger said he had made a decision.

"Arthur said this wasn't going to work," Lelyveld recounted.

Lelyveld said that he was "totally clueless," so much so that he had asked Sulzberger what the "this" was.

"Howell remaining as executive editor," Lelyveld recalled.

Lelyveld said that Sulzberger choked up as they talked. He said the final straw was Raines's plan to share power in the newsroom, the Hail Mary scheme that I had resisted.

Then there was the issue of what would happen to me.

"Arthur said it had been decided that you had to go," Lelyved said. "I would have been willing to have you remain on as managing editor during the interim period, but Arthur said that it had been decided."

I did not believe him. Later I would hear accounts that he was far more involved, in constant conversation with Sulzberger throughout that chaos.

Whether he was or not, I let it go. As we talked, he made no secret of his disdain for Raines and how he ran the newsroom. His one condition for returning was permission to change the typeface on the front page. As if time had stood still, he came back with the same priority he had when he left.

Lelyveld acknowledged that he had failed to keep his commitment to make me his managing editor. At that point, it meant little.

I would reach out to him once again, when I learned that his wife, Carolyn, was losing her battle with cancer. Whatever my difficulties with Joe, I was always fond of Carolyn and their devotion to each other, and I wanted to say good-bye. I went up to her room at Memorial Sloan-Kettering, where I found him keeping vigil.

"Darling," he tried to stir his wife, who rested peacefully as monitors hummed and hissed. "Gerald Boyd is here." She opened her eyes slightly, as if she was acknowledging my presence. Later, he said that was one of the few times that she had responded in weeks. I was glad to be there, with Joe, Carolyn, and their daughters, Nita and Amy, who herself was a new mother. As we chatted outside Carolyn's hospital room, our differences seemed small. All things considered, they were.

I also said my good-byes to Sulzberger. Despite twenty years at the *Times*, I did not know him well. I should have done more to get to know him, but I held back because I always felt uncomfortable around him. And he should have done more to get to know me, if he seriously regarded me as someone who might become the top editor at the *Times*.

We met for breakfast in November 2003, before Raines's *Atlantic Monthly* piece appeared. Sulzberger had called, suggesting that we get together. To avoid media sightings and reports in the *New York Post*'s gossip columns, I invited him to my place. It was the first time he had ever been in my home.

Over bagels, fruit, orange juice, and coffee, we awkwardly revisited the past while trying to focus on the future. His pain was clear and deep, and it caught me off guard. A few days earlier, he had dined with Raines; he was still playing peacemaker.

"One of you needs to reach out to the other," he said. "You have shared so much together over the years."

"Maybe someday," I replied, letting the issue drop.

The last few months had been hell for me, but strangely, I felt sorry for the publisher. He described how he was still trying to get to know Keller and how that effort was complicated by the fact that he had passed him over initially. Then there was the company board of directors. They had demanded an accounting of the newsroom fiasco, which Sulzberger explained in a lengthy, detailed memo. The board was questioning and pressuring him in ways it never had before.

I tried to sound positive. Despite all that happened, I said, we had produced some extraordinary journalism, especially in the months after 9/11. Maybe that was why we were in the newsroom at that particular time, to oversee the most important story of a lifetime. Clinging to that belief comforted me.

Despite exploring the issues repeatedly in therapy, I could not bring myself to ask Sulzberger two questions: *Why did he fire me, and if I had to go, why was there no other job for me at the* Times? Maybe I really did not want to know the answers. Again, that childhood reflex of surviving by shielding myself from the unbearable.

Then there was the issue of race. In my heart, I knew it was a factor in the decision to let me go. The erroneous, anonymous reports declaring me Jayson Blair's mentor would have never stuck had one of us been white. Sulzberger never asked me if they were true, perhaps not wanting a denial to complicate his decision.

———

ON APRIL 5, 2004, I returned to the *Times*. Bill Keller, now executive editor, had phoned the Friday before to invite me to the newsroom for the Pulitzer Prize announcements. I wanted to say a real goodbye to so many who were special to me. The invitation gave me that chance.

Keller said Raines was not invited. "My graciousness has limits," he added. The culture war was still raging, but it seemed far, far away.

I knew that by appearing at an event where Raines was pointedly excluded, I was choosing sides. In many ways, I already had.

I went for the announcements but not the party that followed. I, too, had my limits. To spend the day and then the evening with some who had orchestrated my ouster would have been too much.

As I walked through the newsroom again, my presence caused a slight buzz. Some former colleagues greeted me with an embrace, while others kept their distance. I noticed that like me, my old office was gone. The space was reconfigured with a surrounding area to accommodate John Geddes and Jill Abramson, who each now held the title managing editor.

As Keller began his remarks, he acknowledged my presence to the several hundred former colleagues gathered. I had worried about their reaction. I should not have been. Their prolonged applause touched me deeply.

I listened as Keller spoke. It was his newsroom and his newspaper, and I was now an outsider. I laughed with others at his quips and enthusiastically cheered David Barstow and Lowell Bergman, whose examination of death and injury among American workers because their bosses violated safety rules won the Pulitzer for public service. The *Times* would always be the *Times*, true to its history, culture, and traditions. But in subtle ways, the newsroom had already changed. The place felt different, more mechanical, less emotional. It was as if there were no spirit, no soul.

Standing in the newsroom, looking at the familiar faces, I wondered what role race would play in the paper's future. It was hard to believe the *Times* would be as committed to diversity as it once was. The Blair scandal gave foes or the disinterested a reason to stop the clock.

But I could no longer worry about the *Times*. I received several calls about possible opportunities. One came from Mortimer Zuckerman, the mercurial owner of the *New York Daily News*, who floated the idea of a senior editing position. I made it clear that, at that point in my life, I wanted to run a newsroom and not report to anyone other than the publisher. I no longer wanted to be a number two.

I reached out to other major news organizations and received favorable responses. But no top editing positions were available, I was told.

One friend called with the chance to edit a small paper in the Midwest. But after several talks, he took it off the table, saying he could not believe that the former managing editor of the *Times* could be happy at a place far smaller and with far fewer resources. I did not protest; the idea of such a drastic change in my work and in our lives did not appeal to Robin or me.

I got to know Tavis Smiley, the remarkable young black man who had already made a huge mark with his talk show on BET and then a daily show on NPR. Smiley was forced out of BET in a highly public squabble with owner Robert Johnson, so I felt that he could relate to some of my pain. I was encouraged by how he had branded himself, turning what appeared to be a setback into a huge opportunity to do radio, write books, and make speeches. He was looking for an executive producer for his new radio show out of Los Angeles, and the prospect appealed to me greatly. He talked about the two of us joining forces to produce quality journalism. The conversations came amid my deepest depression. His interest was God-sent, and I was forever grateful. Talks with him helped me start engaging the future.

But I was not ready to change my stripes and move to broadcasting. I felt I still had work to do in print journalism. Returning to a newsroom had the greatest appeal, but that decision was out of my hands. So until something emerged, I thought, I would write my memoir and work part time at Columbia University as director of case studies. In that role, I started developing a series of real-life scenarios highlighting editorial problems that journalists face. The cases were to be set up like interactive games. Students, in the role of an editor, would face a situation or event, such as a local airplane crash. The choices they made would lead to new questions and problems to solve. The goal was to help young journalists sharpen their critical thinking skills. Case studies are popular in business and law schools, and I agreed with the school's remarkable dean, Nicholas Lemann, that such instruction was perfect for the next generation of journalists. I also started a weekly column through the Kansas City–based Universal Press Syndicate explaining how the newsroom worked. Suddenly, I had a full plate.

Still, the past haunted me. Terry McDevitt, the PR strategist whom I was talking to daily and trusted completely, kept insisting that I consent to an interview with Seth Mnookin, the former *Newsweek* correspondent who was writing a book on the *Times*. Mnookin was the reporter who first labeled me as Blair's mentor. His assertions were recycled repeatedly by others in the media who seized on them as the primary reason Blair had survived at the *Times*. When I called Mnookin on the lie, he acknowledged that he got the information from a vague "people who had talked to Blair." He promised to set the record straight but never did.

Now, in an e-mail campaign, Mnookin was demanding that I cooperate with him. Over several months, he sent several messages all but threatening me to play ball. In April 2004 he wrote that Raines and I were the lone holdouts of every *Times* source that he sought to interview, including Sulzberger, Janet Robinson, and the reporters and editors who produced the Blair report the previous year. "I am baffled," he went on, adding that my talking to him could help ensure that my voice was included in "the only objective historical document" about the recent years at the *Times*.

I was determined not to cave in and grew puzzled when my PR rep continued to suggest that I do the interview, since, as she said, nearly everyone else had done so.

After Robin and I pressed her, McDevitt confessed that Mnookin was a longtime friend. I was just as amazed by her ethical lapse as I was by her betrayal of me. I had disclosed so much to her, and I wondered how much of it had already made its way to Mnookin. The damage was enormous. I saw that I had no one to confide in other than Robin and others in my family. I quickly parted company with McDevitt and her firm.

———

AS TIME passed, I found hope and courage in unexpected places. I would look at Zachary, the wonderful son Robin and I had produced, and think about the positives. With Robin and me both working at home, Zachary flourished. He was smart and caring, a fighter who was confident of his worth and abilities. As he saw his life, anything was possible. I took pride in knowing that he was already light-years ahead of where I was at his age. I basked in his company and in knowing that he looked up to me regardless of my title or lack of one. To him, I was simply Daddy.

I relished the summer when Zachary and I began each morning by walking several blocks to the corner where a yellow bus picked him up for day camp in the Bronx. In the fall, I would start my day by walking him to school. Along the way, we talked about everything and nothing. At one point, I was determined to teach Zachary how to ride his bike. He was seven, and that was old enough to lose the training wheels. On a Saturday, we took a taxi across town to Riverside Park, and with a wrench and the assistance of a young man in a nearby bicycle shop, we managed to remove the wheels. For several hours, Zachary tumbled through the park. He wanted to give up, but despite his frustration, he did not. (And if he had tried, I would not have let him.) Then all of a sudden, he got it, riding his bike as if he had always known how. I watched with pure joy. This was my life now, and it was precious.

I learned to depend on Robin, a ferocious defender and a source of my strength. She helped me weather the bouts of depression and encouraged me to not give up on myself. My dependence transformed our relationship. I was no longer the editor who had recruited her to the *Times* and whom she watched rise to managing editor. Looking to her for advice and guidance was now central to our marriage. We were partners who relied on each other completely.

Robin signed a contract to write a second book, this time to work with an entertainment icon on her memoir. After maddening years of fertility treatments and miscarriage, we started the lengthy process to adopt a child, one I hoped to inspire with stories about our families.

I was evolving. As I went into several newsrooms preparing cases for Columbia, I realized how much I wanted to return to work as an editor. I would grow deeply depressed as I interviewed editors, reporters, and executives, wanting so much to be in their shoes. It was difficult to perform a job in which I was a detached observer.

Fortunately, an offer from an old friend led me to a significant newsroom role. Michael Williams, a former colleague from the business side of the *Times*, had become president of publications for Canwest, one of the largest media companies in Canada. Canwest owned two major networks, a national newspaper, and twelve other daily papers in cities across the country. Williams was a remarkable man. Not yet fifty, he had held top jobs at Seagram, the *Times*, and now Canwest. He also happened to be black. He wanted me to become the company's senior editorial consultant, helping him to strategize, troubleshoot, and put his business plan in action.

The job was based in Toronto, with an office in the newsroom of the *National Post*. I eagerly accepted, even though I would not deal directly with the daily report, and even though it required me to commute to and from Toronto every other week. I was so excited to get back in the business in a meaningful way. In the six months I held the position, I glimpsed Canada's attempt to become a multicultural country. Many of the issues that I had seen as an editor in New York were prevalent up north, although Canadians were slow to admit it. One of the biggest stories in Toronto, for example, was gun violence, which was especially rampant in poor, minority communities.

I learned much from Williams, a visionary who understood how journalism and business must evolve—together. He wanted to develop quality content and take it across media platforms. He stressed the need for niche publications to appeal to nontraditional readers, including youth and minorities. He too faced pushback and a demand to generate record profits while investing less and less in operations. In that sense, his challenges were quite similar to those of U.S. news organizations.

After fighting unsuccessfully to get Canwest owners to support his plan, Williams walked away from the job. Since I worked for him, I left too. It was the second time in my career that I had only hours to clear out my office. But this time there was no angst. I had other priorities.

In June 2005, a cousin in California lost a five-year battle with cancer. Claudette Brooks-Cooper, who was practically a sister to my sister, Ruth, had been a lawyer and for the last fifteen years was commissioner of the Alameda County Superior Court's Juvenile Division. Her death brought Gary and me to Oakland, where we stayed with Ruthie in her two-bedroom flat. It was the first time the three of us slept under the same roof since we were children. Gary still dispensed big-brotherly advice, even though, more often than not, his siblings no longer listened. I realized that this was the only way he knew how to let us know he was looking out for us. I found comfort in this. I still needed him.

For the first time, I saw my little sister in a light that made me proud. Watching her raise two teenage girls as a single mother with patience and firmness reminded me of Grandmother's devotion to us knuckleheaded boys. Ruth did not have a lot, but she made good use of what she had. She filled the holes with faith, in a way that made her needs appear minor. Besides the teenagers living with her, she had two adult children. In her, I saw my mother, determined to have a family. They defined her.

Now it was time to define myself. I was no longer a part of the *Times* family, regardless of how much I still thought of the place. My definition was rooted in my life as a husband, a father, a journalist, and an African American. I felt my journey was far from complete, and I was looking forward to where it would take me next.

Early in 2005, Robin and I sold our Upper East Side brownstone, a place that held such symbolism for me, and bought another brownstone uptown, in Harlem. We were now in a neighborhood where it took several calls to finally get the newspaper delivered. But friendly neighbors welcomed us with cookies and pleasant conversation. We found a school that was able to meet Zachary's needs, and Zach joined the Carver Mets, a Harlem Little League team, where he played outfield. We began looking for a church to call home.

My greatest test was yet to come. On a snowy Saturday in February 2006, I collapsed while I watched Zachary run drills at a winter baseball clinic. Doctors said I had a seizure caused by a tumor in my brain. The mass was above the right temporal lobe and would have to be removed by surgery. I accepted the painful news and readied myself for the operation. But several tests and scans later, we learned the nature and the source of the tumor. It stemmed from one of two masses in my left lung. I had cancer.

All my life I had tried to be strong. But the day I heard that word, my strength failed me. As I met with the oncologist, I could not help but cry as he tried to assure me that I would get the best treatment possible.

The signs had been there, but I had thought they were caused by stress. In recent months, I had lost almost twenty pounds—so much that everyone who saw me commented on my weight. I had trouble sleeping and was often tired. My yearly physicals gave no indication of the disease, yet it had been growing in me for a while.

From what I knew, lung cancer was a killer, and death often came quickly. I would learn that so many factors determine the outcome, from the nature of the disease to how the body responds to treatment. So does attitude. It was difficult to be positive as I imagined Robin and Zachary without me, and the rough course I was about to put them through. I thought of how much I still wanted to accomplish—and how much I wanted to see my son grow up—but doubted that I would have time.

I found hope. It started in conversations with Robin about the need to accept life's adversities with faith and fight, advice that Gary, Ruth, and other family members echoed. Gary dispensed daily doses of advice. "You've always been a fighter, and you can't stop now," he urged repeatedly. Robin started researching lung cancer and chemotherapy, and she reminded me that whatever we faced, we faced together. We were on yet another adventure, like so many that marked our courtship and marriage.

In private, I had a range of thoughts and emotions. As a young man I had wondered if I would die early, as my mother had, and I was surprised that I had not. But now I was not so sure. Finally, I was resolved. Whatever happened was a part of God's plan.

I underwent brain surgery, and the tumor was removed. A week later, I had radiosurgery to destroy a smaller tumor. Next, we focused on my lungs.

Because of where the cancer was located and how it had spread, surgery was not an option. How I would respond to chemotherapy, how aggressive the tumors were, would all become clear in time.

This newest journey was taking me further and further from the life that mattered so much to me only a few years ago. Along the way, I became not just different but better. I was much more appreciative of my family, my faith, and my friends, life's gifts. I believed deeply that each step of my life was guided by God, and I tried to recognize the purpose of each joy and each sorrow.

On the morning that Robin and I prepared to discuss the lung treatment with an oncologist, I awoke with a calm that I really cannot explain. I had heard others describe experiencing the presence of God, always listening with a bit of skepticism. But at that moment, I felt him touching me, and then I felt a sense of profound peace. Whatever happened, I knew I was in God's hands and could accept his will. He had brought me Robin and Zachary, and the life that I always wanted. He was there for my remarkable career in journalism, and there when it came crashing to an end. He made it possible to spend priceless time with my son, watching him grow and guiding him as best I could. I never would have had that time with him had I remained at the paper. Nor would I have written this book, a process through which I discovered so much about my family. It was that knowledge that drew me closer to them and helped me see my brother, Gary, and my sister, Ruth, for what they had always been: an essential part of my goodness. In my darkest hour, I realized that I had never been alone. I had family in all parts of the country, praying for me to pull through. I also had God and my past as sources of strength. It was as if I could now close the circle that formed my life.

I had always been fortunate, even when I did not see it. I had a grandmother, Evie, who nurtured us four boys after she had already reared her own five children. She fortified us against a world that could have swallowed us up. It's what family does, she often said. But it was so much more—a decency of the heart that made her know what to do and gave her the strength and courage to do it.

There was Odessa, my mother, who risked her life so her children could have life.

There was Rufus, my father, who did as much as he could for us, and when he could do no more, left us in fine hands.

They were bright lights that guided me, no matter how uncertain, frightened, or confused I was. In the midst of personal tragedy, they led me to my humanity. That, more than anything, allowed me to endure whatever came my way.

AFTERWORD

TWO YEARS, one month, and twenty-six days after Gerald's passing, Zachary and I traveled with one of my best girlfriends to the inauguration of Barack Obama. Zach, twelve, kept warm in his dad's Timberland boots and trapper hat (they fit perfectly) while he used my digital camera to capture the sights and sounds of fellow celebrants huddled on the National Mall.

Ask him what he wants to do when he grows up, and Zachary will tell you that computer technology is his thing. But he knew to intone as he panned the Washington, D.C., crowd: "Here we are on the Mall with hundreds of thousands of others..." and to edit his shots to produce a polished three-and-a-half minute testimony to history, which he posted on his Web site. My son may know the latest in C# programming, but he also has the natural instincts of a journalist. Gerald's legacy continues in this and so many other ways.

To some of his former colleagues at the *New York Times*, that legacy remains as one of the keepers of their institution, the protector of the ideals of fairness and an unwavering commitment to get the story first, get it best, and get it right. Not everybody agreed with his approach, but no one could deny Gerald's loyalty and dedication to the *Times* and to those who worked to uphold the standards that he held dear. I often joked that the Gray Lady was his mistress. Perhaps he cherished her too much, but Gerald rarely did anything halfway.

Others will remember Gerald's collaborative spirit, whether leading teams to produce groundbreaking series or orchestrating the stellar coverage of 9/11 and its aftermath, one of the biggest news stories of his generation. He had a way of being a leader while getting out of the way of those he led so they could do their best work. Gerald's impact on the *Times* was so profound that some in the newsroom still quote him, I'm told. Some ask, "What are we missing?" a question that Gerald posed daily as he assessed and enhanced a story or a strategy, challenging himself to give his readers something they could get only from the *Times*.

To still others, his hand remains in the *Times*' scholarship program, which has sent dozens of deserving high school students of all races and ethnic backgrounds to colleges they otherwise could not afford. As he did with the High School Journalism Workshop, which he cofounded at the Greater St. Louis Association of Black Journalists in 1977, Gerald tried to inspire as many young people as possible to look beyond humble surroundings or perceived limitations to pursue their passions. And if he thought there was even a remote possibility that he could bring another person with promise into his profession, he tried to make his love of journalism contagious. ("Why are you wasting your time in marketing?" he would ask a recent college grad, with all seriousness. "Let's talk about doing something relevant with your life.")

Then there is diversity. To those who truly knew Gerald, it was never solely about race. He preached "diversity of thought," and sought to bring a wide range of experiences and perspectives to the *Times*. That meant attracting more women, young people, people of color, gay people, people from unusual backgrounds, to the mix. "Journalism cannot be rich, smart, or relevant without diversity," he would say. Then he fought to make sure that the *Times*' environment embraced those differences.

Having worked at the Times Company for seven years, I know the newspaper can be a tough place to survive, even with a certain level of education and experience. Gerald was a touchstone in the newsroom for those of us who did not come from privilege or traditional paths; he intruded on any moments of self-doubt to say, "Don't think for a second that you don't belong here." It was a gift to make people believe, as he did, that the *Times* was their newspaper, too.

If I had to identify the most significant aspect of Gerald's legacy at the *Times*, beyond his many firsts and the many awards won on his watch, I would say it was his decency. From sending flowers to celebrate the birth of a reporter's baby to traveling across five states to attend the funeral of the father of another, he showed that he cared about his people in ways small and large. It was a testament to his decency that hundreds of friends, admirers, and former colleagues attended memorial ceremonies in his honor and sent words of condolence to Zachary and me. They recalled his humor, his drive, his integrity, his devotion to journalism and family, his tenderness. In the bitter winter days that followed my husband's death, those heartfelt tributes made me cry and sustained me at the same time. I saved all of the letters and cards in a tan sueded keepsake box, and I hope they will help add new dimensions to the image of the father that Zachary lost at just ten years old.

Gerald's departure from the newspaper that he revered was swift and brutal and ugly. Even at the time of his death, more than three years later, at 4:00 P.M. on November 23, 2006, a relentlessly rainy Thanksgiving Day, the wounds from his severance were still festering beneath old scabs. I don't know if those wounds would have ever healed. But no matter how they stung, he continued to speak only good of the *Times* or not at all. That too exemplified his decency.

Since he passed, Gerald's beloved newspaper and industry have changed dramatically. In response to reform recommendations, the *Times* in late 2003 hired its first ombudsman, an independent editor who reviews readers' complaints. In 2007 the paper moved two blocks from its storied home of ninety-four years to a sleek new tower. And like most U.S. newspapers, the *Times* has endured steep revenue losses as Web sites siphon readers and advertising dollars amid the country's economic crisis. Some papers have switched to publishing only on the Web; some have reduced home delivery; and some have closed shop. For those still in the game, an increasingly Web-centric audience has forced them to think beyond the page, incorporating more video, audio, and interactive features into their news gathering. But buyouts and layoffs have shrunk staffs, forcing journalists to do more with less. Some industry watchers argue that newspapers' business models are obsolete and that making them nonprofit entities may be the only way to save them.

While journalism, like other professions, must evolve with the rest of society, Gerald once wrote, it must keep its roots planted in the bedrock principles of honesty, fairness, and accuracy. That's what separates newspapers from blogs, newsletters, Web "portals," and other avenues of information. Editors must remind the public what makes journalism different from other media, he urged, and then deliver on that difference. That means producing accurate, balanced, relevant news coverage and being transparent in its production.

There is journalism, and then there is home. In our ten years of marriage and two of living together before that, the two were often intertwined. After Gerald died, Zachary and I tried to find a new equilibrium, as I often said to anyone who asked how we were doing. It was the simplest way to explain the impossible. How can you be just two when you are so accustomed to being three? How can you close the gaping hole that such an outsized personality leaves in his wake? As any grieving spouse or child knows, you do so one moment at a time.

It has not been easy. But I take comfort in knowing that Gerald is still with us in many ways. "What the hell are you doing still in bed at 11:30!" I heard him yelling at me one morning a few months after his death. I had shut the blinds and burrowed back under the covers after sending Zachary off to school. This had become an almost daily routine. "Get up! Get going!" he ordered. "You've got work to do!" I burrowed deeper, sobbing, desperately inhaling what little of his scent still lingered on a tie or handkerchief. He saw beyond the fact that I was depressed and missed him terribly. Finally, he whispered, "Don't be afraid." As always, he knew exactly what I was feeling and exactly what to say. He reminded me of my promise to take care of myself and our son.

He's been with me whenever I prepare to write or edit, encouraging me to "write it like you would say it," and always "say what it means." Indeed, as he urged, I continued to get up and get going, and in 2008 completed the editing of two books, including his. Gerald made it possible for me to not have to work nine to five so I could be home to shepherd Zachary through the loss of his father and the beginning of adolescence. I cannot imagine how we might have made it this far without his providing that luxury and necessity, and I thank him for it, and thank God for giving him the foresight to do so.

I think of him whenever I fire up his trusty Weber grill. From a fat steak to cedar-plank salmon to corn on the cob to garlic bread, I know I "burn" well enough to do him proud. I also keep a well-stocked bar— "You never know when you'll have company!" he would chide, lamenting my meager offerings before we merged households. I'm reminded of our precious adventures whenever I linger over the art that graces our Harlem brownstone. The framed photo of sailboats on a languid Lake Michigan, our sole souvenir from our Mackinac Island honeymoon; the colorful Jacob Lawrence print of Frederick Douglass, purchased through an NABJ scholarship campaign; the striking Shona sculpture from a black fine-art fair in Atlanta. "Do you like it?" he would ask, eyeing me over his glasses with that grin, before we took our new treasures home to complement other warm memories.

For major decisions, he reminds me that life is not a dress rehearsal— which is why Zachary and I were in Washington on Inauguration Day. "What would Gerald do?" I asked myself as I weighed the significance of having our son witness the swearing-in of the nation's first black president against the outrageous hotel rates, the slog through D.C. traffic, the throngs of people, the questions about security. There was no question about what Gerald would do, so I booked a room and packed our bags.

Most importantly, Gerald is forever with me in the presence of Zachary. Along with his features and mannerisms, Zach has his dad's charisma and sharp wit, and his penchant for debate. Zachary is a sincere and empathic friend who writes poetry that can bring tears to your eyes. He also has an annoying habit of opening a fresh carton of milk while an already open one is still in the fridge. "Just like your dad used to do!" I fuss at him, rolling my eyes. And we both smile.

Zach is no sports fan like his dad was, and doesn't consider himself an athlete. But he joined the Harlem Little League at Gerald's encouragement and flourished under his father's attention and enthusiasm. As difficult as it was, Zach committed to the Little League season after Gerald passed. In one nail-biter of a game, his base hit sent two runners in to even the score. When the next batter sent Zach home and the team surrounded the plate to greet him with hugs and high-fives, other parents cheered, but I could only cry. I know he was there in spirit, but I so wished my husband could have celebrated that awesome moment with us.

We have not stopped missing Gerald, but somehow we are finding a new equilibrium. It is an ongoing journey. I still love him deeply—I always will—but for Zach's sake and mine, I realized I needed to live in the present instead of continue to grieve for the past. I stopped sleeping with his ties and hankies under my pillow. I journaled and traveled, alone to Spain and to Mexico, with Zachary and my family to the Caribbean and back to our beloved Martha's Vineyard. I began to read his draft of this book, delicately nipping and refining and interviewing folks who could answer questions I would have asked him if he were here. Each time I wavered, heart heavy with the story that unfolded before me, I heard him repeat what he often shared with the young editor he fell in love with, back in the early 1990s, on his Metro desk at the *Times*:

"Just bring your whole self to the job," he would say, as if that was all there was to it. The job of working, the job of living. He truly personified those words. And Zach and I do our best to honor them.

—ROBIN D. STONE

POSTSCRIPT

I N FALL 2003, when Gerald first started the journey of writing his memoirs, I never could have imagined that he would not live to see this book in print. As his reporting led him to St. Louis and Itta Bena, Mississippi, to a greater understanding of his history and himself, he was animated and engaged and back in the game.

I was thrilled to see him become excited again about a major journalistic enterprise, and when he took ill, I was determined that his work find the audience that it deserved. I hope he is pleased with the final product. If he's not, I'm sure he will find some way to let me know.

I cannot speak for Gerald, but I know he would want to acknowledge the many people who by word or deed helped fulfill his dream. On his behalf, I offer a heartfelt thank-you to the following:

Patrik Bass, for passionately championing Gerald and his book, from start to end. Rozalynn Frazier and Sandra Jamison, for their thoughtful research, and Akkida McDowell, for diligently checking the facts. Janice Bryant, for her early and incisive edits. Katti Gray, for lending her poet's ear. Sheila Rule, for reading "before" and "after," and her encouraging words throughout the process.

My agent, Sarah Lazin, for tirelessly knocking on publishers' doors until the right one opened. My editor Susan Betz, for her warm welcome and nurturing at Lawrence Hill Books/Chicago

Review Press, and for protecting the integrity of Gerald's vision. Lisa Reardon, the developmental editor, for her deft hand and eagle eye. The marketing and publicity teams, for their enthusiastic support.

To family and friends, including Gary and Andrea Boyd, Ruth Boyd, Alison Boyd, Aunt Laura Brooks, the late Aunt Rose Boyd, Beatrice Scheinbaum, Carolyn Ellison, Marie Brown, Dorthy Cunningham, and Adam Moss, whose 2007 *New York* magazine piece was the first major media report to portray Gerald as multidimensional and significant to the successes and culture of the *Times*.

To each contributor, your rich and distinct voices and perspectives vividly complement the view of the man who Gerald saw in the mirror and projects in these pages.

And to anyone who may have recounted a story or shared with Gerald some insight that appears in this work, I am deeply and humbly grateful.

—*ROBIN D. STONE*

CONTRIBUTORS

Patrik Henry Bass is senior editor at *Essence* magazine and a contributor to *The Takeaway*, a nationally syndicated radio program.

Soma Golden Behr, a senior editor for many years at the *New York Times*, has been director of the New York Times College Scholarship Program since her retirement from the masthead in 2005.

Gary B. Boyd, Gerald's older brother, lives in the suburbs of Chicago with his wife, Andrea. He is a finance director in the pharmaceutical contract packaging industry.

Dana Canedy is a senior editor at the *New York Times.*

Sidney Cooper was Gerald's first boss.

George E. Curry is a syndicated columnist and former editor of *Emerge* magazine.

Paul Delaney is a former editor and correspondent with the *New York Times* in Washington, Chicago, and Madrid.

Maureen Dowd is a columnist at the *New York Times.*

Margaret Wolf Freivogel and **William H. Freivogel** worked with Gerald at the *Post-Dispatch* in St. Louis and at the paper's Washington bureau. Margaret is founding editor of the *St. Louis*

Beacon (stlbeacon.org). William is director of the journalism school at Southern Illinois University Carbondale.

John Geddes, managing editor for operations at the *New York Times*, worked for and with Gerald for a decade at the paper.

Katti Gray, a contributing writer for *Essence* magazine, spent more than two decades in daily newspapers and has written for several publications.

Michel Marriott, a former longtime reporter at the *New York Times*, is an assistant professor in the department of journalism and the writing professions at Baruch College in New York City.

Jacki (Green) Moffi, a high school classmate of Gerald's, works at Montgomery College in Rockville, Maryland. She uses the word "Gerald" to log on her computer each day.

Christine Moore is a confidential administrative assistant at the *New York Times*.

Gregory Moore, editor of the *Denver Post*, is a member of the Pulitzer Prize Board and a mentor to a number of professional journalists.

Sheila Rule, a book publisher, was Gerald's first wife, his colleague, and his friend for nearly forty years.

William Schmidt is a deputy managing editor at the *New York Times*, where he has been a foreign and domestic correspondent, as well as an editor.

Bernard Weinraub, a former longtime reporter at the *New York Times*, is a playwright.

Michael G. Williams is a former vice president at the *New York Times* and The New York Times Company and former president of Canwest Publications, Inc., the largest newspaper publisher in Canada.

INDEX